Patrick Steiner

# UNLEASH the potential and make it happen

Published and distributed by:
ZIEL AG, Zurich, Switzerland

The use of general descriptive names, trademarks, etc., in this publication, even if the former are not specifically identified, is not to be taken as a sign that such names, as understood by the Trademarks and Merchandise Marks Act, may accordingly be use freely by anyone. While the advice and information in this book are believed to be true and accurate at the date of going to press, neither the author or the editors nor the publishers can accept any legal responsibility for any errors or omissions that may be made. The publisher makes no warranty, express or implied, with respect to the material contained herein.

The final determination of the suitability of any information for the use contemplated for a given application remains the sole responsibility of the user.

All rights reserved. No part of this book may be reproduced or transmitted in any form or by any means, electronic or mechanical, including photocopying or by and information storage and retrieval system, without permission in writing from the publisher.

© 2024 by Patrick Steiner, Zurich. All rights reserved.

Cover design: Rebell Studio, Poznan

Print ISBN: 978-3-9525988-1-8

# Introduction

The last few decades have firmly planted digital as a cornerstone of our existence, yet it remains an enigma for many businesses and leaders. The ubiquitous presence of the digital frontier promises growth, innovation, and success, but it also presents challenges that can be daunting. The truth is, while digital has become an integral part of our lives, its vastness can be overwhelming. This book is not just a guide, it is your compass in the expansive digital terrain.

If the following or similar resonate with you, this book is for you:

'We are pouring money into digital, but are seeing no returns…'

'We are constantly updating with new functionality,
but we do not even have the basics in place…'

'We have digital bits and pieces, but no consistent plan…'

'Our rivals are surging ahead, how do we catch up or better, lead?'

'We start using tools like ChatGPT, RPA but are not maximizing their benefits…'

'Digital is limitless, we want to explore it to the max…'

When you open the pages of this book, you are not merely flipping through printed words. What you hold in your hands is a pledge to digital transformation and success. Every chapter, every insight is designed with one purpose – to **empower you with the knowledge and tools needed to excel in the digital age**.

By the time you reach the final page, digital challenges no longer will daunt you. Instead, you will approach tasks with **reliability** and a deep understanding of risk mitigation, ensuring that every step you take is both confident and secure.

But it does not stop at just execution. As you dive deeper into the content, you will uncover strategies and techniques to operate with **unparalleled efficiency,** leveraging proven approaches from companies around the globe. The age-old adage, 'time is money', holds especially true in the fast-paced digital space, and this book serves as your guide to maximizing every second.

And as the world of digital continues to expand and evolve, staying ahead of the curve is paramount. Through this book, you will not only keep pace but lead the charge within your company and your industry. It introduces you to invaluable shortcuts, helping you accelerate your **digital success**. More importantly, it hones your foresight, enabling you to anticipate opportunities even before they come into the limelight.

Lastly, championing the digital transformation is not just about leveraging tools or adopting the latest technologies. It is about nurturing talent, fostering a culture of continuous learning, and enhancing the overall effectiveness of your organization. This book is your manual to not just navigate but to lead the charge in people development, amassing a reservoir of **digital know-how,** and bolstering your organizational effectiveness.

This book is not just a read, it is a journey. A journey from being a participant in the digital age to becoming its champion. Dive in and discover your path to digital mastery. Think of this book as a compass, a trusted confidant, and a seasoned mentor, all combined into one cohesive package. Every section, every chapter has been curated and structured to serve as your guidepost, illuminating the diverse and intricate landscape of the digital world.

You will be introduced to the many **facets of digital success**, helping you understand its multi-dimensional nature. But success rarely comes without its challenges. This book does not shy away from addressing the potential **barriers** that can, at times, seem insurmountable. Instead, it equips you with the tools and strategies to confront them head-on, turning obstacles into steppingstones.

One of the book's most invaluable resources lies in its detailed breakdown of the **7 Digital Success Levers and 14 Digital Success Modules**. These are not just theoretical constructs but actionable strategies that have the power to unlock a reservoir of potential for your organization and you. Each lever and module is a key, opening doors to unprecedented digital mastery.

While the tactile experience of a print copy has its own charm, serving as a tangible companion in your journey, we understand the importance of accessibility in today's fast-paced world. That is why, you can obviously download this content in an eBook. Whether you are on a bustling train or waiting for a meeting, this digital counterpart ensures you are always a tap away from invaluable insights.

But your journey does not end at the last page of this book. To enrich your experience and offer a platform for continuous learning, the **Digital Arena** extends an invitation  to a vibrant community. This is not just a platform, it is a growing melting pot of experts, professionals, and enthusiasts, all united by their passion for the digital opportunities. Here, the opportunity to learn is limitless. Exchange insights with peers, seek guidance from seasoned experts, share challenges, and celebrate successes. The portal transforms the book's wisdom into a living, breathing ecosystem of knowledge, expanding horizons well beyond the written word.

This book is not an endpoint but a gateway – a gateway to a world of digital excellence, collaboration, and continuous growth. Dive in, and let the journey begin. Embrace this book, immerse yourself in its information, and emerge as the digital hero you are destined to be.

# Table of Contents

# 1   Make digital your success

In an era where the boundaries of possibility are constantly redrawn by the digital brushstroke, navigating the vast expanse of the digital reality has become more than just an endeavor – it is an imperative. Every click, swipe, or interaction a user makes is not merely an action, but a testament to the evolving nature of human connection and communication. Digital Success is not just about dominating a market or pushing a product. It is about understanding the delicate relationship between technology and humanity.

Why is driving Digital Success paramount? Because today, 'digital' is not just a platform or app, it is where aspirations meet innovations, where visions turn into revolutions, and where every organization can transform challenges into unprecedented opportunities. In a world interwoven with codes, algorithms, and data, our commitment to **Digital Success defines our relevance, resilience, and readiness for the future.**

With every Byte of data, with every line of code, we are not just building software, we are shaping cultures, carving out communities, and crafting experiences. Driving Digital Success means not just surviving but thriving, leading, and redefining the contours of tomorrow. The stakes are high, but the rewards – limitless. So, as we stand on the precipice of what is next, we must ask ourselves: Are we just participants in the digital age or are we pioneers, leaders, and architects of the digital future? The choice is ours, and the journey towards Digital Success awaits.

Let us enjoy some inspiration from companies that are leading the way.

---

**Tuning Life's Soundtrack: Spotify's Digital Symphony**

In 2006, Stockholm birthed Spotify, started reshaping music's global voyage. Its freemium model struck chords of inclusivity, evolving listeners into loyal premium subscribers. Tailoring melodies with artful algorithms, Spotify masterfully fuses data and desire, deepening engagement, and forging bonds.

Spotify is not just about melodies, it is a collaborative canvas. Friends worldwide compose playlists, kindling digital bonfires of shared emotion. From Stockholm's streets to the world's corners, it is a universal stage, bridging cultures through strategic licensing agreements.

Across devices, Spotify's seamless integration choreographs life's rhythm. Its virtuoso lessons echo: embrace a user-centric ethos, compose innovative monetization, orchestrate data's harmony, create platform unity, expand via global partnerships, and cultivate a resonant community.

Beyond tunes, Spotify's tale harmonizes technology, data, and creativity. Its global melody celebrates the language of music's connective power, uniting hearts, erasing boundaries, and amplifying life's vibrant symphony.

---

**Catalyst of Connection: Tencent's Digital Journey**

In China's dynamic tech landscape, Tencent's ascent illustrates a catalyst of digital innovation since 1998. With a portfolio spanning social media, gaming, entertainment, and fintech, Tencent epitomizes a digital ecosystem's essence.

At the heart of Tencent's prowess lies WeChat, a symbol of digital sociability, intertwining payments, e-commerce, and media. This offers a holistic experience for companies to learn from, creating seamless engagement and opportunities for growth.

Tencent's gaming division, with the early introduction of the QQ Tang game already in 2004, fosters immersive communities and interactive boundaries. Embracing gaming pushes companies to cultivate connections and experiences with their customers.

Strategic investments in streaming platforms and original content reshape content consumption. Tencent AI Lab catalyzes AI breakthroughs, a lesson in enhancing user experiences and creating value.

Unconfined by borders, Tencent invests globally, supporting cross-continental collaboration. Expanding companies should seek strategic partnerships for reach and diverse perspectives.

Tencent's narrative harmonizes technology and human connection, orchestrating a digital journey shaping communication and evolution, underscoring potential for redefining industries and global connection.

But not just tech-native companies successfully realize digital opportunities, but also conventional companies transform themselves into digital powerhouses.

**Cultivating Progress: The Digital Harvest of John Deere**

In 1837, Illinois witnessed the birth of John Deere, a legend of agricultural innovation. Historically anchored in steel and sweat, today, it is at the nexus of agricultural machinery and digital brilliance.

Through JDLink™, its telemetry system, farmers access real-time data on equipment health, location, and utilization. This is not just machinery, it is a data-driven oracle, forecasting crop yields and machinery maintenance, marrying the might of metal with predictive analytics. But John Deere's story is not confined to furrows and fields, it is a testament to continuous digital evolution. Pioneering in precision agriculture, from its Midwest roots to global farms, Deere drives sustainability by seamlessly integrating AI (Artificial Intelligence), IoT (Internet of Things), and automation into everyday farming.

Across continents, John Deere's blend of mechanics and digital metrics is redefining modern agriculture. Its ethos is crystal: infuse heritage with cutting-edge technology, leverage data-driven insights, promote sustainable farming, and meet the world's growing demands. With John Deere at the helm, the world sees a constructive interaction of tradition and technology, demonstrating that when heritage meets innovation, a more sustainable and bountiful future is crafted.

**Financial Frontiers: BBVA's Digital Odyssey**

Emerging in 1857 from Spain's historic boulevards, BBVA early realized that the future of banking is digital. Swiftly adapting, BBVA launched Garanti BBVA Mobile, a cutting-edge mobile banking app, and incorporated biometric authentication mechanisms, leading the charge in banking security.

Every interaction is enhanced with personalized digital banking experiences, weaving stories of trust in the age of ones and zeros. However, BBVA's journey transcends traditional banking, it signifies a radical digital metamorphosis. Venturing into global markets, BBVA strategically acquired Holvi, Simple, and Atom Bank, strengthening its digital footprint. Championing fintech's potential, it carves out seamless, secure, and innovative digital banking experiences.

With a commitment to leading the digital banking transformation, BBVA's initiatives promise seamless financial transitions across the globe. The bank's dictum: constantly evolve with customer needs, be at the forefront of digital banking innovations, and foster global financial connectivity. At the crossroads of heritage and innovation, BBVA stands tall, embodying a vision, where tradition fuels digital futures, weaving a world of seamless financial empowerment.

**Building Dreams: LEGO's Digital Playhouse**

In 1932, Billund, Denmark, introduced the world to LEGO, the emblem of tactile creativity. Fast forward to today, and LEGO is not just about physical bricks.

With the LEGO Digital Designer software and augmented reality-infused sets like Hidden Side, it marries tactile play with digital wonders. Each set, each brick, represents an evolving universe of interactive digital storytelling and creativity. But LEGO's tale is broader than playful assemblages, it is about digital dexterity in play. From Billund's heart to global digital realms, LEGO has successfully ventured into video games, partnering with global giants to produce titles like 'LEGO Star Wars' and 'LEGO City Undercover'.

Embracing the digital age, they have crafted interactive apps and online communities, inviting fans to build, share, and collaborate. Amidst pixels and plastic, LEGO's intertwined world stands as a testament to endless imaginative possibilities. Their mission? Engage in relentless digital reinvention, bridge tactile with tech, and support global creative communities. In LEGO's universe, each story, be it brick or byte, signifies a commitment to nurturing creativity, highlighting how a classic toy can inspire digital innovations and enrich imaginations across generations.

Now, let us explore how to harness the full potential of these digital endeavors and carve your path towards unparalleled Digital Success.

# 1.1 What is Digital Success

«Success is survival»
Leonard Cohen[1]

Already back in 1972, the Canadian singer-songwriter found a simple definition of success. And it is even more true today. However, in the ever-shifting sands of the digital age, what does it mean to truly succeed? Digital Success is not defined by mere numbers, but by the depth of connections we forge, the barriers we dismantle, and the horizons we expand. Digital Success is the alchemy of turning virtual possibilities into tangible realities.

Despite the broad scope of Digital Success and countless ways of measuring it, a few overarching metrics can help us to gauge a company's overall digital status, to measure its progress in the entire digital transformation and to stay on track with its implementation.

In defining and assessing Digital Success, it is crucial to balance both the expectations of the customers and the strategic goals of the company. At the same time, as Digital Success develops over time, a dynamic view on success metrics from short- to long-term is required – accepting that they are not absolutely sequential. Our simplified Digital Success Matrix presents itself as follows.

---

[1] Leonard Cohen – Canadian singer-songwriter. * 21.09.1934 in Westmount; † 07.11.2016 in Los Angeles

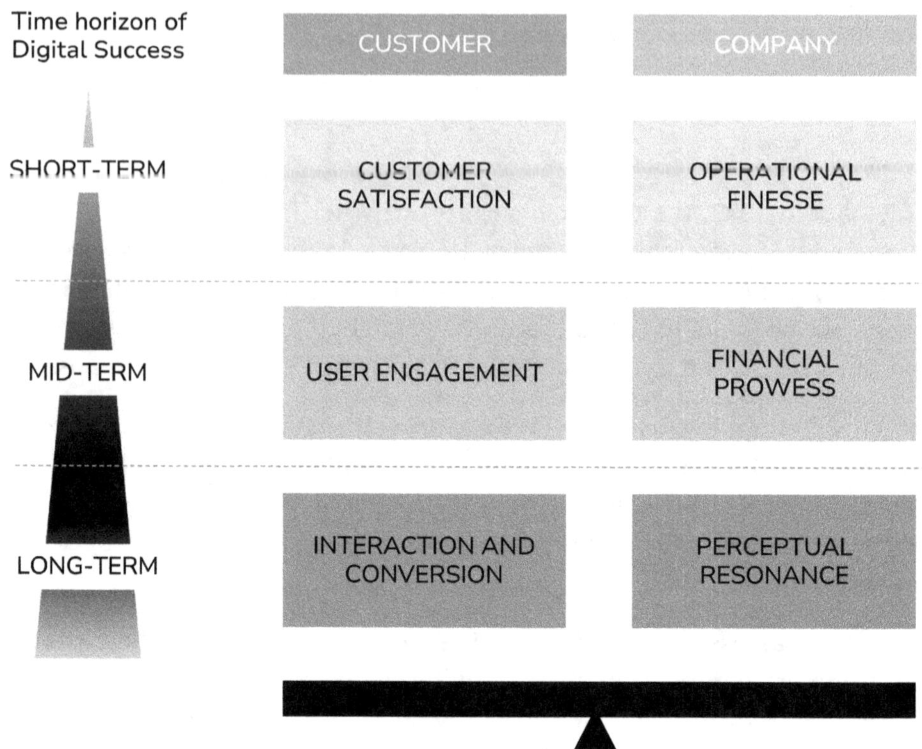


*Figure 1: Digital Success Matrix*

Striking a harmonious balance between customer expectations and company achievements is the key to holistic digital transformation and success. Obviously, there are many more metrics, which help us to develop our digital offering and steer our digital transformation. We will look at them in the individual sections. However, let us start with these overarching objectives.

**Success from the customer's perspective**

Companies must pivot their focus to the customers' vantage point. Satisfied customers do not just engage more, they find their needs met and fulfilled through direct conversions. There are detailed metrics that help us to steer the customer experience in detail, however, overall Customer Satisfaction, User Engagement as well as Interaction and Conversion are the key metrics to look at from a customer's perspective.

**Customer Satisfaction** is the bedrock upon which digital achievements are built. When done right, it can have a short-term effect. Two essential metrics, the Customer

Satisfaction Score (CSAT) and the Net Promoter Score (NPS), offer insights into customers' experiences and their loyalty.

**CSAT** serves as a primary metric for gauging the level of contentment that customers derive from their interactions with your digital channels and offering. By utilizing post-interaction surveys, businesses can effectively quantify this satisfaction level and gain valuable insights into the strengths and weaknesses of their user experiences. The CSAT score, usually expressed as a percentage, directly reflects the proportion of customers who found their digital interactions to be favorable. A CSAT score surpassing 80% holds particular significance, as it expresses that a substantial majority of users have had positive experiences. This benchmark implies that most customers have not only successfully navigated the digital channels but have also found them intuitive, efficient, and aligned with their needs. One exemplary illustration of a company that consistently attains remarkable CSAT scores is Apple. This is a testament to the company's commitment to customer-centric design principles. Apple's emphasis on simplicity, aesthetics, and functionality in its digital interfaces resonates with users. The correlation between high CSAT scores and effective customer-centric design reinforces the notion that investing in user experience yields tangible benefits.

**NPS**, which stands for Net Promoter Score, is a widely used metric that evaluates the overall sentiment and loyalty of customers towards a brand, product, or service. It goes beyond measuring simple satisfaction and expresses customers' likelihood to recommend the offering to others. The NPS framework is based on a single question: 'On a scale of 0 to 10, how likely are you to recommend our [brand/product/service] to a friend or colleague?' Responses to this question are divided into three categories:

1. Promoters (Score 9-10): These are customers who are extremely satisfied with their experience and are enthusiastic advocates of the brand. They are likely to recommend it to others, thereby contributing positively to word-of-mouth marketing.

2. Passives (Score 7-8): Passives are satisfied customers, but they are not as enthusiastic as Promoters. While they might recommend the brand or product if asked, they are less likely to actively promote it.

3. Detractors (Score 0-6): Detractors are customers who are dissatisfied or had a negative experience. They are unlikely to recommend the brand or might even discourage others from using it.

To calculate the NPS, the percentage of Detractors is subtracted from the percentage of Promoters. The resulting score can range from -100 to +100. A NPS at the upper end of the scale generally indicates a more loyal and satisfied customer base, with positive word-of-mouth potential. NPS benchmark figures can vary by industry. In general, an NPS of 0 to 30 is considered good, while an NPS of 30 to 70 is considered excellent. An NPS of 70 or above is exceptional and signifies that the brand has a highly loyal and enthusiastic customer base. An example of a company effectively utilizing NPS is Amazon. With its customer-centric approach, Amazon consistently earns high NPS scores due to its emphasis on fast shipping, reliable customer service, and personalized recommendations. The company's focus on continuously enhancing the customer experience has contributed to its strong brand loyalty and widespread recommendations from its customers. Incorporating NPS into business strategies can lead to a deeper understanding of customer perceptions, guide decision-making, and drive improvements that meet customers' expectations. By leveraging insights from NPS feedback, companies can refine their offerings, strengthen customer relationships, and foster sustainable growth.

Satisfied clients usually start to interact more with the company. So, let us look at the mid-term metric of **User Engagement**. It is the heartbeat of the digital life. Two core metrics, the Bounce Rate and the Average Session Duration, provide insights into how deeply users engage with your (digital) offerings.

**Bounce Rate** is a critical metric of web analytics that provides insights into the effectiveness of a website's (landing) page and user engagement. It quantifies the percentage of visitors who navigate away from a website after viewing only a single page, without interacting further or exploring other pages within the site. A high bounce rate can often indicate that users are not finding the information they need or that the page fails to capture their interest. It might also suggest that the user experience is suboptimal, leading visitors to quickly abandon the site. On the other hand, a low bounce rate implies that users are engaged and interested in exploring more of the website's content. This could be attributed to well-designed landing pages, relevant content, easy navigation, and clear calls-to-action. However, it is important to note that bounce rate should be interpreted in context. For example, a blog post with a high bounce rate might not be a cause for concern if the objective is to provide quick answers or information to visitors. Conversely, an e-commerce site with a high bounce rate on product pages could indicate issues with product descriptions, pricing, or the checkout process. For a blog, a bounce rate of around 70-90% might be acceptable, while for an e-commerce site, a rate below 40% could be a goal to aim for.

The **Average Session Duration**, which typically spans around 2 to 3 minutes, provides valuable insights into user engagement and content effectiveness. It reflects the amount of time users spend on your digital channels during a single session, displaying the level of interest and interaction with your content. This metric is indicative of whether users find your content valuable, engaging, and immersive enough to spend a considerable time exploring it. A longer session duration indicates that users are not only attracted to your digital channel but are also actively consuming your content, which can lead to better understanding and retention of the information you provide. An exemplary illustration of utilizing Average Session Duration to drive user engagement can be found in BuzzFeed's approach. BuzzFeed has mastered the art of captivating users through its interactive and diverse content offerings. By creating a blend of articles, quizzes, videos, and other interactive elements, BuzzFeed encourages users to dive deeper into its content, resulting in extended session durations. This strategy cultivates an environment where users are inclined to explore a variety of topics and formats, leading to increased customer satisfaction as well as interaction and conversion. Incorporating strategies to enhance the Average Session Duration can yield diverse benefits, such as improved search engine rankings, increased ad revenue, and higher potential for conversions.

**Effective digital strategies culminate in interactions and conversions.** The Click-Through Rate (CTR) and the Conversion Rate serve as illuminating metrics that shed light on how users interact with your content and advertising, providing valuable insights into the efficacy of your digital initiatives.

The **Click-through Rate (CTR)** is a vital metric in digital positioning that measures the effectiveness of your digital efforts or campaigns. CTR quantifies the percentage of people who click on a specific link out of the total number of individuals who viewed the content containing that link. They continue the journey. This metric is instrumental in gauging the resonance of your content, the relevance of your offers, and the overall effectiveness of your marketing strategies. A higher CTR is indicative of a well-crafted and compelling message and journey flow that aligns well with your target audience. It signifies that your content succeeded in capturing the attention and interest of viewers, motivating them to take the desired action, whether it is clicking on a link, visiting a specific page, or exploring a product further. To illustrate the importance of CTR, consider email marketing campaigns. A high CTR in an email campaign implies that the subject line and content were engaging enough to prompt recipients to open the email and click on the links within it. This, in turn, drives traffic to your website, increasing the chances of conversions. For digital advertising, a high CTR is crucial for optimizing return on investment. Platforms like Google Ads use CTR as a factor in determining ad relevance and quality score. A higher CTR can lead to lower advertising costs and better ad placements, thereby improving your digital efforts' overall efficiency.

Even further, a higher **Conversion Rate** is a testament not only to user engagement but also to the persuasive impact of your content and design. This metric reflects the percentage of visitors who take a desired action, such as making a purchase, filling out a form, or subscribing to a newsletter. A higher Conversion Rate indicates that your content and overall user experience is effectively encouraging visitors to take the desired actions you have outlined. For e-commerce businesses, in particular, a healthy Conversion Rate is a significant goal. E-commerce entities often target a Conversion Rate in the range of 5-10%, although this can vary based on the industry and the nature of the products or services being offered. A real-world example of achieving remarkable Conversion Rates can be observed in the success of Shopify. Shopify, as a leading e-commerce platform, has demonstrated expertise in optimizing online stores for conversions. By offering customizable and user-friendly templates, efficient checkout processes, secure payment gateways, and responsive design, Shopify has empowered online businesses to create compelling and trustworthy shopping experiences. As a result, Shopify has helped many businesses achieve impressive Conversion Rates, contributing to their growth and success. Enhancing Conversion Rates involves a combination of elements such as persuasive copywriting, compelling visuals, clear calls-to-action, trust-building elements (such as customer reviews and trust badges) and streamlining the user journey. It is important to continuously analyze user behavior, conduct A/B testing, and refine your content and website design to improve Conversion Rates. Monitoring the performance of different pages, checkout flows, and calls to action can provide valuable insights into what works best for your audience.

The insights unearthed from these metrics paint an overall picture of how effectively a company's digital endeavors align with the preferences and needs of its customers. But while the customer is first, it is important to balance Digital Success also in the context of the company's ambitions.

**Success from the company's perspective**

As Digital Success unfolds from a company's perspective, a panoramic triad of lenses – operational finesse, financial prowess, and perceptual resonance – unveil a multidimensional view of success.

**Operational finesse** takes center stage in achieving Digital Success with a short-term perspective. It encompasses the efficiency, accuracy, and seamlessness of your operational processes, both customer-facing and behind the scenes. By employing metrics that gauge operational excellence, you gain a comprehensive understanding of how well your business functions at its core, setting the stage for enhanced customer experiences and overall growth. One crucial operational metric is **Order Fulfillment Time**. This metric evaluates the time it takes for an order to be processed, packed, and shipped to the customer – be it physical or virtual. A shorter Order Fulfillment Time not only satisfies customer expectations for fast deliveries but also reflects the efficiency of your supply chain and inventory management, with this lowering the operating expenses and ensuring effective resource allocation along the delivery chain. Another essential metric is **Customer Support Response Time**. In the digital landscape, customers expect timely assistance. Measuring how quickly customer inquiries or issues are addressed highlights your commitment to exceptional service. A shorter response time fosters trust and loyalty, contributing to positive word-of-mouth and customer retention. Additionally, **Data Accuracy** plays a significant role. Inaccurate data can lead to misinformed decisions and customer dissatisfaction. Regularly auditing and maintaining data accuracy supports better decision-making and helps build a foundation of trust with customers. These operational metrics collectively contribute to a smoother customer journey, and reduced friction and effort within the company. A 15-20% reduction in operational costs, like General Electric's success during its early transformation, signifies a mastery of streamlined execution, supported by digital means.

**Financial Prowess** plays a pivotal role in steering businesses towards success. Navigating the digital challenges effectively involves not only making strategic choices but also investing resources wisely. **Return on (digital) Investment (ROI)** stands as a compass guiding the profitability of digital ventures. This metric serves as a yardstick to measure the gains generated in relation to the investments made. By quantifying the ratio of gains to investments, ROI provides a clear picture of the financial health of various digital and non-digital initiatives. A positive ROI indicates that strategic decisions have led to tangible returns, exemplifying the effectiveness of your investment choices. For aspiring financial success, a coveted benchmark is the 5:1 ROI ratio, reminiscent of Google Ads' impressive performance. This ratio signifies a remarkable fivefold return for every dollar invested. The achievement of such a ratio speaks volumes about the astute financial navigation that underpins Google's advertising strategies. It emphasizes not only the significance of returns but also the importance of optimizing investments for maximum impact. **Customer Lifetime Value (CLV)** stretches beyond individual initiatives. It encapsulates the broader scope of a customer's relationship with your brand and company, encompassing factors like loyalty, repeat engagements, and referrals. CLV quantifies the total value a customer brings to your business over the course of their engagement. When CLV surpasses the cost of customer acquisition (CAC), it not only signifies sound financial stewardship but also harmonizes with customer-centricity. A noteworthy illustration of leveraging CLV can be found in the success story of Netflix. Netflix's commitment to delivering personalized experiences has contributed to driving high CLV. By curating content recommendations that match individual preferences and consistently exceeding customer expectations, Netflix has transformed mere viewers into loyal subscribers. This exceptional CLV displays how investments made in enhancing the customer journey can yield remarkable returns that echo across every stage of the customer lifecycle.

The Financial Prowess offers a perspective that extends beyond numbers, shedding light on the prudent allocation of resources and the strategic choices that drive mid-term Digital Success.

**Perceptual Resonance** weaves a narrative that shapes how your brand is perceived by the world as a foundation for long-term success. **Social Media engagement** stands as a crucible of connection, a place where your brand's essence meets the pulse of your audience. This metric serves as a direct window into how effectively your brand is liked by the digital community. **Shares, retweets, and comments stand alongside likes as markers of engagement**, offering deeper insights into the intensity of audience interaction. The more users share and comment on your content, the more profound the impact of your brand's narrative. These actions demonstrate an audience's willingness to invest their time and voice in your story. To wield the perceptual resonance effectively, your digital strategies must be engineered to do more than just inform, they must spark conversations, inspire sharing, and foster connections. Craft messages that align with your brand's values and resonate with your audience's aspirations. Use visuals, storytelling, and user-generated content to create an immersive experience that invites participation. By nurturing conversations, and building a digital community, your brand can become more than a product or service, it can become a living, breathing entity in the hearts and minds of your audience.


In conclusion, to steer overall Digital Success, these – or some other overarching – metrics need to be defined and regularly tracked. Often as part of a company's Key Performance Indicator (KPI) and Objectives and Key Results (OKR) frameworks (visit section 3.2.1.3 Digital Dashboards and Targets – the Quantitative View on Digital Assets on page 134 for details on objectives setting). They define the expected outcomes that support the overall business ambitions and objectives. However, it is important that these goals are cascaded and mapped into the organization and into the digital efforts. The following visualization introduces the key Digital Success Levers – much more on them later – and links them to the digital overall objectives, that we have just developed.

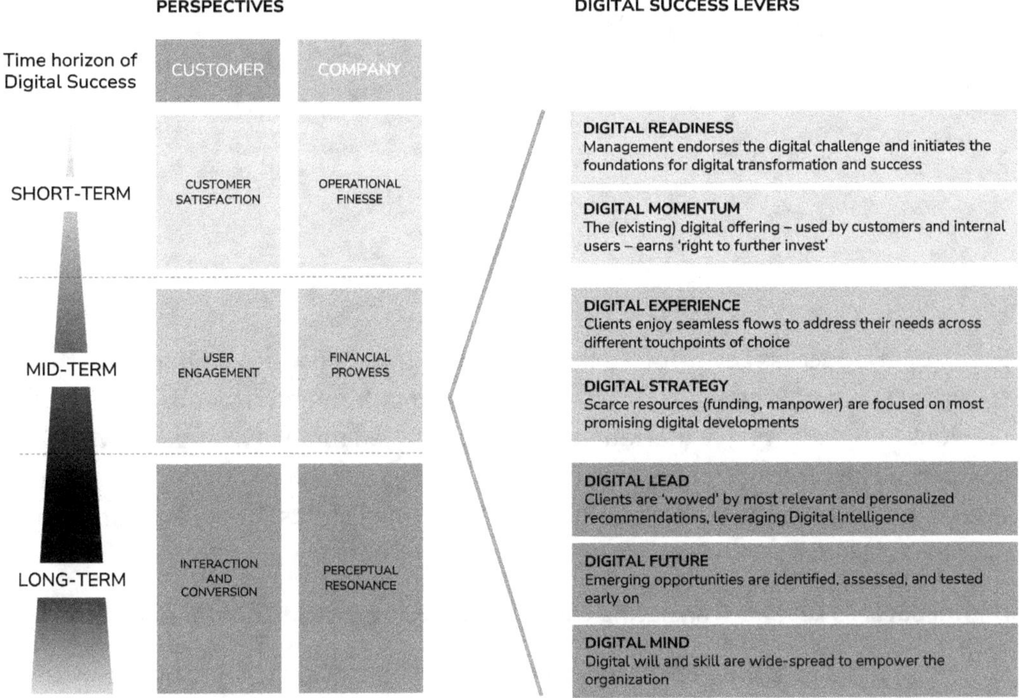


*Figure 2: Mapping Digital Success Levers to Digital Success Metrics*

All these Digital Success Levers directly influence the achievement of Digital Success. For all these Digital Success Levers ambition levels must be set, and quantitative metrics defined – whereas the weight and the exact level of aspiration is driven by the status and the ambition of the company at any given point in time of its digital transformation. This ensures a consistent cascade of objectives throughout the organization, linking Digital Succes to business success.

## 1.2 Digital Success Canvas



Seven **Digital Success Levers** make the difference. They construct a **dynamic pathway to Digital Success**. Progressing from readiness to mindset, each lever builds upon the previous one, creating a narrative of evolution, adaptability, and growth. This comprehensive approach prepares the organization to not only thrive in the digital everyday reality but also to lead and innovate, propelling itself into a future where digital possibilities are harnessed to their fullest potential.

**Digital Success Levers: Translating Digital Success Metrics into Work Areas**

Digital Readiness: Digital Success begins with acknowledging the winds of change. **Management endorsement and a proactive stance towards addressing digital challenges** are the foundational steps. Leaders recognize the disruptive forces at play, including new competitors and changing consumer behavior. This initial acknowledgment creates a sense of urgency that permeates the organization, igniting the journey towards digital transformation. A culture of openness to change and readiness to embrace the digital shift is established, setting the groundwork for future endeavors.

Digital Momentum: As Digital Readiness takes hold, the organization becomes familiar with its existing digital offerings and begins to realize their benefits. This stage is marked by visible progress in digital initiatives, displaying tangible outcomes. Stakeholders witness the positive impact that digital endeavors can have on efficiency, customer engagement, and even profitability. **This momentum breeds excitement and a growing sense of confidence**, catalyzing a cultural shift where digital efforts are celebrated and embraced – and essentially earning the company the right to further invest into its digital future.

Digital Experience: To maintain and further grow Digital Momentum, the emphasis shifts to customer or more generally user experience. The organization channels its efforts into **creating a seamless flow that addresses customer needs across various touchpoints** – the channel of choice for the user. This enhancement of user

---

[2] Karl Popper – Austrian-British philosopher, academic and social commentator. * 28.07.1902 in Vienna; † 17.09.1994 in Kenley

experience fosters trust and loyalty and forms the bedrock for mid-term success. Consistency and personalization become key as customers enjoy an intuitive journey, solidifying their connection with the brand and setting the stage for repeat interactions.

Digital Strategy: Building on this (initial) Digital Experience, the organization strategically allocates its limited resources – funding, manpower, and time – **towards the most relevant digital initiatives** to shape and continue on-going Digital Success, and to reach the North Star. This calculated focus ensures that investments yield the highest returns and are closely aligned with overarching business goals. This stage calls for a clear-eyed assessment and prioritization of where to allocate resources for maximum impact, providing a Digital Road Map for mid-term gains that lay the groundwork for sustained growth and digital resilience.

Digital Lead: As the Digital Strategy is defined, the ambitions rise higher, beyond short- and mid-term. A company can now aspire to lead through digital. Therefore, the organization aims to **deliver personalized and relevant recommendations that always provide a Digital Wow** to users at any given interaction. Leveraging the power of digital intelligence, fully exploring data and analytics drive not only conversions but also customer loyalty and brand recognition.

Digital Future: Leveraging the success of all the above levers, the organization shifts its gaze towards the horizon, **identifying emerging opportunities that can secure long-term growth**, and shape the future industry. This forward-thinking approach involves spotting trends, technologies, and market shifts early on. Rigorous assessment and controlled testing of new avenues ensure the organization is well-prepared to adapt to changing landscapes. This component becomes a cornerstone for long-term viability and proactive innovation.

Digital Mind: To perpetuate success, fostering a Digital Mindset is essential. Empowering the entire organization with digital will and skill becomes paramount. This involves comprehensive training, fostering a culture of experimentation, and recognizing digital excellence. **A widespread understanding of digital's transformative power allows teams to adapt swiftly to changing circumstances**, ensuring the organization remains nimble, innovative, and always at the forefront of digital possibilities.

## Digital Success Modules: Shaping the future of the company

Let us now have a closer look at how Digital Success Modules bring the Digital Success Levers to life. Spanning 14 distinct yet harmoniously integrated units, these modules operate on two pivotal fronts in your voyage towards digital transformation.

We have modules designed to '**unleash the potential**', serving as your visionary guide that sketches the bold contours of what your company should and could attain. They inspire vision, crystallizing the myriad of opportunities awaiting in the digital landscape and helping you envisage a target state that is not just aspirational but grounded in attainable reality.

Conversely, the other cohort of modules dives into the '**make it happen**', mapping out the pragmatic pathway laden with concrete, actionable steps leading your business to its envisaged pinnacle. These modules are the engineers of your digital transformation, crafting plans grounded in reality, ensuring every step is both achievable and in line with your ultimate objectives.

Together, they forge a robust framework, building a bridge between the now and the extraordinary potential of tomorrow, guiding you from conceptualization to realization with unmatched precision and foresight.

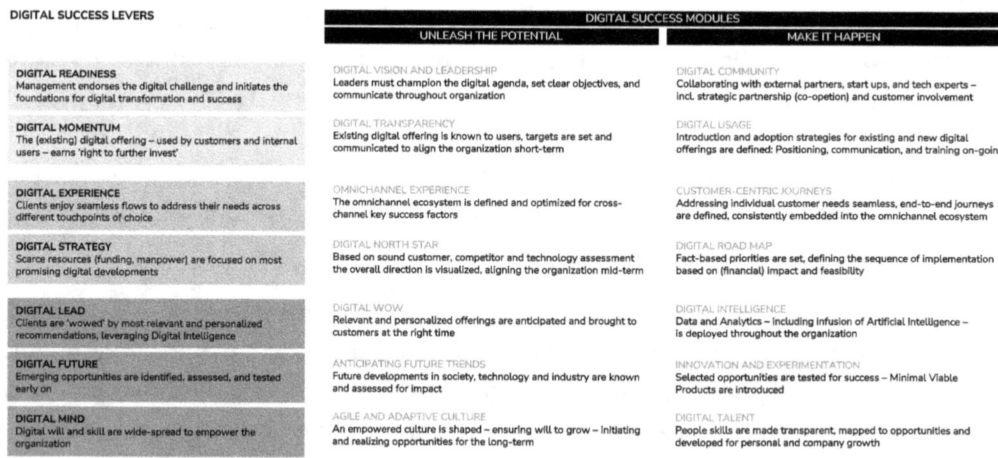

| DIGITAL SUCCESS LEVERS | DIGITAL SUCCESS MODULES | |
| --- | --- | --- |
| | UNLEASH THE POTENTIAL | MAKE IT HAPPEN |
| **DIGITAL READINESS** — Management endorses the digital challenge and initiates the foundations for digital transformation and success | DIGITAL VISION AND LEADERSHIP — Leaders must champion the digital agenda, set clear objectives, and communicate throughout organization | DIGITAL COMMUNITY — Collaborating with external partners, start ups, and tech experts – incl. strategic partnership (co-opetion) and customer involvement |
| **DIGITAL MOMENTUM** — The (existing) digital offering – used by customers and internal users – earns 'right to further invest' | DIGITAL TRANSPARENCY — Existing digital offering is known to users, targets are set and communicated to align the organization short-term | DIGITAL USAGE — Introduction and adoption strategies for existing and new digital offerings are defined: Positioning, communication, and training on-going |
| **DIGITAL EXPERIENCE** — Clients enjoy seamless flows to address their needs across different touchpoints of choice | OMNICHANNEL EXPERIENCE — The omnichannel ecosystem is defined and optimized for cross-channel key success factors | CUSTOMER-CENTRIC JOURNEYS — Addressing individual customer needs seamless, end-to-end journeys are defined, consistently embedded into the omnichannel ecosystem |
| **DIGITAL STRATEGY** — Scarce resources (funding, manpower) are focused on most promising digital developments | DIGITAL NORTH STAR — Based on sound customer, competitor and technology assessment the overall direction is visualized, aligning the organization mid-term | DIGITAL ROAD MAP — Fact-based priorities are set, defining the sequence of implementation based on (financial) impact and feasibility |
| **DIGITAL LEAD** — Clients are 'wowed' by most relevant and personalized recommendations, leveraging Digital Intelligence | DIGITAL WOW — Relevant and personalized offerings are anticipated and brought to customers at the right time | DIGITAL INTELLIGENCE — Data and Analytics – including infusion of Artificial Intelligence – is deployed throughout the organization |
| **DIGITAL FUTURE** — Emerging opportunities are identified, assessed, and tested early on | ANTICIPATING FUTURE TRENDS — Future developments in society, technology and industry are known and assessed for impact | INNOVATION AND EXPERIMENTATION — Selected opportunities are tested for success – Minimal Viable Products are introduced |
| **DIGITAL MIND** — Digital will and skill are wide-spread to empower the organization | AGILE AND ADAPTIVE CULTURE — An empowered culture is shaped – ensuring will to grow – initiating and realizing opportunities for the long-term | DIGITAL TALENT — People skills are made transparent, mapped to opportunities and developed for personal and company growth |

*Figure 3: Digital Success Modules, unleashing the potential, and making it happen*

For all these Digital Success Modules, we will elaborate in detail over the course of this book how we can optimize them to shape the Digital Success of your company – building awareness for its importance, introducing the metrics to assess where your company stands and where it needs to act, and introducing concrete actions for optimization.

But before we can go to optimization, we must acknowledge that in many instances substantial barriers can stand between achieving the Digital Success Levers and executing the Digital Success Modules.

## Possible barriers to Digital Success

Navigating the path to Digital Success is a journey marked by both promise and complexity. However, amidst the exciting possibilities lie challenges that can often act as barriers, impeding the progress of Digital Success Levers and Modules and the realization of ultimate Digital Success.

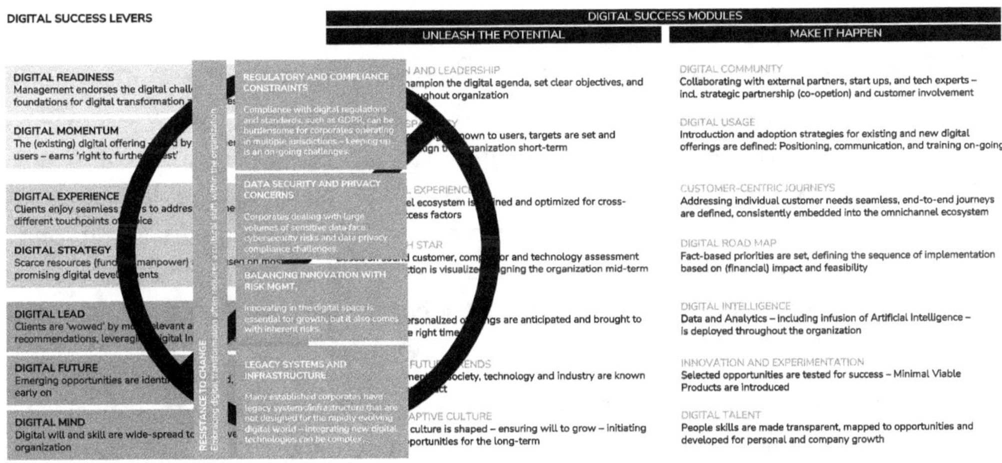

*Figure 4: Possible barriers to Digital Success*

These barriers, often encountered on the road to digital transformation, serve as critical checkpoints that require careful navigation and strategic solutions. By identifying and addressing these hurdles head-on, organizations can pave the way for a smoother transition and a more assured march towards achieving their digital ambitions.

Further down, we will have a closer look at these possible barriers and how to mitigate the risks resulting from them. But let us have an initial introduction here.

**Resistance to Change:** Embracing digital transformation often necessitates more than just adopting modern technologies. It requires a cultural shift within the organization, where traditional mindsets and practices give way to innovative thinking and flexibility. The resistance to change can emerge as a significant hurdle, as employees and stakeholders accustomed to established norms may find it challenging to adapt. Addressing this barrier involves fostering a change-friendly environment through transparent communication, involving employees in the transformation process, and highlighting the benefits that digital change can bring to both individuals and the organization as a whole.

**Regulatory and Compliance Constraints:** In an interconnected world, adherence to (digital) regulations and standards is imperative. Operating in multiple jurisdictions can intensify the complexities of compliance, particularly when regulations like GDPR demand stringent data protection measures. The evolving nature of these regulations means that keeping up with compliance requirements is an on-going challenge. Organizations must establish cross-functional teams, engage legal experts, and leverage technology solutions that automate compliance tracking and reporting. By demonstrating a commitment to data privacy and compliance, organizations can build credibility and trust among customers and stakeholders.

**Data Security and Privacy Concerns:** For corporations handling substantial volumes of sensitive data, the specter of cybersecurity risks and data privacy compliance concerns looms large. Safeguarding data against breaches and ensuring compliance with privacy laws is essential. Organizations must navigate the landscape of cybersecurity solutions, data encryption, and privacy frameworks to establish robust protection mechanisms. Regular security audits, employee training on data handling best practices, and continuous monitoring of network vulnerabilities are paramount in maintaining data integrity and guarding against cyberthreats.

**Balancing Innovation with Risk Management:** Innovation fuels growth, especially in the digital space, where breakthroughs can reshape industries. However, with innovation comes inherent risks, and finding the equilibrium between embracing recent technologies and managing associated risks is a delicate task. Overcoming this barrier requires a dynamic risk management strategy that assesses potential pitfalls while supporting an environment that encourages experimentation and learning from failures. Organizations must establish cross-functional innovation teams, create risk assessment frameworks, and implement processes for rapid experimentation and prototyping. Effective risk management ensures that the benefits of innovation outweigh potential drawbacks.

**Legacy Systems and Infrastructure:** The digital age demands agility, scalability, and interoperability – a stark contrast to the rigidity of many legacy technology systems and infrastructure. The integration of new digital technologies into existing structures can be complex, fraught with compatibility challenges. Legacy systems can hinder the pace of innovation and the ability to respond to market demands swiftly. Addressing this barrier involves strategic modernization initiatives that bridge the gap between legacy and cutting-edge technologies. Organizations can prioritize modular architecture, invest in application programming interfaces (APIs) for interoperability, and adopt cloud-based solutions that offer scalability and flexibility.

Recognizing and surmounting all these barriers is essential for organizations seeking to realize the full potential of their digital endeavors. By acknowledging the challenges presented by resistance to change, regulatory constraints, data security concerns, innovation and risk management, and legacy systems, organizations can proactively devise solutions that propel them past these obstacles.

**Digital Success Canvas**

Combining the Digital Success metrics, linking them to the Digital Success Levers and Modules and being aware of possible barriers establishes the overall Digital Success Canvas to steer your attention and elaborate what needs to be done for your company. Throughout the further chapters, we will use this framework as a point of reference.

**Very simplified the horizontal dimension defines what a company needs to work on, whereas the vertical axis brings it into the context of time** – short- to long-term from top to bottom. A company that has deficits at the upper end of the Digital Success Canvas first needs to **Get the digital basics right**. A company that already is successful at the top, moves further down to **Lead through digital**.

We will use this overall framework, linking all relevant areas of digital transformation to the Digital Success Levers and Modules to elaborate each aspect – to unleash the potential – and to define concrete implementation plans – to make it happen.

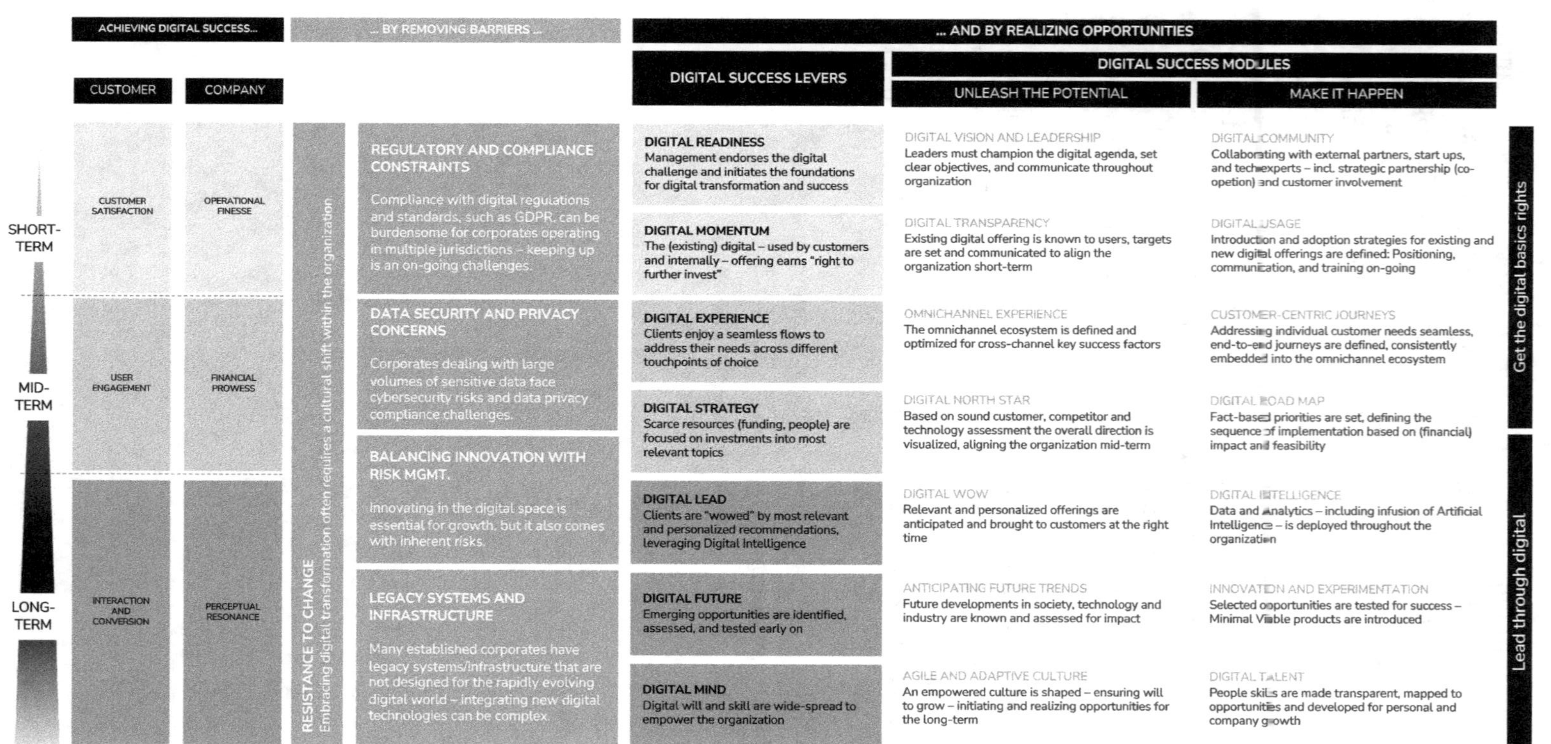


*Figure 5: Digital Success Canvas*

## 1.3 Digital Pulse Check



The Digital Pulse Check helps to fine-tune a company's focus and directing its resources judiciously to foster robust digital growth. Each element of the Digital Success Canvas undergoes rigorous scrutiny, effectively becoming a mirror reflecting the real-time health and future trajectories of your company's status and ambition. Throughout the book we will introduce concrete metrics and markers that can help to assess where your company stands when it comes to achieving Digital Success. For all the Digital Success Modules we will outline possible **metrics and markets** to assess the current status. Based on these assessments a large set of data can be collected and regularly updated. The combination of the most relevant metrics can be used to generate an overall dashboard.

Central to the Digital Pulse Check is the vibrant **Digital Pulse Check Dashboard**, an indispensable tool forged to translate the multilayered analysis into a lucid visual story. Reflecting the structural integrity and nuances of the Digital Success Canvas framework, this dashboard consolidates the expansive data into a heat map-like overview that becomes the heartbeat of your digital transformation. This is a dynamic visual representation system, color-coded to offer intuitive insights at one glance:

- Green emanates from areas displaying high achievement, indicating that the digital solutions implemented have driven growth and nurtured innovation. It represents zones of digital operations where the assessment suggests a fertile ground for further innovation and strides towards greater milestones.

- Amber sheds light on domains where the growth is promising but yet to reach the pinnacle of the pre-defined objectives. It speaks of steady progression, a middle ground that signals caution yet encourages optimism. It is a color that urges a closer look, a deeper understanding, and a calibrated strategy to drive growth and achieve the objectives outlined.

---

[3] Peter Drucker – Austrian-American management consultant, educator, and author. * 19.11.1909 in Vienna; † 11.11.2005 in Claremont

- **Red**, on the other hand, stands as a fervent call to action, reflecting areas where interventions are necessary – urgency depending on a company's status and ambition.

The dashboard's role transcends that of a mere representation, metamorphosing into a dynamic hub that guides informed decisions and strategic pivots. It not only demarcates areas that demand focused attention and action but also illuminates potential avenues for growth, highlighting areas ripe for innovation and development. It effectively becomes a central command center, a focal point where strategy meets data, facilitating an understanding that is deep yet not overwhelming, sophisticated yet straightforward.

Some stereotypical stages of companies on their path of digital transformation are illustrated below with different Digital Pulse Check dashboards.

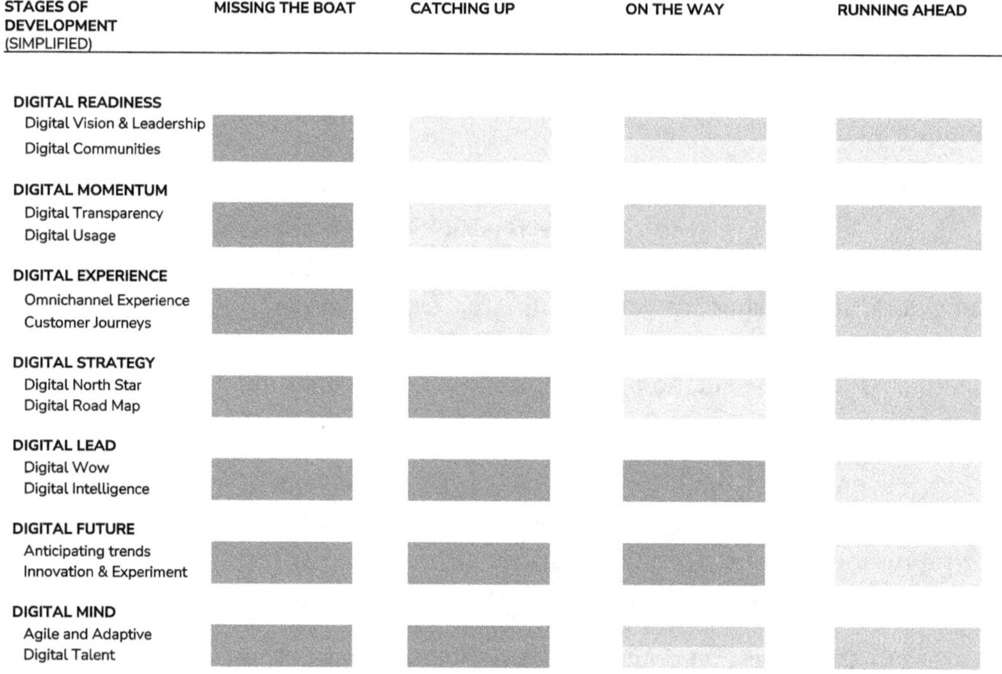


*Figure 6: Illustrative stages of companies' digital status – visualized with Digital Pulse Check dashboards*

Four typical stages can be observed:

**From 'Missing the boat leading' to 'Digital Awakening'**: Companies need to navigate through the complexities of the digital landscape, turning pressure into opportunity. By demystifying digital transformation, they create their own tailored path, aligning it with the current business model to kick-start a seamless digital journey.

**From 'Catching up' to 'Digital Foundation'**: Companies need to solidify their digital basics, earning the right to expand. The must identify gaps, fortify the core, and instill agility, preparing themselves to evolve dynamically. This ensures that strategic adjustments translate into tangible, early wins.

**From 'On the way' to 'Digital Evolution':** Armed with digital basics, it is time to soar. Companies articulate their North Star, designing roadmaps that permeate innovation and efficiency throughout the organization. They accelerate growth, turning visions into lived realities.

**From 'Running ahead' to 'Digital Mastery':** Elevate from having a robust digital offering to becoming a Digital Leader. These companies supercharge their journey, transforming data into insights, and insights into awe-inspiring experiences. They anticipate and harness future technologies to not just meet but exceed customer and market expectations, consistently.

Obviously, each individual company is different, and the exact status and ambition must be assessed individually. The metrics and markets discussed later help to do so for each area of the Digital Success Canvas. The level of aggregation or drill-down can be further refined based on the needs of your company – percentage numbers can be added to the cells to highlight more detailed progress, beyond the simplified color scheme.

More than just an analytical tool, the Digital Pulse Check operates dynamically as a compass, consistently pointing the direction towards fruitful endeavors and guiding resource allocation with a foresight that is both astute and adaptive. The Digital Pulse Check stands as a vigilant sentinel, creating a proactive stance where decisions are not reactionary but crafted with a visionary outlook, maintaining a delicate balance between the present necessities and future potentials.

The Digital Pulse Check culminates as a remarkable tool offering an eagle-eye view of the company's digital heartbeat. It stands as a tangible representation of strategic clarity in the fluid digital landscape, ensuring that a company remains proactively aligned, adapting with agility to the pulsating rhythms of the digital market dynamics.

# 1.4 The Triple-A Approach



«Little strokes fell big oaks»

in Poor Richard's Almanack, by Benjamin Franklin[4]

As we navigate the maze that is digital transformation, it becomes crucial to have a reliable approach to guide us. **The Triple-A approach – Awareness, Assessment, and Action – offers such a structured pathway, adaptable to both macro and micro-level objectives.**

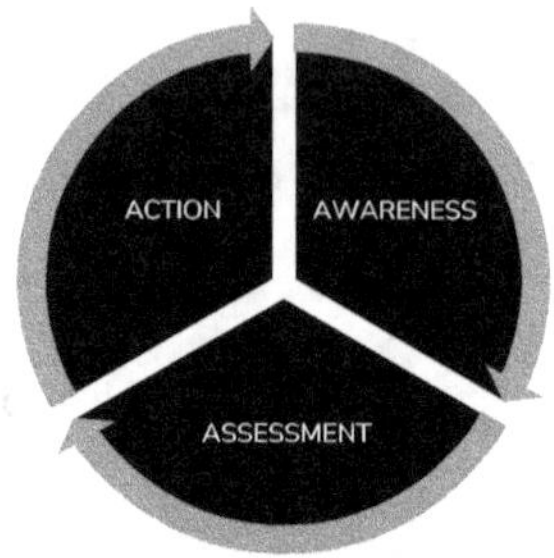


*Figure 7: Triple-A Approach*

The first step towards digital excellence begins with **Awareness**. Senior management and the organization must understand each barrier, Digital Success Lever, and Module. Everyone must grab the scope of each of them, and size the importance and relevance for the company, always cognizant of market trends, customer behaviors, and technological advancements. Getting inspiration from best-in-class companies can help to build the awareness throughout the organization. It acts as the bedrock upon which assessment can be done and action can be introduced.

Once awareness is ensured, the next step is **Assessment.** This involves a deep dive into the current situation of the barriers, Digital Success Levers, and Modules. Assessment is not merely an audit but a detailed evaluation that correlates your digital efforts to measurable outcomes. For each of the Digital Success Modules a set of metrics helps to gauge where a company stands today – also in relation to its ambitions and the competition. The detailed metrics and markers will be introduced in the respective chapters on the Digital Success Levers and Modules. The assessment is also when companies identify gaps or areas for improvement, outlining the need for action and/or the sense of urgency. The results of the detailed assessments of the Digital Success Modules feed into the Digital Pulse Check dashboard.

After gaining awareness and conducting thorough assessments, we arrive at the crucial step of **Action.** This is where plans are executed, strategies are implemented, and theories are tested. Action plans are derived from the insights gathered during

---

<sup></sup>[4] Benjamin Franklin – American polymath who was active as a writer, scientist, inventor, statesman, diplomat, printer, publisher, and political philosopher. * 17.01.1706 in Boston; † 17.04.1790 in Philadelphia

the awareness and assessment stages – also considering inspirations and learnings from best-in-class examples – ensuring they are both data-driven and aligned with organizational goals. Whether it is launching a new digital marketing campaign or overhauling an existing e-commerce platform, these actions are designed to address specific challenges and capitalize on identified opportunities. A set of actions will be introduced for each Digital Success Module throughout this book.

However, the Triple-A approach views action as a cyclical, not linear, process. After implementation of the action, it is vital to loop back to awareness and assessment, to measure the outcomes, and to refine strategies as needed. This creates a continuous cycle of improvement, where actions are regularly evaluated and optimized for long-term success.

**Amazon – Success with a Systematic Approach**

Although simplified in this illustrative case, Amazon's success is no coincidence, but the fruit of systematic work.

**Awareness – Identifying the Need for Customer-Centricity**: In its early years, Amazon recognized the crucial importance of customer satisfaction in the e-commerce space. Jeff Bezos, the founder, made it clear that the company's focus would be on 'customer obsession', as he believed that meeting and exceeding customer expectations would lead to long-term profitability.

**Assessment – Metrics That Matter**: Amazon has always been data-driven, but the metrics it chose were aligned closely with customer satisfaction. The company used data analytics to assess performance indicators like Customer Lifetime Value (CLV), Net Promoter Score (NPS), and conversion rates. This enabled Amazon to understand what was working and what needed improvement from the customer's point of view.

**Action – Implementing Changes**: Based on its assessment, Amazon has continually refined its platform. One of its major breakthroughs was the introduction of Amazon Prime, which offered multiple benefits such as free shipping, exclusive access to movies, TV shows, ad-free music, Kindle books, and more. This feature was developed based on customer feedback and has become a cornerstone of Amazon's business model.

Amazon does not just stop at Action, it creates a continuous feedback loop. It regularly revisits each phase of the Triple-A approach to ensure it is still aligned with customer needs and market dynamics. This adaptability has allowed it to venture successfully into new areas like cloud computing with Amazon Web Services (AWS), and even physical grocery stores with Amazon Go/Fresh and Whole Foods.

Of course, the journey has not been without challenges. Amazon faced significant resistance initially when it introduced Prime due to its annual fee. However, the company mitigated this risk by offering a free trial period, thereby allowing customers to experience the value firsthand. Moreover, Amazon's continuous investment in data security also demonstrates its proactive approach to mitigating operational risks. Today, Amazon stands as a testament to the efficacy of a Triple-A approach. Its customer-centric focus, diligent assessment methods, and decisive actions have not only made it an e-commerce behemoth but also a major player in multiple industries. It demonstrates that with clear awareness, rigorous assessment, and actionable strategies, companies can achieve sustainable growth and remain adaptable in the fast-paced digital landscape.

 Check out further descriptions, updates, and examples as part of the **Digital Arena**. Connect with other professionals to find the best answers for your company.

With the Digital Success Canvas in your hands – understanding the Digital Success metrics, knowing possible barriers, and initially scoping the Digital Success Levers and Modules – we would now be well equipped to explore the individual components in detail, applying the Triple-A approach to each of them. But let us first have a closer look on possible barriers to Digital Success. How can we turn barriers into accelerators?

# 2  Turn barriers into digital accelerators

As we stand poised on the threshold of Digital Success, let us address the challenges that may cloud our vision. These challenges, often dubbed barriers, are not immovable hurdles but invitations to innovation.

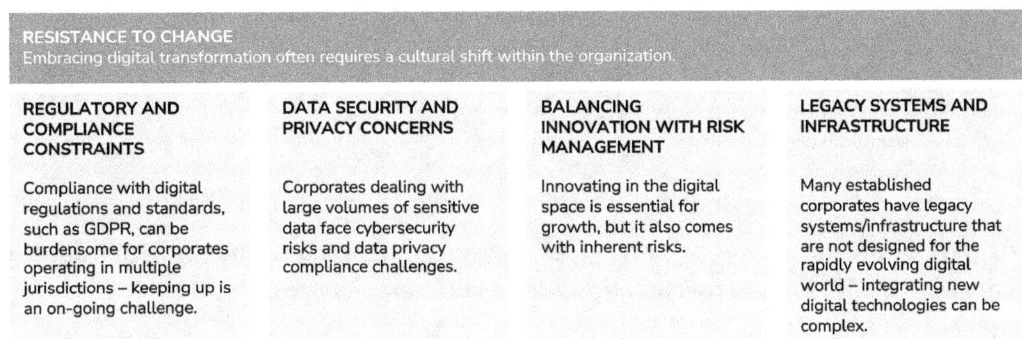


*Figure 8: Possible barriers to Digital Success*

Slightly different in its nature from the other four, Resistance to Change requires primarily a change of mindset, rather than investments into digital solutions and technical developments. At the same time, it often is the biggest possible barrier to Digital Success. Let us start by deep diving into this possible barrier to Digital Success and by exploring ways to mitigate it.

## 2.1   Resistance to Change

«There is nothing more difficult to take in hand, more
perilous to conduct, or more uncertain in its success,
than to take the lead in the introduction
of a new order of things»
Niccolò Macchiavelli[5]

As part of organizational dynamics, resistance to change is a phenomenon deeply
interwoven with human psychology and the cultural tapestry of institutions.

**What the C-Suite needs to know**

1. **The Deep-rooted Nature of Resistance:** Understanding resistance to change means acknowledging its multi-faceted origins. It is essential to be aware that it is deeply anchored in human psychology, organizational dynamics, and fears of the unfamiliar.
2. **Metrics as the Pulse of Organizational Sentiments:** In assessing resistance, comprehensive metrics such as employee digital comfort surveys, project delay frequencies, and digital tool adoption rates become invaluable. They offer a tangible measure of the undercurrents of resistance.
3. **Transparent Communication as the Bridge to Understanding:** When executing actions to counter resistance, clear and consistent communication stands out. Articulating the reasons, significance, and long-term benefits of change helps align the organization towards a shared vision.
4. **Commitment to a Long-term Cultural Odyssey:** A cultural shift is not a sprint, it is a marathon. This journey requires time, patience, collective decision-making, extensive training, and most importantly, unwavering commitment from leadership.
5. **Leadership's Active Role in Modeling Change:** For change to truly permeate an organization, the C-Suite must not merely endorse but actively embody and champion the shift. Their hands-on involvement and dedication set the tone, turning the desired change into a lived reality.

As introduced earlier, let us apply the Triple-A approach to build the awareness,
assess the status and urgency, and to define the right actions to address possible
Resistance to Change.

---

[5] Niccolò Macchiavelli – Italian diplomat, author, philosopher, and historian. * 03.05.1469 in Florence;
† 21.06.1527 in Florence

**Awareness: Unraveling Complexities of Resistance to Change**

 Individuals inherently gravitate towards the familiarity and security of established routines. When faced with digital innovations, these very individuals might experience discomfort, primarily driven by the unpredictability of the unknown. For instance, consider an employee who has been accustomed to a particular software for a decade. The introduction of a new platform can induce anxiety, stemming from the anticipated learning curve and potential errors that might ensue.

This emotional response is not solely restricted to individual behavior, but resonates at an organizational level, giving rise to what experts term as 'Cultural Inertia'. **An organization's culture, built over years, forms a shared set of values and methodologies.** Consequently, any significant deviation from this ingrained culture, especially one that necessitates the acquisition of new skills or embraces novel ways of functioning, is often met with skepticism – let alone changes of entire industry dynamics. A case in point would be a company that has traditionally valued face-to-face interactions. Proposing a change in thinking to digital communication tools, such as Slack or Zoom, might not just challenge logistical norms but also the company's very ethos of communication.

However, resistance is not always a mere reaction to discomfort or cultural inertia. At times, it emerges from genuine concerns rooted in perceptions of threat. **Employees, especially in sectors where digital advancements are rapid, might perceive these changes as direct threats to their job stability or the autonomy they once enjoyed.** The advent of Artificial Intelligence (AI) or process automation tools in customer service sectors serves as a fitting example. Here, representatives could harbor fears regarding their relevance and job security in an AI-driven environment.

Lastly, the role of leadership in shaping perceptions about change cannot be overstated. **Digital transformation necessitates not just the adoption of innovative technologies but also a unified leadership vision.** A lack of coherence among the top brass or mixed signals about the importance of digital initiatives can amplify resistance manifold. If a CEO passionately advocates for digitalization, but is met with lukewarm reception or lack of prioritization from departmental heads, employees find themselves in a conundrum, often defaulting to their comfort zones and resisting change (visit section 3.1.1 Digital Vision and Leadership on page 81 to see how Digital Readiness can be nurtured).

Collectively, understanding these layers of resistance is the first step towards navigating, and eventually mitigating them in the journey of digital transformation.

**Assessment: Diagnosing Resistance**

 Accurately assessing resistance and 'cultural inertia' means diving into both the visible and subtle indicators of hesitation, reluctance, or outright refusal. Let us look at a few indicators.

Begin with the **adoption rate** of any new digital product. The uptake of a novel digital tool over time paints a telling picture. When a new Customer Relationship Management (CRM) system is unveiled and only 30% of targeted employees engage with it in the initial month, despite extensive training, it is clear that there is more than just a learning curve at play, there is palpable resistance. As organizations mine deeper, they can gauge sentiments using **Digital Comfort Surveys**. When employees continually rate their comfort or understanding below a certain threshold, for instance, 2.5 on a scale of 5, the undercurrents of resistance emerge. Such a pattern does not just hint at discomfort – it screams of a significant barrier in accepting or embracing the new. Meanwhile, diving into training sessions can offer a different lens. The nature, frequency, and quality of queries raised offer a wealth of insights. A barrage of repetitive or rudimentary queries often signals that the concept is either not sinking in or is being met with skepticism. Taking a step further, harnessing the **Employee Net Promoter Score (eNPS)**, traditionally a customer loyalty measure, can be a powerful tool in this context. When employees, in response to a query about recommending a new digital tool, give scores below 6 (out of 10), the undertone is evident – there is either disillusionment or active resistance. The digital platforms themselves also share stories through **engagement metrics**. When login rates to a new platform or solutions dip or when there is a stark reduction in the time spent, it is not just about the tool's utility – it is about the users' receptivity. A sharp 40% decline in weekly logins to a newly launched analytics tool, for instance, does not bode well.

However, not all metrics are numerical. **Focus Group Discussions** provide a qualitative touch, capturing the nuances of resistance. The sentiments, concerns, and themes echoing in these discussions flesh out the depth and nature of the hesitations. Lastly, while often overlooked, **exit interviews** can be poignant. When employees single out rapid digital transitions or inadequate training as their reasons to move on, it is a stark reminder that resistance, if unchecked, does not just hinder progress – it drives talent away.

Stringing together these diverse metrics provides an organization with a holistic, multi-faceted view of resistance. It is only with such a comprehensive understanding that companies can craft strategies that do not just combat resistance but also turn it into a catalyst for more inclusive, effective change.

**Action: Orchestrating a Long-Term Cultural Shift to Overcome Resistance to Change**

 Recognizing the profundity of a cultural shift is the first critical action. Cultural changes are not superficial or transient. They are deep-seated evolutions that, once initiated, reframe every facet of the organization. For example, when IBM transitioned from a primarily hardware-based business model to a focus on services, it was not just about new product lines, it was a fundamental shift in the company's identity and values. This understanding underscores the significance of the journey and the commitment it warrants, often spanning years or even decades.

**Central to this transformative journey is clear and consistent communication.** An organization must articulate the impetus for change, emphasizing its foundational importance. When employees see change not as a fleeting phase but as a structural recalibration, their perspective shifts. This perspective shift is essential for the deep-rooted cultural change we seek. For instance, Microsoft's evolution under Satya Nadella required a reframing of company values, emphasizing a growth mindset. This philosophy encourages continuous learning, embracing challenges, and viewing failures as opportunities for growth, rather than setbacks. Nadella's vision was to transform Microsoft from a company that knows it all to a company that learns it all. As a result, this renewed focus aimed to foster innovation, collaboration, and adaptability across the organization[6]. However, **consistent communication is not a monologue but a dialogue.** Embedding regular feedback loops ensures that the organization is attuned to the emotional and psychological resonances of its workforce. These iterative touchpoints, like town hall meetings or digital forums reminiscent of Toyota's continuous improvement philosophy, create a two-way channel, reflecting the collective ethos of the cultural shift.

**Training, in this context, morphs into something grander: empowerment and edification.** Beyond imparting skills, training sessions in a cultural shift scenario are designed to reshape mindsets. They offer insights into the larger vision, underscoring how each digital tool or change is a steppingstone towards that envisioned future. General Electric's corporate training center, the Crotonville campus, established in 1956, stands as a testament to the company's dedication to leadership development and innovation. Often dubbed as the 'epicenter of GE culture', the institute plays a vital role in nurturing talent, encouraging collaboration, and promoting forward-

---

[6] Carmine Gallo in Forbes: "Microsoft CEO Satya Nadella's Clear And Consistent Vision Rallies Employees Around A Common Purpose". Published online 31.03.2018, visited 08.04.2024. https://www.forbes.com/sites/carminegallo/2018/03/31/microsoft-ceo-satya-nadellas-clear-and-consistent-vision-rallies-employees-around-a-common-purpose/

thinking ideas within the organization[7]. Through its diverse and rigorous training programs, Crotonville not only hones the skills of GE's workforce but also helps in shaping the future of leadership in the global business landscape.

**A genuine cultural shift demands democratized decision-making.** This participative approach ensures that decisions are not top-down but are collective, echoing the shared aspirations of the organization. Collaborative platforms or task forces, where diverse teams contribute to the transformation narrative, exemplify this approach. Here, transformation is not dictated, it is co-authored. **Change champions play a pivotal role.** Identifying and celebrating these internal advocates, much like what Unilever did with their sustainability champions, can have a ripple effect. Recognizing and rewarding those who epitomize the evolving culture, who navigate and endorse the new digital norms, sets a resonant example (visit section 3.7 Digital Mind on page 323 to understand how an empowering culture can be established).

**A nuanced understanding of cultural shifts recognizes that change is not just operational – it is deeply emotional.** Engaging change management experts becomes paramount. These professionals, adept at the human facets of transformation, ensure that the journey addresses both the tangible and intangible elements of change. **Leadership's embodiment of the envisioned culture is the linchpin.** When leaders do not just endorse but live the change, it becomes a lived reality for everyone. Their active engagement, be it through using new digital tools or championing transformative initiatives, sends a compelling message about the culture the organization aspires to. For instance, when Alan Mulally took the reins at Ford, he did not just preach collaboration, he practiced it, breaking down long-standing silos. He introduced the 'One Ford' plan, emphasizing a unified vision and cohesive approach across the company's global operations. By promoting open communication, transparency, and shared objectives, Mulally fostered a culture where silos were broken down and teams collaborated effectively to navigate Ford through financial crises and into profitability. His leadership style underscored that collective success at Ford was achievable only through genuine collaboration[8].

**Time, patience, and persistence are non-negotiables.** Cultural shifts are not instantaneous, they are evolutionary. Much like IBM's protracted journey from hardware to services, recognizing that this is a marathon and not a sprint ensures that the organization remains resilient, adaptive, and committed to the course, even when faced with inevitable challenges. In conclusion, initiating a cultural shift to counter resistance is not a mere action plan – it is a visionary commitment. It is about

---

[7] Shlomo Ben-Hur, Bernard J. Jaworski and David Gray in an IMD case study: "Re-imagining Crotonville: Epicenter of GE's leadership culture". Published June 2021, visited 08.04.2024. https://www.imd.org/case-study/re-imagining-crotonville-epicenter-of-ge-s-leadership-culture-a/
[8] Ford company website, visited 08.04.2024. https://corporate.ford.com/about/culture/one-ford.html

envisioning a future where the organization's very ethos is aligned with the dynamism of the digital age. Through transparent communication, empowerment, collective decision-making, and unwavering leadership, organizations can ensure that this cultural transformation is not only initiated but also sustained and celebrated over the long haul.

For almost two hundred years Procter & Gamble has proven that it endorses change and finds new spots to grow and prosper.

In 1837, Nestled along Cincinnati's riverbanks, **Procter & Gamble** (P&G) embarked on a journey, eventually redefining consumer products' global landscape. Its legacy, rich with innovation, crafts narratives of adaptation, transforming resistance into fertile grounds for evolution. At the heart of P&G's alchemy is its commitment to collaboration, manifested in the revolutionary 'Connect + Develop' paradigm, where boundaries blur between in-house genius and external brilliance[9].

But P&G is not merely about products, it is a crucible of cultural evolution. The Leadership Sabbatical Program sends its chieftains on enlightening odysseys, only for them to return as bearers of uncharted insights. From Cincinnati's historic streets to global boardrooms, P&G's footprint, through such initiatives, propagates a symphony of shared vision and renewed vigor.

Across its myriad of brands, P&G's ethos integrates consumer intimacy. Their magnum opus resounds: foster external collaborations, restructure for agility, orchestrate consumer-driven innovations, and cultivate a workforce fortified with adaptability. Beyond the shelves, P&G's tale weaves change management, consumer insights, and strategic partnerships. Their global cadence celebrates the art of transformation, leading the vanguard in navigating change, kindling growth, and elevating life's daily tapestry.

Let us now shift gears and assess the possible barriers that require investments (of people, funds, and time) to address them, in many cases also technical developments. Businesses will inevitably face four fundamental yet interconnected challenges: Regulatory and Compliance Constraints, Data Security and Privacy Concerns, Balancing Innovation with Operational Risk Management, as well as Legacy Systems and Infrastructure. These elements might appear as daunting barriers at a cursory glance. However, with deeper introspection, they unveil themselves as essential facets in shaping a company's Digital Success.

---

[9] Larry Huston, Nabil Sakkab in Harvard Business Review: "Connect and Develop: Inside Procter & Gamble's New Model for Innovation". Published March 2006, visited online 08.04.2024.
https://hbr.org/2006/03/connect-and-develop-inside-procter-gambles-new-model-for-innovation

| REGULATORY AND COMPLIANCE CONSTRAINTS | DATA SECURITY AND PRIVACY CONCERNS | BALANCING INNOVATION WITH RISK MANAGEMENT | LEGACY SYSTEMS AND INFRASTRUCTURE |
|---|---|---|---|
| Compliance with digital regulations and standards, such as GDPR, can be burdensome for corporates operating in multiple jurisdictions – keeping up is an on-going challenge. | Corporates dealing with large volumes of sensitive data face cybersecurity risks and data privacy compliance challenges. | Innovating in the digital space is essential for growth, but it also comes with inherent risks. | Many established corporates have legacy systems/infrastructure that are not designed for the rapidly evolving digital world – integrating new digital technologies can be complex. |

*Figure 9: Focus on barriers that require technical developments to be mitigated*

Primarily, these elements stand not as fleeting hurdles but as enduring realities. Bypassing or minimizing their importance would not only be imprudent but also detrimental. Regulatory compliance, for instance, transcends mere adherence to legal standards. In the interconnected world of today, complying with stringent standards like GDPR is not just a regulatory obligation. Take companies like Apple who, through their privacy-centric campaigns, have shown that adherence is also about building trust. Emphasizing data minimization and on-device processing, Apple ensures that personal information stays largely on the user's device rather than being uploaded to the cloud. Their introduction of features like App Tracking Transparency highlights their commitment to giving users control over their data. Through both hardware and software innovations, Apple's ethos underscores that privacy is a fundamental human right. It is a testament to a company's commitment to respecting the sanctity of personal data, thereby fortifying trust with stakeholders.

It is imperative to acknowledge these challenges not as mere obligations but as potential strategic assets. Beyond their evident complexities, these elements – be it regulatory compliance, robust data protection, a measured risk profile, or system stability – constitute the core of a company's value proposition in a digital age. A company that champions stringent data security, for example, is not merely protecting itself against breaches. Companies like Zoom, post their early security challenges, have emphasized stringent security measures, making it an integral aspect of their value proposition especially in industries where the sanctity of data is paramount.

Yet, recognizing and addressing these challenges necessitates careful consideration, particularly in terms of investments. Resources, though scarce, need to be judiciously allocated. It becomes a balancing act, with companies often at crossroads, weighing the importance of shoring up these foundational barrier elements against the lure of strategic innovations. For instance, Netflix continually straddles the line between investing in innovative content while ensuring platform stability and compliance. As companies navigate these waters, the flexibility in investment decisions might vary –

from being more stringent in areas like regulatory compliance to having more leeway when dealing with legacy systems.

In wrapping up, it is essential to understand that these challenges, though significant, hold the promise of transformative potential. By wholeheartedly embracing these challenges and judiciously allocating resources, businesses can navigate the digital reality not just for survival but for meaningful growth and innovation.

Let us start with the one that is non-discretionary in its nature: Regulatory and Compliance constraints.

## 2.2 Regulatory and Compliance Constraints



**RESISTANCE TO CHANGE**
Embracing digital transformation often requires a cultural shift within the organization.

| REGULATORY AND COMPLIANCE CONSTRAINTS | DATA SECURITY AND PRIVACY CONCERNS | BALANCING INNOVATION WITH RISK MANAGEMENT | LEGACY SYSTEMS AND INFRASTRUCTURE |
|---|---|---|---|
| Compliance with digital regulations and standards, such as GDPR, can be burdensome for corporates operating in multiple jurisdictions – keeping up is an on-going challenge. | Corporates dealing with large volumes of sensitive data face cybersecurity risks and data privacy compliance challenges. | Innovating in the digital space is essential for growth, but it also comes with inherent risks. | Many established corporates have legacy systems/infrastructure that are not designed for the rapidly evolving digital world – integrating new digital technologies can be complex. |

*Figure 10: Barriers – Focus on Regulatory and Compliance Constraints*

International corporations face a major challenge: the intricate web of regulatory and compliance constraints. These constraints, born from an ever-evolving set of regulations and standards, often prove to be significant roadblocks on the path to global Digital Success. Navigating this complex terrain requires strategic foresight, a deep understanding of regional nuances, and a proactive approach to compliance integration.

**What the C-Suite needs to know**

1. Strategic Importance and Diverse Landscape of Compliance: Integrating compliance is a strategic necessity in the global digital reality. With an ever-evolving global regulatory environment, from GDPR in Europe to U.S. industry-specific mandates, non-adherence risks significant penalties and reputational harm. Awareness of these nuances is essential for navigation.

2. Assessment through Measurable Metrics: Utilizing metrics like non-compliance incident frequency and stakeholder feedback scores offers insights into effective compliance and customer trust. These indicators help companies understand regulatory adherence and stakeholder perceptions.

3. Leveraging Technology for Efficient Compliance: Embracing tech-driven solutions, such as regulatory automation, predictive analytics, and secure data management tools, enhances compliance efficiency. These innovations ensure proactive adjustments to regulatory changes and anticipate potential shifts.

---

[10] Paul McNulty – American attorney and university administrator. * 31.01.1958 in Pittsburgh

4.  Cross-functional Collaboration for Comprehensive Compliance: Engaging integrated teams across departments, involving legal, operational, and technical experts, ensures that compliance strategies cover all angles. Early engagement in project planning helps address potential hurdles proactively.

5.  Prioritizing Customer-centric Compliance: Beyond adhering to mandates, transparent communication with customers regarding compliance initiatives fosters trust. Dedicated support for compliance-related concerns and clarity in data handling practices further solidify customer confidence.

Let us build the awareness, discuss ways to assess a company's current status and introduce mitigating actions to ensure compliance.

**Awareness: Decoding the Global Regulatory Labyrinth**

 Governments and industry bodies globally strive to ensure **data security, consumer privacy, fair competition, and even sustainability**. Consequently, they continually update and expand the legal frameworks that govern business operations. This complex regulatory environment poses a multi-faceted challenge, one that international corporation must adeptly navigate to realize successful global digital expansion.

Each geographical region weaves its own distinctive tapestry of guidelines. In Europe, the **General Data Protection Regulation (GDPR)** casts an influential and expansive shadow over data handling practices. It mandates stringent consent management and robust privacy protection for EU citizens, including the right to data deletion and correction. Additional complexity stems from the array of regulations that differ not only between countries but also within a single nation's jurisdictions. As an example, in the United States, corporations must adhere to an array of industry-specific regulations. For instance, the **Health Insurance Portability and Accountability Act (HIPAA)** applies to healthcare data, while the **California Consumer Privacy Act (CCPA),** that has been further developed into the **California Privacy Rights Act (CPRA)** as of 2023, focuses on consumer data protection, partly overlapping in its scope with each other and with the European GDPR regulations.

Non-adherence with the ever-growing and often multi-layered set of regulations can have severe consequences for an organization in the form of direct consequences from the regulators, negative customer experiences and strategic disadvantages.

**Direct consequences from the regulators**: Non-compliance can lead to **substantial fines and penalties** imposed by regulatory bodies, resulting in financial losses that directly impact an organization's financial health. A notable example is the Equifax data breach in 2017, where poor cybersecurity practices led to a significant financial penalty, underscoring the gravity of compliance lapses. Inadequate compliance measures can also trigger **regulatory audits and scrutiny**, consuming valuable time and resources as organizations strive to demonstrate adherence. In 2018, Cathay Pacific faced a significant data breach, exposing sensitive customer data, affecting almost 9.4 million passengers. The aftermath saw a decline in the airline's reputation and share value, coupled with regulatory scrutiny. The UK's Information Commissioner's Office fined the airline £500,000 for inadequate data protection. But more expensive, as a result, Cathay Pacific had to invest heavily in enhancing its data infrastructure and protocols[11]. On top regulatory bodies have the authority to **revoke licenses** or permits vital for business operations. This disruption in business continuity can lead to severe **financial losses**.

**Negative customer experiences**: Non-compliance incidents can severely **damage a company's reputation**, eroding trust and customer loyalty. Negative public perception can have **enduring consequences**, affecting an organization's market standing. Facebook's possible GDPR violations in 2018 damaged its reputation and eroded customer trust due to mishandling of user data. On top, weak data privacy practices can lead to breaches, compromising customer data and resulting in customer **attrition and lost revenue**.

At the same time, emerging regulations, particularly in sustainability and ethical domains, can also open **new avenues for business growth**. Companies that proactively embrace these regulations as opportunities can appeal to conscious consumers and gain a **competitive edge**. For instance, businesses that align with sustainability regulations can tap into a growing market demand for environmentally responsible products and services. Facing increasing global emphasis on sustainability, Unilever launched its 'Sustainable Living Plan' in 2010. This ambitious initiative aimed to halve the environmental footprint of their products, enhance the health and well-being of over a billion people, and source 100% of their agricultural raw materials sustainably, all by 2020. Not only did this align Unilever with international sustainability regulations, but it also led to the creation of eco-friendly product lines that resonated with environmentally conscious consumers. Brands under Unilever like 'Love Beauty and Planet' were developed with an eco-friendly ethos, tapping into a growing market segment, and demonstrating that sustainability can be profitable[12].

---

[11] Michael Cowley on Integrity360: "Cathay Pacific's data breach fine and what companies can learn from it". Published 13.03.2020, visited 08.04.2024. https://insights.integrity360.com/cathay-pacific-data-breach-fine

[12] Unilever company website, visited 08.04.2024. https://www.unilever.com/files/92ui5egz/production/16cb778e4d31b81509dc5937001559f1f5c863ab.pdf

**Strategic disadvantages:** Ignoring or postponing compliance obligations can lead to an **investment backlog.** As these obligations accumulate, they can overwhelm an organization, hindering **operational agility** and the ability to adapt to market changes. Companies like Uber and Lyft have grappled with differing regulatory requirements in various regions, highlighting how compliance complexities can impede business scalability and adaptability.

In this complex regulatory landscape, international corporations must simultaneously safeguard customer privacy, ensure data integrity, and protect their reputations.

**Assessment: Benchmarking Regulatory Adherence**

 Assessing the efficacy of a company's compliance strategy is paramount for ensuring its resilience and strategic alignment. It also helps to right-size the investments into Regulatory and Compliance efforts – scrutinizing the demand for investments and avoiding that every initiative flagged 'regulatory' is simply rubber-stamped during the investment process. By employing a set of metrics, organizations can gain valuable insights into their compliance performance across key impact areas.

A set of indicators help understand, whether **consequences from the regulators** must be expected. We focus on three metrics to assess whether a company has imminent issues, how long it takes to mitigate and how it tries to avoid that new incident surface. Tracking **non-compliance incidents** provides insights into effective and potential gaps in regulatory understanding, implementation, or enforcement. A higher frequency of non-compliance incidents might indicate challenges in translating regulatory mandates into operational practices effectively. A shorter **time-to-remediation** displays the company's ability to promptly address non-compliance issues. Swift remediation demonstrates a proactive approach to compliance management, minimizing potential negative repercussions and mitigating associated risks. And finally, high **completion rates of mandatory compliance trainings** indicate that employees have received essential education on compliance requirements, enhancing the organization's readiness to meet regulatory obligations, and lowers the probability for incidents.

Maintaining customer trust and satisfaction hinges on effective compliance practices. Assess customer-centric compliance through these essential metrics: The **Stakeholder Feedback Score** gauges how stakeholders perceive the company's compliance efforts, reflecting the clarity and effectiveness of its compliance communication and practices. A higher score indicates that the company engages stakeholders well, conveying a strong commitment to regulatory compliance. In addition, a **Customer Trust Index** deep dives on the level of trust customers have in the organization's regulatory compliance practices. A higher index reflects customers' confidence that their data is handled responsibly, positively impacting brand loyalty and customer retention.

**Aligning compliance seamlessly with strategic objectives** is pivotal for sustainable growth. Evaluate strategic compliance integration through the following metrics: The **Percentage of Projects Delayed Due to Compliance** reveals the extent to which compliance requirements are Integrated into project planning early on. A lower percentage implies a well-understood compliance framework, minimizing disruptions to project timelines. In addition, the **Time and Resources Devoted to Compliance Audits** measures the efforts allocated to compliance audits indicates the efficiency of compliance management. Optimal resource allocation demonstrates that compliance audits are conducted effectively, contributing to streamlined operations and cost-effective adherence to regulations.

By utilizing these metrics organizations can proactively address compliance challenges with the appropriate level of investments, improve operational efficiency, and position themselves for growth and innovation.

**Action: Proactive Operationalization for Seamless Compliance Integration**

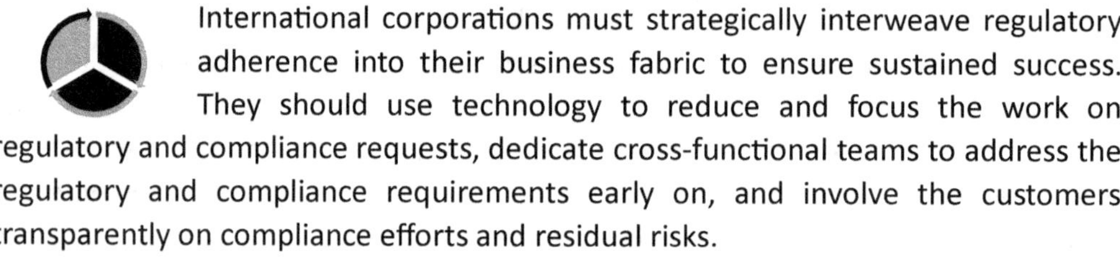

International corporations must strategically interweave regulatory adherence into their business fabric to ensure sustained success. They should use technology to reduce and focus the work on regulatory and compliance requests, dedicate cross-functional teams to address the regulatory and compliance requirements early on, and involve the customers transparently on compliance efforts and residual risks.

**Tech-driven solutions reduce the work of regulatory and compliance topics.** Leverage innovative technology to sculpt streamlined compliance management strategies. The sheer volume of regulatory documents can overwhelm human capacity. **Regulatory automation** utilizes machine learning and natural language processing to parse and analyze complex regulatory documents. This technology assists compliance teams in quickly identifying relevant changes and adapting strategies accordingly. JPMorgan Chase employs software to monitor evolving financial regulations, facilitating swift compliance adaptations. **Automated Compliance Checks** can alleviate the burden of manual compliance monitoring. Automation not only enhances efficiency but also reduces the risk of overlooking critical compliance aspects. Salesforce wields automated compliance checks, infusing data privacy regulations into its cloud services. These automated checks are synchronized with regulatory databases, ensuring timely notifications in case of regulatory changes. Regulations are dynamic and subject to change. **Predictive analytics** utilizes historical data and trends to forecast potential regulatory shifts. By anticipating changes, organizations can proactively adjust their compliance strategies, minimizing disruptions and ensuring continuous adherence. Toyota integrates predictive analytics to preemptively tailor manufacturing processes to stringent emissions regulations. These predictive models analyze regulatory trends, enabling Toyota to optimize processes for future compliance. Compliance often centers around data protection. **Secure data management** solutions encompass encryption, secure storage, and controlled access. These measures not only ensure regulatory compliance but also safeguard customer data, preserving their privacy and earning their trust. HSBC fortifies security and compliance through state-of-the-art data encryption methodologies. The bank employs cutting-edge encryption algorithms to protect sensitive customer information while adhering to international data protection regulations.

Efficient compliance integration mandates harmonious collaborations across internal departments and external partners. Compliance is not solely a legal endeavor, it requires collective efforts across departments. By fostering **cross-functional teams** comprising legal, operational, and technical experts, organizations ensure comprehensive compliance strategies. These teams can assess compliance implications from various angles and swiftly address deviations. General Electric (GE) nurtures integrated teams that ensure compliance with global environmental regulations, reducing the risk of regulatory oversights. These teams meet regularly to assess compliance across various functions and swiftly address any deviations. Compliance is most effective when integrated into the earliest stages of projects – **Compliance by design**. This proactive approach involves cross-functional collaboration between compliance experts and project teams from the outset. By identifying potential compliance challenges during the planning phase, organizations avoid costly retrofits and delays later in the project lifecycle. Airbnb engages its legal and compliance teams early in the product development lifecycle to proactively tackle potential compliance hurdles. By doing so, they ensure that compliance becomes an integral part of the product's DNA. Partnering with **external regulatory experts** or legal consultants enhances organizations' ability to interpret and implement regulations accurately. This collaboration ensures that compliance efforts remain aligned with evolving standards and prevents costly missteps. Air France-KLM enters a strategic alliance with aviation regulators, crafting a compliance fabric that seamlessly weaves through international safety and security regulations. This partnership allows for comprehensive insights into regulatory expectations, guiding compliance strategies.

**Finally, a customer-centric approach to mitigate residual risks.** In an era where customer trust stands as a pillar, organizations must prioritize compliance initiatives that tangibly enrich the customer experience, nurturing unshakable trust and unwavering loyalty. Beyond regulatory mandates, organizations should **proactively**

**communicate** their commitment to compliance, demystifying complex legal jargon and empowering customers to understand how their data and rights are protected. Transparent communication builds trust, as customers feel informed about how their information is used, stored, and protected. For instance, Siemens takes transparency to heart by regularly publishing sustainability reports, outlining its eco-friendly practices and adherence to regulations, supporting a deep bond of trust with environmentally conscious customers. The complexity of compliance regulations can often lead to customer confusion. By dedicating **specialized customer support resources** to address compliance-related queries, organizations demonstrate their commitment to providing accurate and transparent guidance, reassuring customers that their concerns are being heard and addressed. Amazon personifies this with its dedicated compliance support, which consists of a team of compliance experts trained to provide swift and precise assistance to customers facing compliance-related queries, ensuring clarity and confidence.

Salesforce is a shining light on how to turn possible Regulatory and Compliance constraints into an accelerator for its business.

> Salesforce operates in the Customer Relationship Management (CRM) space, where data privacy, security, and compliance are paramount. With the rise of regulations such as the General Data Protection Regulation (GDPR) in Europe and the California Consumer Privacy Act (CCPA) in the U.S., there was a potential for such rules to stifle digital innovation in the CRM industry.
>
> However, Salesforce turned this potential barrier into an opportunity. They integrated these regulatory requirements into their product suite, offering customers 'out-of-the-box' compliance solutions. Instead of fearing the regulations, Salesforce championed them, providing tools and resources that would help businesses navigate these complex compliance landscapes. They launched tools like Salesforce Shield, which provides advanced security, transparency, and compliance features tailored for heavily regulated industries.
>
> By embracing and embedding regulatory compliance into its offerings, Salesforce not only eased the compliance burden for its clients but also differentiated itself in the market. The company's proactive approach to regulations ensured its platforms were always ahead of the curve, transforming potential barriers into competitive advantages in the digital space.

By understanding the nuances of compliance, addressing its implications, and adopting strategic actions, organizations can pave the way for secure, sustainable, and successful digital growth. Compliance, far from being a mere hurdle, becomes a transformative force – a catalyst that propels innovation, enhances reputation, and solidifies an organization's standing in the global digital arena.

However, Data Security and Privacy Concerns are closely related.

## 2.3 Data Security and Privacy Concerns



**RESISTANCE TO CHANGE**
Embracing digital transformation often requires a cultural shift within the organization.

| REGULATORY AND COMPLIANCE CONSTRAINTS | DATA SECURITY AND PRIVACY CONCERNS | BALANCING INNOVATION WITH RISK MANAGEMENT | LEGACY SYSTEMS AND INFRASTRUCTURE |
|---|---|---|---|
| Compliance with digital regulations and standards, such as GDPR, can be burdensome for corporates operating in multiple jurisdictions – keeping up is an on-going challenge. | Corporates dealing with large volumes of sensitive data face cybersecurity risks and data privacy compliance challenges. | Innovating in the digital space is essential for growth, but it also comes with inherent risks. | Many established corporates have legacy systems/infrastructure that are not designed for the rapidly evolving digital world – integrating new digital technologies can be complex. |

*Figure 11: Barriers – Focus on Data Security and Privacy Concerns*

Data security and privacy concerns emerge as high hurdles. Global network interconnectivity and management of sensitive data magnify potential risks. From active dangers – triggered within a company – like data leakage and misuse to reactive challenges – initiated externally – posed by cyberattacks, businesses must comprehend the multi-faceted risk landscape. Recognizing these perils initiates the development of a robust data protection strategy.

**What the C-Suite needs to know**

1. The Complex Landscape of Data Protection: Companies operating globally face a multi-faceted array of risks, including data leaks, breaches, and cyberattacks. Such incidents, like those involving Equifax and Cambridge Analytica, emphasize the importance of safeguarding sensitive data, especially when dealing with international data transfers. Any compromise can lead to significant trust erosion and legal consequences.

2. The Dual Nature of Threats: Data protection risks can be categorized as active – originating from within the company (like internal data leakage) – and reactive – triggered externally (like cyberattacks). Examples like the WannaCry ransomware and the 2013 Target breach underscore the devastating impacts of reactive threats, not just in financial terms but also in reputational damage.

---

[13] Tim Cook – American Executive (Apple Inc.). * 01.11.1960 in Mobile

3. **Measuring Data Protection Effectiveness:** Effective data protection relies on tracking specific metrics, both active (like data leakage incidents and unauthorized access attempts) and reactive (like incident response times and cyberattack frequency). Monitoring and analyzing these metrics help in proactively identifying vulnerabilities and strategizing accordingly.

4. **Best Practices in Data Protection:** Leading companies globally have established effective data protection strategies. Microsoft's data classification, Siemens' encryption protocols, Sony's vendor assessments, Samsung's continuous monitoring, UBS's advanced threat detection, Tesco's vulnerability assessments, IBM's incident response planning, and Commonwealth Bank's transparent communication are notable examples. Emulating such best practices can enhance an organization's data protection framework.

5. **Holistic Approach to Data Security:** Addressing data security challenges requires a two-pronged approach encompassing both anticipatory strategies (like data classification, encryption, and vendor due diligence) and responsive strategies (like real-time threat monitoring, vulnerability assessments, and incident response planning). A harmonized approach ensures comprehensive data protection, bolstering the company's resilience against potential threats.


Let us apply the Triple-A approach to work on the challenges of Data Protection and Privacy.

**Awareness: Embracing Secure Data Protection and Avoiding Pitfalls**

The interplay of data protection regulations, coupled with the escalating specter of cyberattacks, presents formidable obstacles that can potentially derail progress. There are active – risks originate within the company – and reactive – risks are triggered outside of the company – data protection risks to be managed.

Operating on a global scale exposes companies to an array of **active data protection risks**, each with the potential to disrupt operations and damage reputation. Companies handle vast volumes of sensitive data, encompassing customer information, financial records, and proprietary insights, shouldering a profound responsibility. The inadequate safeguarding of this data can lead to breaches, with dire consequences, foremost among them being the erosion of trust and subsequent customer attrition. The complexities of transferring data across international borders add further layers of intricacy to digital operations, necessitating secure and lawful data transfer while upholding data integrity and complying with various regulatory frameworks. Sensitive customer information falling into the wrong hands will erode trust and subject the company to legal repercussions. Moreover, the threat of unwarranted data exploitation, both within and outside the organization, poses a significant challenge. As demonstrated by the Cambridge Analytica scandal, mishandling customer data for unauthorized purposes can lead to severe backlash and public outrage.

**Reactive threats**, exemplified by **cyberattacks**, introduce a layer of immediacy and potential devastation. The interconnected nature of global networks offers cybercriminals ample opportunities to exploit vulnerabilities, potentially compromising sensitive data and eroding customer trust. The WannaCry ransomware attack serves as a chilling example of the havoc that cyberattacks can wreak. This attack paralyzed critical infrastructure and led to significant financial losses. Cyberattacks take various forms, including malware, ransomware, and sophisticated phishing schemes. These attacks are increasingly orchestrated with precision, targeting vulnerabilities in a company's digital infrastructure, and exploiting the all-too-human factor of fallibility. The aftermath of a successful cyberattack extends beyond mere financial losses and operational disruptions. The fallout can potentially irreparably tarnish a company's reputation, leading to a cascading effect of eroded customer trust and damaged brand equity. The 2013 Target data breach demonstrated the impact of a cyberattack on customer trust and financial performance[14]. Cyberattacks can cause prolonged periods of downtime, diminishing customer engagement, and in some cases, even resulting in the loss of invaluable business insights and proprietary information.

**Assessment: Measuring Data Protection and Mitigation**

 Measuring a company's efficacy in addressing data security and privacy concerns involves a comprehensive evaluation of metrics spanning two distinct categories:

**Active Data Protection Metrics**: Monitoring the occurrence of **data leakage incidents**, both internal and external, provides insights into the effectiveness of preventive measures. This metric entails tracking instances where sensitive information inadvertently or maliciously leaves the organization's-controlled environment. A rise in data leakage incidents suggests vulnerabilities in data access controls, employee training, or technical safeguards. Regular analysis of the types of data leaked and the circumstances surrounding each incident informs targeted improvements to prevent future breaches. Tracking **attempts to access sensitive data without proper authorization** offers a gauge of potential internal threats. This metric involves recording instances of unauthorized access to critical databases, files, or systems. A notable increase in unauthorized access attempts might signify compromised credentials, insider threats, or inadequately configured access controls. By examining the patterns of unauthorized attempts and the areas of data

[14] Michael Kassner on ZDNet website: "Anatomy of the Target data breach: Missed opportunities and lessons learned". Published 02.02.2015, visited 08.04.2024. https://www.zdnet.com/article/anatomy-of-the-target-data-breach-missed-opportunities-and-lessons-learned/

targeted, companies can enhance user authentication processes and refine access permission protocols.

**Reactive Threat Metrics**: Monitoring the **frequency of cyberattacks** provides insight into the evolving threat landscape. This metric involves tracking the number of attempted cyberattacks, including malware infections, phishing attempts, and denial-of-service attacks. A surge in cyberattack attempts indicates an escalating risk profile that necessitates proactive countermeasures. Analyzing the tactics, techniques, and targets of these attacks can guide the development of tailored defense strategies. Measuring **Incident Response Time**, the time taken to respond to cyberattacks or security incidents, reflects a company's preparedness. This metric encompasses the time between detecting a security incident and initiating a well-coordinated response. A swift response can mitigate the impact of the attack and minimize potential damage. A prolonged response time might indicate gaps in incident management processes, lack of automation, or inadequate training for incident response teams. Tracking the **duration of downtime** caused by cyberattacks or security breaches quantifies the operational impact. This metric involves calculating the time systems, applications, or services remain inaccessible due to a security incident. Longer downtime affects business continuity, customer trust, and revenue generation. Understanding the financial and operational implications of downtime guides resource allocation for effective recovery and continuity planning.

This assessment ensures proactive risk mitigation and preparedness for emerging threats in the constantly evolving digital landscape.

### Action: Strategies for Data Protection Enhancement and Resilience

Effectively addressing data security and privacy concerns requires a multi-faceted approach that spans both active Data Protection Strategies and reactive Threat Mitigation Strategies.

**Anticipatory Data Protection Strategies:** Following the example of Microsoft, implement **robust data classification mechanisms** that categorize information based on sensitivity (visit section 3.5.1 Digital Wow on page 248 for further details on data infrastructure). Microsoft utilizes automated tools and metadata to classify data into categories like 'public', 'internal', and 'confidential'. This practice allows for different access levels, ensuring that sensitive data is only accessible to authorized personnel with the need-to-know. By employing **granular access controls** and utilizing **role-based access permissions**, companies can minimize the risk of unauthorized exposure and breaches. Emulate the practices of German engineering company Siemens, which employs **encryption** to safeguard data at rest and in transit. Siemens uses industry-standard encryption algorithms and secure key management to encrypt sensitive data stored in databases and during transmission. This measure provides a critical layer of protection against data exposure, rendering stolen data unreadable to unauthorized individuals. Implementing encryption across different layers of the infrastructure enhances security.

**Data Promise – How to Handle Personal Data with Utmost Vigilance**

In the age of digitalization, a company's stewardship of personal data has risen to the forefront of consumer concerns. This has given rise to the 'Data Promise' – an important commitment that companies undertake to safeguard the personal and sensitive information of their customers.

A 'Data Promise' represents a **sacred pact between a business and its clientele**, promoting responsible, transparent, and secure data management. Often articulated in the privacy policies, this pledge not only affirms the adherence to regulatory mandates but fundamentally seeks to foster a bedrock of trust and mutual respect between firms and their customers.

For consumers, the reverberations of a data promise resonate as a shield, safeguarding their sensitive details from potential misuse and creating a landscape of transparency and consent. It facilitates a trust-centric relationship, where customers can navigate a company's offerings with a heart unburdened by privacy concerns, and a reassurance that their preferences and choices are respected. This promise paves the way for personalized experiences, an avenue where customers willingly share information, spawning a tailored service ecosystem that meet their preferences and needs. The data promise allocates the power to the customer.

From the corporate vantage point, honoring a data promise emerges as a powerful catalyst in supporting a robust reputation, establishing the company as a bastion of ethical data practices in a world growing increasingly conscious of data stewardship. A well-articulated and steadfastly upheld data promise can serve as a company's shield, mitigating legal repercussions and aligning the business strategies firmly with regulatory tapestries. Beyond compliance, a data promise opens avenues for rich insights, enhancing business acumen, and creating a culture of innovation propelled by a well-spring of quality data.

A data promise transpires as a beacon of ethical, transparent, and responsible data management, mutually enriching both the company and its customers. It fosters an environment of trust and mutual respect, nurturing a relationship that stands robust in its foundation of ethical engagement. Companies championing a data promise not only sculpt a loyal customer base but steer towards a horizon of sustainable success, leveraging a deeper understanding of market dynamics and creating a nurturing space where customer insights transform into pathways of innovation and growth.

Drawing inspiration from Japan's Sony Corporation, prioritize **third-party vendor due diligence**. Sony employs a comprehensive vendor assessment process that includes security audits, policy evaluations, and contractual stipulations. This scrutiny reinforces the security ecosystem, ensuring that the entire supply chain adheres to stringent security protocols. Companies should establish clear vendor risk assessment criteria, conduct regular audits, and ensure contracts include data protection clauses, specifying security responsibilities.

**Responsive Threat Mitigation Strategies:** Following the example of South Korean tech giant Samsung, implement **continuous monitoring** tools to detect potential security breaches in real time. Samsung employs machine learning algorithms to establish baseline behavior and promptly alerts security teams to deviations, facilitating rapid threat containment. Real-time detection minimizes potential damage by enabling quick response and mitigation. Deploying a Security Information and Event Management (SIEM) system combined with user and entity behavior analytics enhances threat detection capabilities, enabling real-time correlation and analysis.

Mimicking the strategies of Swiss bank UBS, deploy **advanced threat detection solutions** that leverage machine learning and AI. UBS employs real-time monitoring of network traffic combined with behavioral analysis to detect anomalies indicative of potential attacks, enabling swift automated responses – directly built into all interaction channels, such as e-mail or messaging. This approach detects and neutralizes threats before they escalate, safeguarding critical systems and data. Incorporating threat intelligence feeds, endpoint detection and response (EDR) solutions, and anomaly detection algorithms enhances the accuracy and depth of detection.

Taking cues from British multinational retailer Tesco, conduct **regular vulnerability assessments and penetration testing**. Tesco employs automated tools to scan for vulnerabilities in its systems and applications. Timely patch management and proactive vulnerability resolution are integral to Tesco's security strategy. This practice reduces the attack surface by identifying and remediating vulnerabilities before attackers can exploit them. Implementing a vulnerability management process that includes regular scans, risk prioritization, and patching ensures a proactive defense posture.

Following the lead of American technology giant IBM, develop a comprehensive **incident response plan**. IBM's incident response teams are well-trained and conduct regular simulated exercises to refine their response procedures. These practices enhance IBM's readiness to counter cyberthreats. Swift and organized responses mitigate potential damage, minimizing the impact of data breaches and other security incidents. Establish predefined roles, communication channels, and escalation procedures to ensure a coordinated response that includes legal, technical, and communication aspects.

In line with the practices of Australia's Commonwealth Bank, establish **transparent communication** channels for stakeholders in the event of a data breach. Commonwealth Bank promptly notifies affected parties, regulatory authorities, and customers, maintaining trust and complying with data protection regulations. Open communication minimizes reputational damage by demonstrating accountability and commitment to data security. Create a well-defined communication plan that includes legal, public relations, and customer notification aspects, ensuring consistent and accurate messaging during crisis situations.

By harmonizing active measures and reactive strategies, organizations can effectively safeguard their data. Apple stands out as an absolute best-in-class company when it comes to handling data protection and privacy regulations, and they have consistently leveraged their approach as a key differentiator in the market.

**Apple**'s stance on data privacy is not just about being compliant with regulations like GDPR or CCPA, it is central to their brand promise. Their commitment to user privacy is integrated into product design, emphasizing data minimization, on-device processing, and user control over personal data. Apple's marketing campaigns have highlighted their privacy features, turning what could be a regulatory constraint into a unique selling proposition.

Features such as 'Sign in with Apple' emphasize user anonymity, allowing users to log into third-party apps without revealing their email addresses. Apple also introduced the App Tracking Transparency framework, which requires apps to get user permission before tracking their data across other companies' apps or websites.

By making data privacy a cornerstone of their brand and product experience, Apple not only ensures regulatory compliance but also builds trust with its users, turning privacy regulations into a competitive advantage in a data-sensitive digital ecosystem.

Beyond Compliance and Data Protection, it is important to balance Innovation with Risk Management.

## 2.4 Balancing Innovation with Risk Management

«Risk taking is the essence of innovation»
Herman Kahn[15]

**RESISTANCE TO CHANGE**
Embracing digital transformation often requires a cultural shift within the organization.

| REGULATORY AND COMPLIANCE CONSTRAINTS | DATA SECURITY AND PRIVACY CONCERNS | BALANCING INNOVATION WITH RISK MANAGEMENT | LEGACY SYSTEMS AND INFRASTRUCTURE |
|---|---|---|---|
| Compliance with digital regulations and standards, such as GDPR, can be burdensome for corporates operating in multiple jurisdictions – keeping up is an on-going challenge. | Corporates dealing with large volumes of sensitive data face cybersecurity risks and data privacy compliance challenges. | Innovating in the digital space is essential for growth, but it also comes with inherent risks. | Many established corporates have legacy systems/infrastructure that are not designed for the rapidly evolving digital world – integrating new digital technologies can be complex. |

*Figure 12: Barriers – Focus on Balancing Innovation with Risk Management*

In the relentless pursuit of global dominance, businesses stand at the crossroads of innovation and operational risk management (ORM). As they venture into uncharted territories with new products, technologies, and markets, the simultaneous necessity to safeguard assets, reputation, and operational integrity becomes paramount. These two forces – the drive to innovate and the need to manage operational risks – often seem at odds, but in the modern business ecosystem, they must coexist harmoniously.

**What the C-Suite needs to know**

1. Risk-tinged Awareness: Recognize that every innovative stride forward inherently carries operational risks. Understand the delicate combination of operational risk management and the necessity for digital evolution in international business realities.

2. Metrics Illuminate the Scales: Use precise metrics, such as the Innovation Risk Exposure Ratio, to spot areas where the scales between ORM and innovation might be off-balance. Keeping track of Frequency of Risk-Adjusted Innovation Failures can offer insights on whether the organization is pushing boundaries without ample risk considerations.

3. Navigated Innovations: Adopt structured pathways, reminiscent of Google's '20% time' model, to channel innovation efforts within defined ORM parameters. These frameworks should facilitate creativity while ensuring alignment with the company's risk appetite and thresholds.

---

[15] Herman Kahn – American physicist. * 15.02.1922 in Bayonne, † 07.07.1983 in Chappaqua

4.  Leadership – The Balancing Act's Maestro: Leaders must drive the dual mandate of championing innovation while rigorously upholding ORM. By instilling a culture of purpose-driven innovation intertwined with risk awareness, leaders ensure a synchronized approach to innovation and ORM.

5.  Risk-attuned Decisions Shape the Path: Balancing ORM with innovation means making explicit risk acceptance decisions. This involves understanding the potential risks tied to new ventures and ensuring they align with the company's larger risk strategy. Deliberate scenario planning and benchmarking against global players can further sharpen this risk-innovation equilibrium.

Let us dive deeper into the balance of innovation and risk management.

**Awareness: Laying the Landscape – The Thrust of Innovation and the Anchor of Risk**

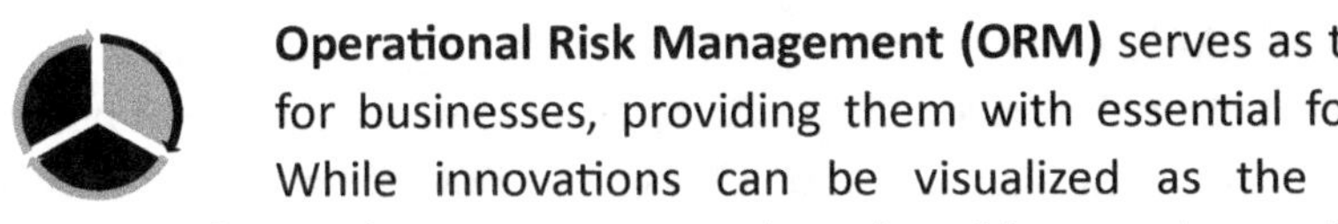 **Operational Risk Management (ORM)** serves as the strategic shield for businesses, providing them with essential foresight and tools. While innovations can be visualized as the engine propelling companies forward, ORM ensures that the ride remains stable, even through unpredictable terrain. For various industries, from finance to manufacturing, this methodology plays a pivotal role. Take the banking sector, for instance, here ORM examines vulnerabilities ranging from potential system downtimes to fraud prevention. For tech giants like Apple, ORM operates in the backdrop, ensuring that any potential supply chain disruptions or risks like the overheating of lithium batteries in iPhones are well-anticipated and preemptively addressed.

In today's era of exponential technological evolution, the relentless drive for companies to continually push boundaries and exceed customer expectations has been termed the '**Innovation Imperative**'. A prime example is Netflix, which evolved from a postal DVD rental service into a global streaming powerhouse. However, every silver lining has its cloud. With vast potential come the **risk realities**. For pioneers like Netflix, every venture into new features or original content production carries with it operational risks. These span from the significant financial investments required to the challenges of navigating global content regulations and potential cultural nuances.

Yet, history bears testament to the **consequences of an imbalance** between innovation and ORM. Consider Boeing's 737 Max crisis, a stark reminder that unchecked innovation, devoid of systematic ORM, can have profound, tragic implications. Conversely, companies drowning in excessive risk aversion can find themselves sinking into the abyss of obsolescence. The tale of Kodak, with its early blueprints of digital camera technology but a hesitance to fully embrace the digital transition due to fears of operational risks, is a testament to this.

The business landscape underscores one fundamental truth: Balance between innovation and ORM is non-negotiable. The spotlight is invariably on those companies that masterfully choreograph their steps, elegantly balancing the dynamism of innovation with the prudence of ORM.

**Assessment: Measuring the Tension – When Innovation Pushes and Risk Pulls**

 It is not enough for companies to merely innovate or manage risks in silos. The interplay between these domains is a nuanced dance, where missteps can lead to significant setbacks, while a harmonious balance can result in unprecedented performance. Operational Risk Management and Innovation must intertwine, and a company's proficiency in managing this delicate balance is often reflected through specific metrics that offer rich insights into its state of equilibrium.

**Innovation-Risk Ratio (IRR)**: Think of this as the pulse rate of a company's innovation heartbeat set against its risk resilience. By comparing the number of innovative projects in motion to the identified operational risks, the IRR offers a quick snapshot of the organization's operational health in relation to its innovation endeavors. A disproportionately high IRR may be an indicator of the 'innovate at all costs' mindset, potentially sidelining ORM. On the other hand, a consistently low IRR might point towards an overly cautious environment, where the shackles of ORM prevent innovative leaps. Successful companies maintain an optimal IRR, ensuring they remain pioneers without jeopardizing operational stability – the concrete IRR level needs to be defined per company within its industry context.

**Innovation Success vs. Risk Incidents Graph**: Picture this as a timeline of a company's journey. By juxtaposing successful innovations against risk incidents over a chronological axis, discernible patterns emerge. A recurrent trend where risk incidents spike following a surge in successful innovations might suggest that the pace of innovation is outstripping ORM's containment capabilities. Such insights can be instrumental in anticipating future challenges and recalibrating strategies.

**Digital Resilience Score**: In an age where digital transformation is not a luxury but a necessity, this score shines a spotlight on a company's fortitude in the digital reality. It assesses not just the digital advancements, but how efficiently risks associated with these advancements are navigated. Consider Amazon's foray into drone deliveries. While this leap displayed immense innovation, the associated operational risks – from technology malfunctions to regulatory challenges – were monumental. Amazon's adeptness in managing these risks, while persistently pushing the digital frontier, enhances its Digital Resilience Score. For any company it can be measured by evaluating a company's ability to innovate and transform digitally while effectively managing the risks associated with these advancements. Factors like the successful implementation of recent technologies and the efficient navigation of operational and regulatory challenges contribute to a higher score.

**Employee Innovation-Risk Perception Survey**: No metric can rival the insights procured from the grassroots level. Frontline employees, those spearheading innovations or managing risks firsthand, possess a unique perspective. Surveying them regularly can reveal whether they feel empowered to innovate or whether ORM protocols hinder their efforts. Alternatively, they might voice concerns that the innovation steamroller is moving so fast that ORM cannot keep pace. These ground truths can guide executive decisions, ensuring that both innovation and ORM remain in tandem.

As these metrics underscore, the combination between ORM and innovation, while intricate, can be both beautiful and strategic when executed with precision.

**Action: Striking the Equilibrium – Directing Innovation within Boundaries of Risk**

The equilibrium between innovation and ORM is a defining attribute. Striking this balance means constantly calibrating risk thresholds with the urge to innovate.

**Explicit Risk Decision Making in Innovation**: Balancing the scales of innovation and risk is a calculated endeavor. Consider Amazon's audacious pivot from being primarily a bookseller to an e-commerce behemoth. Each of its expansion decisions, whether it is the introduction of Amazon Web Services or Prime Video, was underpinned by a detailed risk-assessment mechanism. For instance, before launching Amazon Go or Amazon Fresh, their cashier-less stores, extensive beta testing with employees occurred, ensuring that the technology was foolproof and that any operational risks were minimized before public access. It is important for every company to explicitly manage, and not just accept, risks.

**Innovation Frameworks with Built-in ORM**: Google's '20% time' policy gives employees the creative latitude to explore projects outside their primary job responsibilities. But this freedom is bracketed within ORM bounds. When Gmail was conceptualized as a side project, concerns about data privacy and user trust were paramount. Before its public launch, rigorous ORM assessments, including potential phishing threats and hacking vulnerabilities, were carried out to ensure Gmail's robustness in real-world scenarios.

**Cultural and Leadership Alignment for ORM and Innovation**: When leaders set the tone, organizations follow. When Netflix transitioned from DVD rentals to a streaming behemoth, they did not just look at the technical viability. They also evaluated operational risks like potential content copyright issues, the viability of massive simultaneous streams, and even the implications of differing international censorship laws, ensuring that as they innovated, they were also well-prepared for potential ORM challenges.

**Scenario Planning for Innovative Ventures**: Envisioning future landscapes involves a mesh of innovation foresight and risk anticipation. Tesla's leap into electric vehicles was characterized by this dual vision. Beyond the obvious innovation in battery technology, they also had to anticipate and prepare for risks – like the potential scarcity and price volatility of lithium, the primary element for their batteries, or the infrastructure challenge in setting up Supercharger stations across diverse geographies with differing regulations (visit section 3.6.2 Innovation and Experimentation on page 313 to understand how scenario planning can help to anticipate the implications).

Mastering the dependency between innovation and ORM is about understanding that every step forward is accompanied by a potential pitfall – and planning for both. The balance is not a mere afterthought, it is the choreography that defines sustainable and strategic growth.

Venturing into new industries, while managing risk, is a key factor for Amazon's success.

---

**Amazon: Mastering the Balance of Risk & Innovation**

In 1994, the world met Amazon, emerging from Seattle as a humble online bookstore. Today, Amazon's story is not just about retail, it is about pioneering industries while balancing the scales of risk. With ventures like Amazon Web Services, they demonstrated that bold moves, even outside their core, can redefine market landscapes when approached with calculated precision.

At Amazon's core lies a culture of championing innovation yet accepting the possibility of failure, ensuring that missteps become lessons, not catastrophes. Through diverse undertakings – e-commerce, cloud computing, entertainment, and more – Amazon cushions operational risks, allowing triumphs in one realm to buffer challenges in another. Iterative strategies, such as the limited rollout of products like Amazon Echo, showcase their risk-managed approach to innovation.

From Seattle's shores to global digital frontiers, Amazon collaborates, invents, and refines, always with an eye on the horizon and a foot firmly planted in operational excellence. Navigating the tightrope between innovation and risk, Amazon exemplifies how visionary ambition, paired with astute risk management, can propel a company to stratospheric heights. In the vast Amazon ecosystem, each venture, be it in retail, tech, or entertainment, reflects a commitment to pushing boundaries while maintaining an unerring compass of operational prudence.

---

**As businesses push boundaries, they must also establish boundaries.** This balance is neither about stifling creativity nor about blind ventures, it is about moving forward with an unclouded vision, informed choices, and strategic resilience. By fostering a culture of awareness, rigorously assessing potential pitfalls and imbalances, and adopting proactive actions, organizations can truly harness the power of innovation while staying grounded in operational integrity.

Sometime innovation is limited by existing legacy systems. It is important to keep this in mind.

## 2.5 Legacy Systems and Infrastructure

«Investment in infrastructure is a long-term requirement for growth and a long-term factor that will make growth sustainable»

Chanda Kochhar[16]

**RESISTANCE TO CHANGE**
Embracing digital transformation often requires a cultural shift within the organization.

| REGULATORY AND COMPLIANCE CONSTRAINTS | DATA SECURITY AND PRIVACY CONCERNS | BALANCING INNOVATION WITH RISK MANAGEMENT | LEGACY SYSTEMS AND INFRASTRUCTURE |
|---|---|---|---|
| Compliance with digital regulations and standards, such as GDPR, can be burdensome for corporates operating in multiple jurisdictions – keeping up is an on-going challenge. | Corporates dealing with large volumes of sensitive data face cybersecurity risks and data privacy compliance challenges. | Innovating in the digital space is essential for growth, but it also comes with inherent risks. | Many established corporates have legacy systems/infrastructure that are not designed for the rapidly evolving digital world – integrating new digital technologies can be complex. |

*Figure 13: Barriers – Focus on Legacy Systems and Infrastructure*

As the digital world rapidly evolves, international corporations often find themselves weighed down by the anchor of outdated systems and infrastructures. What were once cutting-edge tools now become significant barriers to embracing newer, more efficient digital strategies. Legacy systems are typically defined by their outmoded technology, lack of adaptability, and inability to meld seamlessly with modern digital tools.

**What the C-Suite needs to know**

1. Modernization Imperative: Legacy systems that were once innovative now hinder progress, creating operational inefficiencies and stifling innovation.

2. Business Impact: Outdated technology, lack of adaptability, and disjointed integration result in fragmented operations, slower decision-making, and compromised customer experiences.

3. Metrics for Assessment: Frequent system outages, escalating maintenance costs, declining productivity, and challenges in integrating new software are indicators of legacy system constraints.

4. Strategic Action Needed: Legacy evolution demands a visionary strategy aligned with Digital Success, modular and scalable system design, cybersecurity focus, employee upskilling, and a culture of adaptability.

---

[16] Chanda Kochhar – Indian Businesswoman. * 17.11.1961 in Jodhpur

5.  **Digital Triumph Opportunity:** Modernizing legacy systems unlocks sustained success by revitalizing operations, fostering innovation, and positioning the company to thrive in the dynamic digital marketplace.

How can the Triple-A approach help us to address the legacy system challenge?

## Awareness: The Relevance and Challenge of Legacy Systems

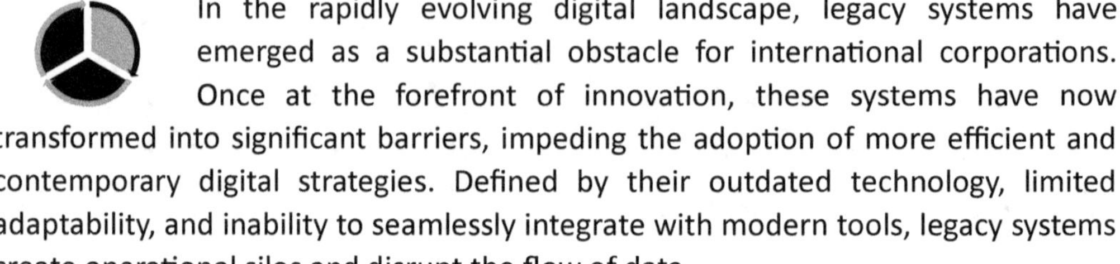

In the rapidly evolving digital landscape, legacy systems have emerged as a substantial obstacle for international corporations. Once at the forefront of innovation, these systems have now transformed into significant barriers, impeding the adoption of more efficient and contemporary digital strategies. Defined by their outdated technology, limited adaptability, and inability to seamlessly integrate with modern tools, legacy systems create operational silos and disrupt the flow of data.

The roots of these legacy systems trace back to a time when today's digital environment was beyond current imagination. Consequently, incorporating new software, applications, and tools has become a formidable challenge. This results in fragmented operations and interrupted data exchanges. Moreover, these legacy systems are ill-suited to match the dynamism and efficiency demanded by today's digital commerce. Manual operations and protracted data input processes hinder quick decision-making and detract from the customer experience. This can lead to a series of barriers to Digital Success:

**Operational risks**: Legacy systems introduce vulnerabilities such as system outages and data leakages, undermining a company's operational reliability and reputation. These systems lack the necessary security updates and patches, making them susceptible to cyberattacks and breaches. Their outdated architecture and protocols cannot withstand modern threats, leaving businesses exposed to operational disruptions. The decline of MySpace serves as a cautionary tale, as the company struggled to keep up with technological advancements and modernize its infrastructure, leading to a loss of relevance and user trust.

**Inefficiencies through fragmentation**: Legacy systems foster disjointed operations, leading to inefficiencies, and duplicated efforts. Data fragmentation across legacy systems hampers real-time visibility and creates silos within an organization. Employees waste time manually reconciling data from diverse sources. Kmart faced inefficiencies in its supply chain management due to fragmented legacy systems, leading to difficulties in inventory management, supply chain optimization, and timely restocking.

**Slowed-down development opportunities**: The difficulty of integrating new components and outdated interfaces stifle innovation, impeding agility in a dynamic digital environment. Legacy systems often lack open APIs (Application Programming Interfaces) and integration capabilities, making it challenging to incorporate recent technologies. Their rigid structure prevents seamless collaboration and hinders the adoption of modern tools. Nokia's reliance on Symbian OS for its smartphones hindered its ability to adapt to the emerging touchscreen trend, causing it to miss out on the smartphone revolution and lose its dominant market position.

**Missed strategic opportunities**: Siloed data and inconsistent flows deprive businesses of holistic insights, hindering strategic decision-making and growth potential. Legacy systems store data in isolated repositories with different formats and structures, making it arduous to consolidate and analyze information effectively. This results in missed opportunities to identify market trends and customer preferences. Blockbuster's reliance on legacy systems prevented it from adapting to changing customer preferences and digital streaming trends, causing the company to miss the opportunity to become a leader in online entertainment.

### Assessment: Metrics to Identify Legacy System Hindrances

 In the journey to achieve digital aspirations, a thorough assessment of legacy infrastructure's impact becomes crucial. This assessment relies on essential metrics that provide tangible insights into whether legacy systems impede Digital Success.

To understand the operational risks, **frequent and prolonged system outages and disruptions** act as indicators. These disruptions not only make daily operations cumbersome but also erode trust among customers, partners, and employees. The frequency and impact of such outages serve as benchmarks to evaluate the capacity of legacy systems to maintain seamless operations and reliability.

Inefficiencies are surfaced by **diminished productivity numbers or increased reliance on manual processes**. In an era that esteems efficiency and automation, the prevalence of manual workflows reflects an inability to adapt to the contemporary digital environment. Sluggish operations hinder growth and impede the company's ability to meet modern consumer expectations. Likewise, customer and employee feedback provide a lens through which to gauge the impact of legacy systems on their experience. Customer and employees interfacing with these systems offer firsthand perspectives on their limitations. Consistently negative feedback signifies that legacy issues are eroding the company's capacity to provide a seamless and modern customer experience.

A limited ability to strategically develop is strongly driven by the **lack of compatibility with new tools.** Persistent conflicts between modern additions and existing systems signal deeper issues. Such incompatibilities hinder the company's capacity to embrace modern technologies, stifling innovation, and agility. Additionally high financial allocation for maintenance vs. innovation offers insights into the influence of legacy systems. If a substantial budget allocation goes towards maintaining existing systems, particularly compared to investments in novel initiatives, it underscores the toll that legacy issues exact. This allocation highlights the diversion of resources from digital transformation and innovation efforts.

To gauge whether your company's data flow is fragmented and inhibiting strategic opportunities, look for **inconsistencies in data across departments**, resulting in conflicting reports and difficulties in generating a comprehensive view of the business. **If your organization struggles to analyze customer behavior holistically due to disconnected systems, it is a sign of fragmented data.** Additionally, observe if decision-making relies on manual data compilation from disparate sources, as this can hinder agility and responsiveness. Identifying these challenges can shed light on the need to address data fragmentation for better strategic alignment and decision-making.

By assessing all these metrics, companies gain profound insights into the impediments presented by legacy systems. These insights guide companies in identifying areas necessitating transformation and empower strategic actions to surmount legacy barriers. On top the metrics also calibrate the level of investments into modernizing the various components of the legacy systems (vs. investment into strategic developments).

**Action: Legacy Evolution – Paving the Path to Digital Triumph**

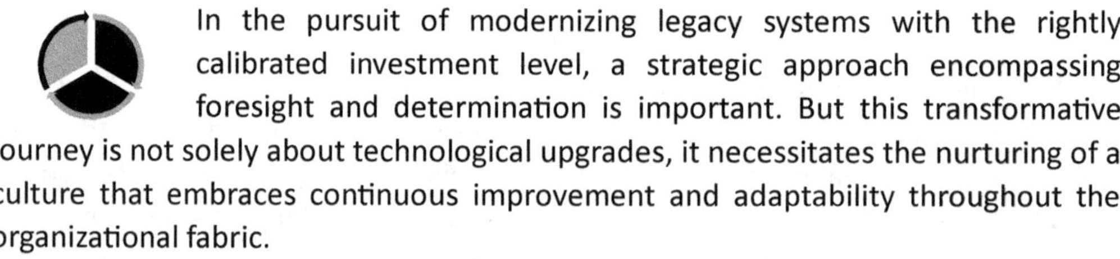

In the pursuit of modernizing legacy systems with the rightly calibrated investment level, a strategic approach encompassing foresight and determination is important. But this transformative journey is not solely about technological upgrades, it necessitates the nurturing of a culture that embraces continuous improvement and adaptability throughout the organizational fabric.

A Target Technology Architecture Blueprint provides transparency throughout the organization. A culture of understanding and broad endorsement of the renewals lay the foundation for a joint direction, whereas a stringent plan and resolute decision making ensures the consequent implementation.

*Defining a Target Technology Architecture Blueprint*

Crafting a **visionary strategy for technology architecture** forms the bedrock of a triumphant transformation. Enterprises must crystallize their interpretation of Digital Success within the context of their technology landscape. This entails understanding existing technology assets, identifying gaps, and envisioning an architectural blueprint that aligns with the organization's digital objectives.

A well-constructed technology architecture blueprint serves as the guiding light for a future-oriented company's transformation. Such a blueprint encapsulates the organization's vision, ensuring that technological decisions are in harmony with business goals. In this context three big rocks need to be addressed by most companies.

A key driver for success in modernizing the legacy systems is the establishment of **consistency and interoperability across platforms and systems**. This involves creating a harmonious technological ecosystem where data flows seamlessly, eliminating data silos and fragmented operations. By embracing standardized protocols and APIs, organizations can facilitate communication between diverse systems, ensuring smooth data exchange and coherent operations. Furthermore, within the context of modern technology architecture, the integration of big data and analytics platforms assumes a fundamental role[17]. These platforms enable organizations to harness the power of data-driven insights for informed decision-making, enhanced customer experiences, and the development of predictive models that drive innovation. Consider Netflix that exemplifies the power of data and analytics integration. Netflix's technology architecture seamlessly integrates data from various sources to offer personalized recommendations and optimize user experiences. Through consistent data flow and interoperability, Netflix enhances its value proposition and drives customer engagement.

**Modularity and scalability** are essential elements of a forward-looking technology blueprint. Organizations should design systems as modular components that can be integrated or replaced without disrupting the entire infrastructure. Scalability ensures that the architecture can handle increased demands and growth without compromising performance. To achieve modularity and scalability, organizations can adopt a microservices architecture. This approach involves composing applications of small, independent services that communicate through APIs, allowing for easier modification, maintenance, and scalability of individual components. Cloud technology often plays a vital role in achieving this scalability. Leveraging cloud infrastructure, such as Amazon Web Services (AWS) or Google Cloud Platform (GCP)

---

[17] Viktor Mayer-Schönberger, Kenneth Cukier: "Big Data – a revolution that will transform how we live, work and think". Published by John Murray, 2013

provides resources on-demand, enabling infrastructure expansion or contraction based on user needs. Implementing DevOps practices introduces automation to deployment, testing, and scaling of applications, fostering agility and enabling rapid iteration and improvements. Take the example of Spotify, which embraces modular and scalable systems. Spotify's microservices architecture enables continuous innovation and rapid feature deployment while maintaining a seamless user experience across a diverse range of devices.

In an era where cyberthreats are pervasive, the technology architecture blueprint must prioritize **cybersecurity and data protection**. This involves integrating robust security protocols, encryption, and access controls. By embedding cybersecurity measures into the very core of the blueprint, organizations safeguard their digital assets and customer trust. Adopting a zero-trust architecture is crucial. This approach treats every user and device as potentially untrusted, implementing stringent access controls, multi-factor authentication, and continuous monitoring. Encryption becomes paramount, with data being encrypted at rest and in transit to ensure confidentiality and prevent unauthorized access. Regular security audits and vulnerability assessments are essential to identify potential weaknesses, prompt vulnerability patching, and stay up to date with the latest cybersecurity threats and best practices. Consider SAP, a global leader in enterprise software, as an exemplar of cybersecurity integration within its technology architecture. SAP's commitment to data security ensures that its solutions are trusted by organizations worldwide, maintaining the confidentiality and integrity of critical business data.

By ensuring consistency and interoperability, modularity, and scalability, as well as cybersecurity within their technology infrastructure, companies lay the foundation for an agile, resilient, and competitive digital ecosystem. However, to be successful, it is important that the blueprint is understood and endorsed throughout the organization, not just with the engineers in the IT department.

### *Cultivating a Culture of Understanding and Endorsement for the Target Blueprint*

Beyond strategies and plans, the transformational journey requires an organizational culture that universally comprehends the paramount importance of infrastructure renewal. This understanding should permeate from top management to the grassroots level. The culture should be one that appreciates that modernization is not merely a technical endeavor, it is a strategic imperative that fuels competitiveness, innovation, and long-term success.

Amid modernization endeavors, the role of organizational culture emerges as a linchpin in the transformational process. A technology-focused metamorphosis is not confined to the IT organization, rather, it infiltrates every facet of an organization's operations, strategies, and aspirations. Such a culture transcends the binary understanding of 'technical' versus 'non-technical' roles, fostering a **collective realization that modernization is integral to the organization's survival and prosperity**.

Education forms the cornerstone of cultural transformation. Organizations must invest in comprehensive **educational initiatives** to bridge the knowledge gap on all levels. These initiatives should not be confined to technical training alone, they should encompass a holistic understanding of how modernization aligns with strategic objectives. Awareness campaigns, workshops, and interactive sessions can demystify the complexities of infrastructure renewal, making it accessible to employees at all levels. Cross-functional collaboration can be nurtured through shared learning experiences, enabling individuals from diverse departments to appreciate the collective significance of modernization.

This in-depth understanding of the necessity and the options, allow the management to accept its **leadership role**. All senior executives, not just the Tech Management, must not only endorse the modernization initiative but also actively communicate its strategic significance. When top management visibly champions the renewal cause, it sends a powerful message about the transformation's gravity and the commitment required from all levels. They should communicate the rationale, benefits, and long-term vision of infrastructure renewal, inspiring confidence, and excitement among the workforces. By leading through example, executives set the tone for a culture that values and supports technological evolution.

A culture of understanding is fortified by the **recognition and celebration** of successes. When milestones are achieved and objectives are met, they should be celebrated as collective victories. Acknowledging and applauding teams and individuals who contribute to the renewal journey reinforces the idea that modernization is a collaborative endeavor that impacts the organization as a whole. By spotlighting successful projects and displaying their positive impact, organizations inspire others to contribute and emulate similar achievements. Recognition creates a sense of belonging and pride, making employees feel valued for their role in propelling the organization towards a more resilient and competitive future.

Microsoft stands as a global exemplar in creating a culture of technological understanding. The company's 'One Microsoft' initiative unified its workforce around a common vision, emphasizing the significance of modernization in realizing that vision. Through transparent communication, education, and recognition, Microsoft has cultivated a culture where employees across disciplines actively engage with and support technological transformation[18].

---

[18] Steve Ballmer on Microsoft company website: "One Microsoft: Company realigns to enable innovation at greater speed, efficiency". Published 11.07.2013, visited 08.04.2024.

Cultivating a culture of understanding represents a foundational pillar of the modernization journey and its implementation.

### *Navigating the Renewal Journey*

Crafting a successful roadmap towards the target architectural blueprint mandates transparency and resolute decision-making. To counter the perennial postponement of infrastructure renewal investments, companies must enact a detailed plan that navigates the journey from the current situation to the envisioned digital infrastructure. This plan necessitates tough decisions and prioritization, ensuring that every step taken aligns with the ultimate goal.

The foundation of a successful renewal plan rests on **transparency**. This also involves clear communication of the vision and the rationale behind the renewal endeavor to stakeholders at all levels of the organization. Transparent communication cultivates understanding, secures buy-in, and rallies the entire organization around the shared objective of technological transformation. The renewal journey begins with a comprehensive assessment of existing systems and applications. This entails a careful evaluation of technological assets, identifying components that align with the future blueprint and those that require replacement or upgrading. This assessment serves as the baseline for the renewal plan, shedding light on the scope, challenges, and opportunities that lie ahead. Once the assessment is complete, organizations can proceed to the evaluation phase, where technological options are carefully examined. This phase involves assessing the feasibility of integrating existing systems, the cost-effectiveness of replacements, and the potential for innovation. Each decision is driven by a commitment to aligning technology with the overarching business strategy.

One of the defining aspects of a transparent renewal plan is the practice of **firm decision-making**. Given the complexity of technology landscapes and the interplay of various components, companies must make tough decisions about which systems to continue or to replace, which to integrate, and which to retire. Each decision contributes to the alignment with the target blueprint. Prioritization is another crucial facet of the roadmap. Companies must prioritize components based on various criteria, including their impact on business operations, potential for innovation, and feasibility of integration. Blind dogma does not maximize the outcome for the company. A methodical approach ensures that resources are allocated to critical areas, preventing dilution, and scattering of efforts. Transparency extends beyond the planning stage, it encompasses the entire renewal journey. Establishing accountability mechanisms ensures that stakeholders remain committed to their roles and responsibilities. Regular progress tracking and reporting foster a culture of ownership and responsibility, keeping all involved parties informed about advancements, setbacks, and adjustments.

Organizations that have successfully embarked on the infrastructure renewal journey offer valuable insights. European aviation leader Airbus executed a comprehensive renewal plan to modernize its IT infrastructure. By transparently communicating the rationale and objectives to its workforce, Airbus navigated the complexities of modernization while minimizing disruptions to business operations. Unilever, a global consumer goods giant, serves as an exemplary model of prioritization and decision-making. Their strategic approach to technological transformation ensured that investments were directed towards areas that aligned with their business strategy, enabling them to achieve seamless integration and enhanced operational efficiency.

In crafting a transparent infrastructure renewal plan, organizations create a roadmap that leads beyond the status quo. Transparency in assessment, decision-making, and prioritization ensures that every step taken is aligned with the ultimate goal of achieving a future-ready technology landscape. This strategic journey not only transforms technological foundations but also cultivates a culture of innovation, resilience, and forward-thinking.

Leading into the new digital age, Deutsche Bank has initiated an ambitious renewal program.

**Deutsche Bank: Pioneering Digital Transformation in Finance**

In 1870, the world was introduced to Deutsche Bank, a beacon of financial stability rising from Germany's heartland. Today, Deutsche Bank's narrative transcends traditional banking, it is a tale of embracing digital metamorphosis while maintaining the bedrock of financial trust. With initiatives like the Digital Factory and a decisive move to modern cloud infrastructures, they showcased the audacious step of reinventing foundational systems, positioning themselves at the forefront of fintech evolution.

Central to Deutsche Bank is a conviction: the fusion of time-honored banking practices with the pulse of technological advancement. By revitalizing its core banking system, entering symbiotic alliances with tech visionaries, and prioritizing cybersecurity, they have ensured that legacy does not mean outdated. Strategic partnerships with tech giants and fintech startups highlight their commitment to intertwining financial acumen with digital prowess.

From the bustling streets of Frankfurt to the global nexus of finance, Deutsche Bank iterates, innovates, and integrates, driven by a future-focused vision yet anchored in unparalleled financial expertise. As they tread the path between tradition and transformation, Deutsche Bank epitomizes how relentless pursuit of digital excellence, complemented by deep-rooted industry wisdom, can redefine a sector's paradigm. In Deutsche Bank's expansive portfolio, every initiative, be it in core banking or digital partnerships, mirrors a relentless commitment to lead, adapt, and flourish in a dynamic digital era.

All these possible barriers need to be actively managed. However, often resources are scarce, and priorities need to be set with an overall perspective.

## 2.6 Balancing Barriers and Priorities in a resource-limited reality



In today's complex business landscape, **corporations are constantly juggling their roles as stewards of resources and drivers of growth**. The challenges of strategically investing in this environment are multi-faceted, primarily due to the need to **balance between perceived barriers and broader strategic development priorities**.

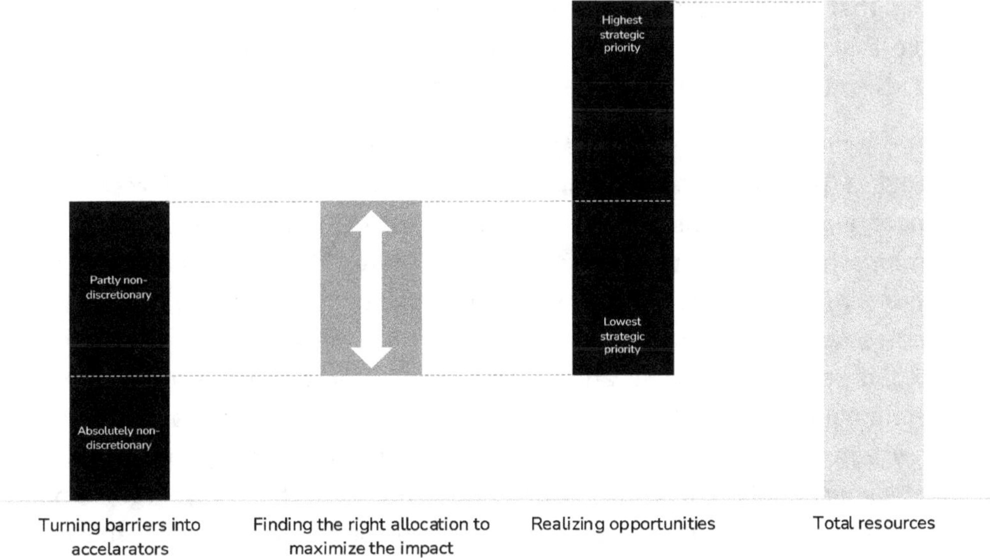


*Figure 14: Investment dilemma*

We are always working in the context of scarce resources. However, it is a fair question to ask, what the **appropriate level of resources is to pursue a company's ambitions**. An optimal investment level does not follow a one-size-fits-all approach but is bespoke, derived from a multi-faceted analysis of various business-specific parameters. A prevalent approach to ascertain this allocation is considering it as a percentage of the company's revenue. Typically, businesses might earmark anywhere from 5% to 15% of their annual revenues for digital innovations and general technology development. However, this allocation should not be arbitrary but

---

[19] Lee Iaccoca – American automobile executive. * 15.10.1924 in Allentown; † 02.07.2019 in Bel Air

anchored in a strategic vision and tangible objectives to foster growth and competitiveness. And an absolute benchmarking is difficult – whereas revenues is a defined number, investments into digital finds different definitions and scope from company to company, e.g., including system maintenance or just focus on new digital developments. However, more comprehensive than the revenue percentage method is a return on investment (ROI) analysis. The essence of ROI analysis lies in correlating every dollar spent on digital solutions with the value it adds to the business, both in the short and long term. This approach extends beyond immediate financial gains to capture enhancements in customer satisfaction, brand equity, market share, and operational efficiencies. **It is not about spending more but spending smartly,** ensuring that every investment yields multiplicative value to the organization. In the pursuit of a more refined strategy, some firms employ a combination of revenue, operational efficiency, and market share metrics to derive a digital investment quotient. This quotient aligns digital spending with key performance indicators (KPIs), ensuring that investments are both substantial and astute. It underscores the principle that investment in digital solutions should reflect a company's strategic objectives and operational needs, driving measurable improvements.

However, regardless of the overall resource level is, it is paramount that corporations carve out a precise understanding **what is needed in terms of resources to transmute existing barriers into robust accelerators.** Understanding that not all investments hold equal merit is fundamental here. There exists a tier of non-discretionary investments, which are non-negotiable and central to the essence of corporate responsibility in the digital era. These include regulatory and compliance norms, data security protocols, and privacy commitments. Contrastingly, areas such as operational risk management (ORM), spearheading innovation, and overhauling legacy systems present a more dynamic spectrum of investment opportunities. Here, the endeavor should be to not just meet immediate needs but to synergize a potent blend of strategic foresight, risk appetite, and a keen understanding of volatile market dynamics. Alphabet's ventures, including notable names like Waymo and Verily, encapsulate this delicate equilibrium between nurturing innovation and mitigating risk. It is not about mere technological overhaul, it embodies a conscientious effort to harmonize age-old infrastructure with burgeoning digital demands, a journey well-charted by industry stalwarts like IBM.

At the same time, corporations stand at a critical juncture where strategic investments no longer remain just a choice but a necessity. It is imperative to maneuver through this path with a delineated strategy that illuminates optimum spheres to channel vital resources towards and realize strategic opportunities that are sustainable and lucrative. **Embarking on this journey demands the crafting of a well-defined hierarchy of priorities,** grounded deeply in the potential business impacts. It necessitates that corporations steer away from static strategies, fostering instead living, breathing frameworks that bring life to every strategic endeavor. At the outset, companies are called upon to immerse themselves in immediate alignment and activation towards high-priority initiatives, giving precedence to those projects that stand tall with a promise of substantial impact. Leveraging the concept of **Minimum Viable Products** (MVPs) becomes instrumental here. By focusing on MVPs, organizations can swiftly move from concept to realization, flexibly adapting based on real-world feedback. It facilitates an early and tangible validation of the projects, preventing the common pitfall of getting mired in exhaustive development cycles. This strategy harbors an agility, nurturing strategies that are robust yet attuned to actual market demands, ushering corporations into a dynamic landscape where potentials are not just identified but rapidly seized and nurtured to fruition. Flowing seamlessly from this stage is the development of a sequential strategy for pipeline augmentation. This strategy extends beyond a structured pathway, evolving into a flexible tool that guides resource allocation while maintaining a rhythm of sustainable growth, responsive to the capricious nature of market fluctuations. The opportunity pipeline thus crafted serves as more than a checklist, it becomes a strategic tool that actively guides resource allocation, creating a harmonious combination between opportunity and strategy, grounded in realistic assessments of potential impacts and feasibility. To truly thrive in this space, corporations must harbor a systematic approach to scrutinizing business cases, fostering a culture where each case undergoes a **rigorous vetting process** to eliminate those merely riding on superficial allure. It involves unearthing opportunities that hold a strong grounding in business acumen and demonstrable potential, avoiding over-optimistic projections that often mask the true viability of a project. This method demands a steadfast commitment to empirical analysis and a deep understanding of market realities.

In conclusion, it is through a judicious and discerning allocation of resources that corporations can indeed steer towards a future of sustainable growth. By forging strategies grounded in reality, yet visionary in approach, companies hold the promise of not just navigating the current landscape successfully but emerging as resilient entities in a fiercely competitive environment, poised for unprecedented success. The pathway to this success is paved with strategic investments that are well-vetted and grounded in a deep understanding of market realities, sculpting a future that is both robust and dynamically attuned to unfolding opportunities.

Having explored the complexities and nuances associated with the aspects of digital transformation, we are poised to transition from understanding and mitigating barriers to seizing opportunities that lie ahead. Each challenge identified and addressed paves the way for a more enlightened, strategic approach to digital integration and innovation. As we turn the page, we embark on an exploration of the strategic Digital Success Levers. Our subsequent discourse will unveil how to adeptly manipulate these levers, aligning them with organizational objectives to build an ecosystem where technology and strategy converge to spawn excellence and value.

# 3 Unleash the potential

Once possible barriers are turned into accelerators, it is time to unleash the potential, and make it happen. We turn our focus on **optimizing the seven Digital Success Levers** with their **14 Digital Success Modules**. One after the other we will apply the Triple-A Approach to build the **Awareness** for what it is, and why it is important. We will discuss metrics and markers to **Assess** the status and level of achievement of a particular company and to identify where it must act. Finally, we will outline key **Actions** a company can initiate and execute to maximize the benefits and to be digitally successful.

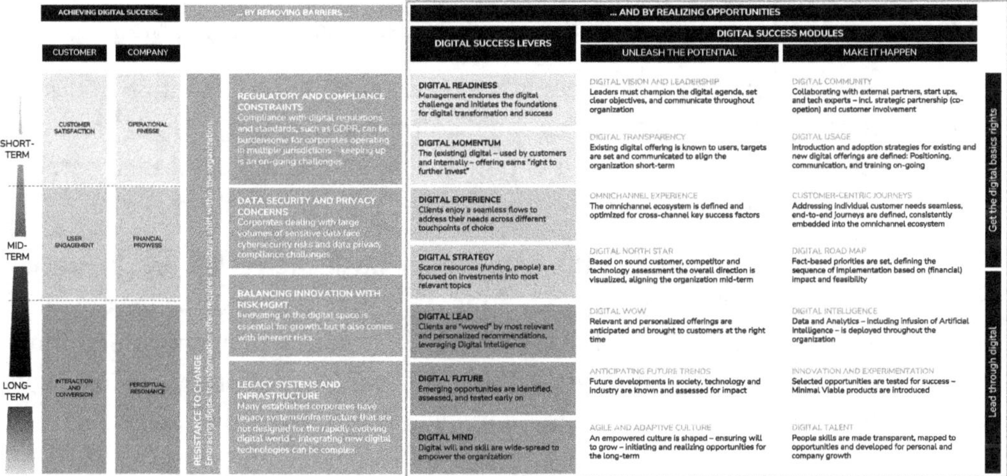


*Figure 15: Digital Success Canvas - Focus on Digital Success Levers and Modules*

For all these levers and modules, you find more information in the **Digital Arena**. Find the latest and connect with like-minded professionals to fully unleash your potential.

At the core of this strategy lies the dual-modules approach, effectively demarcating the digital development into two pivotal stages: 'to unleash the potential' and 'to make it happen'. This approach ensures that companies not only foster visions but also devise actionable approaches to realize them.

**To unleash the potential** is to vividly conceptualize the zenith a company aspires to reach. It embodies in most cases the first module of each Digital Success Lever, where we sculpt the ideal target state echoing the corporate ambitions and the benchmarks they wish to attain. This is the stage where aspirations are translated into tangible goals, crystallizing the 'What' of the trajectory that delineates the pinnacle of achievement that one aims to reach.

Following the laying down of potential directions, we transition into the dynamic phase designed **to make it happen**. This encapsulates for most Digital Success Levers the second module, an operational blueprint that provides the 'How' to the previously established 'What'. It is a systematic approach delineating how to ascend from the current state to the envisioned pinnacle of Digital Success.

As outlined earlier, the pathway to Digital Success for a company is forged through the seamless integration and progressive evolution of the Seven Digital Success Levers, each building upon the previous in creating a transformative digital culture primed for innovation, efficiency, and adaptability. It is worth recapping the core of the framework before we dive into the details of each Digital Success Module.

Digital Readiness sets the foundational stage, establishing a proactive and open culture that recognizes and addresses the disruptive forces in the digital reality of today. It is characterized by management endorsement and a readiness to embrace the digital shift, igniting the company's path towards digital transformation.

Digital Momentum is fostered as the organization begins to realize and appreciate the benefits of its (existing) digital assets. This stage is marked by tangible outcomes and growing confidence, as stakeholders witness the positive impacts on customer satisfaction, operational efficiency, and profitability, thereby encouraging investments into digital developments – earning the right to further invest.

Digital Experience takes precedence next, focusing on enhancing user experience across various touchpoints to build trust and loyalty. It lays the groundwork for mid-term success, emphasizing consistency, personalization, and a seamless flow in the customer's journey, solidifying the brand's relationship with its customers.

Digital Strategy follows, wherein the organization allocates its resources towards the most promising digital initiatives in alignment with its overarching business goals. This stage ensures the highest returns on investments and lays down a roadmap for immediate gains while establishing the foundations for sustained growth and resilience.

Digital Lead comes next, uplifting the company's ambitions to a position of leadership in the digital space. Fully leveraging Digital Intelligence, it focuses on delivering Digital Wow experiences through personalized and relevant engagements. This stage accentuates data and analytics-driven decisions to enhance customer loyalty and brand recognition.

Digital Future evolves by leveraging the success of the preceding stages, with an eye on emerging opportunities for long-term growth and industry shaping. It involves early identification of trends and market shifts, followed by rigorous assessment and testing, setting the cornerstone for long-term viability and proactive innovation.

Digital Mind is the capstone, emphasizing the nurturing of a digital mindset throughout the organization. It creates a culture of experimentation and recognizes digital excellence to ensure the company remains nimble, innovative, and at the forefront of digital advancements.

This comprehensive approach ensures a future where the organization is always prepared to seize emerging opportunities. Let us now focus on all the Digital Success Levers, starting with Digital Readiness. In the prior chapter on possible barriers to Digital Success, we faced 'Resistance to Change' throughout the organization as a possible hinderance, and introduced some mitigating measures (visit section 2.1 Resistance to Change on page 36 to recap on this frequent barrier to success). However, Digital Readiness of Senior Management expands even further. It is the foundation, in many cases the driver for digital transformation and success.

## 3.1 Digital Readiness

«Action springs not from thought,
but from a readiness for responsibility»
G.M. Trevelyan[20]

**Digital Readiness encompasses the senior management's discernment and acknowledgment of both the opportunities and threats triggered by digital developments.** The disruptive potential of digital technologies is double-edged. On one hand, it offers the chance to revolutionize business operations, foster innovative solutions, and carve out new market niches, all of which can potentially lead to a stronger competitive position and enhanced profitability. On the other hand, it poses considerable threats to organizations that remain complacent, including the loss of market share to more digitally agile competitors, outdated business models, and diminished customer loyalty as consumers increasingly gravitate towards businesses that offer seamless digital experiences.

Central to Digital Readiness is senior management's willingness and ability to set a clear **Digital Vision** for the organization, understanding the disruptive potential of digital technologies and championing their integration into the company's core vision. An example is Satya Nadella at Microsoft, who redefined the company's trajectory with a 'mobile-first, cloud-first' approach, harnessing the transformative power of the latest (technical) developments to reshape business propositions and processes[21]. Also, other leaders around the globe and from different industries provide shining examples of **Digital Leadership**. Ana Botín, the Group Executive Chairperson of Banco Santander, pushed the bank into the digital age with the launch of Openbank, an entirely digital bank. Bernard Arnault of LVMH demonstrated digital foresight by investing in e-commerce platforms and digital marketing to democratize luxury retail's reach and personalization. In Asia, Mukesh Ambani transformed the telecommunications landscape in India with the launch of Reliance Jio, providing affordable 4G services and promoting digital inclusivity[22].

---

[20] G.M. Trevelyan – British historian and academic. * 16.02.1876 in Warwickshire; † 21.07.1962 in Cambridge

[21] Chengyi Lin, Benjamin Kessler in an INSEAD publication: "The Rebirth of a Giant: Microsoft's Pivot to Mobile First, Cloud First". Published 11.04.2023, visited 08.04.2024.
https://publishing.insead.edu/case/rebirth-a-giant-microsofts-pivot-mobile-first-cloud-first

[22] Sahil Singh Jasrotia, Roop Lal Sharma and Hari Govind Mishra in IIM Indore: "Disruptions in Indian Telecom Sector: A Qualitative Study on Reliance Jio". Published June 2019, visited 08.04.2024.
https://www.iimidr.ac.in/wp-content/uploads/Vol11-1-03.pdf

Moreover, a distinguishing feature of Digital Readiness is the leadership's recognition that success in the digital age is inherently collaborative – **Digital Communities shape future success.** Whereas Digital Vision and Leadership are the internal ingredients to Digital Readiness, collaborations add the external spices. For instance, Siemens and Alibaba Cloud's collaboration aimed at harnessing the Industrial Internet of Things (IIoT) in China. In the automotive space, the alliance between Nissan, Renault, and Mitsubishi epitomizes how giants can come together to explore electric vehicles and autonomous driving technologies. Further, Unilever's partnership with start-ups through its Unilever Foundry initiative has sparked numerous digital innovations across its consumer goods spectrum. In today's digitally connected world, **senior management must support a culture that values external collaborations**. Such a collaborative stance ensures a continuous influx of fresh ideas and a comprehensive understanding of evolving digital trends and customer preferences.

Digital Readiness encapsulates a forward-thinking Digital Vision and Leadership, as well as a penchant for Digital Communities.

## 3.1.1   Digital Vision and Leadership

Management's role in steering organizations towards meaningful change has taken on a new dimension: Digital Vision and Leadership – from fostering consciousness and conviction to nurturing courage, as well as initiating concrete steps to craft and communicate a compelling Digital Vision. It sounds obvious, but this is where many companies already lack the foundations for Digital Success. **Senior Management does not see the big picture**, how the on-going changes in society and technology will re-shape the economy and the specific industry, drying out traditional pockets of profit, but providing new ones. In lack of this perspective, and driven by short-term pressure for commercial results, misallocations of resources are the norm.

**What the C-Suite needs to know**

1. Prioritize a robust Digital Vision and Leadership: The heart of a successful digital transformation is a far-reaching Digital Vision outlined and led by a future-oriented leadership team. Ensuring that this vision is clearly articulated and reverberates through all layers of the organization is critical to success, guiding every individual towards a unified goal and creating an environment where new digital ventures and existing core processes are nurtured simultaneously in duality.

2. Cultivate Digital Consciousness: Begin with a clear understanding of the foundational pillars of digital transformation. Ground the transformation in Digital Consciousness, recognizing the potential and vital role of digital elements in the current ecosystem and their impact on future industry dynamics, value propositions and business models.

3. **Build and uphold Digital Conviction**: Ensure a deep-seated belief and commitment to the digital pathway your organization is forging. This conviction should be rooted deeply in the organization's core values, historic legacy, and futuristic ambitions.

4. **Encourage and sustain Digital Courage**: Drive your organization forward with a courageous approach to digital transformation. Venturing into new digital territories requires a brave approach where teams are nurtured to explore innovative solutions while adhering to the established (digital) guardrails.

5. **Craft and communicate the Digital Vision Effectively**: Shape a vibrant future through the crafting and effective communication of the Digital Vision. This entails orchestrating a digital transformation journey that not only crafts a detailed path but also leverages a vibrant digital voice, ensuring the resonance of the vision across every level of the organization.

But why are a compelling Digital Vision and an active Digital Leadership so important for Digital Success?

Historic narratives from industry giants such as Kodak and Nokia's mobile business vividly illustrate the perilous journey of companies that remained oblivious to the revolutionary changes ushered in by the digital era. Whereas a generation ago, a 'Kodak moment' was something to cheer about in the family, today it rather frightens managers[23]. Ignoring this critical facet can place organizations at a severe competitive disadvantage, eventually leading to their decline and even oblivion. It is therefore paramount that companies recognize that staying abreast of digital trends is critical to survival, offering them a fighting chance in a fiercely competitive environment.

Concurrently, neglecting the on-going digital transformations can foster operational blind spots, precipitating inefficiencies characterized by **delayed and misguided decisions**. This reluctance to adapt often culminates in the allocation of resources to short-term, superficial projects that only skim the surface of the digital potential, stripping organizations of the impetus for meaningful progress and innovation. Isolated features in the web-presence or Mobile App might be artificially celebrated instead of re-thinking the basic interaction patterns of customers including emerging channels such as messaging and chat bots. A pattern that can be observed in many companies if senior management does not grasp the full scope of digital transformation.

Yet, steering the lens from threats to opportunities, it becomes evident that embracing the digital wave with open arms brings forth a plethora of strategic advantages. By staying attuned to digital shifts, companies can unlock new avenues for business growth, encouraging innovation and enhancing customer experiences

---

[23] Scott D. Anthony in Harvard Business Review: "Kodak's Downfall Was not About Technology". Published 15.07.2016.

through personalized offerings. This proactive stance enables organizations to leverage the evolving digital environment to **stay a step ahead of competitors**, while adapting dynamically to meet fluid market demands.

But what is good Digital Vision and Leadership? True Digital Leaders possess a unique ability to not only understand the nuances of emerging technologies but also to **envision the future possibilities**, inspiring innovation, and adaptability across their teams. Embarking on the journey of digital transformation requires a comprehensive blueprint that is reflective of an organization's ultimate aspirations – this is where the Digital Vision comes into play. Unlike a fleeting slogan or a transitory goal, the Digital Vision is a vibrant, living doctrine, forged from the organization's ethos, and distilled from its grandest dreams and ambitions – it builds on its very own purpose. At its core, a Digital Vision encapsulates **how a company can fundamentally reinvent its value proposition** and overall business model in light of digital advancements. It maps out the long path of transformation, pinpointing milestones that represent progressive realization of the company's future in a digitalized world. It is about envisioning a future state where every operational element – from products to processes to people – is in a harmonious symphony, leveraging digital innovations to deliver **enhanced customer experiences**, open up **new avenues of revenue**, and **forge pathways to untouched markets**.

To paint a more vivid picture, envision a retail company that sees its future not just as a seller of goods but as a holistic service provider, leveraging augmented reality to enhance shopping experiences, using data analytics to personalize offerings, and utilizing AI-driven logistics to redefine efficiency – all integrated into a seamless, digitally-enabled ecosystem that operates with unprecedented efficiency and customer satisfaction. In this envisioned future, digital tools are not just add-ons but are central to the business model, fundamentally altering the way the company delivers value to its customers.

It is obvious that the Digital Vision is broader and more far-reaching compared to a Digital Strategy. While the latter focuses on the allocation of resources to defined short- and mid-term goals, delineating the paths to achieve current objectives, the Digital Vision spans further (also visit section 3.4 Digital Strategy on page 222 for further clarification). The Digital Vision encompasses the reimagination of the business' very essence, delineating a future where digital is not just an enabler but a driver, steering the organization towards a horizon filled with unprecedented opportunities and potentials. It is the rallying cry that unites all stakeholders, giving them not just a direction but a purpose, painting a vivid portrait of what the organization aspires to become, grounded in reality yet reaching for the stars with bold and innovative strategies.

Amazon's Digital Vision is emblematic of a forward-thinking, customer-centric approach that has revolutionized the landscape of e-commerce and beyond. Founded by Jeff Bezos with a focus on delivering unparalleled customer experiences, Amazon's Digital Vision embodies a multi-faceted approach that seamlessly integrates technology, innovation, and a deep understanding of consumer needs.

At its core, Amazon envisions a world where convenience and efficiency are seamlessly intertwined, where customers can access an expansive array of products and services with just a few clicks. This vision is anchored in leveraging cutting-edge technologies to create a frictionless shopping experience that transcends traditional retail norms.

The essence of Amazon's Digital Vision lies in its commitment to data-driven personalization. By harnessing the power of data analytics and artificial intelligence, Amazon tailors recommendations and offerings to individual preferences, enabling customers to discover products they might not have considered otherwise. This vision extends beyond shopping, infiltrating sectors like entertainment and cloud computing, where Amazon's data-driven insights reshape how content is consumed and businesses scale.

Furthermore, Amazon's Digital Vision is synonymous with innovation. The company's dedication to experimentation and risk-taking is epitomized by ventures like Amazon Prime, which redefined loyalty programs and expedited shipping. Its audacious foray into the smart homes with products like Alexa and Echo reflects its drive to integrate technology into consumers' daily lives seamlessly.

Amazon's Digital Vision envisions a world where technology serves as an enabler rather than a barrier. It is a reality where customers' desires are anticipated, met, and exceeded through intuitive interfaces, unparalleled selection, and exceptional service. By consistently pushing the boundaries of what is possible in the digital space, Amazon's Digital Vision has transcended mere retail to become a blueprint for customer-centric digital transformation across industries[24].

**A well-crafted Digital Vision also considers the broader societal impact, fostering sustainability, ethical considerations, and social responsibility**. European automaker Volvo's commitment to safety extends into the digital space through its vision to ensure that no one is killed or seriously injured in a new Volvo car by 2020, underlining the company's dedication to using digital innovation for a larger societal good. While Volvo is proud of what it has achieved so far with its 'Aiming for zero' safety vision, the management is not satisfied yet and will continue on its visionary efforts[25].

**However, outstanding Digital Leadership transcends the confines of crafting a profound Digital Vision**. It encapsulates the nurturing of an environment ripe for innovation and agility, a milieu where ideas flourish and metamorphose from mere concepts to groundbreaking realities. These leaders create environments where experimentation is a regular practice, not a sporadic event, and where taking calculated risks is viewed not as a gamble but a necessary stride towards

---

[24] Steve Case in a New York Times Bestseller: "The Third Wave: An Entrepreneur's Vision of the Future". Published by the New York Times 18.04.2017
[25] Volvo company website, visited 08.04.2024. https://group.volvocars.com/company/safety-vision

revolutionary achievements (visit section 3.6.2 Innovation and Experimentation on page 313 for further inspiration).

In the context of superior Digital Leadership, we see firms that embody the dynamic spirit of agile startups, irrespective of their scale. Companies akin to the innovative Canadian e-commerce company, Shopify, illustrate this principle vividly. Through a proactive approach to remote working, well before it became a pandemic-induced necessity, they demonstrated foresight, adapting seamlessly to changing dynamics, thereby displaying remarkable agility. Similarly, the New Zealand-based accounting software company, Xero, has managed to develop an environment where employees are encouraged to think outside the box, constantly driving innovation. Their open-minded approach facilitates a space where creativity burgeons, intertwining seamlessly with untapped opportunities, offering a prototype for others to emulate.

Stellar Digital Leaders stand as pioneers, exploring new territories and directing their organizations to avenues brimming with growth and prospective innovations. They are not just managers but visionaries with an **unwavering commitment to adapt and evolve**, thereby leading from the front with resilience and determination. These leaders possess the remarkable capacity to bounce back from adversities, stronger and more focused, learning and improving with each step. **A futuristic outlook is a signature attribute of an adept Digital Leader,** possessing the perspicacity to steer adeptly through the tumultuous waves of ever-evolving technological landscapes. They are endowed with a deep understanding of the fluid market dynamics, the shifts in consumer preferences, and the burgeoning technological trends. This visionary leadership guides informed and strategic pivots, constantly aligning with the organization's long-term vision, ensuring that the strategies are not just reactive but proactive, molded with a foresight that is tuned to the pulsating rhythms of the digital era. **Exceptional Digital Leadership symbolizes a harmonious blend of vision and execution,** nurturing a ground fertile for relentless innovation and unwavering adaptation. It is about crafting an ecosystem where new ideas are not just born but are allowed to flourish, reaching their zenith, where employees evolve from being mere executors to becoming significant contributors to the grand narrative.

But how can a company ensure that Digital Vision and Leadership are in place? Let us explore the four stages (Senior) Management needs to go through. Depending on where a company's management stands, we need to strengthen all of them or emphasize one or two specific stages.

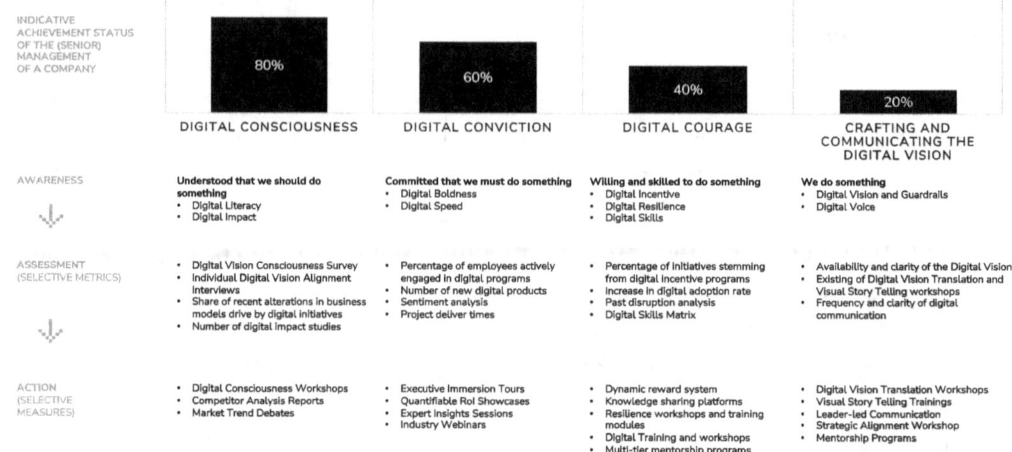


*Figure 16: Four stages to develop Digital Vision and Leadership*

**Digital Consciousness – we understand that we should do something**: This is the foundational stone where management recognizes the indispensable role of digital transformation in steering the company towards success. It is a comprehensive understanding and acknowledgement of both the opportunities ripe for the taking and the threats looming in the digital space. A business steeped in Digital Consciousness is one prepared to navigate the complex digital currents adeptly. Many companies have arrived at this base, but rest on their laurels. Whereas this is intellectually appealing, Digital Consciousness does not drive a company's Digital Success. Real conviction is needed.

**Digital Conviction – we are committed that we must do something**: At this juncture, understanding translates into a compelling need for immediate action. Management and the organization perceive digital maturity not as a choice but a requisite for survival, a tool for carving out competitive differentiation, and a conduit for growth. It speaks to a firm dedication coupled with a judicious allocation of resources, all directed towards harnessing the digital potential to its fullest. Through success examples and competitive pressure, more and more companies settle with this conviction, but still hesitate to move, they need to find the courage.

**Digital Courage – we are willing and skilled to do something**: Embarking on the digital voyage requires more than consciousness and conviction, it demands courage. This entails possessing the expertise to prioritize Digital Success in the company's business agenda. Here, management is equipped not just with the 'will' to forge ahead but also the 'skill' to navigate the intricacies of the digital space, marrying vision with execution seamlessly. When it comes to Digital Courage, we observe a wide range of levels among today's managers of companies. Some have stepped up, and enabled themselves, whereas others are still rather clueless, in many cases convinced that they do not need to learn new tricks, as they have mastered their careers so far without. This is dangerous not just for this particular manager's career, but also for the company's future.

**Crafting and Communicating the Digital Vision – we do something**: This is the pinnacle where intention transforms into a tangible Digital Vision. It is here that Digital Leadership acts and shines, with the top-tier management echoing the digital direction consistently, guiding the organization with a hand that is both firm and enlightened. The shining examples of the digital age, the companies that have increased shareholder value over the past years, have arrived at this stage. They are the lighthouses for the others to follow.

As we dive into these four stages to foster Digital Vision and Leadership, we look at each stage from three angles – as introduced with the Triple-A approach earlier. We deepen the Awareness for the topic, to ensure everyone understands what it is and why it is so important. We run an Assessment of the current status and progress of a company to direct our efforts to the most relevant areas, and we suggest concrete Actions to increase Digital Consciousness, Conviction, Courage and the capabilities to Craft and Communicate the Digital Vision.

### 3.1.1.1 Digital Consciousness – We Understand that we should Do Something

As firms venture into establishing Digital Vision and Leadership, the fundamental step is attaining Digital Consciousness. This stage is central for management to fully grasp the multi-faceted nature of digital transformation, recognizing it as a source of both opportunities and threats. It calls for an immersive understanding of two core aspects: Digital Literacy and Digital Impact.

**Awareness: A Deep Dive into Digital Literacy and Impact**

In the formative stage of defining a Digital Vision, Digital Literacy stands as a pillar that transcends a superficial acquaintance with digital tools and platforms. It demands a **substantive grasp of emerging technologies coupled with an analytical foresight into their broad-spectrum implications for both the industry and a company's prospective trajectory**. At the heart of digital literacy lies the essential ability to discern not just the functionality but the potential transformative impact of digital technologies. It involves understanding the intricate web of digital developments – from AI to blockchain, from Extended Reality to Robotics and 3D/4D Printing – and how they can be harnessed to drive innovation, personalize customer experiences, and streamline operations. Companies like Google have been trailblazers in developing a corporate culture grounded in digital literacy[26]. The firm continually encourages its employees to upskill and adapt to emerging technologies, harboring an environment that is both innovative and forward-thinking. This literacy spawns agility, engendering a dynamic approach where a firm is not just reactive but is proactively maneuvering through the complex and ever-fluctuating digital ecosystem, realigning its strategies with a foresight that keeps it steps ahead in the competitive landscape. Furthermore, it implies nurturing a workforce that can adeptly leverage digital technologies to solve problems, create value, and innovate, facilitating a fluent dialogue between technology and business strategies. Amazon, under the stewardship of Jeff Bezos, manifested this understanding tremendously, ensuring that opportunities presented by digital developments are not merely seized but leveraged to their utmost potential, giving the firm a competitive edge that is both sustainable and forward-thinking. Whereas the digital literacy provides the general understanding, the digital impact takes the digital transformation the to the level of your individual company and what it means for its very own value proposition and service model.

In tandem with digital literacy, **Digital Impact** warrants an astute awareness centered on the comprehensive understanding of how technology can be a game-changer, drastically revolutionizing business models of a company from the ground up. Digital impact makes it more tangible, it takes it to the company level, encompassing a **fundamental rethinking of value propositions, interaction models, and execution setups.** Management understands the concrete influence basic technological shifts have on their company. Successful management shapes the company to leverage opportunities from digital changes. Tesla, spearheaded by Elon Musk, stands as a beacon in leveraging digital dynamics to revolutionize the automotive industry. By envisioning and implementing a strategy deeply ingrained in digital foresight, Tesla has not only been adaptive and resilient but has consistently stayed ahead of market trends, defining the future of transportation[27].

Championing Digital Consciousness as the first stage in the ambit of Digital Vision definition hinges critically on a profound understanding and incorporation of digital literacy and digital impact. But not all companies are at a satisfactory level. Too many managers have not yet established the basic digital literacy or did not spend the time

[26] Vinton G. Cerf in Forbes: "Growing A Culture Of Innovation: 5 Lessons From Google". Published online 16.09.2020, visited 08.04.2024.
https://www.forbes.com/sites/googlecloud/2020/09/16/growing-a-culture-of-innovation-5-lessons-from-google/?sh=7eeb3555d743

[27] David J. Teece in Management and Organizational Review: "Tesla and the Reshaping of the Auto Industry". Published online by Cambridge University Press, 10.09.2018, visited 08.04.2024.
https://www.cambridge.org/core/journals/management-and-organization-review/article/tesla-and-the-reshaping-of-the-auto-industry/5E551257839D03D5E430F61CB93AFA62

to think through the impact for their company. It is worth assessing where your company stands on this crucial foundation.

**Assessment: Gauging Digital Literacy and Digital Impact**

The assessment process stands as the mirror reflecting the current stature of your firm when it comes to Digital Consciousness.

Firstly, fostering a clear understanding of **digital literacy** involves rolling out a comprehensive **Digital Vision Consciousness Survey**. This survey needs to bring senior management into the spotlight, unraveling the depths of their understanding and their viewpoints on the digital sphere. Does your management not just know what the abbreviation AI stands for, but really understand what Artificial Intelligence stands for, and how it will change the company, the industry, our lives? Does your management understand, how Distributed Ledger Technologies (Blockchain) has the potential to disrupt entire value chains and business models? Through this lens, it is possible to vividly illustrate the areas that need nurturing and the pockets of strength that can be leveraged further. A parallel channel of insight can be established through individual **Digital Vision Alignment Interviews**, creating a dynamic feedback loop that encapsulates diverse perspectives within different ranks of the company. This approach not only offers a rounded view of digital literacy but seeds a culture of inclusive digital growth, nurturing a fertile ground for digital ideas to blossom from all corners of the organization.

In the lane of **digital impact**, we steer the lens towards tangible outcomes influenced by digital efforts, we want to see evidence of digital literacy and impact on the steering of the company. This involves orchestrating a focused analysis, deploying metrics such as the **share of recent alterations in business models** driven by digital initiatives. This detailed analysis offers an X-ray view into the beating heart of the business, highlighting the pulse of digital interventions and their success rate, thereby helping to discern the efficacy and pinpoint areas ripe for digital innovation. Equally, engaging with other metrics, including a **reservoir of digital impact studies** with market reports and a thorough competitor analysis, provides a 360-degree view. It aligns a firm with the evolving digital dynamics, helping to foster strategies grounded not just in ambition but in data-driven insights, gifting them the tools to navigate the digital seas with foresight and agility.

Understanding where a company stands in terms of Digital Consciousness helps to initiate the right measures.

**Action: Raising Digital Consciousness with (Senior) Management**

 To cultivate a deep-seated Digital Consciousness among senior management and throughout the organization, a thorough approach, brimming with a series of immersive and knowledge-enriching experiences, should be at the forefront.

The inception is **Consciousness Workshops**, fascinating sessions that not only display real-world success stories but also dissect them to garner actionable insights. Drawing inspiration from GE's commitment to integrating digital technologies with industrial solutions, leaders can indulge in exploratory dialogues, deeply analytical exercises, and hands-on activities that create an environment echoing with creativity and futuristic thinking. The case studies discussed are grounded in reality yet open doors to a visionary future, serving as a beacon of guidance in the digitally conscious corporate landscape[28].

**Digital Thought Leader Seminars** herald the midway point of this enriching journey, establishing a rich ground where thought leaders, with sterling reputations such as Alibaba's Jack Ma, impart knowledge seasoned with experience and laced with forward-thinking perspectives. This platform stands as a lighthouse, shining beams of wisdom derived from personal success stories and building an environment where questions meet answers and curiosity meets knowledge. These seminars are designed as holistic experiences, offering not just lectures but interactive Q&A sessions, supporting a fertile ground for knowledge exchange[29].

**Competitor Analysis Reports** stand as the next crucial juncture in this journey, encapsulating deep dives into the success stories and strategies leveraged by industry stalwarts. By examining a luxury brand's successful path in revolutionizing customer experiences, such as Burberry, leaders get exposed to a kaleidoscope of strategies that have set benchmarks. These reports also encourage leaders to dissect the nuanced approaches adopted by such brands, inspiring them to envisage similar transformative paths for their ventures.

As we continue towards the culmination of this journey, we arrive at the **Market Trend Debates**. These sessions are envisaged as dynamic hubs of intellectual discourse within the company, where insights into emerging market trends and technologies are dissected through the lens of real-world case studies. These debates inspire senior management to craft strategies that are not just robust but deeply

---

[28] GE company website: "GE Reports on Industrial Solutions". Visited 08.04.2024.
https://www.ge.com/news/reports
[29] Jack Ma Interviews on YouTube. Visited 08.04.2024.
https://www.youtube.com/results?search_query=Jack+Ma+interviews.

resonant with market realities, offering a 360-degree view of the market dynamics and encouraging innovative solution crafting.

Through this layered, deeply immersive journey, organizations can cultivate a Digital Consciousness, marked not just by awareness but a deep-seated understanding and foresight into the digital landscape, fostering a culture pulsating with innovation and readiness to spearhead into a future laden with opportunities, thereby steering the corporate ship into waters that promise growth, resilience, and unmatched prosperity.

Whereas many companies in the meantime have established a certain level of Digital Consciousness, we must further focus on building Digital Conviction among the Senior Managers and throughout the company.

### 3.1.1.2 Digital Conviction – We are Committed that we Must Do Something

As we maneuver through the process of consolidating a potent Digital Vision and Leadership, nurturing Digital Conviction emerges as a next cornerstone. This stage epitomizes a robust and determined commitment to immediate and dynamic action in digital transformation, recognizing it not as a supplementary path but as a critical pathway etched in survival, competitive differentiation, and substantial growth. It revolves around a proactive and strategic deployment of resources aimed at propelling the organization to an enviable position in the digital panorama, leveraging the strong dual forces of Digital Boldness and Digital Speed.

**Awareness: Understanding the Vital Elements of Digital Boldness and Speed**

This stage is fundamentally characterized by an **unwavering commitment** from the management to not just envision but ardently drive the digital transformation agenda as a **strategic imperative** and a cornerstone for survival in a digitally dominated marketplace. It represents a deep-seated belief in the transformative power of digital advancements and a **resolute commitment** to steering the organization on a path of continuous digital evolution.

A critical facet of Digital Conviction is nurturing **Digital Boldness**. Here, the management exhibits the courage to venture beyond the conventional paradigms of business operations, encouraging a culture of bold ideation and innovative experimentation. Stepping out of comfort zones and embracing a landscape rife with disruptive solutions signifies a dynamic shift from incremental advancements to **radical transformations**. Companies excelling in digital boldness, like Spotify, have reinvented the wheel, bypassing traditional music distribution models to create a service that is both revolutionary and intensely customer focused. As part of its core values Spotify literally states 'We like being bold'[30]. Management needs to create environments where teams are motivated to ideate without fear, where failure is seen as a **springboard for learning and innovation**. The essence of digital boldness is to craft a future steeped in **audacious visions**, a trajectory that is not restrained by the fear of the unknown but is energized by the unlimited potential that the digital future holds.

Parallelly, **Digital Speed** translates to a **high-velocity approach** towards digital transformation, championing a culture that is agile, proactive, and resolutely focused on being the first mover in the digital sphere. It is about **reducing the timeline from concept to implementation drastically**, facilitating a workspace that is fluid, adaptable, and perpetually ahead in the competitive race. Tech giants like Apple have epitomized digital speed, swiftly adapting to changing landscapes, and continually innovating to remain a frontrunner in the industry. It encompasses an environment that embraces novel tools and strategies, supporting a culture that is not reactive but foreseeing, always a step ahead, driving a pace that sets the industry standard rather than following it. It is about harnessing the potential of rapid prototyping, agile methodologies, and a **fail-fast approach** to stay ahead in the digital race.

In constructive interaction, digital boldness and digital speed create a formidable alliance, operating symbiotically to elevate and accelerate Digital Conviction. Not all companies and their managements have true conviction, beyond paying lip-services with generic statements, which are not followed by action. Hence, it is important to assess where your company really stands.

**Assessment: Unveiling Metrics for Digital Boldness and Speed**

To accurately gauge the progress and efficacy of digital boldness and speed in an organization, implementing a set of metrics is indispensable.

**Digital Boldness** should be measured through a lens that captures both the depth and breadth of initiatives undertaken. Metrics could include the **percentage of employees actively engaged in innovation programs**, the **number of new digital products or services launched** in a year, and a **sentiment analysis derived from employee feedback** on the organization's boldness in embracing digital trends. These can be substantiated with **case studies** that dive into the success stories behind innovative endeavors, giving a qualitative texture to the assessment.

In tandem, **Digital Speed** calls for metrics that track the velocity of the organization in adapting to the digital change. Metrics in this context should encompass **project**

[30] Sally Whatley on Spotify's company website: "Spotify's core values". Published online 02.09.2016, visited 08.04.2024. https://hrblog.spotify.com/2016/09/02/spotifys-core-values/

**delivery times**, focusing on a breakdown that identifies phases of agility and stagnation, alongside a **digital response rate** metric that measures the organization's speed in responding to market changes and technological advancements. **Feedback loop efficiency** is another vital metric, it entails assessing how quickly feedback is integrated into on-going projects, optimizing a rapid iterative cycle that ensures the organization remains on the forefront of innovation. To complement this, **industry benchmark comparisons** can be introduced, where the organization's digital speed is juxtaposed with industry standards, providing a clear picture of where the company stands in the competitive landscape.

By constructing a rich overview of these markers, the assessment phase metamorphoses into a powerful tool, offering deep insights and carving out a pathway grounded in empirical data and qualitative analyses, forging a robust foundation for establishing Digital Conviction.

### Action: Raising Digital Conviction

 As we venture into actions, there emerges a vivid panorama of multi-faceted strategies, each crafting a narrative of steadfast conviction, infused with learnings from industry trailblazers, poised to support a resilient Digital Vision and Leadership.

**Executive Immersion Tours** stand as a cornerstone in driving insightful learning, offering a tangible walkthrough of the endeavors and achievements of industry trailblazers. Leaders can partake in an enriching experience, analyzing the operational nuances of market behemoths like Amazon and Alibaba. Another notable narrative here is the digital transformation journey undertaken by Singapore's DBS, which effectively morphed into a leader in the digital banking space[31].

**DBS: A Bank That Thinks Like a Tech Company**

DBS, once a conventional bank based in Singapore, underwent a transformative evolution by setting its sights on global tech leaders.

Inspired to claim the 'D' in the 'GANDALF' lineup (joining the traditional four GAFA companies, i.e. Google, Apple, Facebook, Amazon, as well as Netflix and LinkedIn), DBS invested not just in innovative technology but also in its people. They established the DBS Academy, dedicated to upskilling employees and supporting a digital mindset. With the launch of digibank, Asia's first mobile-only bank, DBS showcased its commitment to leveraging AI and biometrics to offer personalized banking experiences, significantly reducing the need for physical branches.

By focusing on enhancing over 200+ customer journeys, like home buying or business loan applications, they simplified processes, ensuring a seamless and efficient customer experience. Their transformation

---

[31] DBS company website: "DBS: Leading Digital Transformation". Visited 08.04.2024.
https://www.dbs.com/about-us/who-we-are/awards-accolades/a-world-first/awards-2016

into a technological frontrunner in banking emphasizes that with the right vision and commitment, legacy institutions can redefine industry standards.

In addition to immersion tours, **Quantifiable ROI Showcases** serve as a testament to the potent results that can be achieved through an adept integration of digital strategies. Leaders can take inspiration from the digitization path embraced by BMW, with a specific focus on their futuristic car designs that marry technology and sophistication. Another spotlight in this segment is the Spanish fashion mogul, Zara, which has revolutionized its supply chain through data analytics, by analyzing sales data to forecast demand for products to optimize how much to produce and distribute to each store[32].

Diving deeper, the **Expert Insights Sessions** beckon, offering a rich repository of practical guidance drawn from the experiences of those who have walked the path. An inspiration in this cadre is Vodafone's digital metamorphosis journey, a path laden with strategies derived from real-world experiences.

Rounding off the learning spectrum are the **Industry Webinars**, platforms reverberating with the wisdom of luminaries from various spheres. Hiroshi Mikitani of Rakuten shares his vision and leadership acumen in various interviews available on platforms like YouTube, providing a deep dive into agile leadership. Similarly, witnessing the digital philosophy embraced by the Tata Group can be a learning arc, offering nuances of evolving and adapting in the digital terrain.

Even if Digital Conviction is established, it takes Digital Courage to do something.

### 3.1.1.3 Digital Courage – We are Willing and Skilled to Do Something

In the evolving digital space, nurturing Digital Courage within senior management is fundamental to steering a company towards enduring success. This necessitates a comprehensive approach grounded in an unyielding will and honed skill set, integrating three critical pillars: Digital Incentive, Digital Resilience, and Digital Skills.

**Awareness: Building a Foundation of Incentive, Resilience, and Skills**

**Digital Courage** is a vital disposition that the management must harbor to navigate the turbulent waters of digital transformation successfully. It goes beyond merely adopting new technologies, **it encompasses a willingness to dismantle traditional paradigms, undertake risks, and persistently pursue a digital future with vigor and foresight.**

---

[32] Ankita Varma in The PEAK Magazine: "Zara's Secret to Success Lies in Big Data and an Agile Supply Chain". Published online 02.06.2017, visited 08.04.2024.
https://www.thepeakmagazine.com.sg/lifestyle/zaras-secret-success-lies-big-data-agile-supply-chain/

**Digital Courage is supported by 'Will' and 'Skill'.** Only if management feels comfortable, it will leave its comfort zone and find the courage to move ahead with the digital transformation. Let us start with what influences the 'Will'.

A significant element that contributes to nurturing Digital Will is setting **Digital Incentives**. They are crucial in building a corporate culture that inherently builds a digital-first mindset, where milestones achieved in the digital transformation journey are celebrated and aptly rewarded. They create an environment where the senior management is not only encouraged but incentivized to think and act digitally, facilitating a shift in the core approach towards digital efforts. By embedding digital objectives into their plans, a culture that constantly reveres digital innovation is cultivated, where achievements are not merely recognized but are greeted with tangible rewards, developing a space that breathes and thrives on digital novelty.

But sometimes, best incentives still lead to failures, this is where a culture **Digital Resilience** is required. This is about ingraining a robustness into the corporate ethos that can withstand the myriad of challenges posed by digital disruptions. It is a cultivated ability to anticipate potential roadblocks and formulate strategies that are not just recuperative but leverage setbacks as springboards to drive stronger, more innovative pathways forward. This resilience encourages a perspective that sees failures not as setbacks but as invaluable learning curves, encouraging an adaptable approach that grows iteratively in a digitally vibrant landscape.

Equally important is developing **Digital Skills** at the heart of the organization's senior management. A well-articulated Digital Vision necessitates leaders who possess not just an understanding but a deep mastery over the intricacies of the digital ecosystem. This involves nurturing leadership that can translate consciousness and conviction into concrete visions, leading teams with clarity and inspirational foresight to strive towards a united digital direction. The goal here is to combine a management team proficient in navigating the complex digital environment, capable of guiding every tier of the organization with informed enthusiasm, bridging gaps, and creating cohesive pathways towards realizing the Digital Vision.

Digital Incentive, Digital Resilience, and Digital Skills are not standalone concepts but interwoven facets that give rise to Digital Courage. But not all companies and their management have the courage to drive a Digital Vision. Let us understand where your company stands.

### Assessment: Gauging the Pulse of Courageous Digital Leadership

 To truly drive Digital Courage, it is essential to identify the current standing of a company in the digital development. This involves evaluation and regular feedback loops that assess the three foundational pillars: Digital Incentive, Digital Resilience, and Digital Skills.

A detailed examination of **Digital Incentives** requires a dual approach – quantitative and qualitative. On the quantitative front, it is essential to consider metrics such as the **percentage of initiatives stemming from incentive programs** that have been successfully integrated into the business operations, and the **increase in digital adoption rate post the introduction of incentive systems**. Qualitatively, fostering **focus group discussions and feedback systems** to gauge the morale and responsiveness of the team towards the incentive programs can offer deep insights. It is crucial to engage with the senior management to understand how the incentives have transformed their approach towards digitalization, and whether it has indeed created a culture that reveres digital innovation.

When it comes to **Digital Resilience**, the assessment should be broad, focusing on both **preparedness and response strategies**. Consider the existing protocols for anticipated digital disruptions and analyze the recovery time metric to measure the resilience effectively. The assessment should also encapsulate a **detailed analysis of past disruptions**, the effectiveness of the strategies employed, and the lessons learned. This provides a realistic view of the organization's resilience matrix. Including a feedback loop from various department heads can offer ground-level insights into the operational readiness and responsiveness during disruptions.

Moving on to **Digital Skills**. The assessment necessitates a comprehensive appraisal involving a **deep dive into the existing skill set of the senior management**. In the journey of assessing senior leadership's proficiency in steering the digital transformation, several pragmatic approaches are important. **Structured interviews and organization-wide surveys** serve as foundational tools to gauge the depth of management's **technical knowledge, communication prowess, and strategic insights**. We sit with each leader, engaging in conversations crafted to unveil their perspectives, strategies, and adaptability in the rapidly evolving digital ecosystem. Concurrently, **surveys disseminated across the organization** reveal the grassroot-level perception of leadership's effectiveness in navigating the digital tides. **Feedback mechanisms** are integral to this assessment. We implant **real-time feedback systems** that harvest insights directly from the workforce and stakeholders. These platforms are engines of transparency, capturing the pulse of the organization's sentiment on leadership's responsiveness, communication clarity, and collaborative endeavors in the face of digital transformation scenarios. We transcend surface-level analysis, diving into **action and outcome analysis**. Every strategic move, every decision made in the crucible of digital challenges, is dissected. We explore the relevance, timeliness, and consequential impact of actions to measure their effectiveness and alignment with the overarching digital vision. It is not just about the decisions made but also the **tangible outcomes and value** they engender in the organization's digital narrative. The blend of **interviews, feedback, action analysis, and performance metrics** crafts a multi-dimensional lens, offering a panoramic view of leadership's digital capabilities.

Let us look at some concrete measures to build Digital Courage.

**Action: Embarking to Build Digital Courage**

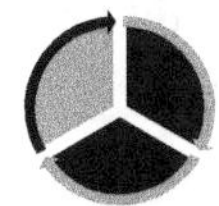 It is quintessential to combine a senior management team that embodies Digital Courage. This mandates actionable and sustainable strategies integrated with real-world success stories to display a pathway that is both encouraging and achievable.

To create an environment of continual innovation, a focus on nurturing **Digital Incentive** is imperative. This approach calls for the creation of a **dynamic reward system** that actively celebrates the small and big digital milestones achieved by both individuals and teams. Taking a leaf from the transformative journey at ING, a transformation characterized by an agile strategy that celebrated incremental progress, can provide substantial guidance[33]. To augment this strategy, establishing knowledge sharing platforms becomes crucial. Microsoft, through its initiative to develop a rich **knowledge network**, leverages the collective intelligence and experiences of its teams, creating a digital-first mindset. The shared knowledge across different teams not only stimulates intellectual curiosity but also maintains a cohesive and collaborative work environment.

Developing **Digital Resilience** stands as a cardinal pillar in this strategy, necessitating the incorporation of **tailored resilience workshops** and training modules. These series of initiatives are designed to create a workforce capable of anticipating, addressing, and adapting to the ever-evolving digital space. Drawing inspiration from Netflix's culture[34], businesses can learn to build an environment of **continuous learning and adaptability**. By encouraging teams to understand and internalize such transformational journeys, a corporate culture of readiness and proactive response to digital disruptions can be cultivated. Implementing regular digital drills to simulate potential disruptions stands as a strategic move to support a culture grounded in

---

[33] Deepak Mahadevan in the McKinsey Quarterly: "ING's Agile Transformation". Published online 10.01.2017, visited 08.04.2024. https://www.mckinsey.com/industries/financial-services/our-insights/ings-agile-transformation.

[34] Netflix company website: "Netflix's Culture Memo". Visited 08.04.2024. https://jobs.netflix.com/culture.

practical insights and foresightedness, ready to navigate the tumultuous digital seas with agility and effectiveness.

The pursuit of **Digital Skills** development unfolds as an on-going journey, where every step is directed towards enhancement and growth. Here, **training programs and workshops** find a central place, designed to imbibe the emerging digital trends and technologies into the core of the organizational ethos. Taking a cue from Google's philosophy of integrating learning with daily job roles[35]. Organizations can construct pathways for teams to stay abreast with the latest developments. Primarily, we channel our efforts into building of a solid foundation of **technical acumen**. This cornerstone equips the leadership with the prowess to not only grasp the nuances of emerging digital trends and technologies but to assimilate them beneficially into the existing corporate structure, creating a vibrant and responsive business environment that is in tune with the dynamic digital heartbeat. The voyage then sails into the waters of **analytical proficiency**, a reality where data is no longer a mere numerical entity but a rich tapestry of insights. Here, the leadership learns to deftly navigate through complex data landscapes, unveiling patterns and predictive pathways that forge a roadmap rich with informed and strategic decisions, finely tuned to reflect evolving market tendencies. As we journey further, we support **agile leadership**, a vital beacon in the turbulent digital sea. This paradigm nurtures a resilience, a readiness to embrace the ceaseless waves of change, guiding the helm with a steady hand and an adaptable mindset, steering the corporate vessel with informed decisions that echo with the pulse of a dynamic market environment (visit section 3.7.1 Agile and Adaptive Culture on page 324 for further details). Woven into this journey is the art of **communication**, a tapestry that narrates the compelling story of the Digital Vision. Here, we sculpt leaders into expert storytellers, capable of crafting narratives that resonate deeply, maintaining a culture where every stakeholder is a vital chapter in the epic of digital transformation, a unified force rallying around a shared vision with engaged enthusiasm and informed perspective. As we dive deeper, we explore the rich landscapes of **collaborative skills**, creating a habitat of synergy and harmony, a space where cross-functional teams flourish in a garden of mutual respect and combined expertise. This nurturing ground enables a convergence of perspectives, a collaborative tableau where ideas blossom into strategies, sowing the seeds for a thriving digital ecosystem grounded in unity and shared objectives. As our journey reaches its crescendo, we embark on the important path of nurturing a **strategic mindset**, a visionary lens that views the digital space with a far-reaching gaze. This acumen builds the ability to envision long-term strategies, a roadmap sculpted with a broad understanding of digital advancements,

---

a guiding star that leads the way, not just to the achievement of short and mid-term goals, but to the realization of a broad, expansive, and overarching Digital Vision.

Adding a deeper layer of engagement is the conception of **multi-tier mentorship programs**, mirroring the innovative strides at Gucci under the leadership of CEO Marco Bizzarri, crafting a repository rich with knowledge and practical insights[36]. This initiative supports a learning environment where wisdom meets fresh perspective, cultivating leaders ready for the digital future. Lastly, championing Digital Courage is integral in steering an organization towards digital maturity. Here, a fundamental step is to create vibrant platforms that encourage interaction between the seasoned management and the digital natives. It seeks to build bridges of understanding and collaborative learning, creating an environment where experiences and viewpoints are not just shared but revered, crafting a learning landscape that is holistically nourishing and grounded in diverse perspectives, nurturing a generation of leaders emboldened with digital courage.

Now, as we have looked at Digital Consciousness, Digital Conviction, and Digital Courage, the company and its management are ready to take some concrete measures to Craft and Communicate the Digital Vision.

### 3.1.1.4  Crafting and Communicating of the Digital Vision – We Do Something

Embarking on a digital transformation journey necessitates visionary leadership that orchestrates the digital duality, where management fine-tunes existing processes while venturing into novel digital territories. This involves crafting a digital case that revolves around Digital Vision and Guardrails as well as a loud Digital Voice, establishing a roadmap steeped in clarity and strategic alignment.

**Awareness: Recognizing the Cornerstones of Visionary Leadership**

As an organization ascends from the foundational pillars of Digital Consciousness, Digital Conviction, and Digital Courage, it transitions into the critical stage of Crafting and Communicating the Digital Vision. This stage beholds the crucial task of crystallizing a vibrant digital perspective, painting it with fine strokes that echo the organization's most treasured values and highest aspirations.

Central to this stage is the careful Crafting of a **Digital Vision** and Guardrails, a task that requires a deep, introspective dive into the very ethos of the organization. It is here that the leadership shapes a vision that is not merely a statement, but a vibrant tapestry woven with threads of the organization's core values, historic legacy, and

---

[36] In European CEO: "Marco Bizzarri is dragging Gucci into the digital future". Published 15.07.2016, visited 08.04.2024. https://www.europeanceo.com/profiles/marco-bizzarri-is-dragging-gucci-into-the-digital-future/

futuristic ambitions. For instance, Tata Motors, an eminent Indian automotive manufacturing company, leveraged this approach to steer its digital transformation, marrying its longstanding legacy with a forward-thinking vision, aiming to bring electric mobility solutions that echo the modern pulse while being grounded in sustainable practices. The crafting process involves delineating a path that is both grand and grounded, where every milestone is a tangible representation of the organization's dreams transformed into achievable targets.

To facilitate this, workshops and brainstorming sessions become crucibles of creation, spaces where vivid ideas are birthed, nurtured, and given a definite structure. **Digital Guardrails** are then etched, serving as firm yet encouraging boundaries that guide teams safely towards the envisioned goals, without digressing into avenues that diverge from the organization's true north. Digital Guardrails translate the Digital Vision into guiding principles for implementation in all areas and on all levels.

Parallelly, the organization embarks on nurturing a vibrant **Digital Voice**, a voice that is harmonious yet resonant, carrying the whispers of innovation to every nook and cranny of the organization. For example, Spain-based fashion retailer Zara adopted a digital voice that mirrored its fast-fashion ethos, utilizing digital platforms to rapidly communicate trends and feedback, thus creating a digitally integrated ecosystem that echoed its business model. This voice becomes a living entity, breathing life into the Digital Vision through carefully curated narratives, visually captivating stories, and dynamic communication channels that foster a two-way dialogue. Leadership training modules might be cultivated to groom spokespersons who carry the mantle of this voice, individuals who are adept at translating the grand vision into everyday language, making it accessible and relatable to every member of the organization. Through a blend of town halls, digital newsletters, and interactive sessions, the digital voice creates ripples of awareness, enthusiasm, and collective ownership, providing a rich overview of insights and feedback that can further refine the digital pathway (visit section 3.2.2.1 Digital Cascades on page 145 for further details on digital communication). But the Digital Voice does not stop at just echoing the vision crafted at the top echelons. It becomes a feedback loop, constantly pulsating with the vibrancy of ground realities, experiences, and insights from every level, sculpting a dynamic vision that is agile and attuned to the evolving market dynamics and organizational needs.

As this potent blend of crafted Digital Vision and vibrant voice melds, it unleashes a powerhouse of engagement where every individual becomes a visionary, nurturing a workspace vibrant with ideas, buzzing with informed conversations, and brimming with a unified zeal to forge ahead into the digital frontier with informed enthusiasm and a clear roadmap.

Often companies are just shy of defining a Digital Vision and of communicating it. Let us assess where your company stands.

**Assessment: Gauging the Resonance of Vision and Voice**

 Transitioning from awareness to assessment involves a critical evaluation of the organization's Digital Vision and Guardrails, along with the Digital Voice, to comprehend the depth of their penetration and influence within the organizational fabric.

For **Digital Vision and Guardrails**, metrics such as the **availability and clarity of the Digital Vision** and the frequency of **Digital Vision Translation and Visual Storytelling Workshops** need to be analyzed. These metrics aid in discerning how effectively the vision is being translated into messages that resonate with the employees, fostering a collaborative spirit and sense of unity in the journey towards digital transformation.

Evaluating the **Digital Voice** entails assessing the **frequency and clarity of communications,** including the direct involvement of senior management. Harnessing tools such as **employee surveys** and **Digital Progress Reporting** can provide valuable insights into the shared understanding and sentiment towards the digital initiatives. It also evaluates the balance in resource allocation between innovative digital ventures and traditional operations, helping to maintain a harmonious balance in the pursuit of digital duality.

**Action: Translating Vision into Tangible Steps and Communicative Leadership**

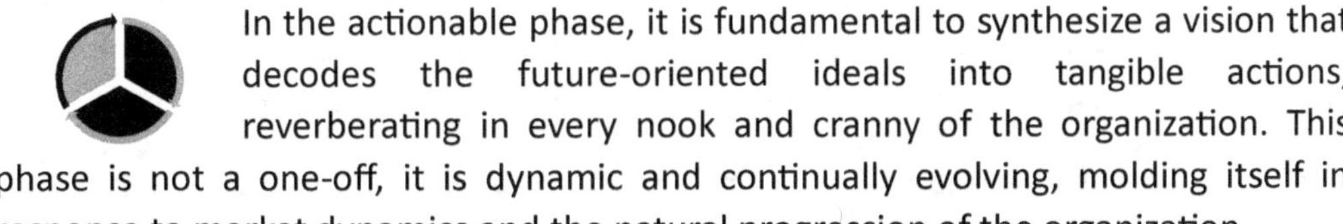 In the actionable phase, it is fundamental to synthesize a vision that decodes the future-oriented ideals into tangible actions, reverberating in every nook and cranny of the organization. This phase is not a one-off, it is dynamic and continually evolving, molding itself in response to market dynamics and the natural progression of the organization.

Frist, we anchor the vision through **Strategic Alignment Workshops** taking inspiration from Amazon's strategy. Here, the Digital Vision becomes harmoniously interwoven with broader organizational goals, defining a pathway characterized by strategic clarity and alignment. It involves creating a symbiotic relationship between the Digital Vision and the organization's core goals, outlining a seamless pathway towards achieving the larger vision[37].

Next, we initiate **Digital Vision Translation Workshops,** a transformative exercise inspired by initiatives at Google, where they conduct 'Google's Sprint Workshops'. This strategy involves the leadership dissecting the broader vision into feasible

---

[37] Amazon company website: "Leadership Principles". Visited 08.04.2024.
https://www.amazon.jobs/content/en/our-workplace/leadership-principles

milestones, thus creating an atmosphere that encourages inclusivity and shared responsibility. The objective is to break down overarching goals into digestible, actionable steps, empowering teams with clear directives and fostering an environment that nurtures collaboration and unity[38].

Subsequently, the emphasis should be on **Visual Storytelling Training**, mirroring Apple's knack for telling compelling visual narratives. At this juncture, the teams are equipped with the tools to craft stories through visuals and stories that meet the audience's expectations, nurturing a culture of cohesiveness and vibrant organizational storytelling. It is about crafting a message that are not only aesthetically pleasing but deeply resonant with the company's vision, leveraging the potent power of visuals to communicate complex ideas effectively[39].

**Leader-led Communication initiative** stands central to this strategy, taking a page from Microsoft's approach under the guidance of Satya Nadella. This strategy emphasizes transparent and regular communication from the leaders, translating the grand vision into a language that resounds with every tier in the organization, creating a genuine sense of shared purpose and belonging. It entails crafting messages that echo with sincerity and heart, nurturing a workspace where every individual feels seen and valued in the grand scheme of things[40].

Deepening this strategy is the introduction of **Mentorship Programs** akin to the nurturing environment developed at General Electric. Here, seasoned leaders mentor budding talents, infusing them with the spirit and knowledge of the Digital Vision, creating a culture of continual growth and learning. This step is crucial in ensuring the developing of future leaders who are steeped in the company's vision and equipped with the skills and knowledge to propel the organization forward.

Lastly, instituting a **Feedback and Refinement Loop** inspired by the Spotify model facilitates a structure that allows the Digital Vision to be agile, continually refined based on real-time feedback, ensuring its relevance in a dynamic market. This strategy is about encouraging a feedback-rich culture, supporting an inclusive and agile approach to digital transformation, where inputs are not just welcomed but actively sought, creating a vision that is vibrant, relevant, and dynamically attuned to the evolving industry landscapes[41].

---

[38] On Google Design Sprints website. Visited 08.04.2024. https://designsprintkit.withgoogle.com/

[39] Thomas Pyczak: "Storytelling mit Bildern: So macht es Apple". Published 10.09.2022, visited 08.04.2024. https://www.strategisches-storytelling.de/storytelling-mit-bildern-so-macht-es-apple/

[40] Satya Nadella with Greg Shaw, Jill Tracie Nichols: "Hit Refresh: The Quest to Rediscover Microsoft's Soul and Imagine a Better Future for Everyone". Published by Harper Business on 26.09.2017

[41] Mark Cruth on the Altassian website: "Discover the Spotify model". Visited 08.04.2024. https://www.atlassian.com/agile/agile-at-scale/spotify

By establishing Digital Consciousness, increasing Digital Courage, and facilitating Digital Courage the pre-requisites to craft and communicate a Digital Vision are put in place – strong Digital Leadership can be provided. However, a well-crafted Digital Vision, defining what a company wants to achieve, requires collective effort for its execution. It is not just about leaders, it is about employees, partners, customers, and the ecosystem – it is about the Digital Community.

### 3.1.2  Digital Community

Articulating a Digital Vision is an essential first step, yet it remains but a skeletal framework without the sinews of collaboration binding it. The collaboration within Digital Communities is not just an additive advantage, but the very force that transforms grand dreams and frameworks into tangible realities through collective vigor.

**While many companies intellectually recognize the power of collaborations, they often only half-heartedly implement a few showcase projects.** This hesitancy typically stems from a fear of sharing information, and the false assumption that they have more to lose than to gain from a partnership. This is often grounded in a tendency to overrate their own standalone capabilities, and not seeing how making the cake bigger, increases the size of the slice for everyone. This approach is not just timid, it is shortsighted and counterproductive. In an age where information flows freely and innovation often happens at the intersections of diverse sectors and skills, hoarding knowledge and avoiding genuine collaboration could be a recipe for stagnation. Failing to commit to meaningful collaborations means missing out on potentially transformative partnerships that could spur innovation and open up new avenues for growth.

**What the C-Suite needs to know**

1. **Imperative of Collaboration:** In the digital age, collaboration is a necessity. Effective collaboration not only enhances efficiency but also fosters innovation, drives growth, and differentiates leaders from followers in the marketplace.

2. **Organizational Synergy:** The Internal Community of digital champions is essential, ensuring effective cross-departmental collaboration – the digital force from within.

3. **Expanding Beyond Organizational Borders:** Collaboration extends outward. Lasting and trust-based partnerships with external experts, from academia to industry specialists, can significantly fast-track digital transformations.

4. **Redefining Ecosystem Dynamics:** Transition from a traditional value chain to an integrated ecosystem. Embrace strategies like coopetition.

5. **Customer-centric Collaboration:** Customers are integral collaborators, not just end-users. Their insights, from ideation to product refinement, are invaluable.

But why are collaborations within Digital Communities so paramount for Digital Success?

At the very outset, fostering collaborations enables **faster realization of projects through readily available resources and the right competences**. Individuals who stand as vanguards of change harbor not just an extensive knowledge base but a readiness to drive transformative changes. It creates a symbiotic environment where organizations can immediately find and allocate the exact resources needed to propel a project from the conceptual stage to realization, thus significantly reducing the gestation period of projects.

Further down the line, it becomes evident that collaboration is not just about speed but quality. When the best competencies converge, there is a natural emergence of **optimized and new innovative ideas**, a phenomenon likened to a treasure trove of innovation. This collaborative intelligence brings to the table a myriad of perspectives that challenges the status quo, encouraging a think-tank approach to problem-solving and innovation. The shared pool of knowledge and skills gives rise to outcomes that are not just better but are more robust, well-rounded, and often unprecedented.

Moreover, collaboration within Digital Communities supports a substantial degree of **risk mitigation**, a byproduct of collective learning from prior successes and failures. Organizations find themselves equipped to steer clear from the pitfalls of repeating mistakes, choosing instead to build upon tried and tested foundations laid by others in the community. This repository of shared experiences acts as a rich resource, helping to avoid known hurdles and navigate towards successful outcomes with fewer risk, creating a pathway that is grounded in wisdom accrued over time.

Beyond the immediate benefits lies a profound advantage that speaks to the future – the assurance of **long-term sustainability**. Collaborative environments champion a culture of continuous learning, nurturing a space rich in knowledge sharing and robust stakeholder engagement. Such communities foster a sustainable ecosystem where learning is an ever-evolving curve, a journey of mutual growth cultivated through open dialogues, brainstorming sessions, and a rich exchange of ideas. Moreover, deep-rooted stakeholder engagement cultivates a reservoir of trust and mutual respect, building relationships that are not transactional but transformative, creating a journey of shared growth and mutual success.

The cohesive fabric of collaborative communities emerges as a necessity. But what makes a powerful Digital Community?

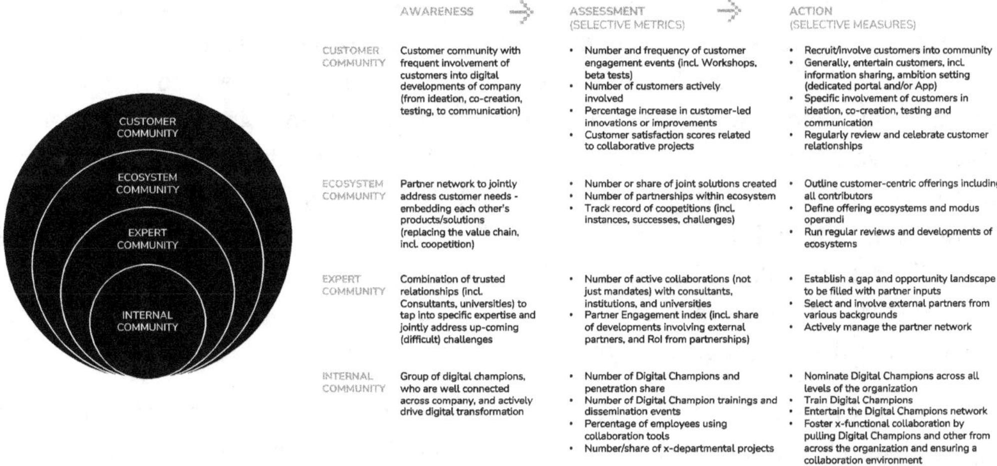


*Figure 17: Complementing Digital Communities*

**Central to any organization's pulse is its human capital**. Digital Visions, regardless of their brilliance, falter if not anchored by these individuals who imbibe the organizational ethos. It is paramount to cultivate champions within. By doing so, organizations ignite a culture where employees emerge as vanguards of change. Such champions, buoyed by intimate organizational knowledge, not only bring digital dreams to fruition but also ensure these dreams are present at every echelon of the organization.

However, the vast expanse of digital expertise is not confined within an organization's walls. Often, the knowledge and tools for a holistic digital transformation reside in the outside world. This external space becomes a source for inspiration when organizations step out and **harness the power beyond their boundaries**. Collaborating with external specialists grants businesses an avenue to diversify their thought processes, integrate avant-garde technologies, and infuse their strategies with insights they may not have internally cultivated. For instance, when Ford partnered with Google in America, it was not just a union of two giants. It was a melding of AI, machine learning, and data analysis prowess with automotive genius to refine manufacturing, invigorate product innovation, and enhance customer experiences.

But in this interconnected age, collaboration is not a binary between an organization and its partners, it is a multi-directional web. Companies are not isolated entities but part of vast **ecosystem communities**. Here, within this mesh of suppliers, industry peers, and even competitors, shared visions emerge. In the digital era, the 'ecosystem play' has developed as an alternative to traditional linear value chains. Unlike linear chains that emphasize internal processes, the ecosystem play underscores collaboration, interdependence, and stakeholder synergy. This approach acknowledges that success is interwoven across partners, customers, suppliers, and competitors. It taps into collective strengths to tackle challenges and seize opportunities within a dynamic network. By adopting the ecosystem play, organizations open doors to innovation, co-creation, and growth. It fosters a collaborative environment where diverse expertise fuels innovation and adaptability, meeting evolving customer needs and market shifts. This shift represents a strategic move from internal focus to shared value creation. Airbus BizLab in Europe exemplifies this philosophy. By launching an accelerator program that melds the ideas of startups with Airbus intrapreneurs, Airbus did not just incubate innovations, it celebrated the collective spirit of European ingenuity[42].

Yet, amidst these layers of collaboration, the heart remains the consumer. Every digital blueprint, while informed by internal champions, shaped by external experts, and delivered through ecosystems seeks to serve and delight the customer. Organizations that transcend the traditional feedback mechanism to **truly engage customer communities** find themselves on a shared odyssey of value co-creation. In APAC, a reflection of this customer-centric collaboration shimmered when Grab, Southeast Asia's ride-hailing titan, intertwined its journey with Singapore's National University Hospital. Together, they launched a dedicated transport solution for expecting mothers, weaving technology with empathy[43].

---

**Salesforce - Redefining Collaboration and Community Engagement in the Digital Ecosystem**

Salesforce, primarily known as a Customer Relationship Management (CRM) leader, has grown to symbolize much more than that. Its community-focused ecosystem and collaborative strategies exemplify a progressive business model that thrives on multi-layered engagement.

**Fostering a robust internal culture for greater efficiency:** Salesforce understands that the key to outward success is inward harmony. The company has nurtured a strong internal community through team-building activities and internal platforms, ensuring its workforce is united in their core values and goals.

**Expanding intellectual horizons through global collaboration:** With events like Dreamforce, Salesforce extends its network far beyond the walls of its offices. Dreamforce serves as a nexus for thought leaders across the globe, providing a platform to share expertise and encouraging collaborative innovation.

**Stimulating growth through symbiotic partnerships:** The Salesforce AppExchange is not just a marketplace, it is a cornerstone of the company's ecosystem strategy. The platform allows third-party integrations that not only enhance Salesforce's existing offerings but create an environment of mutual growth and innovation.

---

[42] On Airbus company website: "Airbus BizLab". Visited 08.04.2024.
https://www.airbus.com/en/innovation/innovation-ecosystem/airbus-bizlab
[43] Jonathan Dyble in Technology Magazine: "Grab to open AI lab with the National University of Singapore". Published online 17.05.2020, visited 08.04.2024. https://technologymagazine.com/ai-and-machine-learning/grab-open-ai-lab-national-university-singapore

**Transforming customer service into community engagement**: Salesforce takes the idea of customer service and amplifies it into community building through their Community Cloud or Experience Cloud. This platform not only solves customer issues but turns those customers into active brand advocates, thus creating a self-perpetuating cycle of positive brand interaction[44].

Let us now explore the four communities that complete the collaboration picture. For each of them we want to understand what it is and why it is so important – building the Awareness for it – but also introduce metrics to run an Assessment where your company stands and outline some Actions your company can undertake to build and maintain successful communities.

### 3.1.2.1    Internal Community – Cultivating Digital Champions Within

In a digitally transforming landscape, organizations need a spearhead, a force that binds various facets of the corporate milieu, ushering in a transformative era replete with innovation, collaboration, and digital acuity. Herein lies the essence of Internal Communities – a powerhouse constituted by individuals, often termed 'digital champions', who embody the fervent spirit of digital transformation. They are the pillars that carry the vision forward, ensuring that every step is a stride towards a future that is digitally sound and profoundly collaborative.

**Awareness: Internal Communities to Harbor the Spirit Inside**

Understanding and fostering Internal Communities is important in nurturing an environment where digital acumen is not just a requirement but a lived reality. These communities are formed of **digital champions**, individuals well-versed and well-connected across different spheres of the organization, acting as the stalwarts steering the firm towards its digital objectives.

Such communities are not just a source of knowledge and expertise, but a vibrant ecosystem where innovation is not the exception but the norm. Companies like Microsoft have leveraged the potential of internal communities to a remarkable effect. Through initiatives like the Microsoft Garage, an outlet for experimental projects and a platform for employees to work on diverse teams and bring their unique ideas to life, they maintained an environment ripe with innovation[45]. This has led to the creation of popular tools and apps, encouraging a culture that values curiosity, exploration, and risk-taking, essential in steering the organization towards achieving its digital objectives.

Companies that have embraced the ethos of internal communities have witnessed transformative success, characterized by agility, resilience, and a proclivity for

---

[44] Salesforce company website. Visited 08.04.2024. https://www.salesforce.com/dreamforce/

[45] Microsoft company website: "The Garage is a program that drives a culture of innovation". Visited 08.04.2024. https://www.microsoft.com/en-us/garage/

pioneering advancements in the digital sphere. **They harbor a culture where collaboration transcends departmental boundaries, pooling together a reservoir of collective intelligence that leads to holistic and optimized solutions**, setting them leagues apart from competitors in a volatile digital space (visit section 3.7.1 Agile and Adaptive Culture on page 324 for further implementation guidance).

Having a pulsating heart of internal communities ensures not just survival but a thriving existence, marked by unprecedented gains and a workplace that breathes innovation and collaboration. But where is your company today?

**Assessment: Feeling the Intensity of the Internal Spirit**

To steer the ship right, it is crucial to take stock of where the organization currently stands in entertaining vibrant Internal Communities. The assessment phase involves an examination of various markers that stand as a testament to the organization's collaborative spirit.

This involves an analytical drill down into the **number of digital champions present** and the **penetration share in the various departments and on all levels**, offering an insight into the depth and breadth of digital integration within the organization. An eye should be kept on the **number and reach of trainings for Digital Champions,** which act as nourishing streams, equipping them to steer forward with confidence and knowledge. At the same time, it is also worthwhile looking at **dissemination events** held by Digital Champions to inspire the rest of the organization.

Further, evaluating the **percentage of employees actively utilizing collaborative tools** paints a picture of the Digital Readiness of the workforce, while keeping a tab on the **number and share of cross-departmental projects** offers a panoramic view of the collaborative landscape within the organization. These metrics act as a lighthouse, guiding the pathway to a collaborative utopia, supporting an environment that breathes innovation, ushering in an era where transformative solutions are a norm, not an exception. But what can your company do to build and maintain Internal Communities?

**Action: Successfully Charting Internal Communities**

To facilitate the blossoming of digital expertise and enthusiasm within an organization, it is essential to undertake well-articulated steps that not only delineate responsibility but also foster an environment that is conducive to learning and collaboration.

Firstly, **nominating digital champions** across various levels of the organization serves as the bedrock in this endeavor. It involves identifying and bringing forward individuals who not only exhibit a knack for digital nuances but also harbor a willingness to become custodians of digital transformation. These individuals, spotted in different departments and hierarchies, become the go-to people, supporting a digital-first mindset, and paving the way for a culture that embraces transformation seamlessly. By nurturing such champions, organizations cultivate in-house experts who can steer their colleagues towards digital proficiency. A fitting example of this initiative is reflected in Adobe's digital champions program[46].

Next in line is organizing holistic **training sessions** for these digital champions. These should not be sporadic events but a continuous learning journey encompassing hands-on workshops, webinars, and seminars that dive deep into the digital trends and tools. This approach ensures a ripple effect, where trained champions become the harbingers of knowledge, sharing their insights and skills with their teams, building a self-sustaining ecosystem of digital literacy. Google, with its comprehensive training and regular workshops, serves as a benchmark in building and disseminating digital skill[47].

A pivotal aspect is to **entertain the digital champions network consistently**, creating a fertile ground where these champions can interact, learn from each other, and grow together. These engagements should be marked with regular catchups, knowledge-sharing sessions, and platforms where they can voice their insights and ideas, creating a vibrant community that breathes innovation and collaborative spirit. Atlassian, with its initiative of forums and regular meetups, stands as an example, illustrating a successful approach to entertaining a collaborative spirit[48].

Encouraging **cross-functional collaboration** stands as another pillar in this structured pathway. Creating avenues where digital champions can come together with others from diverse departments facilitates a melting pot of ideas, driving rich discussions and innovative solutions. Spotify stands as a benchmark in the industry with its system of 'tribes' and 'squads' that support interaction and knowledge sharing across different teams[49].

The **establishment of a collaborative environment** is integral in this journey. It revolves around building spaces, both physical and virtual, where employees feel safe to share, innovate, and work together. Microsoft's commitment to facilitating a

---

[46] Jagpreet Singh on Adobe company website: "Adobe Champion program". Published 12.01.2023, visited 08.04.2024. https://experienceleaguecommunities.adobe.com/t5/adobe-experience-cloud-blogs/adobe-champion-program/ba-p/567208

[47] On Googles company website: "Free Digital Skills Training". Visited 08.04.2024. https://learndigital.withgoogle.com/digitalgarage

[48] On Altassian company website: Team23: "Impossible alone: Charting a new area of teamwork". Visited 08.04.2024. https://www.atlassian.com/company/events/summit-europe

[49] Henrik Kniberg on Spotify company website: "Spotify Engineering Culture". Published online 27.03.2014, visited 08.04.2024. https://engineering.atspotify.com/2014/03/27/spotify-engineering-culture-part-1/

collaborative environment through tools like Microsoft Teams is evidence of the success of such approaches. Lastly, promoting the extensive use of collaboration tools is vital. It is about creating a digital workspace that replicates the physical office environment, offering spaces for discussions, brainstorming sessions, and project management. The integration of tools that enable smooth communication, file sharing, and project tracking ensures that the team stays on the same page, driving efficiency and collaborative success. Slack stands as a prime example of a tool that supports harmony and efficiency in teamwork.

By pursuing each of these actions, an organization carves a pathway that is not only clear and structured but also deep-seated in generating collaboration and digital success. This approach ensures that the organization does not just walk towards digital transformation but does so with a spirit of togetherness and collaborative growth. But sometimes just looking in-house is not enough.

### 3.1.2.2    Expert Community – Harnessing the Power Beyond Boundaries

In the dynamic landscape of the digital age, the traditional boundaries of corporations are becoming increasingly porous, giving rise to the concept of Expert Communities. These are conglomerations of various stakeholders including consultants, academic institutions, and sometimes even competitors, working synergistically to propel innovation and address pressing challenges. Drawing from diverse pools of knowledge and experience, Expert Communities represent a frontier where learning, growth, and innovation are collaborative and exponential. Let us dive deeper into the developmental stages of building these communities, which are segmented into awareness creation, a robust assessment of current standings, and proactive action plans.

**Awareness: The Power of Expert Knowledge**

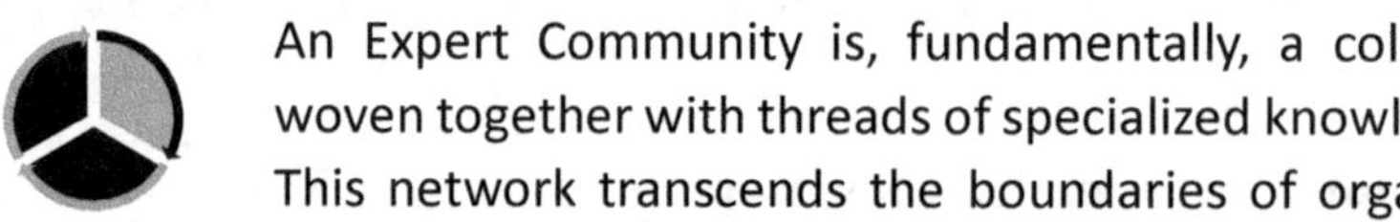

An Expert Community is, fundamentally, a collaborative network woven together with threads of specialized knowledge and expertise. This network transcends the boundaries of organizations, bringing together consultants, academic experts, industry pioneers, and even insightful inputs from competitors to create a vibrant, knowledge-rich ecosystem. The **core strength of an Expert Community lies in its diverse knowledge base**, where the collaboration of varying perspectives and skills leads to more rounded, innovative solutions, catering to a wide array of challenges that the digital era presents.

This collaborative approach is not just about achieving solutions more efficiently, it is about visiting areas previously unexplored, reaching heights previously unthinkable. Companies like Merck & Co. showcase the monumental successes that can be achieved through this collaborative approach, with ventures leading to groundbreaking developments in treatments and therapies. Similarly, collaborations between the Tata Group and prestigious academic institutions like Harvard University have spearheaded innovations in soft robotics, highlighting the transformative potential of Expert Communities.

Thus, Expert Communities stand as a lighthouse of innovation, enabling organizations to navigate the multi-faceted challenges of the digital era with a collaborative, knowledge-rich approach. They foster environments where knowledge is not just acquired but shared, where solutions are not just developed but evolved, leading to a pathway characterized by continuous learning and mutual growth. But the underpinning essence of these communities lies in the **nurturing of relationships built on trust and mutual growth**, characterized by symbiotic alliances that stand to benefit all involved parties. The goal is to create an environment where innovation is not a competitive race but a collaborative journey, where organizations walk hand-in-hand with external experts, jointly addressing and surmounting the complex challenges that the digital space continuously unfolds, and thus steering towards a future rich with innovative solutions and digital success.

This awareness around External Communities goes beyond acknowledging the existence of such communities to understanding the depth of value and the expansive horizon of opportunities that they unfailingly bring to the table. But where does your company stand on Expert Communities?

**Assessment: Identifying Expert Communities**

Understanding where a company stands in maintaining Expert Communities is a cornerstone in crafting a path that is both progressive and sustainable. It involves the assessment that considers a range of metrics to gauge the depth and efficacy of the existing collaborations.

A significant initial metric is the **number of active collaborations** a company maintains with external experts, not just limiting to agreements and (commercial) mandates but a thoughtful analysis of active and fruitful engagements with consultants, institutions, and universities. This facet goes beyond just formal agreements to entail a rich family of relationships that are continuously nurtured and leveraged for mutual growth. It involves maintaining partnerships that are alive with active exchanges, transcending beyond a mere transactional nature to become crucibles of innovation and knowledge sharing.

Following closely is the concept of the **Partner Engagement Index**, an important metric in understanding the health and vitality of an Expert Community. This index is an amalgamation of various critical indicators, including the share of developments involving external partners, which portrays the extent to which collaborations play a role in the organization's new developments and projects. It represents the vibrant synergy achieved through partnerships, showcasing the enriched output born of collective expertise and collaboration. Moreover, within the Partner Engagement Index, a crucial component is discerning the Return on Investment (ROI) from partnerships, a metric that sheds light on the tangible and intangible benefits accruing from the collaborations. It paints a picture of the reciprocal benefits that stem from such partnerships, drafting a roadmap of sustained mutual growth. By deciphering the ROI, organizations can navigate the collaborations more fruitfully, aligning strategies that are both financially and strategically advantageous.

By immersing deeply into these assessment metrics, companies can craft pathways that create a symbiotic growth trajectory leveraging the potent amalgamation of internal and external expertise.

**Actions: Entertain deep-rooted Expert Communities**

 In the journey towards nurturing rich and robust Expert Communities, organizations must initiate well-defined actions that underline not just the collaborative effort but also promote innovation and facilitate shared knowledge growth.

The first critical step in this journey is to **establish a gap and opportunity landscape to be filled with partner inputs.** This action is pivotal as it lays the groundwork for future collaborations. Here, organizations should engage in a thorough analysis to identify the areas where external expertise can be harnessed. It is a matter of pinpointing not only the existing gaps but also potential opportunities where partnerships can drive innovation. Companies akin to Apple have shown proficiency in this arena by continually identifying gaps in their technological advancements and partnering with a diverse panel of experts and organizations to support innovation, effectively filling those gaps, and building opportunities for unprecedented solutions.

Upon establishing this landscape, organizations must move to **select and involve external partners from various backgrounds.** This endeavor should be more than a surface-level engagement, it should aim to build robust relationships with entities bringing varied perspectives and expertise to the table. It calls for collaborations that can offer a fresh set of eyes and potentially ground-breaking approaches to existing challenges. A shining example here is Google's consistent endeavor to partner with academic institutions and technological pioneers to incorporate varied expertise, consequently driving forward in the path of innovation with a rich pool of knowledge and resources at disposal.

Taking the action a notch higher, it becomes imperative to **actively manage the partner network.** This is a rich approach encompassing regular engagements to entertain the relationships formed and to keep the partnerships fruitful. It requires creating platforms for knowledge sharing, setting up regular meetings for updates, and even annual conferences to physically bring together all the bright minds. This helps in maintaining a relationship grounded on mutual growth, a pathway illuminated with shared objectives and collaborative efforts. Amazon, with its extensive network of partners, displays a systematic approach in managing this network actively, ensuring a culture of shared growth and mutual respect, which has indeed created a breeding ground for revolutionary ideas[50].

As organizations stringently follow through on these action steps, they sow the seeds for expert communities that are vibrant with potential, rich with expertise, and grounded on a collaborative ethos. It transforms the landscape from a solitary endeavor to a community-driven pathway, where the journey towards growth is a collaborative narrative, supporting a future where knowledge is not confined but shared, and success is a collaborative milestone.

### 3.1.2.3 Ecosystem Communities – Symbiotic Networks Paving the Path to Success

Successful organizations are recognizing the power of ecosystem communities, a confluence of symbiotic relationships going beyond traditional value chains to create a web of synergistic partnerships. This comprehensive approach, nurturing collaboration even among competitors, is steering the way to unprecedented innovation and robust solutions. Let us explore the fabric of ecosystem communities, delineating awareness, the metrics for assessment, and actionable strategies for a company to nurture these networks.

**Awareness: Ecosystem Communities are Greater than the Sum of their Parts**

Thriving businesses are more than just conglomerates, they are vibrant, evolving organisms interconnected within a web known as Ecosystem Communities. It is here that entities forge relationships not only to survive but to flourish, creating a living, breathing community that goes beyond mere transactional interactions to environments of **co-creation and mutual growth**.

At the heart of these communities lies the revolutionary concept of **coopetition**, where firms, even competitors, cooperate to achieve a common goal, thus superseding the limitations of traditional value chains. This synergistic approach allows businesses to embed their products and services into a cohesive, interconnected matrix, creating solutions that are not just complementary but also enhance each other's value proposition to address the complex, multi-faceted needs of today's customers.

In a world teeming with businesses vying for consumer attention, ecosystem communities stand as a lighthouse of innovation, facilitating a space where

---

[50] Colin Bryar, Bill Carr: "Working Backwards: Insights, Stories, and Secrets from Inside Amazon". Published on 09.02.2021 by St. Martin's Press.

companies can leverage each other's strengths to create products and services that are **greater than the sum of their parts**. By doing so, a company has successfully created a self-sustaining ecosystem that not only meets a wide variety of consumer needs but also **redefines industry standards**, highlighting the enormous potential that lies in collaborative growth.

Another epitome of ecosystem community success is seen in the rapid growth and global footprint of Spotify. Emerging from the Nordic tech scene, which is buzzing with collaborative tech environments, Spotify leveraged shared resources and mutual promotion to create a service that revolutionized the music industry. The secret to their success was not just individual brilliance, but their ability to integrate various music labels, artists, and podcasters into one seamless experience for the user, creating a dynamic and ever-evolving library of audio content that caters to a wide spectrum of tastes and preferences.

The advent of ecosystem communities has reimagined the pathway to digital success, heralding a landscape where collaboration, innovation, and mutual growth are not just encouraged but are fundamental tenets of business strategy. Companies venturing into this landscape must create awareness of the nuanced dynamics of Ecosystem Communities, nurturing relationships characterized by mutual respect, transparency, and a shared vision for the future, to pave the way for a digital future characterized by unprecedented innovation and success.

But is your company already setting up and living in Ecosystem Communities?

**Assessment: Finding traces from Ecosystem Communities**

 It is important for organizations to have a finger on the pulse of their standing in Ecosystem Communities, a strategy that goes beyond just building alliances. Understanding where a company stands in terms of Ecosystem Communities necessitates a deep dive into an array of metrics that surface the extent and efficacy of its collaborative efforts.

Firstly, an essential factor is the **number or share of joint solutions created**. This parameter indicates the successful collaborative outputs that have stemmed from the community. It reflects the innovation and synergy achieved through collective effort. Tracking this metric over time can offer insights into the growth and vitality of the community engagements. Companies should strive to build engagements that yield collaborative solutions, which stand as a testament to the fruitful relationships in the ecosystem community.

Equally important is the **number of partnerships within the ecosystem**. This denotes the scale of the network, highlighting the potential resources and expertise a company can tap into. A vibrant ecosystem community is characterized by a rich combination of diverse partnerships, each bringing a unique value to the table. Companies should be vigilant in nurturing these relationships, supporting partnerships that are symbiotic and yield mutual growth. One must not overlook the **track record of coopetitions**, encompassing instances, successes, and challenges faced during such engagements. Keeping a track record helps to understand the dynamics of such relationships, pinpointing areas of success and avenues for improvement. It aids in sculpting a roadmap for future engagements, crafted from learned experiences and best practices.

An additional marker to consider is the **impact of the collaborations on customer satisfaction**. This involves analyzing customer feedback on joint solutions, as it unveils the direct impact of the ecosystem community on the end-users. Monitoring the fluctuations in customer satisfaction levels post-collaboration can offer valuable insights into the effectiveness of the ecosystem strategy. To navigate the web of ecosystem communities efficiently, organizations should also focus on assessing the alignment of values and visions among the community members. A harmonious ecosystem thrives on **shared values and a unified vision**, which serve as the cornerstone for long-lasting and successful collaborations.

Through a detailed assessment encompassing these metrics, companies can gauge their standings in ecosystem communities, allowing them to navigate a path that is not just reactive but proactive, gearing them towards a journey of sustained growth and collaborative success in the digital space.

### Actions: Combining Ecosystem Communities

 It becomes abundantly clear that fostering a nourishing Ecosystem Community is not just beneficial, but necessary for companies aiming for steadfast growth and sustained innovation. Crafting such communities requires a series of decisive actions that encompass the contributions and coordinated efforts of a network of partners, synergizing to offer a rich, customer-centric value proposition.

The primary step in this endeavor is **outlining customer-centric offerings that involve all or most contributors**. This is where companies not only identify the core value, they aspire to deliver to their customers but also create a platform for seamless integration of offerings derived from various partners. It is about building a collaborative, enhanced value proposition through the synthesis of each partner's strengths, presenting a unified and more potent solution to the end customers. Companies such as Amazon have effectively demonstrated this by integrating a multitude of services and products, ranging from retail to entertainment, into a single customer-focused ecosystem.

Once the offerings have been delineated, the focus shifts to **defining the operating ecosystems and establishing a clear modus operandi**. This stage involves pinpointing potential partners and defining a collaborative framework that sets the operational guidelines. It acts as a blueprint that illustrates the roles and responsibilities of each entity, paving the way for harmonious and productive collaborations. The objective here is to create ecosystems that are flexible and can adeptly evolve in response to changing market dynamics and consumer preferences. Apple's ecosystem, which encompasses a range of devices, services, and platforms, working seamlessly together, serves as an illustrative example of this principle in action.

Building and developing an ecosystem is a perpetual effort that necessitates **regular reviews and iterative developments**. Companies must institute mechanisms for regular assessments to ensure the health and efficiency of the ecosystem. A continuous feedback loop involving all stakeholders, including customers, is at the core of this strategy, facilitating the identification of areas ripe for innovation and improvement. The insights garnered from these reviews ought to steer the developmental strategy, crafting a pathway of on-going improvement and growth. Spotify, for instance, continuously refines its music recommendation algorithms based on user feedback and preferences, creating a more personalized and enhanced user experience over time.

It is equally important to entertain a culture that encourages **innovation and knowledge sharing**. Creating platforms where partners can brainstorm, and nurture new ideas collaboratively is key to nurturing a thriving Ecosystem Community. It should be a space where collective intellect and diverse perspectives are not just welcomed but celebrated, setting the stage for breakthrough innovations that could redefine industry standards. Google has epitomized this through its various collaborative platforms and tools which drive innovation and facilitate knowledge sharing amongst users.

**Leveraging technology to support collaboration** is a necessity. Investment in technology infrastructure that aids seamless collaboration should be a priority. Companies must harness collaborative platforms, AI-driven analytics tools, and secure communication channels to ensure that collaborations are not just successful but groundbreaking, setting new paradigms in the industry. Microsoft, with its suite of collaborative tools such as Microsoft Teams, has set a benchmark in fostering collaboration through technology.

Through a strategic, structured approach focused on collaborative synergies and customer-centric values, companies can explore ecosystem communities that are vibrant, innovative, and geared for sustained growth. However, the main stakeholder is still missing within the communities – the Customer.

### 3.1.2.4   Customer Community – The Quintessential Target of Collaborative Progress

As we venture further into digital integrations, the norms of business-customer relationships are undergoing a seminal transformation. Gone are the days when customers were simply receivers of products and services. Today, forward-thinking companies are evolving to build more inclusive, reciprocal, and engaging relationships through Customer Communities. This network serves as a crucible where creative energies fuse innovations that are finely tuned to meet market aspirations. The road to understanding the importance and developing customer communities embarks from awareness, stretching through assessment, and solidifying in the coherent actions undertaken by a company.

**Awareness: The Immeasurable Value of Customer Involvement**

At its core, a customer community is an orchestrated space, often leveraging digital platforms, where **customers are not just seen as end-users but as valuable partners in a collaborative ecosystem**. This is a ground of mutual enrichment where customers and companies come together, sharing experiences, insights, and even working hand in hand to ideate, design, and refine products and services.

This collaborative approach stands as a pillar of modern business strategy, offering a prism through which companies can view their products and services from various angles, drawing on the rich and diverse perspectives of a wider community, which spans across different demographics and geographical locations. The potency of these communities lies in their ability to **democratize the innovation process**, ushering in a collaborative spirit that extends beyond the company's borders. Imagine a platform where a company not just listens but actively engages with its customers, involving them in every stage from conceptualization, co-creation to the eventual delivery of products and services, in a manner that is transparent, respectful, and inclusive.

Companies, through these forums, can facilitate sessions where customers, experts, and enthusiasts come together to brainstorm and work on the next groundbreaking idea. Such a deep-rooted collaborative approach ensures that the pulse of the market is well understood and integrated into the company's strategy and product development from the get-go. This is not a one-off event but a continuous dialogue where feedback is not only welcomed but actively sought, forging a bond that goes much beyond a commercial relationship, transforming customers into community members – stakeholders in the brand's journey, offering insights and innovations that are ground-up, realistic, and resonate deeply with user expectations.

For instance, platforms like 'LEGO Ideas' have turned consumers into creators, ushering in a truly collaborative era. This program invites LEGO enthusiasts to submit their ideas for new sets, encouraging an open-source approach to innovation. Remarkable designs are not just acknowledged but have the potential to be transformed into commercially available LEGO sets, with the original creators receiving a share of the royalties. It is a vivid testimony to LEGO's commitment to nurturing a collaborative spirit with its customer base, supporting a culture where creativity is rewarded and cherished[51].

Fostering a customer community is akin to nurturing a garden where ideas bloom through collaborative care, where a company and its customers walk hand in hand, shaping a future that is not just profitable but also inclusive, vibrant, and enriched with shared visions and collaborative successes. But has your company already started to work on Customer Communities?

**Assessment: Testing the Customers' Involvement**

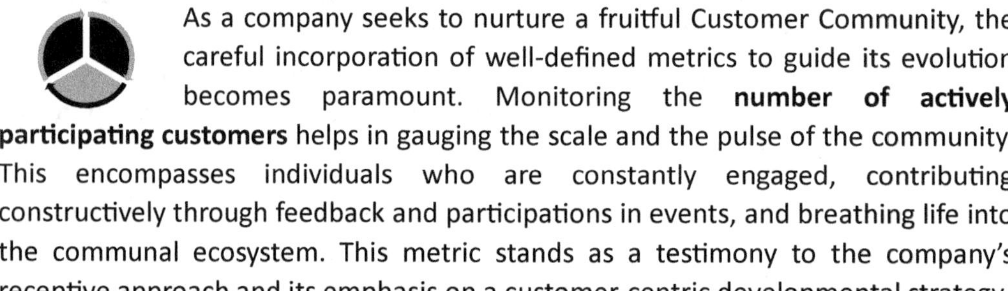

As a company seeks to nurture a fruitful Customer Community, the careful incorporation of well-defined metrics to guide its evolution becomes paramount. Monitoring the **number of actively participating customers** helps in gauging the scale and the pulse of the community. This encompasses individuals who are constantly engaged, contributing constructively through feedback and participations in events, and breathing life into the communal ecosystem. This metric stands as a testimony to the company's receptive approach and its emphasis on a customer-centric developmental strategy.

Moving further, understanding, and analyzing the **nature and frequency of customer engagement events**, including workshops and beta tests, forms the initial step in this endeavor. These events act as a backbone, indicating the vibrancy and health of the community. It reflects the company's dedication to maintaining a spirited, engaged community, setting a tone of collaboration and feedback-driven development.

Yet, the metrics would not be comprehensive without tracking the **innovations and improvements championed by the customer base**. Here, the focus tightens on the reciprocal value derived through the collaborative efforts – highlighting the symbiotic relationship between the company and its community. It mirrors a fertile ground of shared ideas and mutual growth, indicating a healthy, beneficial relationship that sees customers not just as consumers but as vital stakeholders in the company's journey.

Equally important is the incorporation of **customer satisfaction scores connected to collaborative endeavors**. These scores yield insights into the effectiveness of the collaborative projects and the level of fulfillment derived by the customers through their contributions. A high satisfaction score parallels well-executed collaborations,

---

[51] Lego company website. Visited 08.04.2024. https://ideas.lego.com

where customers find their voices heard and their inputs valued, nurturing a relationship of mutual respect and shared vision.

Diving deeper into assessment dynamics, introducing auxiliary metrics such as **sentiment analysis** can provide a richer perspective. It leverages qualitative data to gauge the community's perception, tapping into the undercurrents of customer feelings and areas needing refinement. Complementing this is the focus on the **community growth rate**, offering critical insights into its allure and the potency of strategies deployed for growth.

When harmonized, these metrics craft a lucid, grounded depiction of the community's current standing and its latent potential, thereby laying a solid foundation for a community that is ripe for collaborative growth and mutual enrichment. Here are some concrete measures to build it up.

**Action: Bringing Customers and Companies together**

 To jump-start the formation of a prosperous customer community, it is fundamental for **companies to not only recruit customers but to actively involve them in the community**. This means leveraging data to identify customers who frequently engage with the brand, perhaps those who leave reviews or interact through social media. Once identified, inviting them to an exclusive online forum or community group can be a great first step. Encourage them to invite like-minded peers, turning the community into a growing entity of people who share common interests and affiliations with the brand. Sephora, for instance, managed to build a dedicated space for its customers called the 'Beauty Insider Community', where beauty enthusiasts can share reviews, ask questions, and even post pictures of the products they are using. This community has been a source of invaluable feedback and a hub for sharing expertise, fostering a tight-knit community of brand loyalists[52].

Moving forward, it is crucial to entertain customers adequately by incorporating a rich blend of information sharing and ambition setting through a **dedicated portal or app**. The portal could feature discussion boards for sharing experiences, webinars, and workshops to educate the community about new developments and get feedback on on-going projects. It can host competitions encouraging customers to share their ambitions and potentially see them realized through the brand. Such platforms should be interactive and vibrant, regularly updated with content that is both informative and fun, creating a go-to hub for customers to engage with the brand and each other. Starbucks, for instance, has a robust online community where

---

[52] On Sephora company website: "Beauty Insider Community". Visited 08.04.2024. https://community.sephora.com

it shares behind-the-scenes content, hosts Q&A sessions, and keeps customers updated on the latest happenings. It not only enhances customer engagement but also instills a sense of belonging among its members.

Next, the company needs to **involve customers actively and substantively in processes like ideation, co-creation, testing, and communication**. This could involve setting up collaborative workshops where customers can brainstorm and present their ideas for new products or services. Utilize tools like surveys and feedback forms to understand customer preferences during the creation process, and perhaps even create beta-testing groups where select customers can try out new products and give feedback before a broader release. Companies like Adobe often release beta versions of their products to a select group of customers to garner feedback and make necessary improvements before the official release, ensuring products that are finely tuned to meet customer expectations.

Lastly, it is essential to **continually review and celebrate the relationships formed with customers**. This can involve setting up annual events to celebrate the community, with awards for the most active members or those who have contributed the most valuable feedback over the year. Companies can share success stories highlighting how customer input led to tangible changes and improvements, not only appreciating but publicly recognizing the invaluable contributions made by the community. Regular **feedback sessions** can be hosted, where the community can discuss their experiences, what they feel is working well, and what could be improved, ensuring that the community remains a vibrant, positive, and constructive space. Salesforce, for example, annually hosts the 'Dreamforce' event which not only serves as a platform to announce new products but also celebrates its vibrant community of users, partners, and developers, fostering a shared journey towards success[53].

However, all collaborative efforts, both tempting and potentially harmonious, come with their own set of challenges including potential **clashes of culture, communication breakdowns, and misaligned visions**, as historically evidenced by Nokia's early 2000s aspirations to develop an integrated ecosystem. This initiative was hindered significantly due to internal silos and competitive dynamics among teams rather than creating a collaborative environment. But recognizing and leveraging these challenges can in fact steer organizations to develop strategic blueprints grounded in best practices. One such practice is nurturing a shared vision and values, a strategy which guided the successful launch of Nokia's OZO, a virtual reality camera that embodied Nokia's rejuvenated vision of pioneering in digital realities. Moreover, facilitating open and transparent communication can be seen as

---

[53] On Salesforce company website: "dreamforce". Visited 08.04.2024. https://www.salesforce.com/dreamforce/

the lifeblood of collaborative endeavors, bridging divides and ensuring alignment in pursuits, a philosophy deeply ingrained in Atlassian's operational fabric which encourages open communication through various platforms and tools that support interaction and alignment across diverse stakeholders. In a digital sphere that is constantly evolving, flexibility and adaptability emerge as necessary virtues. The journey of LINE, from a disaster response tool to a multifunctional platform serving millions, stands testimony to the power of adaptability and the fruits of leveraging a vast collaborative network. Emphasizing diversity, not just in expertise but also in background and perspectives, can offer unique and comprehensive solutions, a practice championed by Tata Consultancy Services as they cater to a global clientele, making diversity the keystone of their collaborative efforts. An often underrated yet vital component is the establishment of consistent feedback loops. BBVA's collaborative model, which actively seeks feedback not only from customers but also from internal teams and partners, showcases the critical role of feedback in defining cutting-edge digital offerings.

Looking ahead, we find ourselves at a crucial junction where **collaborative strategies are witnessing a transformation**, evolving to adapt to technological advancements and societal shifts. The collaborative dynamics are changing from straightforward interactions to a rich, multi-dimensional network, co-creating value, shared insights, and amalgamated expertise. Technological advancements, notably decentralized technologies like blockchain, are catalysts to this shift. Estonia's e-Residency program is a beacon in this landscape, facilitating borderless, transparent collaborations grounded in trust, offering a glimpse into a future of unrestricted, transparent collaborations. Moreover, as we forge into the future, we will witness the role of technologies such as quantum computing, extended reality, and artificial intelligence not just as enhancers but as game changers that redefine the very core of collaborative engagements. Yet, it is imperative to navigate the ethical and security challenges that accompany these advancements. Companies like Rakuten are setting a precedent by adhering to ethical standards while integrating AI-based insights across ecosystems, underlining the necessity for trust and mutual respect in collaborative frameworks. As we navigate this landscape, it is clear that future collaborative frameworks will be a complex weave of innovative technologies coupled with humane considerations and agile strategies. While tools and platforms may undergo transformations, the foundational philosophy of creating shared value through cooperative ventures remains the unwavering constant guiding entities through the unpredictable but exhilarating path of our Digital Future, emphasizing a cooperative endeavor that generates shared value, steering us through the dynamic terrain of the Digital Future with a grounded yet forward-thinking approach.

Find more and updated information in the **Digital Arena**. Connect with like-minded professionals to unleash the potential and make it happen.

Digital Vision and Leadership contribute the internal ingredients to Digital Readiness, Digital Communities add the external spices. Based on this we can now turn the page and focus on the second Digital Success Lever – Digital Momentum.

## 3.2   Digital Momentum



Just as momentum in physics denotes the strength or force that allows something to continue or grow stronger as time passes, **Digital Momentum describes the persistent force powered by knowing and using, hence enjoying the benefits of digital tools.** A robust Digital Momentum not only accelerates the adoption of digital tools but also cements a culture of continuous digital evolution. Essentially, Digital Momentum **earns a company the right to further invest** into its digital future.

To drive Digital Momentum, a company needs to provide Digital Transparency about all its digital assets, creating a sense of pride, this helps to unleash the potential ('we know what we have'). Supporting the Digital Transparency is the continuous increase of Digital Usage to make it happen ('we use what we have'). Together they make the Digital Momentum happen but let us start with looking at Digital Transparency.

### 3.2.1   Digital Transparency

At its core, **Digital Transparency is the collective appreciation of what digital assets are available at a company and how every digital tool, platform, and initiative aligns with the organization's vision and mission.** Understanding Digital Transparency transcends technical knowledge. It defines a narrative of how technology empowers businesses, drives innovation, and leads to competitive advantage.

**What the C-Suite needs to know**

1. Transparency is Trust: Digital Transparency cultivates trust, giving stakeholders confidence in the digital trajectory the organization is paving and assuring them of the robustness and reliability of the digital strategies being employed.

2. Digital Story: A living documentation of the firm's digital presence and aspiration, nurturing a sense of ownership and pride – outlining the digital contribution to the business goals.

3. Digital Shelf: Dedicated platform where a company hosts an assemblage of its digital assets, a canvas of digital narratives, accessible for everyone.

4. Digital Dashboards and Targets: Nucleus of insightful engagement, pin-pointing need for action through major gaps, and highlighting opportunities for further development.

---

[54] Gil Penchina – American businessman and investor

5.  **Digital Daily:** Systematic weaving of digital discourse and strategies into day-to-day operations and engagements of a company – driving involvement and empowerment.

But why is Digital Transparency so important?

Digital Transparency goes beyond merely understanding the available digital tools and initiatives, it extends to realizing how these align seamlessly with an organization's vision and mission. Digital Transparency creates a **collective consciousness**, where every individual, irrespective of their role, comprehends, appreciates, and leverages the existence and potential of digital strategies and tools. This broad understanding ensures a **unified drive towards development, enhancing efficiency and heightening customer satisfaction.** It eradicates the barriers that stifle progress, breaking down the silos that hinder communication and collaborative efforts. With that, Digital Transparency aids in initiating **innovation**.

At the heart of Digital Transparency lies **empowerment**. Stakeholders become actively involved, evolving from mere spectators to contributors in the digital development. In a world inundated with information, being able to trust the digital tools and platforms in place is fundamental. **Transparency cultivates this trust, giving stakeholders confidence in the digital trajectory the organization is paving**, and assuring them of the robustness and reliability of the digital strategies being employed.

What does Digital Transparency entail?

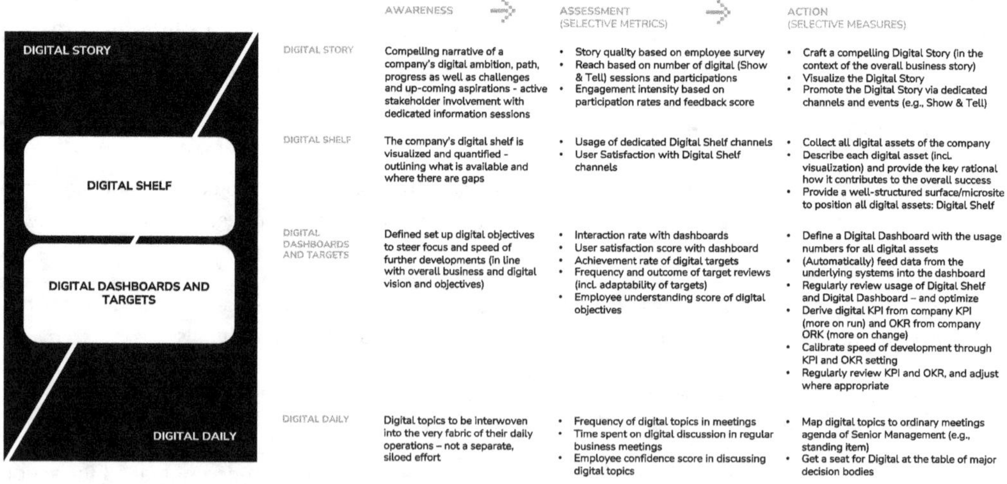


| | AWARENESS | ASSESSMENT (SELECTIVE METRICS) | ACTION (SELECTIVE MEASURES) |
|---|---|---|---|
| DIGITAL STORY | Compelling narrative of a company's digital ambition, path, progress as well as challenges and up-coming aspirations - active stakeholder involvement with dedicated information sessions | • Story quality based on employee survey<br>• Reach based on number of digital (Show & Tell) sessions and participations<br>• Engagement intensity based on participation rates and feedback score | • Craft a compelling Digital Story (in the context of the overall business story)<br>• Visualize the Digital Story<br>• Promote the Digital Story via dedicated channels and events (e.g., Show & Tell) |
| DIGITAL SHELF | The company's digital shelf is visualized and quantified - outlining what is available and where there are gaps | • Usage of dedicated Digital Shelf channels<br>• User Satisfaction with Digital Shelf channels | • Collect all digital assets of the company<br>• Describe each digital asset (incl. visualization) and provide the key rational how it contributes to the overall success<br>• Provide a well-structured surface/microsite to position all digital assets: Digital Shelf |
| DIGITAL DASHBOARDS AND TARGETS | Defined set up digital objectives to steer focus and speed of further developments (in line with overall business and digital vision and objectives) | • Interaction rate with dashboards<br>• User satisfaction score with dashboard<br>• Achievement rate of digital targets<br>• Frequency and outcome of target reviews (incl. adaptability of targets)<br>• Employee understanding score of digital objectives | • Define a Digital Dashboard with the usage numbers for all digital assets<br>• (Automatically) feed data from the underlying systems into the dashboard<br>• Regularly review usage of Digital Shelf and Digital Dashboard – and optimize<br>• Derive digital KPI from company KPI (more on run) and OKR from company ORK (more on change)<br>• Calibrate speed of development through KPI and OKR setting<br>• Regularly review KPI and OKR, and adjust where appropriate |
| DIGITAL DAILY | Digital topics to be interwoven into the very fabric of their daily operations – not a separate, siloed effort | • Frequency of digital topics in meetings<br>• Time spent on digital discussion in regular business meetings<br>• Employee confidence score in discussing digital topics | • Map digital topics to ordinary meetings agenda of Senior Management (e.g., standing item)<br>• Get a seat for Digital at the table of major decision bodies |

*Figure 18: Components of Digital Transparency*

Understanding the magnitude and depth of Digital Transparency necessitates a deep dive into its cornerstone elements, each forging a pathway towards a digitally empowered and conscious corporate environment.

At the top of Digital Transparency is weaving a **Digital Story** – a vivid narrative that encapsulates the company's digital ambitions, victories, challenges, and future aspirations. Building on the future-oriented Digital Vision, the Digital Story connects it with today's digital presence and reality of the company (visit section 3.1.1 Digital Vision and Leadership on page 81 to understand the foundation). This on-going story, narrated through dedicated information sessions, actively involves stakeholders, nurturing a space where they can contribute and align with the company's digital path. It is a compelling biography of the company's digital life that breathes trust and inspires participation from every stakeholder involved, fostering a community bonded through a shared vision and mutual goals.

Whereas the Digital Story, is the tip of the iceberg, the **Digital Shelf** is the large body underneath. It represents a tangible manifestation of the organization's digital assets. Here, every tool and initiative finds its place, outlined lucidly to highlight both the available resources and the gaps that need filling.

**Digital Dashboards and Targets** add the quantitative perspective to the Digital Shelf. For all the (relevant) digital assets objectives are carved in tandem with the business vision. This endeavor shapes the trajectory of digital advancements, focusing on key areas to enhance efficiency and drive growth. These targets stand as lighthouses, guiding the journey and ensuring the organization maintains its course in the vast digital sea, charting paths towards meaningful destinations.

Finally, the **Digital Daily** is where digital topics, i.e. the Digital Story, the Digital Shelf, as well as the Digital Dashboards and Targets, cease to be segregated entities, integrating seamlessly into the day-to-day operations of the organization. It is a woven fabric of digital messages intermingled with daily tasks, where digital discussions become a routine aspect, creating a workplace pulsating with digital heartbeat, encouraging adaptability, and nurturing a naturally digitally inclined workforce. It is about making Digital Transparency not a part of but the culture itself.

In embracing Digital Transparency with an all-encompassing approach, companies are not just building a workplace, they are cultivating ecosystems rich in collaboration, innovation, and relentless pursuit of digital excellence.

**Unilever's Pursuit of Digital Transparency**

**Digital Story:** Unilever has been continually active in sharing their digital and sustainability journeys. This is visible through their comprehensive annual reports, sustainability disclosures, and even through social media campaigns. Their Digital Transparency extends to providing case studies, webinars, and insights that go beyond displaying achievements – they aim to educate their partners, customers, and even competitors about the challenges and solutions related to sustainable growth.

**Digital Dashboard:** Unilever's long-standing mission is to improve health and well-being, reduce environmental impact, and source 100% of agricultural raw materials sustainably. While these aims may not be 'digital' in the traditional sense, Unilever has managed to translate these goals into a digital space. They use a variety of internal and external dashboards to track everything from supply chain sustainability to employee engagement metrics, making these dashboards available to key stakeholders. They have even leveraged blockchain technology to enhance transparency in their supply chain.

**Actionable Digital Targets:** Unilever has set highly specific, actionable targets, often breaking them down by product, geography, or business line. They have committed to big digital shifts, such as moving towards more direct-to-consumer digital channels and leveraging data analytics for better consumer insights. These digital targets align closely with their broader corporate goals, making it easier for stakeholders to see how digital initiatives fit into the larger picture.

It is a compelling example of how even traditional companies can leverage Digital Transparency to build momentum and remain competitive in a fast-evolving landscape[55].

For Digital Transparency to be effective, it cannot be compartmentalized or treated as a periodic initiative. It must permeate every facet of the organization, becoming as intrinsic as the company's culture itself.

Let us now build the Awareness for Digital Transparency on what it is and why it is important, introduce some Assessment metrics and propose some concrete actions to craft a Digital Story, to position the Digital Shelf, to set Digital Dashboards and Targets, as well as to integrate Digital Daily into the everyday business processes.

### 3.2.1.1 Digital Story – Digital Key Messages in the Strategic Context

In the digital epoch where organizations constantly evolve, the act of describing the corporate digital direction emerges as a linchpin in building a sense of unity and alignment within a company's culture. Here, the Digital Story unfurls, not just as a recounting of the company's milestones but as a living narrative imbued with the breaths of every individual in the organization.

---

[55] Paul Hiebert in Adweek: "Unilever's Jennifer Gardner Is Tired of Talking About Transparency". Published online 17.07.2020, visited 08.04.2024. https://www.adweek.com/programmatic/unilevers-jennifer-gardner-is-tired-of-talking-about-transparency/

**Awareness: Appreciating the Power of a Digital Story**

 At its core, a Digital Story is a vibrant, evolving narrative that chronicles a company's path in the digital transformation. It encapsulates the series of transitions, advancements, and innovations undertaken, and it paints a vivid picture of the hurdles overcome and the milestones achieved. It is a **living documentation of a firm's digital presence and aspirations,** outlining not just the directions and technologies but humanizing them through real experiences, personal impressions, and the shared enthusiasm of a workforce steering towards a unified goal. A prime example can be seen in the approach adopted by the South African telecommunications giant, MTN. In narrating their journey towards launching a mobile money feature, they did not stop at just explaining the technology. They highlighted real stories – a farmer buying seeds, a mother sending money to her college-going son, a young entrepreneur paying suppliers – bringing to life the tangible impacts and the societal ripple effects sparked through their digital initiative. It encapsulated not just a service but a story of empowerment and connectivity, creating a vivid chapter in their broader Digital Story[56]. The Digital Story builds a narrative that resonates with the target audience, addressing their pain points, aspirations, and needs, thereby fostering a relationship grounded on trust and reliability. It is this narrative that brings to life the Digital Vision, highlighting how the digital product suite meets or exceeds user expectations and why it should be the preferred choice. Companies like Amazon have exemplified this by constantly evolving their positioning from being a mere online bookstore to a one-stop-shop for a vast array of needs, thereby highlighting the convenience, variety, and reliability it offers to different user segments.

At the heart of the Digital Story is the **unique selling proposition (USP)**, which should be well-articulated for the entire digital product suite and each individual product within. The USP navigates the fine line between highlighting the unique functionalities that set a product apart and emphasizing the benefits that users will gain from using it, thereby creating a substantial difference from competitors. Therefore, the Digital Story demands a profound understanding of the competitive landscape, allowing a company to position its products not just in isolation but in a vibrant market filled with alternatives. It is a continuous endeavor, wherein feedback is constantly integrated to refine the positioning, ensuring it remains relevant, compelling, and aligned with the evolving needs and preferences of the target audience. For instance, Google's search engine in its nascent stages leveraged a USP of providing fast, relevant, and comprehensive search results based on a complex

---

[56] Enzo Scarcella on MTN company website: "MTN's multi-pronged approach to accelerate digital inclusion". Published online 09.06.2022, visited 08.04.2024. https://www.mtn.com/mtns-multi-pronged-approach-to-accelerate-digital-inclusion/

algorithm that was distinctly superior to what was available at that time. It was not just about finding information but finding the most relevant information quickly and efficiently, which underscored its early positioning strategy. In detailing the specifics, the Digital Story encompasses a deep understanding of not just the product's features, but the benefits they confer to the users. It articulates why a product is not just different but better, conveying the tangible and intangible benefits that it offers.

But why is cultivating a robust Digital Story so crucial in establishing Digital Transparency and eventually drive Digital Momentum? For one, it encourages an **active, participatory culture**. It is not just a story told by the leadership, it is a collective narrative, enriched with insights, stories, and experiences of individuals across the organization. This creates a **sense of ownership**, a **pride in being part of a grand development**, encouraging every individual to contribute proactively to the digital endeavor. Moreover, a well-articulated Digital Story serves as a compass, aligning diverse teams and functions under a unified vision. It helps in bridging gaps, developing understanding, and ensuring that everyone, right from the executive suite to the newest recruit, is on the same page, fully aware and engaged in the collective digital voyage. By clearly outlining the digital ambitions and paths, it aids in demystifying complex concepts, breaking them down into relatable narratives that are understood and endorsed by everyone, fostering an environment of clarity and mutual understanding. Renowned Indian e-commerce platform, Flipkart, provides another illustration. Flipkart utilizes their digital narrative not just to spotlight triumphs but to undertake a candid analysis of setbacks. Following a festive sale that did not meet targets, they engaged in a transparent, company-wide assessment, dissecting what went wrong without engaging in a blame game, turning the experience into a learning chapter in their evolving Digital Story, supporting a culture of learning and collective growth.

Furthermore, a Digital Story stands as a beacon, displaying the company's resilience, ingenuity, and the spirit of innovation, often serving to inspire and create a culture of continuous learning and adaptation. It is painting a vivid picture of how each stride in the digital journey equates to progress, not just technologically but culturally, socially, and ethically.

In conclusion, crafting a potent Digital Story is not just an exercise in chronicling a company's digital journey, it is a vital instrument in driving Digital Transparency, nurturing a culture of inclusivity, collaboration, and shared vision. It stands central in driving Digital Momentum, fueling the enthusiasm and shared dedication needed to march towards a future of digital success, one that is carved through collective efforts, unified dreams, and a shared sense of purpose and direction.

But where does your company stand when it comes to a compelling Digital Story?

## Assessment: Reading the Digital Story

 Assessing the state of a company's Digital Story is a nuanced process that involves measuring various aspects that demonstrate how well the narrative is supported within the organization and possibly even beyond. This assessment ensures that the story is not just compelling but also coherent, grounded in realities, and shaped with inputs from a wide spectrum of stakeholders, fostering a deeper connection and a sense of ownership among all involved.

It is valuable to consider **qualitative assessments**, diving into feedback received to understand the depth of engagement. Are employees identifying with the stories shared? Are they feeling more connected with the organization's digital journey? It should probe whether the story articulates the vision, the progress, and the roadmap effectively while reflecting the collective journey and the shared dreams and aspirations of the workforce. Furthermore, the quality assessment could involve evaluating how well the story portrays the tangible impacts of the digital initiatives, weaving in personal narratives and testimonials to forge a deeper connection. These feedback statements can serve as a goldmine of insights, helping to sculpt a story that is not just compelling but also deeply personal, creating a strong sense of belonging and pride among the employees.

Moreover, a deep dive into the **clarity and comprehensiveness of the USP**, both for the overarching digital product suite and for each individual product therein. This involves scrutinizing how lucidly the USP communicates the unique attributes and advantages that set the products aside in a crowded marketplace. It is essential that both internal and external communications illuminate the USP in a manner that meets the target audience's preferences and needs, establishing a unique space in the competitive arena. After this is an evaluation of how the Digital Story supports **differentiation from the competitors**. A robust Digital Story not only highlights what is different about a product but articulates those differences in a manner that exhibits added value to the users. Here, the focus is on embodying a degree of innovation in the products and elucidating the unique benefits users will reap from choosing these offerings over others in the market. The analysis should encapsulate customer feedback and reviews, underscoring what users perceive as distinctive, thereby delineating a clear path of value in the user's journey.

Lastly, focusing on the Digital Story's **reach** is paramount. The number of digital 'Show & Tell' sessions organized and the participation in these sessions give a concrete indication of how well the story has permeated through the organization. Tracking attendance and the diversity of the attendees can help in understanding whether the story is reaching all corners of the organization, fostering a company-wide discourse. Moreover, analyzing the frequency of these sessions can indicate whether the organization maintains a consistent engagement rhythm, keeping the message fresh and updated in the minds of the employees.

Through this detailed process, a company ensures that its Digital Story remains vibrant, relevant, and deeply rooted in the shared experiences and the collective heartbeat of the organization, steering it towards a future of digital success borne out of shared dreams and united efforts. Let us now explore how your company can craft a compelling Digital Story.

**Action: Crafting a Compelling Digital Story**

Drafting a Digital Story is an endeavor that requires not just clarity of purpose but a systematic approach that supports connectivity and a collective sense of pride in the digital milestones achieved by the organization.

A company must craft a Digital Story with a **set of compelling messages,** seamlessly woven with the broader narratives of the company's vision, mission, and the business roadmap charted. These key messages need to be clear, precise, as well as catchy. Prioritization on key topics is required. This is not just about corporate objectives, it is about **human stories**, about moments that matter, challenges to overcome, and the journey that everyone undertakes within the larger digital voyage of the organization. Companies such as Procter & Gamble have mastered this by narrating the human stories behind their digital transformation, taking their stakeholders on a journey through their efforts to leverage technology in enhancing consumer experiences and operational efficiencies. It paints a rich tale of human experiences and aspirations weaving through the technological milestones achieved[57]. Leaders should not shy away from sharing setbacks, as well as triumphs, detailing how the organization rallied to overcome challenges and evolve stronger. Companies like Siemens have adopted a transparent approach in narrating their digital journey, showcasing not just the highs but the learnings derived from the lows[58].

In the dynamic arena of digital products, establishing a firm ground demands orchestrated actions rooted deeply in the facets highlighted during the assessment phase. To start with, one must compile the **overall product suite's positioning** in the marketplace. A compelling case in point is Adobe, which framed its Adobe Creative Cloud to cater to different creative professionals, leveraging its deep-rooted legacy in the creative software domain. This is evidenced in their detailed product descriptions and success stories highlighted on their official site, where they have

---

[57] Some of the stories are outlined in the 2021 annual report, visited 08.04.2024.
https://us.pg.com/annualreport2021/
[58] Stories on Siemens company website, visited 08.04.2024.
https://new.siemens.com/global/en/company/stories.html

distinctly positioned each product in their suite. Further, each individual product should be subjected to a careful process to sharpen its **unique selling proposition (USP)**. In the area of e-commerce, Amazon is a frontrunner with products like Alexa, which is positioned not just as a smart home device but a personal assistant that evolves to offer personalized experiences, a detail vividly portrayed through user testimonials and product details on their official site[59].

A crucial next step is to **visualize this story**, making it tangible, palpable, and alive through vibrant visual interpretations. Key visuals, which are recognized throughout the organization are of immense value and ensure some consistency of the Digital Story. DHL, the global logistics company, has accomplished this through a vibrant combination of videos, infographics, and reports detailing their digital journey, guiding stakeholders through their commitment to digital innovation, painting a vivid picture through visual narratives that chart their digital milestones and future aspirations.

But crafting and visualizing the story is only half the endeavor. It is important to **promote the Digital Story actively through dedicated channels and events**, creating platforms where the story can be narrated, celebrated, and lived. LEGO stands as a stalwart example here, promoting its digital and sustainability journey through events and a dedicated section on its website[60].

Companies should also leverage digital platforms to narrate this story, creating dedicated spaces in the corporate intranet, newsletters, or even a dedicated podcast series that periodically narrates the chapters of this digital story, fostering a **continuous engagement with the story**. Nestlé, for instance, shares its digital journey tales through newsletters and dedicated sections on their website[61].

Moreover, maintaining a **collaborative culture where every employee becomes a storyteller**, sharing their subjective experiences of the digital journey, through platforms that encourage sharing, be it digital storytelling contests or collaborative digital boards where employees can pin their stories, developing a collective story that is rich with individual experiences and insights.

Through a systematic crafting and nurturing of the Digital Story, organizations can create a culture where transparency is not just a corporate objective but a lived reality, where each stakeholder feels a personal connection to the digital message,

---

[59] developer.amazon.com/alexa. Visited 08.04.2024

[60] On YouTube: "Our LEGO® Stories Episode 3 - Building Digital Relationships". Visited 08.04.2024 https://www.youtube.com/watch?v=Se-iKz1ZaLk

[61] Theodora Stanciu on SocialInsider: "Nestlé's Social Media Strategy - Learn from the World's Largest Food Company". Published online on 14.10.2021, visited 08.04.2024. https://www.socialinsider.io/blog/Nestle-social-media-strategy/

supporting a spirit of collective ownership, pride, and a unified stride towards Digital Momentum and success.

The Digital Story is the tip of the iceberg, but there is much more underneath: The Digital Shelf of a company.

3.2.1.2    Digital Shelf – Comprehensive Overview of the Digital Assets
To have a reliable basis, organizations are constantly on the lookout to offer a detailed picture of what digital products, tools and platforms are available and used. Understanding and leveraging the Digital Shelf becomes an essential endeavor in this context. Let us dive into the various facets involved in building and nurturing a Digital Shelf.

**Awareness: Discovering the Layers of the Digital Shelf**

 A Digital Shelf serves as a dedicated collection where companies host an assemblage of their digital assets, providing a detailed depiction of their digital competencies. This **repository** includes a company's digital interaction channels with clients, applications, bots that facilitate service, and other digital tools, which act as a testament to the company's digital prowess. It also highlights the customer journeys that a company enable to satisfy customer needs. The presentation is enriched through vivid and detailed visualizations, making it a transparent and interactive platform. An organization that has employed this concept proficiently is American Express, a globally recognized financial services corporation. Through their sophisticated digital customer service ecosystem, American Express unveils a robust Digital Shelf on their website and mobile app that outlines a multitude of digital avenues through which they engage with their customers. It encompasses a variety of features such as chat bots that assist customers around the clock, AI-driven recommendations for personalized offers, easy-to-navigate FAQ sections, and secure messaging channels for detailed queries, among other features.

The Digital Shelf stands as a **canvas of digital narratives**, a space where a company unfurls the vivid tapestry of its digital assets, seamlessly woven to narrate a brand's journey in the digital epoch. It is far more than a static presentation, it embodies a dynamic visualization of a company's digital odyssey, encapsulating every milestone and strategy that underscores its commitment to digital evolution. In this vibrant space, companies do not just map out functionalities, they narrate the stories behind each tool and channel, articulating their commitment to leveraging digital advancements to foster a connection that is deep, and trust infused. It reflects a culture of transparency, a shared understanding that nurtures a relationship of trust and mutual growth with its client base. It is a living entity, displaying an organization's relentless pursuit of digital excellence, a beacon highlighting a philosophy of growth and the on-going journey of innovation.

But where is your company when it comes to the Digital Shelf?

## Assessment: Exploring the Digital Shelf

 To build an efficient and transparent Digital Shelf, assessment is a first step that offers an insightful analysis based on a variety of metrics which are essential in shaping a strategy that aligns with the business goals and caters to the user needs proficiently.

Analyzing the **usage of dedicated Digital Shelf platforms** involves a granular approach to data analytics. Companies should look into the segmentation of users, understanding their behaviors, preferences, and patterns such as the devices they use, the time they usually log in, and the kind of content they consume the most. Diving deeper, one can assess the bounce rate, the pages that are most visited, and also the pathways through which users discover these channels, be it through organic search, referrals, or social media platforms. The **user satisfaction with Digital Shelf channels** should be assessed through comprehensive user feedback systems, incorporating star ratings, reviews, and possibly heat maps to understand user engagement on the pages. It is beneficial to include mechanisms for users to provide feedback easily, encouraging them to articulate both the strengths and areas for improvement, facilitating a roadmap for future developments that is directly aligned with user needs and preferences.

There are concrete measures to position the Digital Shelf.

## Action: Building a Digital Shelf

 To foster Digital Transparency by positioning a robust Digital Shelf, your company should commence with the **collection of all its digital assets**. This is not limited to the major platforms but extends to every microservice, API, and bot that facilitates customer interaction. Organizations should emulate companies like Airbnb, a forerunner in integrating a plethora of digital assets ranging from its primary rental platform to community-driven blogs and user-friendly mobile applications. These assets are clearly delineated, each highlighting its unique value proposition.

Upon gathering these assets, the next imperative step is to **describe each digital asset clearly**, including a visual representation and a detailed rationale explaining how each contributes to the overarching business strategy. Companies like Microsoft have excelled in this, offering a rich library of digital assets, each accompanied by a detailed narrative elucidating its functional capacity and the value it adds to the organization[62].

---

[62] On Microsoft company website: "Microsoft Learn. Spark Possibilities". Visited 08.04.2024

Following this, **craft a well-structured surface or microsite to host your Digital Shelf**, where all digital assets are displayed elegantly, with rich content detailing their functionalities and benefits, enhancing the user experience through easy navigation and intuitive design. These platforms can be made available for internal and possibly external users. A potent illustration is Adobe's Digital Shelf, which is carefully structured to offer an intuitive and enriched user experience, allowing visitors to seamlessly navigate through a broad array of assets[63].

Making the numbers of the Digital Shelf dynamic leads us to the Digital Dashboard and Targets as the next component of the overall Digital Transparency.

### 3.2.1.3  Digital Dashboards and Targets – the Quantitative View on Digital Assets

Companies find themselves navigating a complex web of technologies and strategies to stay relevant and competitive. In such a dynamic environment, having well-defined Digital Dashboards and Targets becomes a pre-requisite in guiding organizations towards a future that is not only successful but sustainable. The essence of Digital Dashboards and Targets lies in creating a focused pathway, grounded in transparency and strategic foresight, which drives every individual towards collective objectives.

**Awareness: Shared Direction based on Digital Dashboards and Targets**

 The **Digital Dashboards** stand tall as the nucleus of insightful engagements, offering a comprehensive aggregation of data that breathes life into a company's Digital Shelf. This tool serves not just as a representation but as a powerhouse, substantiating the stories crafted in the Digital Shelf with empirical evidence – a dynamic ensemble of numbers, trends, and insights that serve as the blueprint to an organization's digital storyline. Digital Dashboards transcend beyond merely being data aggregators, they are interpreters of data, transforming raw data into narratives that fuel informed decision-making, offering a dynamic visualization of the company's trajectory. It serves as a trusted advisor, a guardian overseeing a company's digital landscape, ensuring that narratives are not just spun from creativity but are rooted in data, offering a **transparent, dynamic, and insightful visualization** of the journey thus far and the road ahead.

Going beyond the transparency provided by Digital Dashboards, **Digital Targets** necessitates a deep dive into two fundamental yet distinct components that shape them, namely Key Performance Indicators (KPIs) and Objectives and Key Results (OKRs).

---

**KPIs**, or **Key Performance Indicators**, are the metrics that echo the heartbeat of an organization's day-to-day functioning, giving life to the constant 'run' that maintains its vitality (visit section 2.5 Legacy Systems and Infrastructure on page 63 to better understand why stability and performance of the digital platforms are crucial). KPIs offer a snapshot into the health of a company, enhancing daily operational fluency through a systematic and structured analysis of performance metrics. They serve as reliable markers that help in gauging the efficiency of digital tools and strategies deployed, thereby streamlining processes, and promoting a culture of continuous improvement and transparency.

Complementing the KPIs, we have the **OKRs**, which stand for **Objectives and Key Results**, steering the organization towards transformative goals that drive innovation and growth. Encompassing the 'change' initiatives, OKRs open vistas of opportunities and pathways grounded in clarity and visionary leadership. They provide light directing efforts and energies towards unified, aspirational goals that align with the broader objectives and values. Through OKRs, organizations articulate ambitious yet attainable goals, supporting a narrative of transformative change and agile responsiveness to market dynamics.

The ensemble of KPIs and OKRs create a vibrant ecosystem of Digital Targets that act as guiding forces in the journey. Together, they create a culture of Digital Transparency that goes beyond numerical analytics to tell a vivid story, portraying the why, what, and how of digital endeavors, showcasing the impacts and the substantial value derived from insightful digital investments. Moreover, Digital Targets support an inclusive work culture where every individual becomes a stakeholder in the digital narrative, nurturing a workplace where insights are openly shared, fostering collaborative innovation, and cultivating shared Digital Transparency and eventually driving Digital Momentum.

But does your company manage with transparent Digital Dashboards and Targets?

**Assessment: Measuring Digital Dashboards and Targets**

 Exploring the **employee interaction rate with dashboards** involves a close monitoring of the usage patterns among employees. It is important to understand not only how frequently they interact with the dashboards but also the nature of these interactions. Evaluations should consider the efficiency brought in by using the dashboards – does it save time, does it facilitate better communication, and does it support a culture of data-driven decision making? The next metric to ponder upon is **user satisfaction score with the dashboard**. Here, businesses must dive deeper into feedback regarding the visual appeal, the ease of locating information, the speed of the dashboard, and the relevance of the data presented. The feedback collection process should be on-going, welcoming

suggestions for features that can be added or enhanced to augment user satisfaction continually. Evaluating the **breadth and depth of the dashboard** is about striking the right balance between offering a comprehensive overview and not overwhelming the user with excessive information. It involves ensuring that the dashboards provide a 360-degree view of all the vital metrics while also offering the option to drill down to more detailed views, thereby catering to both novice and experienced users efficiently. Keeping tabs on **data recency or time-to-update metric** should entail diligent monitoring of the data pipelines ensuring a smooth flow and prompt updating of data resources. Moreover, this metric should also cover the processes in place for error handling and debugging to maintain an elevated level of data accuracy and reliability. Finally, the **user accessibility metric** extends beyond just the user interface to encompass a wide range of aspects including multilingual support, adherence to accessibility standards to cater to differently abled individuals and ensuring compatibility with various devices and browsers to offer a seamless user experience to a broader audience.

Beyond the Digital Dashboards, let us also assess the quantity and quality of the **Digital Targets**. This involves a holistic approach to creating and maintaining balanced digital target metrics that revolve around assessing the quality of the targets set, understanding the efficacy of the regular reviews and adjustment of targets, and gauging the effect Digital Targets must steer and motivate the organization. At the helm of this strategy lies the **achievement rate analysis**, a critical element that embodies the very essence of goal setting. This encompasses a diligent tracking of the **target attainment ratio**, a metric that gives a snapshot of the targets achieved versus those that were set over a specific period, the aim being to attain a balanced score that reflects well-placed ambitions and realistic expectations. Targets set too low, do not support ambitious development, targets set to high de-motivate the organization. As part of OKR, a target achievement rate of 80% is often discussed. However, in organizations where (financial) incentives are traditionally linked to 100% achievement, a change of mindset is required. This analysis is further deepened by a comprehensive **gap analysis**, where the distances between the achieved and set targets are not just identified but thoroughly examined to understand the underlying reasons for any discrepancies, laying a rich foundation for insightful future strategies.

As we progress, it becomes evident that the strategy cannot be static, paving the way for the incorporation of **regular reviews and adjustment metrics**. This segment is piloted by a firm grasp on **review consistency**, which implies measuring the regularity of the review meetings with a keen eye on maintaining a frequency that facilitates timely tweaks while avoiding a culture of incessant alterations. It is vital to be complemented by **adjustment impact analysis**, a process to quantify the repercussions of the modifications instigated post reviews, thereby understanding if the refinements genuinely fostered better alignment and increased success rates.

While strategies and reviews form the framework, the key success factor holding it together is the organization's pulse, the **employee understanding and engagement**. Understanding and motivation metrics come into play here, encompassing a regiment of periodic **employee engagement surveys** to keep a tab on the level of comprehension and alignment with the digital objectives, always targeting high engagement scores reflective of a well-informed and motivated task force. This analysis is enhanced by scrutinizing the **feedback loop efficiency**, which involves a systematic evaluation of the feedback mechanisms in place, honing in on aspects such as response times and resolution rates, and even venturing into the qualitative depths of the feedback received.

By accentuating each metric with a proficient level of detail, the assessment process evolves into a clear picture where an organization needs to improve in the context of Digital Targets.

### Action: Steer with Digital Dashboards and Targets

 Merely having a vast array of digital tools and strategies is insufficient. It is crucial to steer the organization towards well-articulated and actionable Digital Dashboards and Targets that resonate with the overall objectives, akin to carefully plotted waypoints on a navigator's journey.

The subsequent critical step involves **defining a digital dashboard that succinctly presents the usage statistics of all your (main) digital assets**, offering a snapshot of the performance metrics and creating a narrative that encourages stakeholders to dive deeper. Shopify stands tall as a beacon in this area, offering a dashboard that not only presents real-time insights but encourages users to analyze these metrics deeply, fostering a culture of informed decision-making. Diligent sourcing of data into the dashboards cannot be underestimated. Often information is stored in different siloes and with different formats and definitions. To orchestrate a seamless sourcing and cleansing flow ensures a reliable and efficient data base.

To enrich the Digital Dashboards with a future-oriented perspective, Digital Targets need to be defined. The initial phase in this strategic path is to **derive digital KPIs from the overarching company KPIs**. This process is about creating a symphony where the digital elements complement and enhance the broader corporate metrics. Consider how Amazon constantly revises its digital KPIs to echo the company's customer-centric philosophy. They leverage big data and customer feedback to refine these KPIs continually, steering their Digital Strategy in a direction that is always aligned with customer satisfaction. As we navigate further, it becomes pivotal to **calibrate the speed of change through OKR setting**. This methodology ensures a paced yet flexible approach towards achieving digital targets. The approach taken by tech giant Google is a testament to the efficacy of this strategy. Google's use of OKRs, a practice they adopted from Intel, has been extensively documented, including in 'Measure What Matters' by John Doerr, where it outlines how this strategy has been crucial in driving their products to success with a well-paced development strategy[64].

Ensuring a dynamic and responsive strategy necessitates **regular reviews and recalibrations of KPIs and OKRs,** to not only track progress but also adapt to the rapidly evolving digital environment. A resonant example of this is seen in Microsoft's growth under the leadership of Satya Nadella. The company realigned its targets, and embraced a culture of learning and adaptability, focusing not just on quarterly revenues but emphasizing learning and customer satisfaction, a strategy detailed extensively in Nadella's book 'Hit Refresh'[65].

Lastly, creating a culture of continuous improvement through the regular review and optimization of your Digital Dashboard and Targets is important. This involves systematic monitoring and iterative enhancements based on the insights garnered, promoting a collaborative environment conducive to sustained growth. Salesforce, with its systematic approach to regular reviews facilitated through its tableau tool, serves as an excellent reference point.

However, Digital Story, Digital Shelf, and Digital Dashboard and Targets only come to life if they are integrated into a company's daily processes.

3.2.1.4    Digital Daily – Part of Everyday Business and Considerations
In an era where the Digital Shelf as well as the Digital Dashboards and Targets are continuously evolving, organizations are faced with the imperative task of harmonizing digital tools and strategies with their daily operations. Digital Daily, the practice of embedding digital discussions and considerations into the daily discourses of a business, stands as a cornerstone in this endeavor. It steers away from isolated digital engagements and strides towards a culture where **digital deliberations are central to every conversation and every decision**, marking a transformative approach to operational strategies.

Before diving deep into the nuances of this practice, it is crucial to delineate its critical facets – understanding its profound implications, outlining the modalities of its assessment, and carving a path for action that resonates with the organization's vision.

---

[64] John Doerr: "Measure What Matters". Published by Penguin Business, 2017
[65] Satya Nadella with Greg Shaw, Jill Tracie Nichols: "Hit Refresh: The Quest to Rediscover Microsoft's Soul and Imagine a Better Future for Everyone". Published by Harper Business on 26.09.2017

**Awareness: The Power of Digital Presence in Daily Business Processes**

 The concept of Digital Daily stands tall as an illustration for organizations aiming to stride boldly into the future. This dynamic practice refers to the **systematic weaving of digital discourse and strategies into the day-to-day operations and engagements of a company**. It is about fostering a habitat where digital initiatives are not relegated to quarterly reviews or isolated strategy sessions but find a heartbeat in every conversation, every decision that shapes the organization's journey.

Digital Daily envisages a workspace where digital dialogues are not an annex but form the primary script, transcending departments and hierarchies. It promotes a scenario where even a casual coffee-break conversation could potentially spiral into a brainstorming session on the next digital breakthrough, nurturing a fertile ground for innovation. To underpin the importance of Digital Daily, one must appreciate that we are in an era where digitalization is not just a trend but a revolutionary force reshaping industries. This is a transformative period where artificial intelligence, machine learning, Internet of Things (IoT), and augmented reality are no longer buzz words but have practical implications and potential impacts on businesses. It is where big data is not just about the vast quantities of information, but an insightful resource that can dictate market trends and inform business strategies.

An integral facet of Digital Daily is to build Digital Literacy, where individuals, irrespective of their role, hold a foundational understanding of the digital domains pertinent to their function, allowing them to engage confidently and constructively in digital discussions. The goal is to create an organizational ecosystem where digital aptitudes are as fundamental as any other skill set, nurturing a cadre of employees who do not just execute digital strategies but live and breathe them, creating a culture of curiosity, adaptability, and continuous learning (visit section 3.1.1 Digital Vision and Leadership on page 81 to understand how Digital Literary is essential for Digital Readiness).

Moreover, it marks a move towards breaking down silos that often exist, encouraging cross-functional teams to engage in digital dialogues, thereby triggering a collaborative and informed decision-making process. By establishing an environment that promotes daily digital dialogues, organizations instill a sense of digital democracy, where ideas do not just flow top-down but can bubble up from any corner of the organization, setting a stage for organic innovation and informed decision-making rooted in digital acumen.

But is your company integrating digital topics into everyday operations?

**Assessment: Listening to the Digital Voice throughout the Company**

 Gauging the degree to which digital aspects are integrated into a company's daily routines goes beyond mere statistical analysis, it involves a critical, in-depth exploration of the various facets that constitute the Digital Daily landscape.

Beginning with the **frequency of digital topics in meetings**, this metric necessitates more than a casual glance at the agenda, It calls for a detailed, item-by-item breakdown of discussions facilitated in different gatherings, from high-level board meetings to small team catch-ups. Imagine diving into a discussion regarding a marketing strategy, and assessing the extent to which digital platforms are perceived as vital tools in reaching target audiences. Questions such as 'How often is the digital perspective brought up?' or 'Are digital approaches centrally positioned or are they afterthoughts?' help in painting a vivid picture of the current scenario. The analysis could be amplified further through a qualitative lens – for instance, evaluating the depth of insights shared, the innovative digital strategies envisioned, and the alignment with overarching corporate goals, thus allowing the firm to weave a richer, more vibrant digital narrative through regular discourse.

Equally crucial is measuring the **time spent on digital discussions in regular business meetings**. This goes beyond just clocking the minutes allocated to digital dialogues. It could entail scrutinizing the robustness of the digital dialogues – are they superficial run-throughs or deep, enriching conversations that spur innovative thinking? Here, one can look at how meeting times are utilized to foster a digital mindset, perhaps through showcasing successful case studies, initiating brainstorming sessions for new digital initiatives, or even carving out time for digital literacy segments, thus nurturing a fertile ground for digital innovation to flourish organically. To deepen this analysis, feedback from meeting attendees can be systematically collated and analyzed to grasp the perceived value derived from these discussions, paving the way for more enriched and focused dialogues in the future.

The pillar holding up this structure is arguably the **employee confidence score in discussing digital topics**. This metric, obtained perhaps through nuanced surveys or interactive feedback sessions, illuminates the comfort and proficiency levels of employees in engaging with digital topics dynamically. The focus here should be on understanding the individual experiences of employees – are they comfortable articulating digital strategies, do they possess the digital vocabulary to engage substantively in discussions, and what barriers do they encounter in this process?

The path towards a mature Digital Daily environment is anchored in a deep-seated understanding of the current landscape through a lens that is both detailed and empathetic, paving a pathway towards a digitally fluent and responsive organization, constantly evolving in tune with the digital rhythms of the modern world.

**Action: Integrate Digital into Everything, Every Day**

 As organizations journey towards seamlessly writing the digital message into their daily operations, it is incumbent upon them to initiate structured, purposeful actions that guide them in this path, taking bold strides that amalgamate the vigor of the digital sphere into the heartbeat of daily engagements.

A foundational step in this process is to **map digital topics to the ordinary meetings' agenda of senior management**, positioning them as standing items that command dedicated focus and discussion, together with the business topics. This transcends mere periodic updates and ventures into establishing digital checkpoints in every meeting. It means navigating discussions on market dynamics through a digital lens, examining customer feedback in the context of digital experiences, and evaluating strategies with a keen eye on digital advancements and possibilities. Companies like Salesforce have pioneered this approach. Marc Benioff, Salesforce's CEO, regularly dedicates time in management meetings to evaluate the company's digital initiatives and strategies, effectively mapping digital topics into the regular discussion agenda. Such an approach ensures that the digital story is not just a guest at the table but a permanent resident, actively influencing discussions and decisions.

Securing a **seat for digital at the table of major decision bodies** signifies recognizing and asserting the indomitable force that digital has grown to become in today's business landscape. This involves identifying champions within the organization who embody the digital spirit, harboring deep expertise and insights in the digital landscape, and embedding them into major decision-making bodies. These individuals would serve as the digital compass, steering discussions and strategies through the digital landscapes, thus fostering a culture where digital insights are not just included but revered. Microsoft stands as a beacon here. They have created a culture that integrates digital champions at various levels of decision-making, ensuring that digital insights have a significant role in steering the company's strategy. This proactive move was guided strongly by their CEO, Satya Nadella, encouraging digital inclusivity and innovation. This proactive move has ensured that the digital narrative is robust and resonant in all its strategic imperatives. Implementing this could encompass a formal induction process for digital experts into core teams, coupled with sustained development programs to ensure these champions are abreast of the evolving digital trends, thus enabling them to serve as robust pillars of digital knowledge and expertise.

Moreover, collaborative platforms could be instituted, where digital champions from different divisions convene periodically to share insights and learnings, leveraging digital wisdom that permeates throughout the organization.

Enabling the fruition of a Digital Daily ethos demands a harmonized rhythm where digital perspectives are not mere additions but integral chords in the organizational symphony, orchestrating a future where every note resonates with the deep tones of digital understanding, developing a culture that is not just reactive but proactively strides ahead, grounded in digital prowess, tuned to the pulse of the digital heartbeat, and poised to seize the boundless opportunities that lie in the vibrant digital transformation that unfolds before us.

While the Digital Story, Digital Shelf, Digital Dashboard and Targets, and Digital Daily lay a robust foundation for cultivating Digital Transparency, building a truly digitally fluent organization requires more: Digital Usage.

### 3.2.2   Digital Usage

**Digital Usage brings the digital product suite to life**, acting as a catalyst in realizing the innate potentials and benefits designed for both internal and external users.

**What the C-Suite needs to know**

1. Digital Usage Contributes to the Right to Further Invest: Digital Usage increases customer satisfaction, allows straight-through processing, and hence operational efficiency, and ensures the realization of target Return on Investments on digital developments.

2. Digital Cascades: A communication roadmap characterized by a harmonized chorus of messages relayed through the most effective channels, sculpted to reach diverse market segments and target audiences.

3. Digital Adoption: The work does not stop at product launch. It is crucial for companies to continuously refine and adapt their digital products based on on-going user feedback and evolving market needs. This is a cyclical process that involves regular updates, training, and addressing issues to ensure sustained user engagement and adoption.

4. Digital Introduction: More than just launching a product, it is about strategically weaving the story of a new digital product and presenting it to the potential user base in a manner that is not just informative but also emotionally resonant. You never get a second chance to make a first impression.

5. Leverage User Communities and Ambassadors: Building and nurturing digital user communities can provide valuable insights into customer needs, promote feature adoption, and even identify potential brand ambassadors. These organic advocates can play a critical role in enhancing product adoption and sustaining long-term customer relationships.

But why is Digital Usage so important for Digital Momentum?

Higher Digital Usage results in **increased customer satisfaction** as it meets and often exceeds the key needs of its user base through digital solutions. By fully integrating the insights and feedback from the users, companies can tailor products that align perfectly with the users' requirements, offering solutions that are both intuitive and highly functional. Furthermore, Digital Usage significantly enhances operational efficiency. Through **straight-through processing** based on digital applications, companies can streamline workflows, reducing manual interventions and thereby mitigating errors. This culminates in a smoother, faster, and more efficient process that benefits both the users and the company. An additional evident merit of higher Digital Usage is the realization of a positive **Return on Investment (ROI) on digital developments**. With a surge in Digital Usage, companies witness a rise in the customer base and hence, profitability. It is a cycle of growth, the more the digital solutions are utilized, the higher the returns, paving the way for further investments in technological advancements. Moreover, maintaining a vibrant Digital Usage culture incubates a sense of **pride and satisfaction throughout the organization**, especially among the product owners. This nurturing environment builds the momentum that propels the organization to greater heights.

Contrastingly, low Digital Usage brings about a host of unfavorable consequences. One significant peril is the **loss of credibility in digital efforts**. Organizations may face a grim scenario where business cases remain unrealized, leading to skepticism towards future digital endeavors. The inability to meet projected goals creates a ripple effect, where trust dwindles, and the enthusiasm for new digital initiatives dampens. Moreover, a stagnant digital situation leads to **widespread frustration among users**. They find themselves navigating through products that are unsupported, leading to a cumbersome user experience characterized by unmet needs and unresolved issues. This, unfortunately, extends to product owners who, despite their efforts in building the products, find their initiatives underutilized and undervalued, casting a shadow of discontent and disappointment. One of the most severe repercussions is the **lack of Digital Momentum**, as companies may find themselves trapped in a cycle of unsatisfactory digital products with no drive to invest in strategic areas. This stagnation can trigger a dangerous standstill in a world that continuously evolves at a breakneck pace.

Salesforce stands out as a leader in driving digital usage, going well beyond merely providing a Customer Relationship Management (CRM) solution. The company's investment in 'Trailhead', an online learning platform, is designed to help users understand the full breadth of Salesforce's ecosystem. Trailhead serves as a user-friendly gateway to the Salesforce universe, offering interactive tutorials that guide users through everything from the basics to advanced functionalities.

What sets Salesforce apart is its focus on continuous engagement. The platform regularly updates Trailhead with new learning modules and offers extensive customer support. A vibrant community of users shares tips, insights, and best practices, thereby ensuring that users are not just onboarded but continually engaged.

The company excels at creating business-centric narratives around their tools. Through case studies, webinars, and customer testimonials, Salesforce does not just describe what their software does but demonstrates how it solves specific business challenges. These narratives serve as much more than marketing material, they provide real-world, actionable insights that help businesses understand the value of adopting and using Salesforce's suite of tools.

One of the most compelling aspects of Salesforce's approach is its culture of celebrating customer successes and learning from failures. They encourage users to share their own 'Trailblazer stories', which are case studies of how they have successfully implemented Salesforce solutions to solve business problems. These stories serve dual purposes: they validate Salesforce's offerings and act as a how-to guide for other customers who face similar challenges.

Salesforce also employs gamification techniques to incentivize usage. As users complete modules and tests within Trailhead, they earn badges and points, which can be displayed on their professional profiles. This not only encourages continued use but also instills a sense of achievement and community among users.

Finally, the real-time dashboards and analytics offered by Salesforce serve as an invaluable tool for businesses to gain instant insights into customer interactions. These dashboards are more than mere statistical displays, they offer a narrative of a company's customer relationship journey and serve as a constant reminder of the utility of Salesforce's tools.

By weaving these multiple threads into a cohesive strategy, Salesforce ensures that the adoption of its tools is a continuous journey rather than a one-time event. This approach has made Salesforce not just a product provider but an integral partner in its customers' success stories[66].

But let us understand what really drives Digital Usage.

Sailing forward on the usage journey, we encounter **Digital Cascades**, a communication roadmap characterized by a harmonized chorus of messages relayed through the most effective channels, sculpted to reach diverse market segments and target audiences. It is here that the Digital Story and the communication assets come to life, providing a lens to view the depth and breadth of what the products offer, bridging gaps and fostering understanding, laying down paths adorned with engaging and informative signposts guiding users to realize the business priorities encapsulated in the digital offerings.

As the narrative unfolds, the spotlight shifts to encouraging a nurturing relationship through **Digital Adoption of existing (digital) products**. Picture a gallery where success stories are the masterpieces on display, offering users glimpses into potential use cases and benefits, with detailed case studies serving as guides, narrating tales of efficiency and achievement. It is an open dialogue where feedback is not just welcomed but sought, an avenue where testimonials become learning experiences, encouraging others to explore the rich shelves that the digital products offer.

Next, we traverse the domain of **Digital Introduction of new products and features**, a well-orchestrated ballet where new digital offerings are unveiled not just with

---

[66] On Salesforce company website Trailhead: "Für die Zukunft qualifizieren". Visited 08.04.2024. https://trailhead.salesforce.com/de

fanfare but with support systems including comprehensive workshops and training modules. Envision a space where resources are not just available but easily accessible, promising a smooth journey for the users, a beginning marked with enthusiasm and guided exploration, built up through feedback and continuous iterations, ensuring a path devoid of obstacles from the get-go.

For a smooth implementation of all the Digital Usage measures it is vital to understand the **symbiotic relationship between centralized and decentralized units within an organization**. Think of centralized units like headquarters, global product owners or central marketing as the conductor of Digital Usage. They are responsible for formulating the overarching strategies and core brand messages, using insights drawn from comprehensive market research and data analytics. They also ensure that communication assets are produced once, leveraging synergies across the markets. Decentralized units, such as Digital Field Forces or regional offices, function like the instruments. They specialize in localization and implementation, fine-tuning the strategies and messages created centrally to meet local tastes, cultural nuances, and market conditions. To create a well-oiled machine that operates at peak performance, companies must orchestrate effective collaboration between these central and decentral units. To sum up, it is not just about what the central units dictate or what the decentralized units prefer, it is about creating a balanced, responsive system where both entities contribute to the greater organizational goal – in this case, driving the Digital Usage of company products.

Let us now look at these components of Digital Usage to ensure we understand what they are – we are building Awareness for it. Further we can Assess where your company stands and understand what Actions your company can initiate to drive them.

### 3.2.2.1 Digital Cascades

The rapid digitalization of industries necessitates a symbiotic evolution in communication strategies to harness the complete potential of digital products. Digital Cascades emerge as a pivotal element in this narrative, forming a structured, well-orchestrated communication strategy that progressively unveils the Digital Story, including information from the Digital Shelf and the priorities derived from Digital Dashboards and Targets, through layered communication targeted at diverse audience groups.

**Awareness: Communication throughout the Organization**

One of the salient features of Digital Cascades is their dynamism, representing a living, evolving approach that facilitates a continuous flow of information – whereas the overall Digital Story is more passive, acting as a stable backbone. Cascades strategically integrate a variety of elements – right messages targeted at the apt audiences through the most befitting channels, all while creatively leveraging communication assets to enhance the impact and reach. This multi-faceted approach not only amplifies the resonance of the communication but nurtures a connectivity that is deep-rooted, engaging the audience in a manner that is both sustained and meaningful.

Why is this so crucial? Firstly, it brings the digital products suite to life, functioning as a vital conduit that relays the benefits and utilities of the digital offerings to the audience in a manner that is tangible and relatable. It creates a vibrant, living story that fosters a sense of anticipation and engagement, ensuring that the audience is continuously looped into the evolving digital development, contributing to a Digital Momentum that is self-sustaining and energizing.

Moreover, it empowers the organization to build a communication strategy that is not stagnant but dynamically aligned with the business priorities, ensuring that the digital messages are not just heard but understood. It creates a rich experience, ensuring that the digital communications are not a one-off event but a continuous dialogue that builds a relationship grounded in trust and mutual growth.

Digital Cascades stand as a starting point in the context of Digital Usage, promising a communication strategy that is rich, dynamic, and created through a deep understanding of the digital dynamics and its audience. But where does your company stand?

**Assessment: Hearing the Digital Messages in the Organization**

An integral facet of nurturing a thriving digital ecosystem through Digital Cascades is the rigorous assessment of the strategy through carefully delineated metrics that offer insight into the effectiveness of the communication approach.

A vital barometer here is the pure **availability of an orchestrated communication plan** that weaves the key digital messages through time in a manner that meets the overall business communication objectives. This metric offers an incisive view into the effectiveness of the digital message, exploring whether the communication plan is strategically positioned to channel the digital stories optimally, offering a window into the strategic depth of the plan and its resonance with the audience at every touchpoint.

In parallel, the **comprehensiveness of the communication plan** takes precedence, presenting a multi-faceted overview that spans the appropriateness of messages, the integration of the most conducive channels, and the creative incorporation of digital assets. This metric, thus, necessitates a deep dive into the structural integrity of the communication plan, evaluating whether it exhibits a harmonized alignment across various parameters, thereby promising a communication strategy that is not only robust but is finely tuned to meet the diverse needs of different audience groups[67].

Engaging with the audience is a continual journey, one that demands a sustained flow of communication. Here, the assessment metric of **continuous flow of digital communication** over time stands central, evaluating whether the strategy fosters a living dialogue with the audience. It seeks to understand whether the Digital Cascades create a continuum of engagement, nurturing a relationship with the audience that is not transient but sustained, encouraging a Digital Momentum that is vibrant and matches the corporate objectives in a manner that is engaging and progressive.

**Action: Run Digital Cascades throughout the Organization**

Initiating a robust Digital Cascades strategy commences with the **definition of the key messages**, a process steeped in extensive research and a deep understanding of the market landscape. These key messages, which are finely aligned with the overall Digital Vision and Digital Story position the individual digital products. In line with the company's priorities and supported with the transparency from the Digital Dashboards and Targets, the products to be communicated, are selected. For each of these products the essence is distilled and formulated as a compelling message. A testament to the sheer brilliance in delineating key messages can be observed in Apple's launch of the iPhone 12, where the central message of '5G speed' was emphasized consistently across all digital platforms, reiterating the groundbreaking features that set it apart in the competitive market.

To infuse a dynamic synchronization between the business priorities and the digital narratives, a careful **mapping of digital key messages with the business priorities** over the months and years becomes imperative. This is not merely about aligning strategies but creating a symbiotic relationship between business goals and Digital Cascades, envisaging a narrative that breathes life into business strategies through digital messages that are both compelling and strategically aligned to develop deep engagement with the target audience at every crucial juncture. After all, the digital products shall support the achievement of the business objectives. With the aligned

---

[67] Martina Lauchengco: "Loved – How to rethink marketing for tech products". Published by John Wiley & Sons Inc., 2022

messages, we define the timeline for the digital cascades, the horizontal axes in the communication plan matrix.

An in-depth understanding and segmentation of the **target audience groups** becomes pivotal next. The outline of these groups requires the integration of market research data and consumer insights to craft a tailored approach that addresses the unique needs and preferences of each segment and target group. It is also important to define the best sequence in reaching these target groups – usually, warming up internal stakeholders, before reaching out to external customers. Crafting a list of target groups that acknowledges the diversity of the audience ensures a dialogue that is not just inclusive but offers a spectrum of perspectives, enhancing the depth of engagement. The list of target audiences builds the vertical axes in the communication plan matrix.

As we now have established a matrix structure, outlining the key messages horizontally over time, and listing all target audience groups vertically, it is then important to **map the interaction channels** into that matrix, an approach that leverages the inherent strengths of diverse platforms, be it the immediacy of social media, the formal structure of corporate communication channels, or the immersive experience of multimedia platforms – the best channel to reach the target audience. Understanding the unique dynamics of each channel enables a strategy that is tailored to leverage the strengths of each platform to support a rich and nuanced dialogue.

Central to the Digital Cascades strategy is the **creation of a rich repertoire of communication assets**, which can be fed into the various channels, bringing across the messages to the target audience. From visual storyboards to interactive webinars, the assets should encompass a range of mediums to cater to diverse audience preferences. Developing these assets is a collaborative effort, leveraging both internal creativity and possibly engaging external agencies to bring forth a rich collection of assets that promise a narrative that is vibrant and pulsating with creativity.

The **compilation of the overall communication plan** emerges as a critical juncture, a point where a strategic blueprint comes to life. It involves the crafting of a detailed matrix that not only sequences the key messages over time but delineates the target audience in a vertical cascade, creating a blueprint that is both strategic and responsive to the evolving market dynamics. It is a roadmap that promises an engagement strategy that is fluid yet structured, offering a dynamic message that evolves in response to the changing landscape.

To drive a strategy that promises seamless integration, it becomes critical to align with both **external and internal corporate communications** to orchestrate the execution. This alignment promises a strategy that speaks in a unified voice, developing a story that is coherent and synergized, leveraging the strengths of diverse departments to create a communication strategy that is vibrant, engaging, and promising a rich potential for growth.

By engaging deeply with each of these facets, an enterprise sets a foundation for Digital Cascades that promise not only a vibrant dialogue but nurtures a deeply connective and engaging relationship with the audience.

Communication is the basis, but dedicated efforts are often required to drive Digital Adoption.

### 3.2.2.2 Digital Adoption

Digital Adoption, a term that has gained pronounced importance in the rapidly evolving digital space, stands at the core of a company's Digital Momentum. It encapsulates the process where individuals are not just acquainted with existing digital tools but are adept at utilizing them to their fullest potential.

**Awareness: The Importance of Using the Existing Digital Assets**

 As much as we would love that digital products are developed, and immediately fully used by internal and external users, reality is, that efforts are required to bring products and users together. Digital Adoption emerges as the cornerstone for sustaining and enhancing Digital Usage. It goes beyond introducing users to existing digital solutions, it entails **facilitating users in understanding, embracing, and utilizing the full spectrum of functionalities embedded in a digital product suite to the fullest potential**. It marks a transition from a superficial acquaintance with digital tools to an immersive experience where the users are adept and comfortable in navigating the rich feature sets, thereby incorporating these tools seamlessly into their daily operations.

Importantly, Digital Adoption is essential in **driving customer satisfaction**, a critical facet in the broader spectrum of Digital Momentum. It ensures that the development of a digital product suite is aligned with the users' core needs and preferences, fostering a user-centric approach that stands as a testament to a company's commitment to delivering value and driving satisfaction. The approach appreciates and leverages the diversity in a user base, recognizing the varied learning curves and preferences, and thus delineating pathways that facilitate both the external and internal stakeholders in mastering the digital suite at a pace and manner that resonates with them.

Moreover, the role of Digital Adoption in **ensuring a robust return on investment (ROI)** of digital developments cannot be overstated. It guarantees that the fruits of digital endeavors are realized and capitalized upon, creating a cycle of success that not only encourages further investment but engenders a sense of pride and satisfaction across the organization. By advocating for a robust digital adoption strategy, companies ensure that the trajectory of digital products is characterized by momentum rather than stagnation, carving out a path characterized by growth, satisfaction, and an ever-evolving digital landscape that promises to meet and exceed user expectations time and again.

Digital Adoption shapes an environment where products are not just developed but lived, facilitating a culture of adept utilization, continuous learning, and a forward momentum.

But let us look at where your company stands when it comes to Digital Adoption.

**Assessment: Measuring the Usage of Digital Assets**

Corporations are recognizing the undeniable impact of Digital Adoption in driving growth and innovation. To grasp the current standing of a company in the reality of Digital Adoption, an in-depth exploration of various dimensions is essential.

First and foremost, understanding the **focus of adoption efforts** and precisely identifying where to initiate is vital. This step requires an organization to delineate the areas where a digital overhaul could impart the most significant impact, effectively setting the trajectory for the forthcoming phases of the adoption journey. A discerned start, grounded in systematic research, forms the bedrock of a successful digital transition, guiding efforts in a focused direction that echoes with the organization's overarching objectives.

Building upon this, it becomes critical to deep dive into the **depth of understanding of the users**, unraveling the barriers and trigger points that govern their experiences. Does your company really understand the detailed needs of the customers when it comes to the usage of the digital products? By leveraging tools such as user interviews and data analytics, companies can fine-tune their strategies to mirror the needs and preferences of the user base, maintaining a digital landscape where user convenience is not an afterthought, but a driving force.

Equally significant is establishing **concreteness in the adoption measures**, which translates to crafting narratives that are tangible and grounded in reality. Are the measures pragmatic? Sharing compelling success stories and spotlighting the unmistakable benefits accruing from digital adoption can build an environment where the measures are not just theoretical constructs, but tangible pathways delineated through vivid, relatable narratives, highlighting the transformative potential of digital integration.

As the story unfolds, attention must be steered towards the **realistic sequencing of measures**, a step vital to avoid the pitfalls of information overflow. A strategic rollout, conceived and executed in a phased manner, can guarantee a transition that is not just smooth but also strategically sound, ensuring each stage incrementally builds upon the last, thus creating a streamlined pathway of transition that is devoid of bottlenecks and information overload.

Finally, the blueprint remains incomplete without allocating **sufficient resources**, a pillar that stands testament to the organization's commitment to nurturing and advancing the digital adoption roadmap. Does your company allocate sufficient resources? Ensuring a focused management attention coupled with resource allocation not only signifies a readiness to adapt but a forward-thinking vision that is aligned with the rapid digitalization engulfing the business landscapes globally.

In encapsulation, analyzing and understanding the current Digital Adoption landscape is a multi-faceted endeavor.

**Action: Driving Digital Adoption**

 An orchestrated series of actions is paramount to encourage an uptick in the utilization of a company's digital assets. The initiation point is leveraging the Digital Shelf as well as the Digital Dashboards and Targets to pinpoint where the focus should be directed in enhancing digital adoption. By closely monitoring the digital environment where your products reside, you create an advantageous position to spur increased usage. It can involve a systematic assessment of data analytics derived from user interactions and behaviors, offering invaluable insights that drive strategy formation. For instance, consumer goods companies like Procter & Gamble utilize digital shelves to optimize product visibility and accessibility for consumers, enhancing their shopping experience and increasing digital adoption.

Understanding your audience forms the backbone of this initiative. Here, the key action involves **identifying target groups in detail**, with a reliance on analytics to grasp profiles displaying specific needs and triggering points. It is a deep dive into consumer personas, harnessing data to fathom the unique characteristics, preferences, and pain points of different user segments. The objective is to tailor strategies that resonate profoundly with each group, ensuring a higher success rate in adoption initiatives. Companies like Netflix, for example, leverage big data and analytics to understand the preferences and viewing habits of different user segments, allowing them to create personalized experiences and content recommendations that match the expectations of their audience. Equally critical is **spotting the barriers and hurdles that currently inhibit higher usage levels.** This step demands a keen eye on the prevailing issues and complaints, holding them under a microscope to understand the root causes of lower adoption rates. It is a diagnostic approach, identifying symptoms, and tracing them back to underlying issues, facilitating a comprehensive understanding that guides the subsequent steps. Here, hospitality giants like Marriott have effectively utilized customer feedback to address barriers in the digital booking process, enhancing usability and increasing customer satisfaction.

With the hurdles clearly mapped out, the next important stride is **formulating mitigating measures that empathetically address these barriers**. Here, the strategies bloom from a deep understanding of the issues at hand, crafting solutions that are both empathetic and effective. The narrative leans heavily on highlighting tangible benefits, articulating compelling use cases, sharing success stories, and even mobilizing peer pressure positively to encourage adoption. It is a concerted effort to build a story that is both persuasive and grounded in reality, encouraging users to overcome apprehensions and embrace the digital assets. Organizations like IKEA utilize augmented reality apps to provide customers with a tangible sense of how their products would look in the consumers' own spaces, effectively addressing barriers related to online furniture shopping.

Success in this endeavor hinges on **creating comprehensive packages that intertwine communication, training, and motivation harmoniously.** These are not isolated elements but work in a symbiotic relationship, building an environment conducive to digital adoption. Communication delineates the value proposition clearly, training equips users with the necessary skills and knowledge, while motivation and incentives add that extra nudge, encouraging users to step out of their comfort zones and embrace the new digital platforms. E-commerce platforms like Amazon effectively utilize communication and training modules, along with a reward system, to engage users and encourage them to use digital assets more comprehensively.

Finally, **planning and executing dedicated adoption campaigns**, which are in tandem with Digital Cascades, come to the fore. These campaigns carry the mantle of all the preparatory work done in the previous steps, bringing to life strategies that are both deep and wide, reaching different user segments with messages that encourage adoption. Leveraging insights from the Digital Cascades ensures a harmonized approach, where messages flow seamlessly, creating a ripple effect that encourages users to adopt the digital assets progressively. In this context, campaigns like Spotify Wrapped engage users by personalizing the experience and encouraging them to interact more with the platform, driving higher digital adoption rates.

Each step in this action plan is carefully crafted, ensuring a strategy that not just identifies the areas requiring focus and the hurdles to overcome but actively engages with users, encouraging them to adopt digital assets through campaigns that are both empathetic and compelling, promising a higher success rate in digital adoption initiatives.

Driving Digital Adoption helps with the usage of the existing products, but also new products require a well-crafted introduction plan.

### 3.2.2.3 Digital Introduction

Digital Introduction stands as a crucial moment in the journey of a product from its conceptualization to becoming a tool, a solution, or a companion in the user's daily life. It is that juncture where a product is presented to the world, ready to create impressions and trigger engagements. Let us dive deeper into understanding this critical phase in the product life cycle.

**Awareness: You Never get a Second Chance to Make a First Impression**

 At its core, Digital Introduction is more than just launching a product, it is about strategically weaving the story of a new digital product and presenting it to the potential user base in a manner that is not just informative but also emotionally resonant. This involves detailed planning, which considers the unique selling propositions of the product and designs a campaign that is both compelling and holistic, covering all facets of the product, from its functionalities to the benefits it promises to bring into the users' lives.

This process involves systematic planning where every detail matters – from the visual aesthetics in the advertising materials to the tone of voice used in the communication. It is about crafting a **narrative that speaks directly to the users**, addressing their needs, their aspirations, and potentially, their pain points that the product aims to solve.

But why is this process so essential? Firstly, it sets the **initial perception of the product** in the potential users' minds. A well-articulated Digital Introduction supports a positive perception, laying a solid foundation for a successful product life cycle. Secondly, it assists in **differentiating the product in a saturated market**. In the digital space, where numerous products are vying for the users' attention, a Digital Introduction that stands out can carve out a unique space for the product, setting it apart from the competition. Furthermore, it serves as the Initial point of engagement between the product and the potential users, establishing a relationship that, if nurtured correctly, can evolve into loyalty and advocacy. It is the moment where the users are invited to embark on a journey, a voyage of discovery where they explore what the product has to offer, initiating a dialogue that promises mutual growth and evolution.

Moreover, a thoughtfully designed Digital Introduction campaign can **inculcate trust** in the user base. Through clear communication of the product's benefits and functionalities, it can establish a transparency that assures users of the product's reliability and efficacy, building a trust bridge that promises a product that delivers on its promises.

The Digital Introduction is the **herald of the product's journey in the market**, a journey that promises not just functionalities but solutions, not just features but experiences, setting the stage for a relationship that is built on trust, engagement, and mutual growth. It is about creating not just a launch, but a grand entry into the users' world, promising a product life cycle that is rich, fulfilling, and resonant with the users' needs and aspirations.

But where does your company stand when it comes to Digital Introduction?

**Assessment: Gauging the Efficacy of Digital Introduction**

Companies must deep-dive into various facets to understand the penetration and reception of their Digital Introduction endeavors. One fundamental metric is the **prioritization of highest impact business introductions**. It involves discerning which product introductions hold the most potential for making a significant impact in the market. Does your company have the right focus? The criterion here is to focus on new products, not minor enhancements, leveraging campaigns to bring them to the forefront while ensuring that smaller improvements are intuitive and do not require extensive marketing and communication efforts.

A second critical metric is the **clarity of the message** for new products, including defining the unique benefits for users and crafting compelling calls-to-action. This metric evaluates how well the campaign communicates the distinctive advantages of the product, urging potential users towards adoption through clear and resonant messaging.

Yet another vital metric is scrutinizing the **comprehensiveness of the introduction packages**. This encompasses a detailed examination of the entire array of introduction materials and strategies, ensuring that they holistically cover all the necessary aspects, providing potential users with a full-fledged understanding of what the product has to offer.

Moreover, striking a balance between **central preparation for efficiency and decentralized implementation** for a close-to-user rollout is essential. It involves cultivating a strategy that harmonizes central planning with localized implementations, facilitating a rollout that is both efficient and resonant with local preferences and nuances. To achieve a seamless balance, the involvement of field forces becomes indispensable. These teams should have a keen understanding of the local markets to tailor the introduction strategies, ensuring alignment with the central vision while resonating with local nuances and preferences.

Through a systematic assessment process that is grounded in clearly defined metrics, companies can craft Digital Introduction strategies that are not just well-articulated but also dynamic and resonant, promising a product introduction that is both comprehensive and engaging, setting the stage for a product lifecycle that promises growth, engagement, and sustained success in the market.

**Action: Roll out Successful Digital Introductions**

 The first decisive step is to **prioritize new digital developments for dedicated introduction campaigns**. The focal point here is to align the introductions stringently with the overarching business objectives, creating a roadmap that unequivocally focuses on new and promising products. A stellar example of this is Apple's launch of its iPhone series where every new model comes with a dedicated, well-planned introductory campaign, emphasizing the unique features and improvements over the previous versions. This strategy has been important in establishing the iPhone as a premium product in the smartphone market[68]. It necessitates a discerning eye to separate the game-changing products from the regular updates, channeling efforts, and resources to where they can create a substantial impact.

An essential part of this stage is **crafting compelling messages for new digital products and features**. For instance, when Slack was introduced, it positioned itself as more than a communication tool, portraying itself as a collaboration hub that can 'replace email and make teamwork seamless', which was a strong message showcasing its value proposition and distinguishing it from other messaging apps[69].

Moreover, it involves **preparing a multi-faceted introduction approach**, which not only encompasses communication strategies but also lays down a framework for access to products, including outlining the required rights, facilitating training and learning modules, and establishing feedback loops. A notable example here would be how Zoom ensured easy accessibility and offered comprehensive guides and tutorials amidst the COVID-19 pandemic, simplifying the onboarding process for a surge of new users globally.

Lastly, the spotlight shifts to the breadth and depth of **product positioning kits** available for each entity within the digital product suite. These kits should embrace

---

[68] Hitesh Bhasin on Marketing91: "The Marketing Strategy of Apple: A Sneak Peek". Published online 11.01.2019, visited 08.04.2024. www.marketing91.com/marketing-strategy-apple
[69] Hiten Shah in the nira blog: "How Slack Became a $16 Billion Company by Making Work Less Boring". Visited 08.04.2024. https://nira.com/slack-history/

a spectrum of materials that adeptly convey the USPs and the distinguishing facets of each product. It encompasses evaluating the diversity of content formats available and discerning how proficiently they voice the USP and other benefits. An important facet of this process is understanding how these kits harmonize with the overarching Digital Story, offering a cohesive narrative that aligns with business objectives and goals.

To ensure a well-rounded reach, the introduction strategy necessitates an **orchestrated approach combining central and decentralized plans,** including localization of introduction campaigns. A case in point is Spotify's expansion strategy, tailoring its service to local markets with region-specific content and localized marketing campaigns, ensuring resonance with diverse audience groups globally[70].

By embarking on a path where each step is planned and executed, companies can navigate the complex digital space efficiently, crafting introduction strategies that are not just well-planned but resonate deeply with the target audience, fostering a Digital Introduction landscape that is both vibrant and effective, promising a strategy that is poised for success in a competitive digital marketplace.

However, let us consider one additional element that spans across all measures of Digital Usage. In today's interconnected world, **the role of digital user communities and ambassadors becomes paramount** in sustaining long-term user engagement and advocacy. Community building starts with the setup of digital platforms where users can congregate, share experiences, and offer feedback. These platforms should be initiated by central units, given they possess the technological resources and the overarching brand narrative that unifies all users. A prime example of this is the French cooking platform Marmiton, which engages its users by providing a space for local recipe exchanges. This platform does not just offer a service, it offers a community of like-minded individuals who share a passion for cooking. Identifying ambassadors from your user base can amplify your brand's reach and credibility. This process should be centrally coordinated using data analytics to identify users who are not only active but also influential within their circles. Once identified, they can be given exclusive access to features, early product releases, or even enlisted for beta testing, adding value back to the product based on their experience. German car maker Audi, for example, identifies brand ambassadors among its customer base who exemplify the brand's values, offering them perks and exclusive insights into upcoming innovations. These ambassadors naturally evangelize the brand, encouraging new users to engage with the digital product. The digital user

---

[70] Gennaro Cuofano: "How Does Spotify Make Money? Spotify Freemium Business Model". Published 04.10.2023, visited 08.04.2024. www.fourweekmba.com/spotify-business-model/

communities and ambassadors thus serve a dual purpose: they are both a feedback mechanism and a promotional channel. Their engagement not only adds a layer of trust and social proof but also provides invaluable insights for product development and improvement. Effective community building and ambassador identification are the icing on the cake for companies aiming to drive Digital Usage (visit section 3.1.2 Digital Community on page 103 to understand how necessary collaboration is for Digital Readiness).

 Find more and updated information in the **Digital Arena**. Connect with like-minded professionals to unleash the potential and make it happen.

Digital Transparency and Digital Usage drive the Digital Momentum. In many companies there is a lot to gain already with the existing digital assets. This momentum earns the right to further invest. It paves the way to further develop the Digital Experience.

## 3.3  Digital Experience

«Make the customer the hero of your story»
Ann Handley[71]

Traditional approaches to customer engagement no longer suffice In meeting the ever-increasing needs and expectations of the modern consumer. This is where the role of a harmonized Omnichannel Experience and well-thought-out end-to-end customer journeys come into play.

**Omnichannel Experience** is the ultimate outcome. Customers today interact with companies through various touchpoints. A disjointed experience across these platforms can result in lost opportunities and diminished brand loyalty. On the contrary, an integrated omnichannel strategy ensures a consistent and personalized customer interaction, regardless of the medium.

Contributing to a seamless Omnichannel Experience are **end-to-end customer journeys**, which involve understanding and optimizing every stage of the customer lifecycle – from initial product interest and engagement, through purchase and use, to eventual advocacy or repurchase. By focusing on these journeys, companies can identify pain points, eliminate bottlenecks, and create a frictionless experience that not only attracts but retains customers in the long term.

### 3.3.1  Omnichannel Experience

The customers decide where and how they want to interact with the company. Location, timing, availability of devices and other circumstances may trigger different channel preferences. However, the person behind and the needs often remain the same. Therefore, it is **essential that the experience remains consistent across the channels** – across omni-channel, meeting clients where they are.

#### 3.3.1.1  Navigating the Omnichannel Landscape for Digital Mastery

Omnichannel strategy refers to a comprehensive and integrated approach to customer engagement and sales that focuses on providing a **seamless and consistent experience** of messages, visuals, and positioning statements across all available touchpoints. With an omnichannel approach, customers can transition effortlessly between various channels such as self-service (incl. social media, websites, Mobile Apps) and all touchpoints with in-person interaction with the company (incl. messaging, e-mail, digital meeting, physical brick-and-mortar branches and stores)

---

[71] Ann Handley – Writer, digital marketing pioneer, and author

while receiving a cohesive and personalized experience at every step, also supporting a consistent brand recognition.

However, still many companies run multi-channel or even single channel approaches, often developed as legacy over years, but often also supported by organizational structures and lack of client-centric thinking.

The primary differences among these approaches lie in their scope, integration, and customer experience:

| | **Omnichannel** | **Multi-Channel** | **Single-channel** |
|---|---|---|---|
| Scope | Encompasses a unified strategy that seamlessly integrates all channels, both online and offline. | Involves using multiple separate channels, often with minimal integration. | Focuses exclusively on a single channel, without considering other potential touchpoints. |
| Integration | Channels are integrated, sharing customer data, and offering a consistent experience as customers move between them. | Channels might not be integrated, leading to fragmented customer experiences and inconsistent messaging. | Limited to one channel, with little to no integration with other customer interaction points. |
| Customer Experience | Prioritizes a seamless, personalized, and convenient experience for customers across all channels. | May provide varied experiences across channels, making it less convenient for customers to switch between them. | Offers a consistent experience within the chosen channel but lacks flexibility for customers who prefer different channels. |

An omnichannel strategy stands out for its **holistic, customer-centric focus**. It surpasses the limitations of both multi-channel and single-channel approaches by harmonizing various touchpoints to meet the evolving expectations of modern customers.

Adopting an omnichannel approach offers numerous advantages, allowing your company to meet customers where they are, provide exceptional experiences, and build lasting relationships that translate into business success. Although it is crucial that a company covers the full channel ecosystem, it is at the same time important to note – particularly in a world of scarce resources – that not all use cases and functionalities necessarily need to be covered in all channels. Customers have specific needs and preferences where they would like to do what. Immediate transparency and simple execution use cases are often addressed best in self-service channels, whereas more complex, advice-intensive topics are better covered in channels that allow for in-person interaction.

Certainly, customers' preferred channels can vary based on factors such as demographics, industry, and the nature of the business. However, here are some main channels that customers often prefer to use. In many cases it is a continuum of channels from self-service to customer-employee interactions.

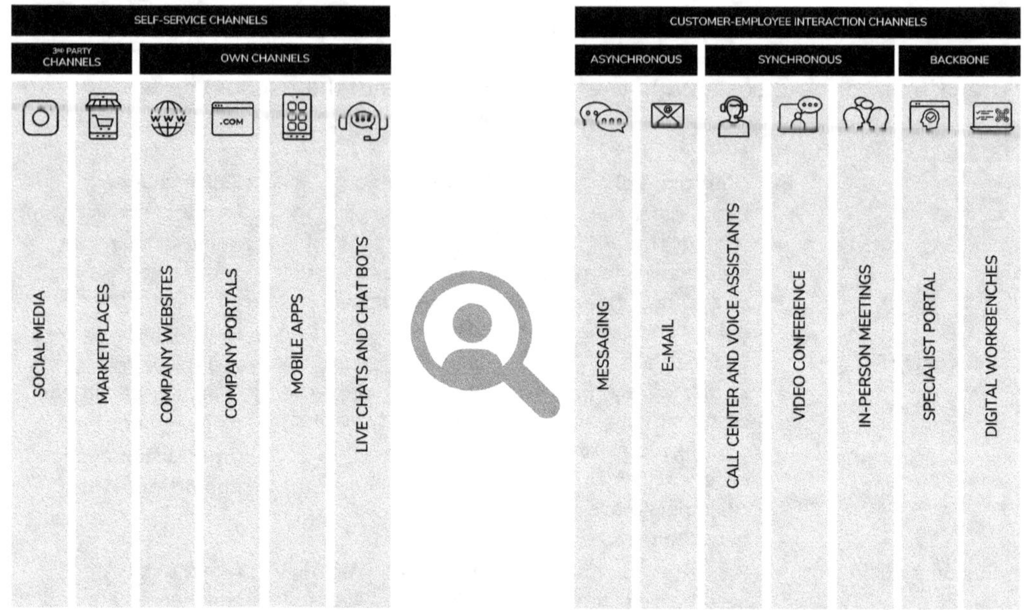


*Figure 19: Omnichannel ecosystem*

Let us have a close look at all these channels and touchpoints, as they are often the window of a successful digital approach. Self-service **channels** have become more relevant for most users, and their use will further grow over the coming years.

### 3.3.1.1.1 Social Media – Connecting People with People and Companies

Social Media refers to online **platforms and websites that enable users to create, share, and interact with content, as well as connect with other users**. These platforms facilitate communication and engagement through various forms of content, such as text, images, videos, and links.

*Figure 20: Large and growing number of social media*

Main use cases of Social Media include communication and networking (incl. Facebook), content sharing (incl. YouTube, Instagram), information dissemination and Influencer/Thought leadership (incl. X), entertainment and engagement (incl. TikTok, Twitch), business marketing and branding as well as recruitment and job search (incl. LinkedIn), and more. Social Media has

160

become an integral part of modern life, enabling individuals, businesses, and organizations to connect, communicate, and share information on a global scale.

Its applications span personal, professional, and organizational spheres, making it a transformative force in how we interact and communicate in the digital age.

**What a company should consider to maximize benefits from Social Media**

- Platform-Specific Algorithms: Understand and adapt to the unique algorithms that drive visibility on each social media platform. This involves optimizing posting schedules, engagement metrics, and content formats.

- Real-Time Engagement: Leverage real-time features like Instagram Stories or Facebook Live to interact with your audience. Be prepared to actively monitor and respond to comments and questions during these events.

- Virality Factors: Create content with the potential for virality, focusing on emotional resonance and shareability. Consider elements like humor, relatability, or topical relevance to encourage sharing.

- Direct Customer-to-Customer Interaction: Use social listening tools to monitor conversations among customers. Be ready to intervene or guide the conversation when necessary to maintain brand image and values.

- Influencer Collaborations: Identify key influencers whose followers match your target audience. Establish clear performance metrics to evaluate the success of these collaborations.

- User-Generated Content (UGC): Encourage satisfied customers to post about their experiences with branded hashtags. Curate this content for display on your own platforms, adding a layer of social proof to your brand.

Social Media extend the company's reach to billions of people, however selecting the target groups and the right channels – based on the intention – is critical to success.

### 3.3.1.1.2 Marketplaces – Integrating to Broaden the Reach

Digital marketplaces are online platforms that **connect buyers and sellers, facilitating transactions for goods, services, or information**. These platforms provide a virtual space for several types of transactions, often enabling a wide range of products and services to be bought and sold. Digital marketplaces have gained prominence due to their convenience, global reach, and ability to streamline the buying and selling process.

Digital marketplaces have become powerful platforms that connect sellers and service providers with a vast audience. Amazon, for example, has set a gold standard by offering a wide array of products – ranging from electronics to groceries – and allows sellers to tap into its enormous customer base. eBay, on the other hand, has pioneered the auction-style format, providing a space for individuals and businesses to buy and sell new or used items through bidding or direct purchases. In the space of travel and lodging, Airbnb has disrupted traditional hospitality by linking travelers with hosts, offering everything from rooms to entire homes for a more local experience.

The gig economy also finds its champions in digital marketplaces. Upwork and Fiverr serve as conduits between businesses and freelancers, offering a gamut of services such as writing, graphic design, and software development, while TaskRabbit provides a versatile platform for hiring individuals for various chores and tasks. These platforms democratize talent acquisition, allowing businesses to hire specialized skills for project-specific needs. For those interested in unique, handcrafted, or vintage items, Etsy provides a niche marketplace focused on artisanal products.

Furthermore, the service industry is not left behind. Platforms like Uber and Lyft, or Grab and Gojek in Asia, have revolutionized transportation through their app-based ride-sharing services. Each of these marketplaces has leveraged digital platforms to meet specific customer needs, effectively changing the way we shop, work, travel, and more.

**What a company should consider to maximize benefits from Marketplaces**

- **Search Algorithm Optimization:** Understand the search ranking algorithms unique to each marketplace. Optimize product listings with high-quality images, keyword-rich titles, and detailed descriptions to improve visibility.

- **Customer Reviews and Ratings:** Actively manage and solicit customer reviews, as they have a major impact on purchasing decisions and marketplace search rankings. Implement automated follow-ups post-purchase to encourage reviews.

- **Pricing and Promotional Strategies:** Utilize dynamic pricing tools to adjust your prices in real-time based on supply, demand, and competitor pricing. Time-limited promotions can stimulate buying urgency.

- **Inventory Management:** Employ real-time inventory management tools to ensure product availability aligns with listing information. Inventory issues can severely impact your marketplace ratings and customer trust.

- **Multi-Channel Fulfillment:** Understand the delivery and fulfillment options available on the marketplace, from 'Fulfilled by Amazon' (FBA) to in-house fulfillment. Choose options that align with your cost, speed, and customer experience goals.

- **Seller Performance Metrics:** Keep close tabs on key performance indicators specific to online marketplaces, such as Order Defect Rate (ODR) or Late Shipment Rate. Falling below certain thresholds can result in penalties or even suspension.

These examples illustrate the diverse applications of digital marketplaces, from buying and selling products to accessing services, accommodations, and more. Digital marketplaces offer convenience, efficiency, and access to a global customer base, making them an integral part of modern commerce.

### 3.3.1.1.3 Company Websites – A Show Case Window to Start a Customer Journey

Many customers start their purchasing journey by visiting a company's website. They provide a centralized space where visitors can learn about the company, its products or services, mission, values, and contact information. For many industries, the vast majority of customers, particularly shoppers, start their search online.

Too many websites are still siloed presentations of individual contents mainly in three areas:

| Company information | Product information | Other information |
|---|---|---|
| Websites serve as a hub for disseminating essential **information about the company**, such as its history, leadership team, mission, and values.<br><br>**Investor Relations** information usually is presented and updated with media updates.<br><br>**Event Promotion:** Companies use websites to promote events, conferences, webinars, and workshops. Visitors can find details about upcoming events and register to attend.<br><br>They also provide **contact details** for inquiries and support. | Companies use websites to **display their products** or services in detail. This may include product specifications, images, videos, and user reviews, enabling potential customers to make informed purchasing decisions.<br><br>**Online transaction** opportunities: Many companies use their websites as e-commerce platforms, allowing customers to browse and purchase products or services directly. This can range from physical products to digital goods or subscriptions. | **Customer Support and FAQs:** Websites offer dedicated sections for customer support, frequently asked questions (FAQs), and troubleshooting guides. This assists customers in finding solutions to common issues without needing to contact support.<br><br>**Recruitment and Careers:** Companies use websites to advertise job openings, provide information about company culture, and offer insights into potential career paths. This helps to attract and engage potential employees. |

It is, however, important to remember that customers usually do not just look at company websites for pure entertainment but with a concrete need in mind. Therefore, company websites are in many use cases the **starting point for an actionable customer journey** with direct links to other channels for execution. So, it is important to already design websites with end-to-end customer journeys in mind, ensuring an easy flow and actionable execution to satisfy the visitors' needs.

When done the right way, websites can be powerful show case windows to generate leads, and drive product sales. In addition, websites collect valuable information to enrich the company's understanding of each customer by gathering data on user behavior, website traffic, and engagement.

**What a company should consider to maximize benefits from Company Websites**

- **SEO and SERP Positioning**: Optimize on-page and off-page elements to improve your search engine ranking (Search Engine Optimization: SEO). This includes meta tags, content optimization, and backlinks. Use analytic tools to regularly monitor your website's performance on search engine results pages (SERPs).

- **User Experience (UX) and Design**: Focus on creating an intuitive, easy-to-navigate interface with responsive design. This involves optimizing page load times, simplifying navigation, and ensuring mobile friendliness.

- **Conversion Rate Optimization (CRO)**: Implement strategies to convert website visitors into customers. This can involve A/B testing of various elements such as call-to-action (CTA) buttons, landing pages, or checkout processes.

- **Content Strategy**: Produce high-quality, relevant content that addresses customer pain points and highlights your products or services. Employ a content management system (CMS) to update and manage your content efficiently.

- **Analytics and User Behavior Tracking**: Utilize web analytics tools to track key performance indicators such as bounce rates, session duration, and conversion rates. Use the data to fine-tune the website elements and improve user engagement.

- **Security and Compliance**: Implement robust security measures to protect customer data and ensure compliance with regulations like GDPR or CCPA. Security breaches can severely harm your brand reputation and customer trust.

For many use cases the websites are just the starting point, to allow personalized servicing and execution, the customers seamlessly continue to browser-based portals, authenticating at the point of entrance.

### 3.3.1.1.4 Company Portals – Secure Environment for Information and Execution

These are digital platforms that are **owned and managed by a specific company** or organization. Users are **required to authenticate** their identity, often through registration, login credentials, or other secure methods, to access the content and services offered. Authentication helps ensure privacy, security, and personalized experiences for users interacting with the company's digital presence. In some industries, e.g., financial services, regulators establish specific requirements such as Two-Factor-Authentication.

These company-specific portals are usually accessible through a browser and can be accessed from many devices, in most cases from desktop computers, laptops and tablets – supporting a big screen experience.

In the current digital age, companies globally are focusing on deepening customer engagement through dedicated online platforms. One key development is the rise of **Customer Portals**, exemplified by Amazon's dashboard for shoppers, Vodafone's phone plan management system, and Alibaba's comprehensive user interface.

Equally impactful is the emergence of **Online Communities**, where brands like Xiaomi and LEGO foster direct interactions and co-creation with consumers. Another significant transformation is seen in **Healthcare Portals**, such as the NHS App in the UK and Apollo Hospitals' patient portal in India, which offer convenient access to medical records, appointments, and prescriptions. **Financial Services Portals** have revolutionized financial transactions, as seen with Barclays' robust online banking and Safaricom's M-Pesa internet banking in Kenya. **Subscription Services** like Netflix and Spotify have reshaped consumer access to content, offering exclusive libraries to their subscribers. Finally, personalization stands as a critical component in enhancing user engagement, demonstrated by e-retailers like ASOS, Tokopedia, and Takealot that offer tailored shopping experiences based on user behavior. Overall, the digital transformation across sectors underscores the need for businesses to invest in innovative, convenient, and personalized online platforms to build stronger relationships with their customers.

**What a company should consider to maximize benefits from Company Portals**

- User Authentication and Access Control: Employ strong authentication methods to verify users and ensure that they have appropriate levels of access. This can include multi-factor authentication (MFA) and role-based access control (RBAC).

- Search and Navigation: Implement an intuitive search and navigation system that allows users to easily locate the information or tools they need. This could involve an advanced search algorithm, a detailed FAQ section, or a chat bot for immediate assistance.

- User Experience (UX) and Personalization: Create a user-friendly interface that also allows for personalized content and notifications based on the user's role, preferences, or history. This makes the portal more engaging and useful.

- Data Security and Compliance: Ensure that all data stored or transmitted through the portal is encrypted and complies with relevant regulations, such as GDPR for personal data or HIPAA for healthcare information.

- Scalability and Performance: Design the portal to handle varying amounts of traffic and user load. Use load balancing and cloud resources to ensure high performance and availability.

- Integrated Functionality: Implement APIs and integrations with other enterprise tools like CRM systems, HR software, or data analytics platforms to provide a comprehensive set of functionalities within the portal.

- Feedback Mechanisms and Support: Incorporate options for users to provide feedback or seek help. This can range from a simple 'Contact Us' form to more complex support ticket systems integrated into the portal.

In many cases customers prefer more mobility when they access a company portal. This is where Mobile Apps come into play.

### 3.3.1.1.5 Mobile Apps – Tailored Experiences for On-the-Go use cases

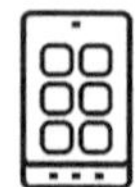 Mobile apps have not just become commonplace, they have seamlessly integrated into our daily lives. They offer on-the-go solutions that cater to a myriad of our needs, making tasks easier, more efficient, and enjoyable.

Mobile apps are specialized software applications crafted specifically for mobile devices. Their intrinsic **value comes from their portability, allowing users to access vast functionalities and services anytime, anywhere.** App stores, whether it is Apple's App Store or Google's Play Store, house millions of such apps, each striving to provide a unique user experience.

In today's digital age, the power of convenience is at the consumer's fingertips. Mobile devices have evolved into dynamic hubs for a plethora of activities, from shopping to event ticketing. These transformations are made possible by sophisticated mobile applications tailored for intuitive, user-centric experiences. Take shopping, for instance. The very essence of retail has shifted with the emergence of mobile commerce, condensing the expansive aisles of shopping malls into the compact screens of smartphones. The global e-commerce giant Amazon exemplifies this revolution. Its mobile app, with intuitive navigation, personalized product recommendations, and a seamless checkout process, sets the gold standard for mobile shopping. Not just confined to purchasing, features like user reviews, wish lists, and real-time order tracking enrich the overall consumer experience. At the same time, in Asia, Alibaba's app stands as a testament to integrated e-commerce (and so does Tencent's WeChat). Beyond its vast product range, the app weaves in payment and logistic solutions, crafting a holistic shopping journey. Further south, Africa's retail landscape is painted with the colors of Jumia. Catering to the unique needs of African consumers, Jumia's app integrates localized features, such as the 'JumiaPay' option for mobile money transactions, capturing the continent's digital pulse. The mobility sector too has been overhauled, with transportation and food delivery apps reshaping our commuting and dining habits. Uber and Lyft, predominant in the US and many global regions, have simplified transportation. The ease of hailing a ride, combined with transparent fare estimates, route tracking, and driver reviews, has revolutionized daily commuting. Southeast Asia offers a different flavor with Grab or Gojek. More than mere transportation apps, Grab and Gojek are digital ecosystems, encompassing ride-hailing, food delivery, digital payments, and even financial services in one cohesive mobile interface. When it comes to food, apps like Uber Eats have reimagined the dining paradigm, allowing users to enjoy diverse cuisines, place orders effortlessly, and track their meals in real-time. Lastly, the reality of events and entertainment has been democratized by mobile apps, making ticketing queues a thing of the past. India's BookMyShow is a game-changer in this space. Beyond ticketing, it offers a comprehensive entertainment guide with integrated reviews, trailers, and synopses. Europe, on the other hand, has its champion in Ticketmaster. More than a booking platform, it is a holistic event companion, offering everything from seating layouts to real-time ticket availability and directions to venues.

**What a company should consider to maximize benefits from Mobile Apps**

- User Interface (UI) and Experience (UX): Prioritize an intuitive and visually appealing UI and ensure the UX is tailored for small screens. Incorporate touch-friendly elements, easy navigation, and fast loading times.

- Platform-Specific Optimization: Develop or adapt your app to work seamlessly on different operating systems (iOS, Android) and device types (smartphones, tablets). This may involve using native development or cross-platform frameworks.

- App Store Optimization (ASO): Optimize the app's title, description, and keyword tags to improve its visibility in app stores. Monitor and encourage user reviews, as they significantly influence download rates.

- Push Notifications and In-App Messaging: Implement personalized and timely push notifications or in-app messages to engage users. However, be mindful of frequency to avoid annoying users and prompting uninstalls.

- Security and Data Privacy: Implement strong security measures like SSL, data encryption, and secure authentication. Ensure compliance with privacy regulations like GDPR or CCPA for data collection and storage.

- Real-time Analytics and Monitoring: Use mobile analytics tools to track user behavior, engagement metrics, and crash reports. This data is crucial for on-going app improvements and understanding ROI.

- Offline Accessibility: Design the app to provide essential features or content even when offline. This improves usability and retains users who might otherwise abandon the app during connectivity issues.

From streamlining critical business engagements and curating knowledge pathways to enriching our personal expectations of entertainment and self-expression, mobile apps have truly sculpted the digital age. They have redefined accessibility, personalized experiences, and bridged global divides. In this interconnected mosaic, each app, irrespective of its category, contributes to a larger narrative: a narrative of innovation, adaptability, and an ever-evolving human experience.

### 3.3.1.1.6 Live Chats and Chat Bots – The Digital Conversationalists

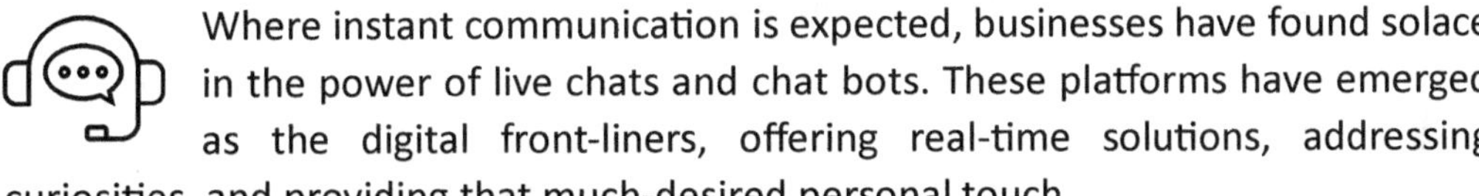 Where instant communication is expected, businesses have found solace in the power of live chats and chat bots. These platforms have emerged as the digital front-liners, offering real-time solutions, addressing curiosities, and providing that much-desired personal touch.

When it comes to **customer support**, live chats have bridged the gap between query and solution, enabling real-time problem resolution. Companies like Amazon and

Zara employ live chat options, helping users navigate through product inquiries, technical glitches, or even making real-time recommendations. Meanwhile, chat bots, with their **24/7 availability**, redefine the idea of 'working hours'. It is common for users to get their queries addressed at the oddest hours by businesses like Sephora and H&M. Through bots, these companies cater to global audiences, addressing concerns instantaneously irrespective of time zones.

**Order assistance** takes on a new meaning in the digital age. Instead of navigating through pages and FAQs, customers of companies like Domino's Pizza can now use chat bots to place their orders. Simultaneously, service-oriented businesses, from local salons in Paris to wellness centers in Mumbai, are integrating chat bots for **appointment scheduling**, ensuring users can book slots without any human intervention.

**Personalized product recommendations** have changed the way consumers shop online. ASOS, a UK-based fashion retailer, employs chat bots to analyze user preferences, making shopping an experience rather than a chore. On the flip side, bots have made **FAQs and self-service** a breeze. A user's query can be addressed without any wait time, reducing the load on human support, and driving efficiencies.

Businesses are constantly on the lookout for potential customers. Through **lead generation** capabilities, chat bots offer an innovative approach. They not only engage website visitors but also capture important data, subtly pushing potential customers through the sales funnel. Real estate companies like Zillow in the US and Zoopla in the UK utilize chat bots to interact with potential home buyers, guiding them through listings and even setting up viewings.

Companies are also leveraging chat bots for **onboarding and training**. For instance, SAP uses chat bots to guide users through product functionalities, making the onboarding process smoother. Bots do not stop at external users. **Employee support** sees chat bots stepping in, aiding in HR inquiries and policy clarifications, acting as digital HR assistants in firms across Asia, including TCS in India. Businesses thrive on feedback, and chat bots are at the forefront of **data collection and analysis**. Whether it is gathering feedback post-purchase or gauging the pulse of the customer post-interaction, bots ensure every piece of information is captured, ready to be analyzed. This data-driven approach has been employed by African telecom giants like MTN to improve customer experiences continually.

**What a company should consider to maximize benefits from Live Chats/Chat bots**

- Instant Response and Availability: For live chat, ensure agents are available during peak hours or when users are most active. For chat bots, make sure they are capable of 24/7 automated responses to the most common queries.

- Contextual Understanding and Personalization: Equip chat bots with Natural Language Processing (NLP) for better contextual understanding and personalize interactions based on user data for both live agents and chat bots.

- Clear Escalation Paths: Provide a straightforward way for users to escalate from a chat bot to a live agent for more complex queries. This should be a seamless transition, preserving the chat history and context.

- Data Security and Compliance: Implement secure data storage and transmission protocols for sensitive information exchanged via live chats or chat bots. Ensure compliance with data protection regulations like GDPR or CCPA.

- User Interface and Experience (UI/UX): Design the chat interface to be intuitive and user-friendly. This includes easily accessible chat buttons, prompt message notifications, and a clean, readable layout.

- Analytics and Performance Metrics: Utilize analytics tools to track key performance indicators such as response time, resolution rate, and customer satisfaction scores. Use this data for on-going optimization.

- Multi-Channel Integration: Ensure that your live chat and chat bot services are integrated with other customer service channels like email, phone, and social media. This offers a seamless customer service experience.

Live chat solutions and chat bots are not mere tools but essential cogs in the expansive machinery of modern businesses. From enhancing user experiences and personalizing interactions to streamlining processes, they are setting new standards in customer engagement, retention, and support.

However, despite the growing importance of the self-service channels, a **company must not forget that still a large number of customers expect direct exchanges with a human being**. All channels supporting this customer-employee interaction remain highly important. The art is to build these channels in a way that the augment the employee to serve the customer best possibly.

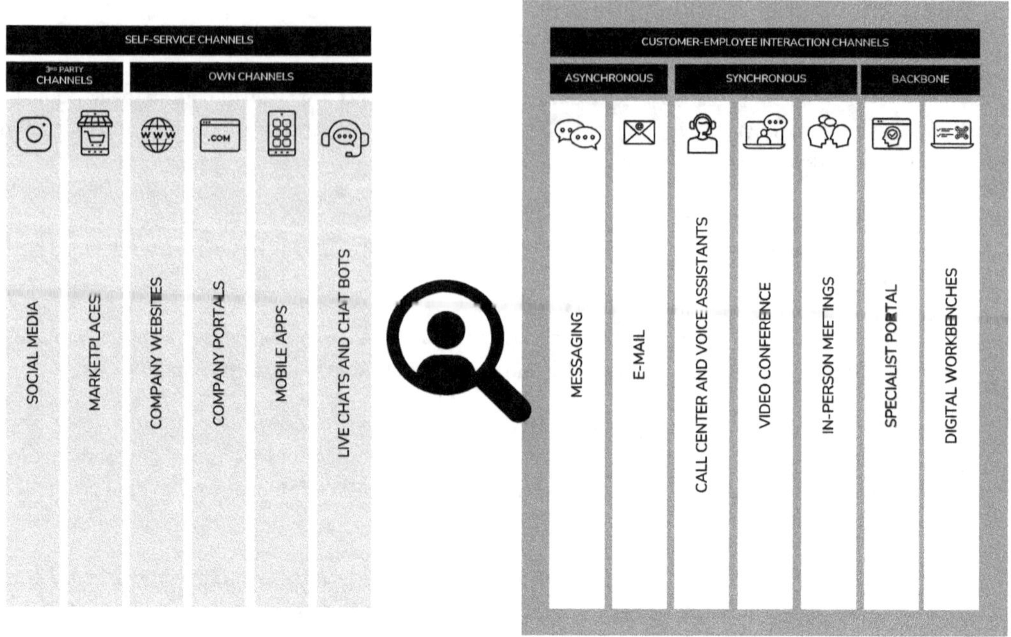


*Figure 21: Omnichannel ecosystem: Focus on Customer-Employee interaction channels*

A wide range of **customer-employee interaction channels** run in parallel to support asynchronous and synchronous interaction.

### 3.3.1.1.7 Messaging – Facilitators of Enhanced Customer Interaction

Messaging apps have become cornerstones of contemporary customer interaction. Boasting billions of global users, these platforms provide businesses a direct and highly personalized means to engage their clientele.

WhatsApp Business has emerged as a transformative tool, replete with features specifically tailored for businesses. This allows companies to craft a business profile, dispatch automated responses, and seamlessly integrate it into their CRM system. An apt example is KLM Royal Dutch Airlines, which harnesses WhatsApp Business to disseminate boarding passes, provide real-time flight updates, and cater to customer queries in the respective language of the customer. In China, WeChat has evolved from a mere messaging app to a multifunctional platform, integrating features like payment gateways, shopping interfaces, and mini programs. Starbucks China, for instance, leverages WeChat comprehensively, utilizing it for processing payments, offering rewards, and orchestrating special campaigns – all while keeping the customer within the app's ecosystem. LINE holds a dominant position in markets like Japan, Thailand, and Taiwan. Its business-oriented iteration, LINE for Business, empowers companies to broadcast news, updates, and promotions. Brands, such as Uniqlo, harness LINE not just as a marketing conduit but also as a real-time customer service channel. Viber, popular in Eastern Europe, provides Viber Business Messages,

170

a feature that lets companies send rich promotional messages. McDonald's Ukraine uses Viber to share promotions and updates with customers. Telegram emphasizes security and offers channels for businesses. These channels allow brands to broadcast messages to vast audiences. Companies, like TechCrunch, deploy Telegram bots to disseminate daily digests and breaking news to their subscribers. Messenger by Facebook is not just for personal chats. Brands use it to offer personalized shopping experiences. For example, Sephora's Messenger bot delivers product reviews, tutorials, and booking services. Signal, valued for its robust encryption, attracts businesses dealing with sensitive data. Firms such as law consultancies use Signal or Threema to maintain confidentiality in client conversations.

To truly unlock the potential of messaging apps, businesses need to be unwaveringly customer centric. This requires a commitment to ensuring that every interaction, whether driven by automation or human intervention, is anchored in meeting the customer's needs and providing unparalleled convenience.

**What a company should consider to maximize benefits from Messaging**

- **Privacy and Encryption:** Make sure to adhere to the highest levels of encryption and data security, especially when sharing sensitive information. Compliance with privacy regulations like GDPR is critical.

- **Localized Content and Language Support:** Tailor your messaging to the local language and customs if you are dealing with an international audience, as many messaging apps are popular in specific regions.

- **Quick Replies and Instant Service:** Leverage the real-time nature of messaging apps to provide instant customer service. Use features like read receipts and last seen to better gauge customer engagement.

- **Multi-Media Support:** Take advantage of the multimedia features like voice notes, video clips, and image sharing to provide a richer, more interactive customer experience.

- **Integration with CRM and Analytics Tools:** Sync the messaging app with your CRM system to maintain detailed customer profiles. Use analytics to monitor engagement metrics and optimize strategy.

To sum it up, while messaging apps offer a powerful avenue for businesses to intimately connect with their clientele, the true key to success lies in a combination of strategic foresight, technological integration, and a relentless focus on customer experience.

### 3.3.1.1.8    E-mail – The Time-Tested Channel for Direct Customer Engagement

 In a dynamic digital age marked by fleeting trends and rapidly evolving technologies, e-mail stands tall as a **steadfast pillar of communication**. It is not just the familiarity but the inherent characteristics of e-mails that cement its significance. Whether for a young startup or a global conglomerate, e-mail

represents a blend of formality, personal touch, and direct reach, something other platforms often struggle to emulate. A distinct advantage of e-mail is its **universality and accessibility**. Unlike newer platforms that cater to specific age groups or demographics, e-mail cuts across age, profession, and even geographic divides. It is not subjected to the unpredictable whims of social media algorithms, ensuring that a well-crafted message reaches its intended recipient in its entirety. Additionally, its asynchronous nature permits a depth of conversation, allowing both businesses and customers the luxury of time to articulate their messages comprehensively

In today's marketing, the strength of e-mail lies in its **potential for deep personalization**. Amazon from the US sets a global standard by pushing e-mail recommendations that echo a user's unique browsing and buying behavior. Similarly, European fashion powerhouse ASOS dispatches curated fashion suggestions, resonating with an individual's style and past purchases. Asia's e-commerce leader, Lazada, leverages e-mail to highlight geo-specific promotions, ensuring relevance to its vast user base. Flutterwave from Africa taps into regional financial trends, offering insights tailored to local preferences.

An often-underestimated power of e-mail is its role as a **channel for curated content**. Publications like The New York Times compress a world of news into succinct e-mail digests. The Guardian offers a range of newsletters, each fine-tuned to diverse reader interests. Nikkei Asian Review from Japan presents comprehensive market rundowns, and Africa's Mail & Guardian delivers sharp political insights, all directly to the e-mail inboxes of eager subscribers.

Beyond marketing, e-mails serve as a trusted channel for **customer support and feedback collection**. American tech icon Apple furnishes post-purchase support, guiding users from unboxing to advanced features. Airbnb emphasizes the feedback loop, encouraging guests and hosts alike to share their experiences, ensuring service quality remains uncompromised. Asia's trade behemoth Alibaba employs e-mail as a primary channel for addressing trade disputes, while Takealot from South Africa exemplifies e-mail-based customer service, swiftly responding to customer inquiries.

E-mails are irreplaceable for **transactional updates**, ranging from order acknowledgments to delivery alerts. Walmart ensures transparency with its customers by consistently updating them about order progress. Zalando walks customers through every step post-purchase, including returns and refunds, ensuring clarity. Flipkart elevates the user experience by integrating order tracking links within e-mails. Jumia reassures its vast customer base with prompt confirmations and delivery timelines.

## What a company should consider to maximize benefits from E-Mails

- **Segmentation and Personalization:** Divide your email list into various segments based on customer behavior, demographics, or purchase history. Tailor content and offers to each segment for a more personalized experience.

- **Content Relevance and Value:** Ensure that email content provides value to the recipient. This can range from educational content and product recommendations to exclusive offers and news updates.

- **Automated Campaigns and Triggers:** Implement automated email campaigns that activate based on specific triggers like customer behaviors or milestones (e.g., abandoned cart, account anniversary).

- **Mobile Optimization:** Design emails to be easily readable and functional on mobile devices, where a sizable percentage of emails are now opened. This includes responsive design and easy-to-click call-to-action buttons.

- **Deliverability and Timing:** Ensure emails reach the inbox by adhering to best practices that avoid spam filters. Pay attention to the timing of email sends, optimizing for when recipients are most likely to open and engage.

- **A/B Testing and Analytics:** Regularly perform A/B testing to optimize elements like subject lines, content layout, and calls to action. Use analytics to measure key performance indicators such as open rates, click-through rates, and conversion rates.

E-mail remains a significant tool, and its efficacy is tied to judicious and strategic use. As attention spans shrink in the digital age, ensuring every e-mail offers relevance, value, and respect will guide businesses to continued success.

### 3.3.1.1.9    Call Center and Voice Assistants – The Voice of Customer Engagement

The modern call center is a **sophisticated amalgamation of technology, processes, and human skill**, working in tandem to offer unparalleled customer service. From the first point of contact to post-call analysis, the path of customer interaction is lined with various digital tools and platforms. These have transformed traditional call centers into dynamic, responsive hubs of communication that transcend geographical boundaries and cultural nuances. As we explore these tools, we will unravel the layers of complexity that are now considered standard in leading call centers across the U.S., Europe, and Asia.

Establishing a strong rapport with customers is pivotal. This is where **Customer Management and Interaction Platforms** shine, laying the foundation for a personalized, dynamic, and efficient communication model. At the heart of this platform lies **Customer Relationship Management (CRM) Software**. CRM tools have revolutionized the way businesses perceive and interact with their customers. With the capability to consolidate an ocean of data into a single interface, these software solutions are indispensable for a holistic view of customer interactions and tailored assistance. Salesforce is a testament to the transformative power of cloud-based CRM solutions. Its innovative approach has become a benchmark, assisting numerous organizations in maintaining an extensive reservoir of customer data and facilitating superior interactions. SAP, headquartered in Germany, offers its own brand of CRM expertise. As part of its comprehensive suite of business applications, SAP's CRM solution is recognized for its robustness and versatility. Meanwhile Zoho has carved a niche for itself by providing a comprehensive cloud CRM solution that caters to businesses, whether they are budding startups or large corporations.

But the customer's journey often begins even before they connect with a representative. Here, **Interactive Voice Response (IVR) Systems** play a critical role. As the digital gatekeepers, IVRs are more than just a series of pre-recorded options. They are a bridge, guiding callers through an array of self-service options, potentially resolving their concerns without requiring any human intervention. Such systems bring to light the marvel of automation coupled with intuitive design. Genesys, from the U.S., is one of the trailblazers in this domain. Their robust IVR solutions have redefined what it means to offer self-service options to customers. Journeying to Europe, Avaya has left a significant footprint across the continent. Their IVR technology is not just about streamlining customer interactions, it is about elevating the entire customer experience. And the narrative of IVR would be incomplete without mentioning Ameyo from Asia. Headquartered in India, Ameyo's suite of call center solutions, which prominently features their IVR system, has been catering to diverse industries with a promise of efficiency and innovation. Together, CRM and IVR systems illustrate the fusion of technology and customer-centric strategies. They exemplify how modern businesses can harness digital tools to ensure that the voice of the customer is not just heard but is also responded to with precision and personalization.

Amidst the hum of a bustling call center, the core challenge remains: how do we connect customers to the right representative swiftly and efficiently? The answer lies in the strategic orchestration of **Call Routing and Optimization tools** that serve as the backbone of effective call center operations. Taking center stage in this domain are **Automatic Call Distribution (ACD) Systems**. These systems analyze factors such as agent availability, expertise, and the nature of the customer's query, and then intelligently route the call to the most suitable agent. The result? Substantially reduced wait times, maximized agent productivity, and a smoother experience for the caller. Cisco, a renowned tech giant from the U.S., has crafted an ACD solution that stands as a beacon of efficient call distribution. Their technology ensures that not only are calls routed promptly but are also matched with the agent best equipped to handle the inquiry. Not to be left behind, Europe offers its own stalwart in this sector: Alcatel-Lucent Enterprise (ALE). Headquartered in France, ALE's OmniGenesys

Contact Center solution offers a robust ACD feature, ensuring seamless call connectivity.

Yet, in the world of call centers, outbound calls are just as crucial. **Predictive Dialers** have emerged as a game-changer for businesses aiming to reach out to their clientele. By leveraging historical data and agent availability, these systems optimize call rates, ensuring agents spend less time waiting and more time connecting. Five9, an industry leader from the U.S., offers a predictive dialer solution that epitomizes efficiency. With its cloud-based technology, businesses can achieve faster connections and improved hit rates. Europe's contribution in this space is marked by DialApplet, a Spain-based company. Their software not only automates call dialing but also promises a rich set of features to boost agent performance. On the Asian front, Drishti-Soft offers Ameyo Predictive Dialer. Their solution promises reduced idle time, intelligent call assignments, and improved operational efficiency. The constructive interaction of ACD systems and predictive dialers underscores the importance of intelligent call management. Their adoption illustrates how forward-thinking businesses are placing their bets on technology to optimize customer interactions, ensuring that each call, inbound or outbound, is an opportunity for meaningful engagement.

In the dynamic environment of call centers, sustained excellence hinges not just on innovative tools but also on the systematic evaluation of performance and a commitment to continuous improvement. **Performance Analysis and Quality Assurance** tools serve as the foundation, offering in-depth insights and actionable feedback to call centers worldwide. Central to quality assurance are **Call Recording and Quality Monitoring** tools. They allow managers to capture agent-customer interactions, fostering an environment of training, compliance, and feedback. The U.S.-based NICE Systems has been a front-runner in this space, offering solutions that not only record calls but also analyze them for various performance metrics. Meanwhile, Audiocodes brings to the table VOIP-based call recording solutions that integrate seamlessly with various enterprise communication platforms. Asia's own Ozonetel from India champions this domain, with its cloud-based recording tools that allow businesses to store, manage, and evaluate vast volumes of call data. Moving deeper into analytics, **Speech Analytics** tools are revolutionizing the way businesses understand their customers. By analyzing recorded calls, these tools can gauge sentiments, extract trends, and measure satisfaction levels. Verint Systems from the U.S. has been pioneering in this domain, with solutions that can sift through hours of calls to derive actionable insights. Europe's CallMiner, on the other hand, provides a comprehensive suite of speech analytics tools that convert customer interactions into operational intelligence. From Asia, Singapore's HelloSoda stands out with its unique approach, leveraging both speech and text analytics to derive a holistic view of customer interactions. Lastly, the overarching need for comprehensive insights has bolstered the importance of **Reporting and Analytics** platforms. They compile data from various touchpoints to provide managers with a bird's-eye view of operations. Cisco from the U.S. is exemplary here, with its Unified Intelligence Center offering customizable reports, dashboards, and real-time analytics. Europe's tech powerhouse, SAP, brings forth its analytical solutions tailored for call center operations, ensuring data-driven decisions are always within reach. Meanwhile, the Asian market sees Ameyo taking the lead, integrating powerful reporting capabilities into its call center suite. To sum up, Performance Analysis and Quality Assurance tools underscore the belief that excellence is an on-going journey. Through continuous monitoring, insightful analytics, and actionable feedback, businesses can fine-tune their strategies, ensuring they not only meet but consistently exceed customer expectations.

**What a company should consider to maximize benefits from Call Support**

- Skilled and Well-Trained Agents: Ensure your agents are knowledgeable about products, services, and common customer issues. Regular training and performance reviews are key.

- Queue Management and Call Routing: Implement advanced queue management systems to reduce wait times. Route calls to the most appropriate agents based on the issue or customer profile.

- Real-Time Monitoring and Analytics: Use software solutions that allow real-time monitoring of call metrics such as call duration, hold times, and first-call resolution rates for on-going optimization.

- Customer Verification and Data Security: Employ secure and efficient methods for verifying customer identity to protect sensitive information. Compliance with data protection regulations like GDPR is essential.

- Multi-Channel Integration: Ensure that call center services are integrated with other digital touchpoints like email, chat, and social media for a seamless customer service experience.

The call center has emerged not just as a point of contact but as a strategic asset for businesses. **The fusion of technology and human expertise**, as highlighted through our exploration, displays the future of customer service – adaptive, predictive, and ever-responsive.

### 3.3.1.1.10 Video Conference – Real-time Customer Engagement

The importance of forging authentic and impactful connections with clients and customers cannot be overstated. As part of a holistic omnichannel strategy, video conferencing has surged to the forefront as an ever more important channel. It offers an unparalleled blend of personal interaction and digital convenience, thereby evolving the traditional paradigms of relationship-building. The essence of a successful video conference is predicated on three critical phases: detailed preparation, vibrant and dynamic interaction, and diligent post-conference follow-through.

**Comprehensive Preparation**: Prior to a video conference, businesses must understand their client's unique needs and expectations. This phase is facilitated by intuitive platforms such as Cisco Webex in the U.S. and GoToMeeting in Europe, which feature user-friendly agenda-setting modules. Embedded within these modules are robust workflows that easily pull pertinent information, like product details, directly from integrated systems. This allows for the seamless creation of customized and up-to-date presentations, proposals, and talking points. Additional features such as pre-meeting surveys and customizable invite templates gather initial data, allowing businesses to tailor the dialogue even further. Sharing advance materials or even interactive product demos ensures that clients are engaged and prepared, fostering an atmosphere conducive to meaningful conversation – a meeting reminder notification completes the picture.

**Immersive and Interactive Engagement**: The core of the video conference should be as interactive and engaging as an in-person meeting. Sophisticated tools, such as those offered by Zoho Meeting in Asia, offer real-time screen sharing and augmented reality demonstrations. Note taking and joint adjustments of product proposal defines the minimum standard. But the interactivity does not stop there. Businesses can also leverage real-time polls, breakout rooms for focused discussions, and even gamified elements to boost engagement. Additional analytics, based on Natural Language Processing (NLP), can help to understand sentiments, or detect opportunities to support the employee real-time. Interactive Q&A sessions and live feedback tools make it possible to address client queries and concerns instantaneously. Where possible additional experts can be pulled into the conversation immediately. The aim is to entertain a vibrant dialogue, underpinned by active listening and real-time responsiveness, to build trust and solidify the relationship.

**Strategic Post-Conference Actions**: Once the meeting concludes, swift and structured follow-up is crucial for sustaining the momentum generated during the interaction. Platforms with integrated CRM systems enable immediate updating of client profiles. Additionally, advanced analytics and transcription services, like those from Kaltura in the U.S., break down the conference into actionable insights. The crucial aspect here is capturing key activities and next steps. Whether it is assigning responsibilities for follow-up actions, setting deadlines, or scheduling subsequent interactions, no stone should be left unturned in the comprehensive capturing of action items and commitments. In addition, efficient archiving of the customer interactions can contribute additional benefits.

By attending to these three phases, businesses can elevate video conferencing from a mere communication tool to a vital cog in their omnichannel client engagement strategy. This not only enhances immediate client interactions but also sets the stage for longer-term relationship-building and client satisfaction.

**What a company should consider to maximize benefits from Video Conferencing**

- Secure Connections: Employ robust security measures including end-to-end encryption and secure meeting links to protect sensitive information discussed during the call.

- User-Friendly Interface: Choose a video conferencing tool with an intuitive user interface to minimize technical hiccups and facilitate a smoother experience for customers who may be less tech-savvy.

- Preparation and Agenda: Always have a clear agenda and be prepared with all necessary materials, including slides or demos. This shows professionalism and respect for the customer's time.

- High-Quality Video and Audio: Ensure that the technology used delivers high-quality video and audio to prevent glitches that can interrupt the flow of conversation and impair communication.

- Screen Sharing and Interactive Features: Utilize features like screen sharing, virtual whiteboarding, and real-time polls to make the meeting more interactive and engaging for the customer.

- Follow-Up and Documentation: Record the meeting with the customer's permission for future reference and send a follow-up email summarizing key points and next steps. This enhances the customer's experience and makes it easier to track actionable items.

In the delicate relationship of client and customer interaction, video conferencing provides businesses with the tools they need to lead. Effective preparation, rich interaction, and structured follow-through make these digital interactions resonate, ensuring that businesses can cultivate and sustain thriving relationships in a digital age.

### 3.3.1.1.11 In-person meetings – Personal Touch Augmented by Technology

In a world increasingly dominated by digital channels, the enduring value of in-person, physical meetings should not be underestimated. As a crucial element in an omnichannel strategy, face-to-face interactions bring a level of nuance, authenticity, and trust that is often hard to replicate through digital means. The success of in-person meetings, however, also hinges on three vital components: rigorous preparation, dynamic engagement, and strategic post-meeting actions. The features outlined as part of the video conferences in the prior section also apply to physical in-person meetings. But in addition, the personal contact allows for some more emotions.

**In the Preparation Stage, Digital Tools Take the Lead**: As you gear up for an important in-person meeting with a prospective client, your Customer Relationship Management (CRM) system is the star player. Through machine learning algorithms, it auto-generates a tailored meeting agenda, which is shared with your team through an **Integrated Workflow System**. This digital platform is robust, pulling in real-time data, past interaction history, and product information to create a highly customized plan. You use **Screen Sharing** features to conduct a preparatory meeting with your team, ensuring everyone is aligned. While the primary preparation is digital, a **Tactile Information Pack** is prepared to serve as a tangible enhancement. These are physical materials – like product samples or high-quality printed brochures – that are aligned with the digital content.

**Digital Dominates the Actual Meeting, with Tactile Enhancements**: When it comes to conducting the meeting, digital tools are front and center. You utilize a tablet connected to **Interactive Digital Dashboards**, allowing for real-time updates and data-driven discussions. The power of **Screen Sharing** and **Augmented Reality (AR)** features allows you to present complex product models and real-time data, enhancing both understanding and engagement. At strategic moments, you introduce the physical elements from your **Tactile Information Pack**. Whether it is a fabric swatch relevant to the discussion or a 3D printed model, these tactile elements serve to amplify the digital interaction rather than replace it.

**Post-Meeting: Digital Tools Seal the Deal, with Tactile Follow-Up**: The meeting may be over, but the digital machinery is far from done. Your **Voice-to-Text Service** converts meeting notes into digital records, which are immediately processed by your **Next Best Action Algorithm** in the CRM system. It is this system that orchestrates your follow-through, generating not just emails but also setting tasks for sending out a tactile **Follow-Up Pack**. This pack serves as a physical memento of the meeting, perhaps containing a small product sample or a hand-written thank-you note that complements the digitally generated meeting summary.

**What a company should consider to maximize benefits from In-person meetings**

- **Secure WiFi and Connectivity**: Ensure that the meeting room has secure and reliable WiFi for all attendees, especially if the meeting requires live demos or remote participation.

- **Digital Agenda and Pre-Meeting Material**: Use digital platforms to send out agendas, background materials, or presentation slides ahead of the meeting, allowing attendees to come prepared and engage more effectively.

- **Real-Time Collaboration Tools**: Implement tools that allow participants to collaborate on a document or project in real-time during the meeting, helping to capture ideas and assign tasks immediately.

- **Interactive Displays**: Utilize smart displays or projectors that allow for interactive presentations, brainstorming sessions, or Data Visualization, thereby enhancing the quality of discussion and engagement.

- **Remote Participation**: Have a reliable setup for high-quality video conferencing for stakeholders who cannot attend in person but still need to be a part of the decision-making process.

• **Meeting Recap and Action Items:** Use digital tools to quickly summarize the meeting and distribute action items to all attendees, ensuring everyone is aligned on next steps and responsibilities.

In this way, digital tools and platforms form the backbone of your client engagement strategy. Tactile elements are not an afterthought but a well-integrated part of the whole, serving to enhance the impact of the digital interactions. This creates a rich, multi-layered experience that leverages the best of both worlds, epitomizing what a modern, digitally led yet human-centric approach to client engagement should look like in a successful omnichannel ecosystem.

### 3.3.1.1.12 Specialist portals – Technical Support, Medial or Legal Consultations

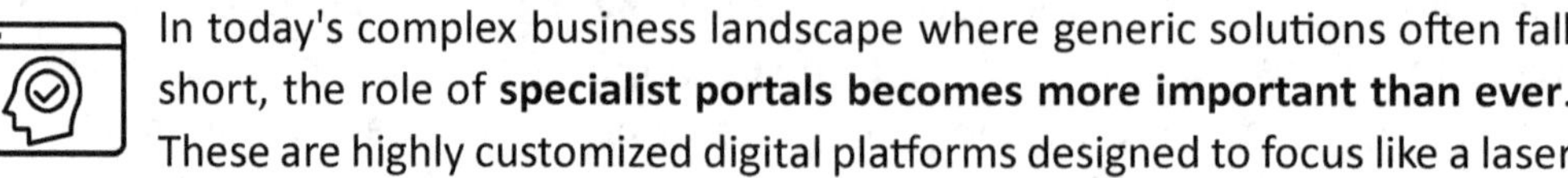

In today's complex business landscape where generic solutions often fall short, the role of **specialist portals becomes more important than ever**. These are highly customized digital platforms designed to focus like a laser on the unique needs and challenges faced by specialists within various fields. They provide an unparalleled level of expertise and problem-solving capabilities, far removed from the jack-of-all-trades approach of generalist platforms.

The importance of these platforms lies in their ability to tackle specific issues that general tools simply cannot handle. Whether we are talking about advanced medical diagnoses, complex engineering calculations, or specialized legal research, specialist portals offer a streamlined, in-depth resource. What sets them apart is their ability to seamlessly integrate with existing enterprise systems like Enterprise Resource Planning (ERP) or Customer Relationship Management (CRM). This seamless integration is key, creating an ecosystem where data flows freely and specialists have immediate access to precisely the resources, they need without navigating through irrelevant options or interfaces.

Another hallmark of these platforms is their efficiency of design. Tailored for quick and precise problem-solving, the user interface and experience are fine-tuned to the needs of specialists. Customizable dashboards, real-time analytics, and predictive modeling tools are often standard features, all designed to enable specialists to work not just hard, but smart, arriving at solutions with speed and accuracy.

**What a company should consider to maximize benefits from Specialist Portals**

• **Role-Based Access Control:** Implement a role-based access control system to ensure that users can only access the resources and tools that are relevant to their specific job functions or expertise level.

• **Customizable Dashboards:** Offer customizable dashboards that allow experts to tailor the user interface to display metrics, tools, or data most relevant to their individual tasks.

• **Advanced Search and Filtering:** Include powerful search features with advanced filtering options to enable users to quickly find documents, data sets, or previous cases that are relevant to their current work.

- Collaboration Tools: Integrate collaboration features like chat, forums, and file-sharing capabilities to facilitate real-time interaction and teamwork among experts who may be geographically dispersed.

- High-Performance Computing Resources: For portals that require data-intensive tasks, ensure the availability of high-performance computing resources, and make it straightforward for users to request and allocate these resources.

- Workflow Automation: Include features that automate repetitive tasks and integrate with existing systems (like CRMs or ERPs) to streamline the overall workflow and reduce the administrative burden on experts.

- Secure Data Storage and Transmission: Ensure robust security measures, including encryption and multi-factor authentication, to protect sensitive or proprietary information. Also, make sure to comply with industry-specific data protection and privacy regulations.

- On-going Training and Support: Provide comprehensive training resources, including webinars, tutorials, and documentation, to help users get the most out of the portal. Also offer robust customer support options, including live chat or a dedicated helpline.

So, what does this mean for organizations striving to solve complex challenges? It means that the role of specialist portals should never be overlooked. They offer a depth of resources and tools that generalist platforms cannot provide. And it is not just about having more features or more data, it is about having the right features and the right data. In that sense, these platforms become an indispensable part of a holistic organizational strategy, filling in the gaps left by more general tools to ensure that no stone is left unturned in the pursuit of solving complex, specialized problems.

### 3.3.1.1.13 Digital Workbenches – The Core of Customer-Employee Interactions

When the inundation of data can be overwhelming, the rise of digital workbenches for client management emerges as a necessity for clarity and efficiency. These platforms are more than mere tools, they are expansive ecosystems that combine various facets of client interaction into a singular, accessible space, allowing for a holistic and informed approach to client relationships.

Central to the effectiveness of these platforms is the **Customer Profile**. This is not just a digital card of contact details, it is a comprehensive overview of a client's journey with a business. Take, for instance, the approach of luxury brands like Ritz-Carlton or Mercedes-Benz. For them, knowing a client means understanding their preferences, recalling their previous purchases, and predicting their future needs. This intimate knowledge stems from detailed client profiles that form the backbone of their impeccable service.

The **Communication History** is another pillar of excellence in client management. In a world where interactions span across multiple mediums and platforms, it is essential to have a unified view. Imagine the smoothness in Apple's after-sales service, when a customer walks into an Apple Store, their entire communication, from emails to support calls, is at the fingertips of the service representative, enabling continuity and understanding.

**Task and Activity Tracking** brings precision and accountability to client interactions. The Asian tech giant, Samsung, for instance, is renowned for its punctual product launches and timely customer support. Behind this timeliness is likely a robust system that tracks every task, deadline, and activity, ensuring that every cog in their vast machinery moves in synchrony. Understanding a client's **Transaction History** is not about numbers, it is about narratives. Each transaction tells a story of a need, a desire, or a problem faced by the client. Companies like Amazon excel in this domain. Their recommendation engines, backed by a client's transaction history, often predict needs even before the client fully realizes them.

The essence of **Notes and Annotations** lies in capturing the intangible. While data provides the what, these notes often provide the why. Major consulting firms, such as Deloitte and KPMG, rely heavily on such annotations. When dissecting vast volumes of data for a client, these notes serve as contextual markers, guiding the narrative and providing depth to the analysis.

**Document Management** goes beyond mere storage, it is about accessibility and relevance. When a client queries a past proposal or contract, the swiftness with which a company, like Siemens, retrieves and navigates this document can be the difference between a continued partnership or a lost opportunity.

Deep dives into **Engagement Insights** transform raw data into actionable strategies. Digital marketing firms, especially in saturated markets like Europe, harness these insights to tailor their campaigns. By understanding past client behaviors and engagement patterns, they can craft messages that resonate and drive action.

Today's clientele, especially in niche sectors, seeks personalization. **Customization and Personalization** tools in workbenches allow businesses to shape their services like clay, molding them to fit the unique contours of each client's requirements. This is evident in the bespoke experiences offered by luxury brands such as Hermès or Bentley, where products and services are often tailored to individual tastes.

**Collaboration Tools** bridge departmental silos. For instance, when Tesla releases a new car model, the synchrony between its design, engineering, sales, and customer support teams is palpable. Such inter-departmental harmony is often orchestrated on platforms that promote collaborative inputs and shared insights.

Finally, as remote work and global operations become the norm, **Integrated Communication Channels** and **Reminders and Alerts** become the nerves and sinews holding operations together. They ensure that distance does not dilute engagement quality. The agility of companies like Zoom or Slack in weaving these tools into their offerings highlights the evolving nature of workplace communication.

**What a company should consider to maximize benefits from Digital Workbenches**

- Task Management and Prioritization: Integrate task management tools that allow employees to set, track, and prioritize their tasks for the day. A visual drag-and-drop interface can make this easier.

- Single Sign-On (SSO) and Integration: Use Single Sign-On to enable seamless access to various tools and resources without requiring multiple logins. Integrating commonly used applications can boost efficiency.

- Real-Time Collaboration and Communication: Include chat and video conferencing capabilities to facilitate real-time collaboration. Shared workspaces and document editing features can enhance teamwork.

- Customization and Personalization: Allow users to customize their dashboard according to their workflow and job responsibilities. Elements could include KPI trackers, calendars, or industry news feeds.

- Data Analytics and Insights: Provide data analytics tools that can offer insights into workflow efficiency, resource allocation, and even personal productivity metrics.

- Automated Workflow: Incorporate workflow automation features to handle routine tasks automatically, freeing up employees to focus on more complex, value-added activities.

- Security and Compliance: Implement strong security measures such as multi-factor authentication and encrypted data storage. Ensure the platform complies with data protection regulations relevant to your industry or geography.

- Training and Support: Offer tutorials, FAQs, and customer support to help employees get acquainted with the platform. Live support should be readily available for any troubleshooting.

To sum up, digital workbenches elevate the space of client management from a task to an art. With their array of tools and functionalities, they empower businesses to not just engage with clients but to enchant them. They are the canvases on which businesses paint their client relationships, ensuring every stroke is informed, intentional, and impactful.

Across all these channels, we find a set up **overarching key success factors**.

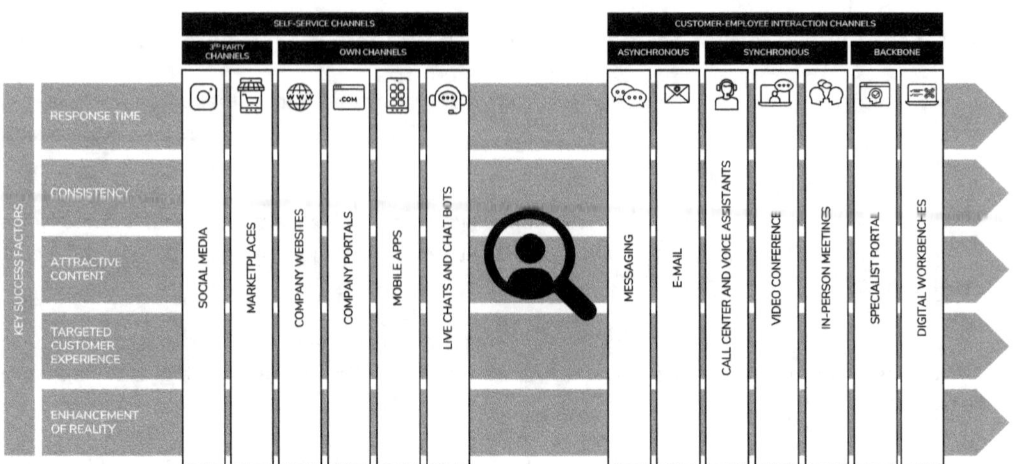

*Figure 22: Omnichannel key success factors*

### 3.3.1.2    Omnichannel Success factors

Beyond optimizing the individual channels – where the key topics to consider have been listed in the respective sections – overarching omnichannel success factors need to be addressed. It is worth-while to have special emphasis and possibly even dedicated teams looking at shortenings the response time, connecting disparate data, optimizing the target user experience, making the content attractive and exploring new ways of interactions and touchpoints such as Augmented and Virtual Reality, well into the Metaverse.

### 3.3.1.2.1    The Pivotal Role of Response Time in the Digital Channel Ecosystem

In an age where the digital world pulsates with activity around the clock, customer interactions occur at an unprecedented pace. Amidst this bustling landscape, **the crucial determining factor for customer satisfaction and brand loyalty hinges on one thing: response time.** We are talking about the milli-seconds it takes to up-load a screen, the seconds ticking away as a chat message goes unanswered, the minutes it takes for an email reply, and the hours that pass without acknowledgment on social media platforms.

**Awareness: No Time to Waste**

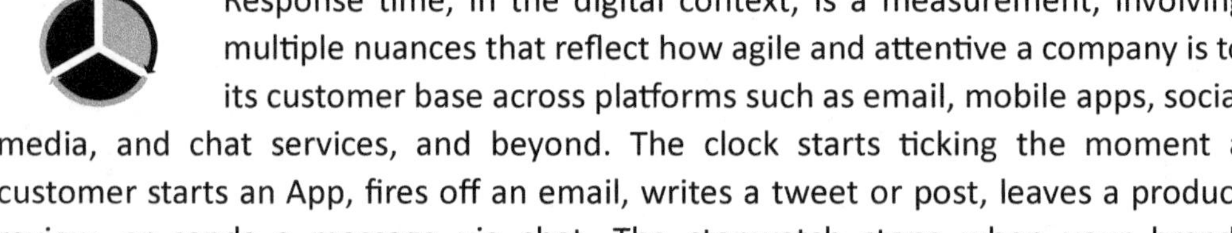

Response time, in the digital context, is a measurement, involving multiple nuances that reflect how agile and attentive a company is to its customer base across platforms such as email, mobile apps, social media, and chat services, and beyond. The clock starts ticking the moment a customer starts an App, fires off an email, writes a tweet or post, leaves a product review, or sends a message via chat. The stopwatch stops when your brand, represented by either human customer service agents or AI-powered tools, steps in to offer a reply or resolve an issue.

Response time takes on an enormous weight in the digital sphere because **it not only influences immediate sales but also has long-term repercussions on brand reputation**. A slow response time is not just a momentary frustration, it contributes to an evolving narrative about your brand being unresponsive or uncaring. This can lead to negative reviews, detrimental word-of-mouth, and ultimately a decline in customer retention rates. In contrast, swift and efficient responses create an impression of a brand as reliable, considerate, and engaged. When customers know they can rely on you for quick solutions, they are more likely to return and recommend your services, thereby enhancing customer lifetime value. Additionally, in a world accustomed to real-time gratification, the speed of your response can set you apart from competitors who are slower off the mark.

Let us understand where your company stands when it comes to Response Time.

### Assessment: Testing the Speed of Interaction

Understanding that response time is mission-critical, how does a business go about assessing its performance? Here, **analytics software** that can provide granular insights into your digital channels' performance becomes invaluable. You will want to configure these tools to provide specific metrics such as 'average email response time', 'social media engagement rate', and 'live chat resolution time', and many more.

In digital channels, the response time is not just a singular metric, it is a mosaic of various sub-metrics. For instance, in the case of email, you have 'time to acknowledgment', which is how quickly an automated email is sent to let the customer know their message has been received. Then there is 'time to first human reply', capturing the period it takes for an actual person to intervene. For chat systems, you might measure 'time to bot response' and 'time to human escalation' separately.

It is not enough to simply know your numbers, you need to know what these numbers mean in a broader context. **Industry benchmarks** give you a comparison point to understand if your response times are competitive, below average, or industry leading. Likewise, periodic internal audits can also offer qualitative insights, such as the correlation between response time and customer satisfaction levels or churn rates.

## Action: Ensure Immediate Responses

 In a reality where customers demand immediate gratification, **maintaining system stability and stellar performance** is not just a priority but an absolute necessity. Leading companies such as Amazon have been known to invest heavily in this, ensuring their platforms maintain high-speed responses, according to numerous studies available on www.websitebuilderexpert.com, a site offering comprehensive statistics and insights on various websites and platforms. Recognizing the vital role of swift response times, businesses are urged to evolve, optimizing both lead and load times by decentralizing their server and platform infrastructure, strategically aligning them closer to the end-users. Companies such as Google have constantly worked on this by optimizing their server infrastructure globally. This strategic relocation ensures that customers experience significantly reduced waiting times when initiating applications, loading screens, or executing transactions.

Stepping into the modern era necessitates leveraging **real-time automated workflows**, an approach that stands powerful in the face of an influx of customer interactions. Salesforce has successfully exemplified the proficient use of real-time automated workflows. By assigning interactions to the apt departments or individuals based on predefined criteria, it filters and prioritizes tasks seamlessly. It adeptly identifies high-priority clients and elevates critical technical issues to teams specialized in swift resolutions, ensuring no concern falls into oblivion and crafting a framework where response times are optimized at every junction (visit section 3.3.1.1.9 Call Center and Voice Assistants – The Voice of Customer Engagement on page 173 to review some available technology).

In a world brimming with digital interactions, **AI-driven chat bots** cease to be a luxury and stand as a vital entity, a necessity steering the helm in managing a barrage of incoming queries through digital conduits. OpenAI, among other, has been at the forefront in this sector, developing sophisticated AI chat bots capable of understanding and handling multi-step interactions. They exhibit a deep understanding of contextual nuances, allowing them a timely and intelligent delegation of complex issues to human agents. This strategic integration of AI capabilities with a human touch not only brings down average response times significantly but fosters a reality of synergy where efficiency meets empathy.

---

**Leveraging the potential from AI-enhanced customer service bots**

AI-enhanced customer service bots have carved a niche, redefining the interface between businesses and their clientele. At the core of this transformation lies the potent combination of machine learning and natural language processing (NLP), enabling these bots to decipher complex human interactions and respond with unprecedented precision and personalization. One compelling exemplar is OpenAI's GPT models. These are not just programmed responders but intuitive entities, trained on a myriad of datasets, capable of interpreting a spectrum of inquiries and crafting responses that are contextually aligned and highly relevant. They interpret, analyze, and converse, transcending the traditional scripted interactions to deliver a bespoke conversational experience.

In the context of e-commerce, the advent of AI has pioneered a multitude of refined customer interaction paradigms. A query about a product morphs into a personalized interaction where the bot, empowered by AI, offers detailed insights tailored to the specific inclinations of the shopper. Real-time updates on order status and expected delivery times are communicated with accuracy, amalgamating live data analytics and instant response mechanisms.

For those seeking solutions, AI bots are the frontline troubleshooters. They diagnose issues, offer step-by-step solutions, and have the acumen to escalate complex scenarios to human agents, ensuring that each interaction is tailored, efficient, and solution oriented. The bots are not just problem solvers, they are bridges to enhanced customer satisfaction.

Every interaction with an AI bot is an echo of personalization. They sift through customer preferences, browsing patterns, and behavioral nuances to offer recommendations that are not just relevant but bespoke. This is not just technology at play, it is technology intertwined with a deep understanding of individual customer preferences, delivering a shopping experience that is as personalized as it is efficient.

The story does not end at product recommendations. AI bots are adept at navigating through the complexities of billing and payment queries. Customers seeking clarity are met with instant, detailed, and accurate responses, a synergy of technology and human-like interaction that enhances trust and builds a rapport anchored in reliability and efficiency.

AI is not just a technological tool, it is a catalyst that transforms customer service from a functional necessity to an enriched, interactive, and value-added experience. Each interaction is a learning curve, each response, a step closer to refined customer engagement where technology and human interaction converge to script a narrative of enhanced customer satisfaction and loyalty[72].

**Empowering customer service teams** with instantaneous access to a wealth of customer data, inclusive of past interactions and a well-rounded database of pre-approved responses to recurrent queries, stands paramount. Firms like Zoho have showcased how integrated CRM systems can revolutionize customer service. Integrated CRM systems offer a vault of information at the agent's fingertips, enabling them to devise solutions that are not just quick but deeply personalized, resonating with the customer's unique needs and history. It creates an environment where solutions are not just about speed but about understanding the customer in depth, offering solutions that are tailor-made, swift, and heartwarming.

---

[72] Helen Feng, Maria Morel on IBM company website: "How AI-powered chat bots are transforming marketing and sales operations". Published online 02.08.2023, visited 08.04.2024.
https://www.ibm.com/blog/how-ai-powered-chat bots-are-transforming-marketing-and-sales-operations/, and
Bernhard Marr in Forbes: "How Artificial Intelligence Is Making Chat bots Better For Businesses". Published online 18.05.2018, visited 08.04.2024.
https://www.forbes.com/sites/bernardmarr/2018/05/18/how-artificial-intelligence-is-making-chat bots-better-for-businesses/?sh=1d21af3a4e72

Understating the role of response time in the vibrant digital channel ecosystem would be a glaring oversight. It is a defining pillar in the perception of your brand, a silent yet potent communicator of your business ethos. Leaders in the industry like Apple have consistently shown an understanding of this critical aspect, adopting strategies to enhance response times. Companies that nurture an understanding of this critical facet, continually evaluating and honing their strategy stand to win in this digital race. Reducing response times is not a mere tactic, it is a strategic orchestration reverberating through every facet of the business, echoing in the halls of customer satisfaction, painting perceptions of your brand, and scripting stories of long-term profitability through satisfied smiles and loyal customers.

### 3.3.1.2.2   Consistency: Unifying Data and Crafting Seamless Experiences

In the digital age, the key to offering unparalleled customer experiences lies in the harmonious blend of data unification and seamless omnichannel strategies. This section dives into the crucial aspects of this integration, focusing on the stages of Awareness, Assessment, and Action to guide businesses in achieving a consistent and customer-centric digital presence.

**Awareness: Grasping the Essence of Data Unification and Omnichannel Synergy**

The power of unifying disparate data is not just in aggregating information but in transforming it into actionable insights that shape customer behavior and drive business growth. Data unification involves amalgamating fragmented data from varied digital touchpoints – be it social media, mobile apps, e-commerce platforms, or email marketing. This process is critical not only for ensuring data compatibility and integrity but for enriching the data with a level of depth and usability that goes beyond mere transactional information. It encompasses emotional data points, like sentiment analysis from social comments or in-app behavioral cues, which add nuanced layers to the customer profile. By weaving together these diverse data strands, businesses can create a comprehensive and dynamic portrait of their customers, revealing not just what they do but why they do it.

Parallel to data unification is the concept of **omnichannel integration**. Omnichannel goes beyond providing multiple channels for customer interaction, it is about creating a seamless, unified experience across all platforms. Each channel must not operate in isolation but rather as part of a cohesive whole, working together to deliver a consistent and continuous customer journey. In an ideal omnichannel ecosystem, customer interactions on one channel should effortlessly lead to the next, akin to a well-orchestrated symphony where each instrument contributes to a harmonious whole. Each touchpoint is not just a standalone interaction but a **'digital handshake'** that seamlessly passes the customer to the next touchpoint. This is akin to a relay race where the baton is smoothly passed from one runner to the next, keeping the momentum going. The bar for customer expectations is perpetually rising. This constructive interaction is crucial in today's digital milieu where customer journeys are increasingly complex and non-linear. A customer's interaction with a brand could start from an online search, move through various digital platforms, and culminate in a physical store purchase. Understanding and optimizing these varied touchpoints require a holistic view of the customer journey – a view that is only possible through effective data unification and omnichannel strategies.

Moreover, this integrated approach is vital in anticipating and meeting the rising expectations of customers. For instance, when a customer adds an item to their cart on a mobile app, they expect to see that update reflected when they switch to the browser-based version. This level of seamless transition across channels is not just a convenience but a fundamental expectation in today's digital world.

Let us assess where your company stands when it comes to consistency across channels.

**Assessment: Evaluating the Current State of Consistency**

 A comprehensive **data audit** is the foundation of this phase. Businesses need to employ specialized software to scrutinize existing data repositories, assessing for fragmentation, data silos, and inconsistencies. This audit should map out where each type of data is stored – whether in a CRM system for customer details, analytics tools for website behavior, or social media monitoring platforms for engagement metrics. The audit helps in identifying gaps in data collection and integration, which are essential for a coherent understanding of the customer journey.

In terms of omnichannel experience, the assessment involves leveraging **analytical tools** to track and understand customer navigation paths across various platforms. This is not just about knowing where customers come from, it is about comprehending their entire journey and interaction with the brand. Examining metrics like conversion rates, cross-channel engagement rates, or multi-platform customer retention rates reveals patterns and potential bottlenecks in the customer journey.

This assessment should also include a detailed **mapping of the customer journey** across all touchpoints. This mapping acts like a blueprint, outlining each possible customer interaction, and importantly, the interconnections between these touchpoints. The aim is to understand not only the standalone impact of each channel but also how they collectively contribute to a seamless customer experience. This could involve drawing lines of data flow, preference synchronizing, and emotional continuity across channels, serving as a script for the customer experience.

Another key element in this phase is **benchmarking the company's processes** against industry standards or competitors. Tools like Google Analytics Benchmarking or industry reports provide comparative data that is invaluable in understanding where a company stands in its data unification journey. This benchmarking should focus on specific metrics relevant to the company's goals and industry norms.

Lastly, direct **human feedback** plays a crucial role in the assessment phase. Despite the wealth of data and analytics available, the value of customer feedback, gathered through surveys, feedback forms, or interviews, cannot be overstated. This feedback offers nuanced insights into customer satisfaction and experience that may not be captured through quantitative data alone.

### Action: Unify Data and Craft Consistency

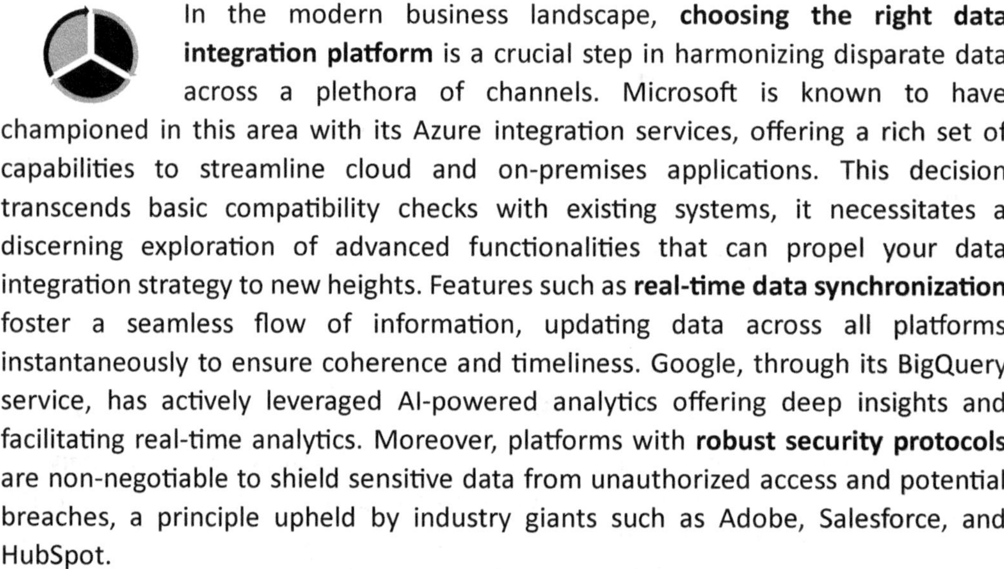

In the modern business landscape, **choosing the right data integration platform** is a crucial step in harmonizing disparate data across a plethora of channels. Microsoft is known to have championed in this area with its Azure integration services, offering a rich set of capabilities to streamline cloud and on-premises applications. This decision transcends basic compatibility checks with existing systems, it necessitates a discerning exploration of advanced functionalities that can propel your data integration strategy to new heights. Features such as **real-time data synchronization** foster a seamless flow of information, updating data across all platforms instantaneously to ensure coherence and timeliness. Google, through its BigQuery service, has actively leveraged AI-powered analytics offering deep insights and facilitating real-time analytics. Moreover, platforms with **robust security protocols** are non-negotiable to shield sensitive data from unauthorized access and potential breaches, a principle upheld by industry giants such as Adobe, Salesforce, and HubSpot.

Parallel to technological prowess, crafting a **structured data governance framework** emerges as a cornerstone in the data unification journey. IBM has been championing strong governance frameworks to ensure data quality and security. This blueprint should outline protocols governing data safeguarding measures and usage policies, orchestrating a harmonious flow in data handling processes. An iterative nature of this framework ensures it evolves with your data unification strategy, remaining receptive to enhancements and refinements. Regular audits stand as a vigilant guardian ensuring the system's agility and readiness to adapt to emerging necessities (visit section 3.5.2.3 Infrastructural foundation – Providing the Systems and Platforms for AI on page 286 to better understand the data infrastructure).

At the heart of any consistency is a robust database that captures the essence of each customer through data points gathered from every interaction across all channels. This is the **Single Client View (SCV) database**. More than just a data repository, it acts as a dynamic profile that updates in real-time, ensuring that any interaction across any channel is informed by the most current and complete data available. Amazon utilizes SCV databases to enhance the customer shopping experience, leveraging a vast amount of data to make smart product recommendations based on individual browsing and purchasing histories.

**Single Client View: A Concrete Intersection of Regulatory Adherence and Technological Elegance**

Single Client View (SCV) is both an art and a science, a synthesis of regulatory precision and technological innovation. In the complex environment of financial services, it emerges as a strategic linchpin anchoring institutions in an environment of enhanced compliance and enriched customer insights.

Regulatory landscapes, marked by their stringent and dynamic nature, necessitate a fluid and responsive data management system. For instance, in the wake of regulations like GDPR in Europe or CCPA in California, institutions are mandated to offer clients not just access to their data but insights and control over its usage. SCV, in this context, is not a luxury but an imperative.

Technologically, the SCV narrative is woven into the sophisticated fabric of data architecture and management. Consider a global bank with a diverse clientele spread across multiple geographies and segments. The challenge is not just data volume but its variety, velocity, and veracity. A robust data architecture lies at the core, where technologies like Hadoop and Spark enable the handling of massive datasets with agility, although some of the expectations are not yet met. For example, a client's transaction data, social media interactions, and customer service records are ingested and processed in real-time. Data lakes come into play, storing petabytes of data, making it accessible and ready for analytics. The management processes are the unsung heroes. For instance, an automated system might flag inconsistencies in a client's data – perhaps conflicting contact information. The process ensures data validation and cleaning, assuring that the SCV reflects accuracy and consistency. Every interaction, transaction, and engagement is logged, and analytics tools sift through this data to offer insights.

Imagine a wealth management advisor having access to an SCV that reflects a client's financial transactions, investment preferences, risk appetite, and even sentiments expressed during customer service interactions. The advisor does not just see numbers but a narrative that informs personalized service delivery.

The integration of AI amplifies SCV's potency. Machine learning models, for example, analyze a client's transaction patterns to predict future behavior. A client making frequent international transactions might be offered a customized package with reduced forex fees and enhanced global access. SCV is not a static concept but a dynamic asset, bridging regulatory adherence and technological sophistication. It is a story of informed decision-making, where compliance meets innovation, and every piece of data is a golden thread weaving the harmonious tapestry of personalized and compliant financial service delivery.

Acknowledging that data unification is a continuous, adaptive journey paves the way for a strategy that is both dynamic and resilient. SAP stands as a testament to the on-going effort in adapting to technological innovations and fluctuating customer anticipations, laying down the bedrock for a customer-centric strategy that is resilient and evolving. Through efforts in integrating data across all conceivable digital touchpoints, businesses lay a foundation for a strategy envisioned to stand resilient, gracefully evolving to meet challenges head-on, sculpting a pathway steeped in endurance and success over time. Data unification is far from a static, one-time process. It is an evolutionary journey that adapts and grows with both technological advancements and shifting customer expectations. By taking calculated steps towards integrating data across all digital touchpoints, businesses are not merely streamlining their operations, they are laying down the cornerstone for a customer-centric strategy that stands the test of time.

As the unification system reaches a zenith of proficiency, the focus shifts to leveraging this consolidated database to enhance customer experiences exponentially. Adobe has been at the forefront in using unified data for more personalized customer experiences. Strategies should be envisioned that sculpt algorithms capable of analyzing unified data, segmenting customers with precision, and crafting marketing campaigns that resonate with targeted demographics.

**Case persistence across channels** ensures a seamless continuation when and where a customer wants. The days of re-keying data are long gone, updates on conditions must now be made transparent to maintain a high level of customer satisfaction. Apple, a leader in this field, allows users to switch between devices seamlessly, maintaining all data and activity status without any issues. The handoff feature stands as a testimony to this.

Omnichannel strategy is not a one-time setup. It demands **regular A/B tests, performance reviews, and customer satisfaction surveys**. Detailed reports generated from these tests and surveys should be analyzed and acted upon to ensure the Omnichannel Experience remains top-notch. Netflix excels in utilizing customer feedback and A/B testing, continually tweaking its platform for a customized and enjoyable user experience.

Effective omnichannel systems modify content dynamically across platforms based on the customer's behavior, embodying fluid personalization. A finely tuned system could, for instance, lead a company's desktop website to display products related to sustainable living after a user reads a related blog post on the mobile app. Etsy successfully utilizes this strategy, enhancing user experiences and boosting sales through data-driven insights.

### 3.3.1.2.3   Attractive Content: The Universal Magnet for Digital Engagement

Content is your first impression, and on-going relationship builder rolled into one.

**Awareness: The Importance of Attractive Content**

Think beyond generic blog posts and consider a multi-media approach that combines video, podcasts, infographics, and interactive quizzes.

Engagement hinges on content that draws attention, encourages interaction, and is memorable. Crafting such content requires a kaleidoscope of multimedia, interactive features, and personalized touches, transforming each piece into a distinct experience, tailored to diverse audiences.

**Multi-media content** has transcended being a nice-to-have and is now a cornerstone of digital engagement. Companies akin to BuzzFeed demonstrate mastery in this domain. BuzzFeed crafts a mix of content types, from quick, engaging quizzes to in-depth articles and visually arresting infographics, each piece carefully curated to cater to varied audience preferences and informational appetites. The brand's success emanates from its ability to balance entertainment and information, ensuring that each content piece, regardless of its format, offers tangible value and fosters engagement.

The narrative of **personalization** is being rewritten, with platforms like Netflix leading the charge. It is no longer about superficial customizations, it is a combination of algorithms and insights. Netflix employs sophisticated machine learning algorithms, crafting recommendations that echo with individuals' specific viewing patterns, preferences, and contexts. Every suggested movie or series is a testament to the platform's commitment to offering bespoke viewing experiences, ensuring users feel seen, heard, and valued.

As we traverse the digital content landscape, the **adaptation of content to diverse platforms** emerges as a cardinal element. Coca-Cola exemplifies this strategy, weaving a narrative that, though consistent in its core message, is tailored in its delivery to resonate with the distinct audience and contextual nuances of each platform. It is a symphony of storytelling that is as diverse as it is unified, ensuring the brand's message permeates, engages, and captivates across the digital spectrum. Amidst this content renaissance, the **'Skim, Swim, and Dive' approach** embodies the stratification of content depth to cater to diverse audience inclinations. It is a story of breadth and depth, where 'Skim' caters to the quick browsers, offering succinct, visually engaging content. 'Swim' delves deeper, offering richer insights for those seeking a balance between depth and brevity. 'Dive' is an odyssey of comprehensive, in-depth content for the audience segment craving detailed, exhaustive insights. This layered approach ensures that content is a dynamic dialogue, resonating across the spectrum of audience engagement preferences.

In this enriched landscape, digital content morphs into a mosaic of experiences. It is a canvas where multimedia interactivity, profound personalization, platform-specific adaptation, and depth diversification converge. Each content piece is not just a component but an experience, not just seen or heard but felt and remembered, echoing in the crowded corridors of the digital space, ensuring every interaction is not just a touchpoint but a landmark in the audience's digital journey.

Does your company already prepare and provide attractive content?

**Assessment: Challenging the Attractiveness**

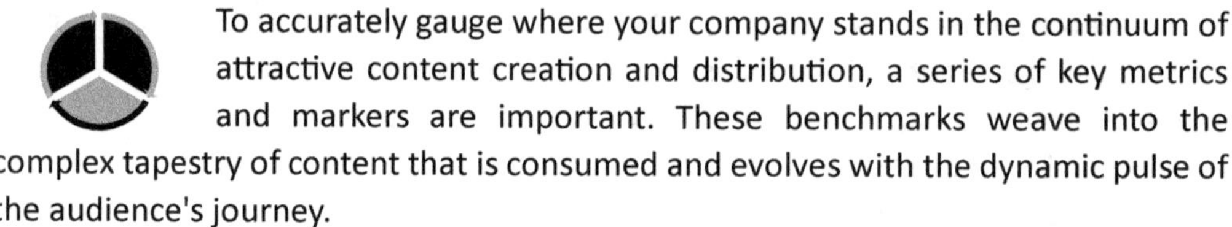 To accurately gauge where your company stands in the continuum of attractive content creation and distribution, a series of key metrics and markers are important. These benchmarks weave into the complex tapestry of content that is consumed and evolves with the dynamic pulse of the audience's journey.

**Engagement Metrics** are the soul of assessing content's resonance. These metrics transcend traditional analytics, diving into interaction rates, audience participation, and content sharing frequencies. Tools akin to Google Analytics and social media insights offer a panorama of data, highlighting content pieces that ignite conversations and encourage community engagement.

**Content Diversity Index** can be a good starting point. This metric evaluates the variety and balance in the types of content produced – from videos and podcasts to infographics and interactive quizzes. Organizations can perform a **content audit**, categorizing and analyzing each piece to measure diversity and identify gaps. For instance, if an enterprise mirrors the BuzzFeed model, a high index value would indicate a rich, diversified content portfolio.

The narrative of **personalization efficiency** is told vividly through **Customization Effectiveness Ratios**. This metric, inspired by the likes of Netflix, quantifies the alignment between content personalization and user engagement. It is not just about views but how well audiences connect with tailored content, evident in prolonged engagement durations and repeated interactions.

**Platform Adaptation Quotient** unveils the story of content's adaptability across diverse channels. Like Coca-Cola's nuanced storytelling, this quotient measures the consistency and customization of content narratives across platforms. **A/B testing** and multi-channel analytics can illuminate the effectiveness of platform-specific content strategies, ensuring brand stories are as compelling as they are cohesive.

The **Content Depth Engagement Metric** evolves from the 'Skim, Swim, Dive' approach. It evaluates audience engagement at various content depths. Analytics tools can segment audience interactions, offering insights into preferences for quick reads, moderate dives, or in-depth explorations. This stratified analysis illuminates the content's acceptance across diverse audience inclinations.

**User Experience Surveys** and **feedback mechanisms** are indispensable. Direct audience insights unveil the tangible and intangible elements that transform content consumption into experiences. These insights, coupled with **behavioral analytics**, weave a story of content that is not just seen and heard but felt and remembered.

The journey to assess attractive content production and provision is paved with analytics, direct audience feedback, and strategic insights. It unveils a narrative of content that lives and breathes with the audience, echoing in the corridors of digital spaces, marking not just touchpoints but significant landmarks in the audience's engagement journey. Every metric, every insight is a thread in the beautiful tapestry of content that engages and transforms the digital audience experience.

**Action: Deliver Attractive Content**

In the quest to produce engaging content, precision, and comprehensive actions are crucial. Each aspect, from employing robust analytics to carrying out detailed content audits, warrants an enhanced focus.

**Harnessing Advanced Analytics** takes a leaf from organizations like Airbnb that go beyond mere data collection to its deep analysis. Companies should establish a dedicated analytics team to comb through every strand of data. Using tools like Google Analytics or Mixpanel, initiate regular training sessions for teams to extract actionable insights effectively. Create weekly or bi-weekly reporting systems and monthly strategic review meetings to pinpoint and act on emerging trends, ensuring each content piece is a by-product of informed insights.

**Strategic Content Diversification** mirrors the multi-faceted approach of brands like LinkedIn. Begin by developing audience personas, conducting surveys, and utilizing AI-driven tools to glean deep insights into audience preferences. Form a creative team, comprising content strategists, writers, and multimedia creators, tasked with producing a diversified content aligned with the identified personas. Establish monthly review sessions to assess engagement levels and tweak content strategy accordingly.

**Platform-Specific Customization** can take inspiration from Nike's bespoke content approach. Initiate platform audit sessions to ascertain the distinctive dynamics of each. Establish platform-specific content teams equipped with customized tools and training to tailor content adeptly. Regularly review and adapt content strategies based on platform-specific analytics and user feedback, ensuring likability and engagement are optimized.

In **Content Depth Stratification**, The New York Times' model of varied depth can be instructional. Implement audience engagement surveys and use AI tools to analyze and categorize audience preferences. Develop editorial teams with specialists in creating 'skim', 'swim', and 'dive' content. Institute quarterly reviews to assess the engagement metrics of each content depth category and refine strategies to heighten relevance and interaction.

**Leveraging AI and Machine Learning** is about strategic implementation akin to Spotify's personalized playlists. Identify AI implementation areas, conduct pilot projects, and measure impacts. Employ AI specialists to optimize machine learning algorithms. Regularly review and enhance AI strategies through bi-monthly strategy refinement sessions, ensuring AI-driven personalization continually evolves, mirroring dynamic audience preferences.

---

**Navigating the World of Content Management Systems**

In the dynamically evolving digital landscape, having a powerful online presence is fundamental, and at the heart of this lies the strategic selection of a best-in-class Content Management System (CMS). A CMS is a software application that facilitates the creation, management, and optimization of digital content. In a world where companies are vying for digital prominence, the choice of CMS is often a notable change.

A crucial element of an effective CMS is a **user-friendly interface**. The platform must be intuitive and navigable, enabling users, including those with limited technical expertise, to manage content efficiently. WordPress excels in this area, offering a streamlined, user-centric interface that demystifies content management. **Flexibility and customization** are also vital. Companies should choose systems that enable tailoring of content and design to connect with the brand identity and audience preferences. Drupal stands out for its modular approach, offering a plethora of plugins and themes that cater to a diverse array of requirements, ensuring that each digital platform is a unique reflection of the brand it represents. In the context of **enterprise-grade solutions**, Adobe Experience Manager emerges as a formidable contender, offering a suite of tools designed for companies seeking to consolidate and elevate their content, delivering personalized experiences across various channels.

**SEO optimization** is another cornerstone in the context of digital visibility. The CMS should be ingrained with features that amplify SEO efforts, ensuring that content is not only engaging but highly discoverable. Joomla is renowned for its innate SEO features, serving as an ally in propelling businesses to the summit of search engine rankings. Security, in the digital expanse, is non-negotiable. Shopify and Squarespace are examples of CMS platforms known for robust security protocols that safeguard the website and user data, cultivating a digital environment where users interact with confidence.

The landscape of CMS is enriched by the entry of Censhare, a universal content management platform that prioritizes contextualization of content, delivering tailored experiences that match the specific nuances of diverse audience segments.

Moreover, a **strong support network and active community** is a treasure trove of resources and assistance. Platforms like WordPress provide access to a vast array of tutorials, forums, and customer service, ensuring that businesses navigate challenges with agility and efficiency. However, the journey is dotted with pitfalls. Overly complex systems can become an albatross, hampering operational efficiency. **Hidden costs** associated with additional features or plugins and scalability issues are other common challenges. In a world driven by mobile interactions, a CMS like Wix, known for its **exemplary mobile optimization**, emerges as a sanctuary, ensuring that the mobile user experience is as seamless and engaging as the desktop version.

It is about ensuring that the CMS reflects the business's unique needs and objectives, a robust, adaptable, and engaging foundation in the dynamic digital ecosystem.

**Collaborative Content Creation** draws inspiration from Google's collective creativity. Develop cross-functional content creation teams, facilitate regular brainstorming sessions using tools like Miro or Stormboard, and promote a culture of diverse input. Evaluate the diversity and creativity metrics of content through quarterly creative reviews, ensuring each piece is a harmonious blend of varied insights and creativity.

**Periodic Content Audits**, as exemplified by Shopify, are essential. Form audit teams with members from content creation, analytics, and strategy sectors. Implement tools like SEMrush or Ahrefs for detailed content performance analyses. Schedule bi-monthly audit meetings to delve into audit findings and create action plans for content refinement, ensuring content remains aligned with audience engagement patterns and SEO benchmarks.

Thus, with these enriched, detailed steps, businesses are equipped with a concrete, actionable plan. It is a roadmap where content, enriched by profound insights, creativity, and strategic precision, becomes a dynamic entity. Here, each content piece is not just created but orchestrated, ensuring the digital space is not just populated but enriched, echoing the vibrant, diverse, and evolving needs of the dynamic audience.

### 3.3.1.2.4 The Pinnacle of Business Strategy: Targeted User Experience

In the world of digital interactions, the influence of design extends far beyond mere aesthetics.

**Awareness: Making the Customer Happy**

Customer Experience (CX) creates the power of the user's journey, interweaving elements of visual appeal, navigational ease, and emotional resonance. Here, design elements are not isolated graphics or text, they are individual cogs in a complex machine built to deliver an unparalleled user experience (UX).

While visual elements often take center stage, **sensory experience design** expands the scope to include audio cues, haptic feedback, and even timing and animation. For example, consider a mobile app that emits a subtle 'ding' sound and vibrates slightly upon successfully completing a transaction. This engages multiple senses, reinforcing a sense of accomplishment and enhancing memorability.

**Design can function as an emotional accelerant**, amplifying the impact of every interaction. Is not just about the what, it is profoundly about the how. How does the customer feel during a webpage transition? How does the choice of color palette affect the user's emotional state? By recognizing the role of design in evoking specific emotional responses, brands can curate experiences that transcend mere transactions, metamorphosing into emotionally charged relationships.

But does your company fulfill the criteria for good Target User Experience?

**Assessment: Stress-testing the Target User Experience**

Start with an in-depth **design audit** that reviews every pixel of your digital interfaces. Go beyond just asking if the site is visually pleasing or easy to navigate. Ask how each design element contributes to the overarching user experience and emotional journey. Heuristic evaluations provide more analytical data, allowing you to identify gaps between your current design strategy and best practices in UX/UI design.

Typical analytics can tell you what a customer does, but they cannot tell you how a customer feels. **Emotional design metrics** aim to fill this gap. Sentiment analysis on customer feedback, heatmaps indicating where users spend the most time, and eye-tracking studies revealing where users look first on a page are some of the more advanced methods to quantitatively assess the emotional impact of your design choices.

The crown jewel in your assessment arsenal is the raw, **unfiltered reactions of real users** interacting with your digital touchpoints. By employing methodologies like user interviews, focus groups, and A/B testing of distinctive design elements, you gain a 360-degree view of the emotional landscape traversed by your customers. This is not just data, it is emotional cartography, mapping out the highs and lows of the user journey.

**Actions: Design Good Target User Experience**

In laying the foundations for an exceptional Target Customer Experience (CX), it is important to acknowledge that your target audience encompasses a diverse range of individuals. Commence by crafting **detailed customer personas**, leveraging deep insights and data analytics to sketch vivid representations of different customer groups. Companies should strive to be as insightful as Amazon in this respect, using personas to inform and enrich user experiences through targeted content and personalized recommendations, enhancing the shopping journey significantly[73]. Employ features such as interactive quizzes to engage younger demographics and graphical elements like detailed infographics to satisfy data-driven segments.

A next critical step involves the careful **layering of diverse design elements**, including strategic color choices and font styles to evoke desired emotional responses and shape user perceptions effectively. Taking cues from industry leaders like Apple, which ingeniously leverages the principles of color theory and typography to project an identity of innovation. Consider a palette that elicits trust and displays brand personality while ensuring typography mirrors the brand's identity to create a resonant visual harmony.

Dive into the finer details with **micro-interactions**, these are subtle design elements, such as animated buttons that change color upon interaction, or intuitive gestures that facilitate user navigation. Platforms like Airbnb serve as a great benchmark in this domain, presenting a delightful array of micro-interactions that not only guide users but also inject moments of joy in the user journey. These aspects can transform waiting times into engaging experiences, holding the user's attention, and enhancing their overall interaction with your platform.

Building trust through design should be a non-negotiable pillar in your strategy, **incorporating transparent data protection mechanisms and clearly displayed trust signals**. Taking a leaf from Shopify's book with their trust badges offering, can guide you in building a website that communicates safety and reliability effectively. Pair this with an easily accessible yet non-intrusive customer service chat bot to foster a reassuring and responsive environment.

---

**A Deeper Dive into Design Language**

The world of Design Language is not merely an artistic endeavor, it is a strategic orchestration of visual, interactive, and emotional elements, each engineered to craft a memorable, engaging, and consistent brand experience. Every color, shape, texture, and sound is a precise choice, a deliberate stroke in a larger masterpiece that transcends aesthetic appeal to encapsulate the brand's essence, ethos, and values.

In this sophisticated dialect, the nuances matter as much as the overt expressions. For instance, the subtlety of a shadow effect in the user interface, the fluidity of a transition animation, or the tactile experience of a physical product are all articulations of a brand's Design Language. These are not accidental but are the outcomes of rigorous research, iterative design processes, and user testing to ensure that every element not only resonates with the audience but is also anchored in usability and functionality.

---

[73] Chris Dawson on ChannelX: "The three Personas of Amazon Prime Members". Published online 16.07.2019, visited 08.04.2024. https://channelx.world/2019/07/the-three-personas-of-amazon-prime-members/

Apple's renowned Design Language offers a rich tapestry of details. Each product, from the sleek MacBook to the intuitive iPhone, embodies a harmonious blend of form and function. The choice of materials, the tactile experience, the visual aesthetics – every detail is a harmonized expression of Apple's commitment to quality, innovation, and user experience. Consider the iconic iPhone interface. Each icon is designed with precise geometry, the color choices are tested for visibility and emotional response, and the touch interactions are engineered for responsiveness and intuitiveness. These are not just design choices, they are strategic decisions that encapsulate Apple's brand identity and promise. Apple's use of sans-serif typography, for example, is not a mere aesthetic choice. It reflects the brand's commitment to clarity, simplicity, and elegance. The typeface is carefully chosen and tested to ensure readability, accessibility, and aesthetic harmony across different contexts and devices.

In a digital application or website, the navigation menu, the layout of content, the interactive elements – each is a strategic component of the Design Language. It is akin to a symphony where each instrument plays a critical role. When a user interacts with a brand, the transitions, the feedback sounds, the visual cues – each interaction is an opportunity for the brand to communicate, engage, and build a relationship.

A well-articulated Design Language goes beyond visual aesthetics and enters the domain of emotional and psychological engagement. It creates a sense of familiarity and predictability. Users know where to find what they are looking for, they know what to expect, and this consistency fosters trust, loyalty, and engagement.

Evaluation metrics like user engagement levels, time spent on the platform, and user feedback are critical in assessing the effectiveness of a Design Language. They offer insights into how users are responding, where the gaps are, and how the design can be optimized to enhance the user experience and engagement.

In the competitive landscape of branding, Design Language is not a peripheral element but a core strategy. It is the visual, interactive, and emotional embodiment of the brand's identity, values, and promise. It is a dialect that speaks silently yet powerfully, crafting experiences that linger, stories that convince, and bonds that endure in the ever-evolving inter-dependence of brand and audience engagement.

Steer clear of static designs, instead, opt for **real-time feedback mechanisms** that dynamically adapt to user behaviors, thus building a supportive and interactive user environment. Netflix's user interface stands as a testimony to the effectiveness of such strategies, evolving based on user preferences to offer a personalized browsing experience. Such mechanisms can include dynamically appearing help buttons that offer timely assistance, maintaining a nurturing and supportive digital environment.

An on-going, data-driven strategy is key to crafting a Target Customer Experience that is not just satisfying but truly enchanting. Companies like Google have paved the way in this endeavor, pioneering a culture of continuous refinement based on user feedback and emotional metrics. It involves a systematic approach to data analysis to ensure that the customer journey is not just enchanting but also emotionally compelling and strategically nuanced, promising a standout presence in a fiercely competitive digital space.

When we discuss the next level of digital engagement, it is impossible to overlook the sweeping influence of Augmented Reality (AR), Virtual Reality (VR), and the burgeoning Metaverse – Extended Reality (XR). Companies like IKEA have already made groundbreaking progress by incorporating AR into their IKEA Place app[74]. This app allows customers to virtually 'place' furniture items in their homes via their smartphone screens, solving a major pain point in furniture shopping – the uncertainty around how a piece will fit or look in a given space. In the virtual reality space, Oculus Rift and HTC Vive are offering fully immersive 3D environments, allowing users to climb Mount Everest or explore underwater worlds without ever leaving their living rooms.

**Awareness: What is Real, in the Future?**

 AR and VR technologies began as tools for gaming and simulation. However, these technologies have found critical applications in various fields. In healthcare, VR is being used to simulate surgical procedures, providing medical professionals with safe and realistic training grounds. The Metaverse, meanwhile, is evolving beyond a gaming space, it is turning into a fully functional digital society. Platforms like Roblox and Second Life offer virtual real estate, digital economies, and even governance structures.

In this digital renaissance, **AR and VR are acting as catalysts to merge the physical and digital worlds**. Snapchat has democratized the use of AR through its filters, enabling users to transform real-world environments or facial features in real-time via smartphones. Virtual conferences and meetings in the Metaverse are doing away with geographic limitations, redefining how corporate interactions occur.

Is your company already preparing its channels for the future?

**Assessment: Spotting Opportunities for Digital Enhancement of our Reality**

 Traditional key performance indicators (KPIs) like click-through rates or screen time do not capture the nuanced engagement levels that AR and VR can offer. New metrics have emerged, like 'User Engagement Depth', which measures how interactively and meaningfully a user is engaged in a virtual environment. Specialized analytics tools from platforms like Unity offer details, like 'heatmaps', which show where a user looked the most during a VR experience or which virtual objects were interacted with the most during an AR simulation.

---

[74] On IKEA company website: "Mit der IKEA App per Augmented Reality einrichten". Visited 08.04.2024. https://www.ikea.com/de/de/this-is-ikea/corporate-blog/ikea-place-app-augmented-reality-puba55c67c0

Feedback is not just about star ratings or textual reviews anymore. AR and VR platforms are incorporating in-experience feedback mechanisms where users can provide reactions while still being in the virtual world. Eye-tracking technology and emotional response analysis are among advanced techniques being used to collect granular feedback.

Several tools and platforms offer insights into competitive AR, VR, and Metaverse strategies. Companies should employ intelligence tools like SimilarWeb or SEMrush, tailored to track competitor activities in these areas. Case studies, whitepapers, and technical audits are valuable resources for understanding how your competitors are implementing or benefiting from AR, VR, and the Metaverse.

**Action: Explore the Limits of Reality Enhancement**

Before sinking significant resources into a full-blown experience, companies should focus on creating a Minimum Viable Product (MVP) – a scaled-down, functional version of the envisioned experience – to validate the concept. For instance, using platforms like Apple's ARKit or Google's ARCore can allow you to build and test a simple AR prototype that lets users preview how a new coffee machine would look in their kitchens. This MVP approach reduces financial risks and allows for flexible adjustments based on real-world testing.

Usability in the digital reality spectrum is unlike any other medium. Designers must consider factors like preventing motion sickness in VR experiences or ensuring information is not cluttered in an AR overlay. Software like Adobe XD and Sketch are now offering AR/VR-specific design functionalities. Businesses need to invest in specialized UX/UI talent who understand the unique design philosophies these new realities demand.

Technologies like AR, VR, and the Metaverse are in a perpetual state of evolution, driven by constant user feedback and rapid technological advancements. Companies need to establish robust mechanisms for frequently updating their Digital Experiences. For example, VR game developers often release weekly updates, which not only fix bugs but also add new features based on community feedback. The specialized nature of AR, VR, and Metaverse technologies often means that in-house teams lack the necessary expertise to fully realize a project. Collaborating with external agencies or technology providers can add invaluable dimensions to a project. For instance, Apple's collaboration with Pixar to create the USDZ format has helped to standardize AR experiences across various platforms and devices.

The journey to a stellar Omnichannel Experience is about recognizing the individuality of each customer, understanding the intricacies of their journey, and ensuring that the brand's voice remains harmonious throughout. By championing these principles, businesses set the stage for an experience that is not just seamless but also resonant.

### 3.3.2  Customer-centric Journeys

With today's learned behavior of users, the end-to-end customer journey has become a critical framework for understanding and enhancing the **complete experience a customer has with a brand**. This journey encompasses every interaction, from the first moment of brand discovery to post-purchase interactions, and even the potential for repeat business. Its scope is vast, but so too is its importance. Apple, for instance, has masterfully crafted a journey that spans not just its innovative products but also the in-store and after-sales experiences. Walk into any Apple store, and you are immediately greeted by the seamless fusion of product design, technological assistance, and even educational sessions. This comprehensive approach applies across the markets and has become synonymous with the brand's identity. Similarly, IKEA is not just a furniture store, it is an experience. From the moment customers step into an IKEA showroom, they are taken on a journey. It starts with inspiring room setups, moves to easy product selection, and culminates in the famed DIY assembly, making customers feel a deeper connection to their living spaces. Alibaba has reshaped the e-commerce landscape. Their platform is not just about buying, it is an end-to-end journey of product discovery, entertainment, digital payments, and even travel bookings. The Alibaba experience reflects the integrated lifestyle of the modern consumer in China.

**What the C-Suite needs to know**

1. Strategic Differentiator: The customer journey has evolved from a simple operational element to a key strategic differentiator. Well-mapped and optimized journeys can set a brand apart, fostering loyalty, driving engagement, and bolstering the bottom line. It is not just about the product or service anymore, it is about the entire experience wrapped around it.

2. Adaptive Evolution: Customer journeys are not static, they continuously evolve based on market trends, technological advancements, and consumer behavior shifts. Constant evaluation and adaptation are crucial. Being proactive, rather than reactive, ensures that the brand remains at the forefront of customer expectations.

3. Comprehensive Customer Understanding: The Digital Journey Canvas provides an all-encompassing view of the customer experience, emphasizing the importance of detailed insights into every interaction. This understanding is critical for creating a unified and personalized customer journey that drives satisfaction and loyalty.

4. Strategic Optimization and Integration: Utilizing advanced analytics and cross-functional collaboration, the Canvas allows for the meticulous evaluation and optimization of customer touchpoints and journeys. Ensuring seamless integration of these journeys and clear ownership of the process is vital for delivering a cohesive and resonant customer experience.

5. Digital Product Journeys are essential to fostering enriching customer experiences, they should be meticulously designed and continuously refined based on detailed assessments like Journey NPS,

emotional feedback, journey duration, abandonment rate, and path analysis to ensure each touchpoint is effective and contributes to a seamless, harmonious product flow akin to Tesla's integration of software and hardware for an unparalleled automotive experience.

6. Crafting a 'Product North Star', which harmonizes customer expectations, company goals, competitive insights, and technological advancements, guiding the development of seamless digital product journeys and ensuring alignment with strategic objectives and customer satisfaction is essential.

7. A product journey roadmap is a strategic narrative that integrates detailed feature mapping, minimalistic MVP development, and iterative enhancements based on customer feedback and market insights. It is a living entity that requires agility and flexibility, adapting to dynamic markets and evolving customer preferences to ensure market success and customer delight.

8. The product backlog is a critical, adaptive document that organizes features, enhancements, and requirements, allowing for organized flexibility, strategic prioritization, and collaborative refinement. It is essential to harness cross-functional team insights and align with customer expectations and market trends, making customer involvement in ideation and co-creation a cornerstone of the product development process.

But why are Customer-Centric Journeys so important?

The secret to capturing and holding attention is the creation and development of customer-centric journeys. Understanding this can be likened to acquiring the golden key that unlocks a treasure trove of opportunities for both customers and companies (visit section 1.1 What is Digital Success on page 13 to understand how much customer journeys contribute to Digital Success). At the heart of these journeys is an emphasis on customer satisfaction, a pillar built on the dual foundations of simplicity and efficiency. Imagine a digital pathway where every step is intuitive, where services and products are easy to find, to understand, and to use. It is a journey that anticipates the customer's needs, presenting solutions before they even formulate the questions, thereby creating a frictionless and joyous interaction at every juncture. It offers not just satisfaction, but a delightful experience characterized by ease and efficiency, building a relationship where customers feel genuinely understood and catered to. The journey is also crafted to foster deep **engagement through the relevance of each step**. This is not just about bombarding the customer with information but curating experiences that are tailor-made, relevant, and deeply personal. It means engaging narratives that meet individual preferences, creating a rich overview of interactions where each touchpoint feels like a dialogue rather than a monologue, encouraging active participation and engaging a community where every voice is valued. Moreover, these pathways are designed to naturally lead to **conversion**, guided by a structure that offers direct execution capabilities at every conceivable point. Picture a journey where every step feels natural, where one action flows seamlessly into the next, creating a symphony of interactions that lead customers naturally and almost inevitably towards a satisfying conclusion, be it a purchase, a subscription, or another form of conversion, achieved not through pressure, but through understanding and fulfilling genuine needs and desires.

From a corporate lens, the customer-centric journey approach is not just outward-facing, it also nurtures **operational finesse within the organization**. It engenders a workflow that is like a well-oiled machine, optimizing processes to eliminate redundancies and drive efficiency from the front end to the back end. Think of it as a straight-through process that is free from unnecessary bumps, a highway that leads straight to the destination without unwarranted detours, saving time, energy, and resources, and creating an environment where every task is performed with a precision that speaks of mastery and understanding.

**Financial prudence** is another inbuilt advantage as well, allowing companies to focus their investments on areas that genuinely matter, avoiding the wasteful dispersion of resources and ensuring that every dollar spent is a step towards enhancing **perceptual resonance**, creating a harmony between the customer's expectations and the company's deliverables. It is a finely tuned instrument where every note plays to enhance the customer's experience while simultaneously achieving the company's objectives, creating a melody of success that resonates with both parties. Venturing into the vibrant landscape of the digital market with a customer-centric approach is the beacon that guides businesses to the shores of Digital Success.

But what makes good Customer-Centric Journeys?

We need to establish an overview of all journeys, to ensure a seamless flow despite dependencies among products. Enters the **Digital Journey Canvas**. Within the holistic view of the canvas develop the individual **Digital Product Journeys**, where each product owner is responsible for crafting seamless flows when customers are exploring the respective product.

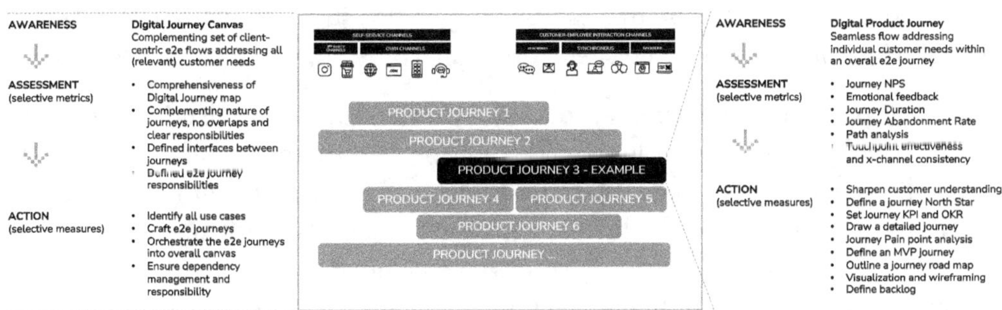


*Figure 23: How the Digital Journey Canvas and Digital Product Journeys play together*

### 3.3.2.1 Digital Journey Canvas – Comprehensive View of Customer Experiences

At its core, the canvas encourages a **holistic view of the customer's journeys**, emphasizing the interdependence of various stages and touchpoints in the customer's interaction with the business. This approach facilitates a deep connection with customers, building a symbiotic pathway that triggers trust and satisfaction.

**Awareness: A Comprehensive View of the Digital Customer Experiences**

The Customer Journey Canvas emerges as a great instrument that encapsulates the broad connection between businesses and their clientele. It is a **visual map** that illuminates the multi-faceted interactions customers have with a company, marking an important first step in the path of optimizing customer experiences. It weaves a tapestry of complementary pathways that not only enhance the depth of engagement with the clientele but also nurture a robust and enduring relationship, presenting a rich, uninterrupted, and seamless customer experience.

The canvas is crafted with insight and precision, portraying an overview of the **customer's holistic journey**. This ensures that there is a **consistent narrative**, avoiding overlaps and ensuring that each product journey within the canvas complements each other, creating a coherent and synergized pathway towards customer satisfaction and engagement. Next to each other the product journeys are mutually exclusive, together they are collectively exhaustive[75]. Every touchpoint, interaction, and experience is illustrated, offering an in-depth understanding of the customer's pathway from initial exploration, through engagement to conversion and loyalty. Touchpoints, emotions, and experiences are laid bare, offering a granular view of the customer's interactions and emotional connections at each juncture. The importance of this tool in gaining insights into customer behaviors, preferences, and pain points cannot be overstated. It is like a magnifying glass that reveals not only the path the customers take but also the emotions and motivations that underline their journey. Every area of the canvas reveals not just actions but the deeper sentiments, aspirations, and the silent, often unexpressed, needs of the customers.

In strategic planning, the Customer Journey Canvas becomes a wellspring of insights. It goes beyond surface-level interactions, diving deep into customer's emotions, expectations, and latent needs. With this tool, businesses no longer need to rely on assumptions or generic data. Instead, they are equipped with precise, targeted insights that form the bedrock of personalized and impactful engagement strategies. In a world where customization is king, the canvas ensures that every interaction,

---

[75] Barbara Minto on the McKinsey Alumni Center website: "MECE: I invented it, so I get to say how to pronounce it". Visited 08.04.2024. https://www.mckinsey.com/alumni/news-and-events/global-news/alumni-news/barbara-minto-mece-i-invented-it-so-i-get-to-say-how-to-pronounce-it

every message, and every offering is tailored to meet the individual customer's needs and desires. It transforms every touchpoint into an opportunity to enhance satisfaction, instill loyalty, and augment the overall customer experience.

The Digital Journey Canvas is indispensable in crafting the overall customer experience that is not only satisfying and enjoyable but also deeply personal and resonant, striking a chord with customers at every touchpoint, and fostering a relationship that is built on customer engagement and satisfaction.

But where does your company stand when it comes to a comprehensive Digital Journey Canvas?

**Assessment: Testing the Quality of Digital Journey Canvas**

The genesis of this exploration is rooted in the grounded understanding of the company's existing placement on the digital journey canvas. Every stroke and contour of the current journey maps come under scrutiny, aided by a variety of metrics that serve as the compass, guiding the evaluation of their maturity and effectiveness.

One of the first ports of call is the evaluation of **the depth and breadth of the use case inventory**. Visualize this process as peeling back the multiple, complex layers of an onion. Every layer reveals a new dimension of customer insights, stretching from explicit customer preferences to the subtle yet impactful nuances of seasonal market trends and behavioral shifts. This exploration involves leveraging advanced analytical tools and methodologies. Implement AI and machine-learning algorithms to deeply mine customer data, extracting patterns and insights that are not just rich but actionable. Every piece of data, every customer interaction, is a puzzle piece, contributing to the complete, holistic image of the customer's use cases. Gap analysis is the compass in this exploration. It is not just a tool but a strategic ally, illuminating the obscured or often overlooked opportunities Nestled within the paths of customer interactions. The canvas of customer engagement is vast, and within its expansive boundaries, lies potential areas teeming with growth prospects – waiting to be discovered, nurtured, and optimized. A suite of specialized tools and metrics including customer friction points, conversion rates, and engagement levels become the magnifying glass in this endeavor. Each tool is selected with precision, tailored to unveil specific intricacies and areas that are ripe for refinement and optimization. Customer friction points are identified through detailed **customer feedback analysis and user experience testing**. Every feedback, comment, or complaint is a valuable insight, pointing towards the areas requiring immediate attention. Implement real-time feedback collection systems, utilize AI-powered sentiment analysis, and conduct user testing sessions to capture and analyze these friction points in-depth. **Conversion rates** are another crucial metric, shedding light on the efficacy of the customer's journey from awareness to purchase. Dive into analytics – segregate data based on demographics, behaviors, and interactions. Utilize tools like Google Analytics and Adobe Analytics to capture, analyze, and interpret this data, translating numbers into actionable strategies for enhancement. **Engagement levels** are the pulse of the customer's journey. Monitor interactions across digital platforms – social media, websites, or mobile apps. Implement tracking pixels, use heatmaps, and analyze user navigation paths to understand how customers are interacting, what is attracting their attention, and where they are dropping off. In the orchestration of these evaluations, **collaboration and cross-functional alignment** emerge as the keystones. Involve teams from marketing to IT, customer service to product development. Foster a culture of collective insights, where data and findings are shared, analyzed, and acted upon collaboratively. This synergy is instrumental in not just identifying but effectively addressing and optimizing the identified gaps and opportunities.

As the journey spirals deeper, the **harmonization of different product journeys within the canvas** takes precedence. It is a ballet of sorts, where each product journey, with its unique rhythm and melody, is evaluated for its contribution to the grand symphony of customer experience, to the Customer Journey Canvas. The **integration index** stands as a testament to the symbiosis and constructive interaction amongst diverse product journeys, a metric echoing the harmonious or discordant notes within the customer experience symphony. The narrative of assessment is enriched by the incorporation of **dependency management**. Here, metrics like **error rate, system downtimes, and bottleneck analysis** are the silent sentinels, vigilantly monitoring and signaling any impending disruptions or obstacles that could mar the fluidity of the customer journey. In the context of **interface mapping**, touchpoint effectiveness score and customer feedback transform into the architects and sculptors, shaping and refining the bridges that connect various stages of the journey. They are not just structural entities but artistic expressions of the brand's commitment to seamless, intuitive, and enriched customer interactions.

The **feedback loops** are the lifeblood of the continuous evolution of the Customer Journey Canvas. Metrics like **customer feedback scores and the rate of feedback implementation** into the system are the catalysts propelling the dynamic, adaptive, and responsive nature of the customer journeys, ensuring they are not static but living entities, pulsating with the evolving rhythms of customer expectations and market trends.

As the curtain falls on the assessment, the spotlight shines on **end-to-end journey responsibilities**. Metrics such as **team performance scores, role clarity indices, and individual accountability matrices** morph into the litmus tests. They evaluate the clarity, definition, and orchestration of roles and responsibilities, echoing the harmony or dissonance within the internal teams navigating the dance of delivering exemplary customer journeys.

Traversing the path of understanding your company's stance in developing a digital journey canvas involves a mosaic of metric analyses. Now, what can a company do to establish a comprehensive Digital Journey Canvas?

**Action: Paint the Digital Journey Canvas**

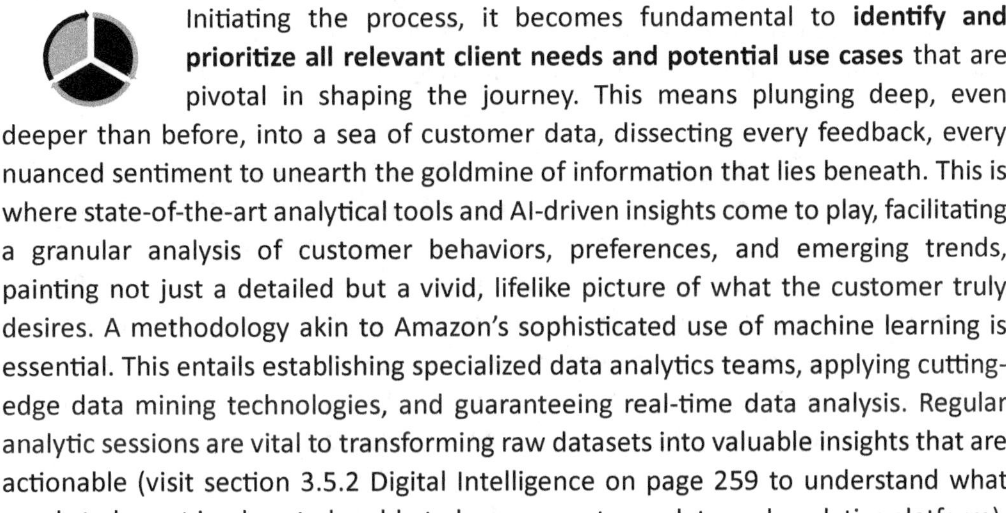

Initiating the process, it becomes fundamental to **identify and prioritize all relevant client needs and potential use cases** that are pivotal in shaping the journey. This means plunging deep, even deeper than before, into a sea of customer data, dissecting every feedback, every nuanced sentiment to unearth the goldmine of information that lies beneath. This is where state-of-the-art analytical tools and AI-driven insights come to play, facilitating a granular analysis of customer behaviors, preferences, and emerging trends, painting not just a detailed but a vivid, lifelike picture of what the customer truly desires. A methodology akin to Amazon's sophisticated use of machine learning is essential. This entails establishing specialized data analytics teams, applying cutting-edge data mining technologies, and guaranteeing real-time data analysis. Regular analytic sessions are vital to transforming raw datasets into valuable insights that are actionable (visit section 3.5.2 Digital Intelligence on page 259 to understand what needs to be put in place to be able to leverage a strong data and analytics platform).

Next on the canvas comes the exhilarating role of high-level sketching **e2e journeys** – details will follow in the section on Digital Product Journeys – each embodying a living, breathing path, vibrant with minutiae and animated with boundless possibilities. This step is likened to being an avant-garde artist with a palette of endless colors, choosing each hue with heightened precision to depict a journey that is not only functional but aesthetically gratifying, akin to a masterpiece. Apple highlights this through its product ecosystem that offers a seamless user experience, with devices and services that work impeccably together, offering a blend of technology and aesthetics that is unparalleled. Companies should organize multi-disciplinary workshops, use prototyping tools, and focus on iterating designs to achieve an optimal blend of functionality and aesthetics.

As the individual journeys take shape, the spotlight graciously turns to integrating all relevant product journeys into a consistent, fluid, and overall Digital Journey Canvas. Picture it as a well-curated gallery, where each painting, rich with detail and narrative, tells a part of the grand, overarching story, and yet, they all resonate with a harmonious, unifying theme. This stage employs visual analytics and evocative graphic representations to bring forth a vibrant mosaic of journeys, where each piece is a work of art, yet together they narrate a compelling, heart-grabbing story that matches every customer's aspirations and needs. In the domain of **weaving individual paths into a cohesive overall journey canvas**, ensuring a seamless alignment of various customer journeys is critical. Adopting a strategy reminiscent of Airbnb's tailored experiences requires the creation of visual storyboards and routine cross-functional team collaborations to refine integration points. Here, **dependency management** becomes crucial. Companies need to identify and map out the interdependencies among individual Product Journeys. Creating a matrix that outlines these dependencies, routinely updating it, and employing it as a dynamic tool for cross-functional collaborations ensures that Product Journeys are not siloed but are harmoniously interwoven, delivering a seamless, unified customer experience.

Anchoring this complex structure demands establishing **clear responsibility for the Digital Journey Canvas**, confiding in a maestro, perhaps a product owner or an initiative lead, who stands tall with a visionary gaze, orchestrating every minute element with a maestro's grace and expertise. They ensure a rhythmic flow of experiences, perfectly tuned to reflect the customer's heartbeat, creating a symphony of harmonious melodies that touch the soul. In addition, the ownerships for the underlying Digital Product Journeys need to be established (visit section 3.7.1 Agile and Adaptive Culture on page 324 to understand empowered product organizations).

As we step back to admire this overall structure, what unfolds before our very eyes is a digital journey canvas that stands as a testimony to relentless pursuit, unabating passion, and a depth of expertise that is simply unmatched. It narrates a saga, a story vibrant with details, rich with engrossing narratives, where every stitch tells a compelling story, every hue narrates a profound emotion. Disney stands as a hallmark in this domain, creating theme park experiences that go beyond mere amusement, encapsulating deeper emotional messages, fostering connections, and creating cherished memories that connect with visitors on a profound level, promising not just a journey but a transcendent and profoundly satisfying experience.

Within the Digital Journey Canvas, the individual Digital Product Journeys can be brought to life.

### 3.3.2.2 Digital Product Journey- Seamless Product Flow

Diving even deeper, we commence breaking down this vibrant picture further, dissecting the overall e2e journeys into contributing product journeys with defined interfaces, a task akin to sculpting a masterpiece from a block of pure, untouched marble. Every chisel, every alteration is deliberate, transforming a solid block into a marvel of details and enigmatic pathways. This endeavor demands defining pathways and nodes of interaction, establishing a rich matrix of responsibilities **that ensure a seamless combination of elements, each moving gracefully, synchronized in perfect**

**harmony, a ballet of exquisite execution.** Tesla's approach to integrating software and hardware offers an unparalleled automotive experience, ensuring that every aspect of the vehicle is harmonized, offering an elegant and innovative solution that pushes the boundaries of what is possible[76].

Let us dive deeper into understanding the Digital Product Journeys, their assessment metrics, and the strategic measures companies can adopt to bring these dynamic journeys to life.

**Awareness: A Seamless Flow Around One Product**

**Digital Product Journeys stand as a cornerstone in carving out enriching customer experiences.** These are designed pathways that steer customers seamlessly through a series of interactions and engagements with a digital product, driving not only user satisfaction but delight. Key components of the Digital Product Journey can be summarized in an overall **product compendium**, outlining the North Star, the OKR, the journey map, as well as the back log.

The genesis of these journeys lies in a clearly articulated **Product North Star**, a visionary compass that encapsulates the ultimate ambition and the core value that the product intends to offer its customers. Like the overall company North Star also the Product North Stars must be grounded on the strategic foundations of customer expectations, company objectives, competitive arena, and technical opportunities. Each product owner must be on top of these developments for the respective product. Imagine a digital wellness application that uses the North Star of 'holistic wellbeing', every feature, blog post, and notification would reflect this central theme, perhaps offering integrated meditation sessions, nutrition guides, or encouraging notifications to keep users aligned with their wellness goals.

To bring this North Star to fruition, it is critical to set forth with clearly defined **Product Objectives and Key Results (OKRs)**. This goal-setting framework, utilized by companies like Google, ensures that the entire team is synchronized in their efforts, aligning their micro-objectives to echo the central mission. It serves as a rudder steering the developmental efforts, keeping them focused and on track. For instance, an e-commerce platform might set a quarterly OKR to reduce the cart abandonment rate by enhancing the checkout process, thereby aiming to provide a smoother and more reassuring path to purchase.

As the blueprint of this immersive customer experience, the **journey map** comes next, visualizing each interaction point a customer might have with the product.

---

[76] On Tesla company website: "Introducing Software Version 10.0". Visited 08.04.2024. https://www.tesla.com/blog/introducing-software-version-10-0

Beginning with a **Minimum Viable Product (MVP)**, the initial focus is to satisfy the principal needs of the customers with a basic yet functional product. Imagine a simplified version of a travel booking app that allows users to book flights and hotels. As insights start pouring in from real users, gradual optimization begins. Through a series of iterations, features such as personalized recommendations, virtual tours, and AI chat bots for instant assistance are woven in, elevating the app from a booking platform to a comprehensive travel assistant. An integral part of this journey mapping is emphasizing **artificial Intelligence (AI) integration**. AI technology can be leveraged to anticipate customer needs even before they articulate them. For example, utilizing machine learning algorithms, a financial management app could analyze spending patterns to offer tailored savings advice, or a health app could suggest personalized fitness plans based on a user's activity levels, making the journey not just responsive but even predictive. In addition, AI contributes to smoothen the pathways, eliminating hurdles and driving efficiency. Further efficiency gains along the entire Product Journey can be realized through **Robotic Process Automation** (RPA).

An undeniable facet of Digital Product Journeys is the fluidity and the scope for continuous enhancement. This involves being receptive to feedback, both quantitative and emotional, and translating it into actionable improvements. A fluid **product roadmap** allows for adaptations based on real user experiences, ensuring the journey remains relevant and empathetically aligned with evolving customer needs. For instance, evolving the earlier example of a wellness app, incorporating user feedback might lead to the introduction of features such as virtual yoga classes, a community forum for users to interact, or a mood tracker that helps individuals keep a check on their mental wellbeing, thereby offering a more rounded approach to holistic health.

Digital **Product Journeys translate insights and technologies into tangible experiences**, narrating a story through a combination of well-coordinated touchpoints. These journeys stand as living entities, continuously evolving, and adapting, promising not just a service, but a relationship grounded in understanding, empathy, and trust. Each update, each new feature, comes as a testament to the brand's commitment to offering nothing but the best, most intuitive, and fulfilling experience to its customers, entertaining a relationship that goes beyond transactions to touch lives genuinely.

But where does your company stand when it comes to Digital Product Journeys?

## Assessment: Pressure-test the Product Flow

 The assessment of Digital Product Journeys is a rich, multi-faceted process that can unearth deep insights and shine light on opportunities to elevate the customer experience to unprecedented heights. A detailed assessment acts as the canvas on which a vibrant, living portrait of the customer's journey is painted, each metric adding a stroke of depth, color, and texture to the evolving masterpiece.

The **Journey Net Promoter Score (NPS)** is the starting point, guiding firms in understanding the pulse of customer satisfaction and loyalty. It moves beyond mere numerical analysis to envelop an understanding of the narratives woven behind the scores. For example, analyzing patterns in scores can lead to identifying a product feature that stands out in eliciting customer satisfaction. But it goes a step further – inviting open-ended feedback can provide a space for customers to express detailed sentiments and experiences, providing rich data for qualitative analysis. A deep dive into this ocean of stories can unveil underlying patterns – stories of delight, messages of friction, and even hidden expectations, each unraveling avenues for enriching the journey.

Equally significant is the analysis of **emotional feedback**, which taps into the reservoir of feelings experienced by the customers during their journey. This feedback can be captured through creatively designed surveys using emoticons for various touchpoints or incorporating AI tools that analyze facial expressions during user testing sessions. Such a rich palette of emotional responses can foster a deeper understanding of moments that truly resonate with the users. For instance, in a digital library application, a feature allowing users to share the joy of finding a long-sought book through emotive reactions can be a window into the highs of their journey, helping in crafting moments that evoke joy, surprise, and delight, thereby painting a landscape of emotionally resonant experiences.

A critical dimension to consider is the **journey duration**, which involves a breakdown of the time spent across various stages of the journey. Utilizing heat maps or session replays to visualize where users spend most of their time can be a rich avenue for insights. For instance, if a travel booking app finds that users spend a disproportionate amount of time in the payment section, it may signal a complexity that needs to be addressed, possibly paving the way for a one-click payment feature to simplify the process, thus promising a swift, seamless transition through stages.

The **journey abandonment rate** presents an urgent call for introspection, urging businesses to dive deep into the stages where users choose to abandon the journey. Here, tools like exit surveys can be instrumental in understanding the triggers behind abandonment. In a digital health platform, users abandon a nutrition tracking feature midway because of its complexity. Understanding this can spur a redesign, making it more intuitive and user-friendly, thus turning potential points of exit into milestones of engagement.

The **path analysis** unveils the labyrinthine pathways traversed by users, offering a detailed blueprint of the most and least traveled paths. With techniques like sequential pattern mining, a business can discover frequently occurring sequences of events that lead to a purchase, aiding in the careful crafting of journeys that naturally lead to conversion. It is like understanding that users of a culinary app often traverse from a recipe video to a grocery shopping feature, revealing a potential for integrating a smooth pathway that bridges content consumption with actionable purchases, creating a landscape ripe with opportunities and convenient transitions.

Lastly, ensuring **touchpoint effectiveness and cross-channel consistency** is akin to orchestrating a symphony where each instrument (or touchpoint) plays in harmonious rhythm, offering a composition that is delightful and resonant. Here, utilizing AI-powered analytics can help in crafting personalized experiences across touchpoints, analyzing real-time data to offer suggestions, reminders, or offers that are in tune with individual preferences and past behaviors, creating a tapestry of experiences that feel personally crafted for each user.

As we see, diving deep into these assessments opens a rich canvas of opportunities, a mosaic where data, technology, and human experiences intertwine to offer a landscape brimming with understanding, delight, and unprecedented resonance.

**Action: Design Seamless Digital Product Journeys**

To initiate and lead digital product journeys, a profound understanding of each step is crucial to craft a pathway that is truly centered on the customer. At the outset, diving into the scoping of the client-centric product journey is vital. This involves developing comprehensive profiles of your customer segments, pondering their habits, preferences, and challenges encountered while interacting with comparable products. A profound analysis facilitates the creation of pathways that seamlessly guide customers towards pre-identified goals. Airbnb systematically segments customer journeys into smaller, more manageable steps, integrating features like intuitive search and reviews.

As we proceed to the customer understanding stage, immersing oneself in deep research becomes important. Leveraging tools such as customer interviews, surveys, and data analytics will provide a wealth of insights into the customer's perspective. A fitting example to follow is Spotify's 'Year in Review' feature, which showcases a deep understanding and acknowledgment of their customers' choices, crafted through detailed data analysis.

***Crafting a Stellar Product North Star: A Symphony of Strategy and Innovation***

The creation of a Product North Star stands as the quintessential act of harmonizing **customer expectations, company ambitions,** the **competitive arena,** and **technological opportunities** (visit section 3.4.1.1 Strategic Foundations on page 226 to validate what needs to be taken into consideration). The first step is immersing in the world of the customer. By dissecting feedback, analyzing trends, and engaging directly through surveys or interviews, a rich tapestry of customer expectations is woven. This tapestry, intricate and revealing, becomes the stage upon which the product's journey unfolds. Parallelly, the curtains are drawn to reveal the grandeur of company ambitions. Every product is a narrative, a story that should reflect the epic tale of the company's overarching visions and goals. Here, alignment and synergy are the watchwords, ensuring each product is a chapter that enriches and elevates the company's saga. Yet, no performance is complete without acknowledging the audience, and in the world of product development, the competitive arena plays this pivotal role. An in-depth, analytical gaze into competitors' strategies and market positioning unveils the unique niches and stages where the product can perform its mesmerizing dance, captivating the audience with its unparalleled value and innovation. In this grand theatre of product development, technological opportunities are the magical elements, the special effects that transform a performance from ordinary to extraordinary. The spotlight here is on emerging technologies, their incorporation an act of alchemy that transforms base elements into golden experiences.

With these foundational pillars, the act of **sketching the Product North Star** is akin to composing a symphony. A team of cross-functional maestros is assembled, each a virtuoso in their field, coming together in a conclave of creativity and strategy. Insights, data, and aspirations are the notes, and their harmonious integration composes the melody of the Product North Star. **Stretching the ambition** is where the composition elevates, each note reaching higher octaves, embodying aspirations that are both grand and attainable. It is a performance of balance, where innovation, feasibility, and aspiration are the chords that create a melody of unparalleled resonance. The final note, the crescendo, is the formulation of the North Star. A statement of eloquence, precision, and inspiration, it encapsulates the essence of the product's destined journey. A journey where every step, every movement is a combination of strategic alignment, customer delight, competitive distinction, and technological innovation.

Derived from the North Star and the status of a company, formulating **Product Journey KPI and OKRs**, the crafting of tangible metrics, is central to the process of making it happen. Platforms such as LinkedIn have ingeniously centered their KPIs around user engagement and connections, creating a space of professional growth and knowledge sharing.

In the silent aftermath of this symphony's composition, what remains is not just a statement but a guiding light. The Product North Star, a compass that directs, inspires, and illuminates every step of the product's odyssey from conception to the grand applause of market success and customer accolades.

### Unleashing Mastery in Detailed Journey Mapping

In the world of crafting enriching customer experiences, the creation of a **detailed journey map** is akin to composing a symphony, where every touchpoint is a harmonious note resonating with precision, empathy, and innovation. It is a process where technology and human insights unfold, scripting a story of engagement, delight, and excellence. The **delineation of customer touchpoints** stands as the first act in this grand composition. Each touchpoint is a world of interaction, a universe where customer expectations and product offerings meet. Here, data analytics, customer feedback, and real-time interaction monitoring intertwine to unveil a landscape of engagements that are as diverse as they are dynamic.

**Salesforce's Journey Builder tool**, housed under the renowned Salesforce Marketing Cloud, acts as a dynamic tool devised to orchestrate and streamline customer journeys, offering a personal touch at every engagement node. This easy-to-use tool transforms the way businesses interact with their customer base, laying down pathways laden with personalized experiences that carry the potential to forge deeper connections and usher in digital success.

Diving into the essence of Journey Builder reveals it as a conduit that facilitates the design, automation, and management of marketing campaigns and customer journeys. Leveraging a rich reservoir of customer data, it empowers companies to craft and coordinate cross-channel journeys that resonate on an individual level, nurturing relationships that span vast arrays of customers, all with a touch of personalization that feels both genuine and insightful.

The journey embarks with a data-driven approach to personalization, harvesting insights from a myriad of sources to piece together narratives that echo with relevance and understanding. This crafting of personal pathways ensures that every touch feels not just familiar but intuitively attuned to individual preferences, striking a chord that fosters relationships built on understanding and relevance.

A notable pillar supporting this grand architecture is multichannel integration, a feature that harmonizes messages across a spectrum of platforms including emails, mobile interfaces, social networks, and web portals. This creates a symphony of interactions where each touchpoint sings in harmony, delivering a unified message that enhances both the relevance and impact of each individual engagement.

As the journey unfolds, customers find themselves engaged in real-time, a dynamic landscape where actions meet instantaneous responses, creating a journey that adapts and evolves to echo individual behaviors and preferences. It is a conversation that flows naturally, a dialogue that reflects understanding and responsiveness, creating a collection of experiences that feel deeply personal and engaging.

Integral to sustaining this dynamic pathway is the tool's encouragement for continuous optimization. Companies find themselves equipped with the ability to monitor and adjust the crafted journeys, steering them with a firm hand guided by real-time data and feedback. This ensures that the pathways pulsate with life, adapting to embrace changing needs and preferences, constantly resonating with relevance and effectiveness.

Looking inward, we find the tool championing enhanced operational efficiency, offering a streamlined playground where diverse departments converge in unity to design and implement the carefully crafted journeys. It is a symphony of operations, where strategies harmonize and echo with unified objectives, promising a cohesive approach that elevates the customer experience to unprecedented heights.

Salesforce's Journey Builder tool emerges as an architectural maestro in the space of customer engagement, an entity that champions the crafting of personalized customer journeys[77].

In this multi-faceted landscape, the **documentation of the process flow** emerges as an essential element. Platforms like ARIS play the role of scribes, capturing, mapping, and documenting every touchpoint, every emotion, and every data point. Each documented element is a blueprint, offering a tangible narrative that is both strategic and operational. Yet, the world of detailed journey mapping is not just about capturing the present but envisioning the future. Here, the magic of AI and RPA (Robotic Process Automation) unveils a universe where each interaction is dynamic, where the customer journey is an evolving story of adaptive engagements and automated efficiencies. **AI** breathes life into the journey map, infusing each touchpoint with adaptive intelligence, where interactions are personalized, and pathways are responsive. Every element of the customer journey evolves, echoing the silent yet dynamic rhythms of individual customer's needs, preferences, and emotions. **RPA** unveils a world of efficiency and precision, where mundane and repetitive tasks transform into automated symphonies of speed and accuracy. It is an effort of technology where every automated process ensures that the customer experience is not just engaging but efficiently seamless.

In this grand theatre of detailed journey mapping, **feedback loops** and **evaluation metrics** are the watchful eyes, the vigilant guardians ensuring that the journey map is a living entity. Every piece of feedback is a gem of insight, and every evaluation metric a pulse of performance, each woven into the journey to ensure it is evolving, adaptive, and resonating with the dynamic combination of customer expectations and market trends. This grand composition unveils a detailed journey map that stands as a masterpiece of the harmonious dance of human insights and technological prowess. Every touchpoint is a note, and every interaction a melody, each resonating with the grand rhythms of the Product North Star's silent yet potent symphony.

---

[77] On Salesforce company website: "Meet Journey Builder". Visited 08.04.2024.
https://www.salesforce.com/eu/products/marketing-cloud/journey-management/

***Navigating the Nuances: Elevating the Art of a Dynamic Product Journey Roadmap***

Embarking on the task of crafting a stellar product journey roadmap unfolds a reality where precision, insight, and adaptability converge. It is akin to drafting a treasure map, where every milestone, every feature, and every iterative refinement becomes a crucial landmark guiding the product's expedition towards market ascendancy and customer acclaim.

Every roadmap begins its genesis with a **structured timeline**. In the heart of Shopify's acclaimed methodology lies the delicacy of integrating each product feature and enhancement into a sequential flow. It is more than a chronological arrangement, it is the weaving of each feature into a time-bound narrative, where strategic release timelines are harmonized with market readiness and customer anticipation.

The product journey roadmap blossoms through **detailed feature mapping**, an act of artistry where each feature is not just delineated but carefully aligned with customer needs, market trends, and competitive landscapes. In Shopify's world, features unfold like chapters of an engrossing narrative, each endowed with functional elegance and strategic fit, ensuring merchants navigate a landscape marked by intuitive design and enhanced user engagement.

As the eyes wander towards the **crafting of the MVP**, the essence of minimalistic elegance and strategic focus comes to the fore. Taking a leaf from Dropbox's playbook, it is about the art of embracing indispensable features that echo the core value proposition, whilst skillfully sidestepping the allure of cluttered functionalities[78]. Each feature within the MVP is a careful selection, akin to a jeweler choosing gems, ensuring the product signals purity, value, and functional elegance. However, the MVP is not a static masterpiece. It is an overview of **iterative enhancements and refinements**, where feedback is the brush, and insights are the colors, each stroke adding depth, vibrancy, and relevance to the product's journey. Here, each piece of customer feedback, market insight, and technological innovation is treated as a sacred script, guiding the enhancement of features, user experience, and value proposition.

In the world of dynamic markets and evolving customer preferences, the roadmap becomes a living entity, marked by **agility and flexibility**. It is a dynamic masterpiece that breathes adaptability, where features, strategies, and timelines are fluid, each adapting, evolving, and resonating with the silent yet potent rhythms of external influences and internal innovations. The lifeblood circulating through this evolving entity is the **integration of feedback loops**. In this world, feedback is not just

---

[78] Mary Ann Azevedo on Tech Crunch website: "Playbook, where 'Pinterest meets Dropbox' for designers". Published 19.04.2022, visited 08.04.2024. https://techcrunch.com/2022/04/19/playbook-where-pinterest-meets-dropbox-for-designers-closes-on-18m-in-funding/

received, it is celebrated, analyzed, and woven into the roadmap's DNA, ensuring the product does not just meet the market but greets it with innovation, relevance, and adaptative elegance.

The product roadmap emerges as a lyrical symphony, where each note, each rhythm, and each pause is a harmonious blend of strategic foresight, operational precision, customer insights, and adaptive innovation. In the silent echoes of this melody, the product's journey unveils not just a path but a narrative – a soul-stirring sonnet of market success, customer delight, and competitive ascendancy.

### *Elevating the Craft of Visualization and Wireframing*

In the expansive universe of product development, there is a pivotal moment where abstract ideas and outlined features transcend into a visual, interactive incarnation. This metamorphosis is catalyzed in the **visualization and wireframing phase,** a process echoing the delicate balance of art and science, precision and creativity, function and form.

As the journey unfolds, we immerse ourselves in the initial step of **crafting the skeletal structure of the product's interface.** This is not merely a technical exercise but a nuanced art form where strategic placement and aesthetic appeal converge. Every button, navigation bar, and interactive element is carefully placed, echoing both the functional necessities and the subtle artistry that elevate user engagement. Each component is strategically positioned to facilitate ease of access, intuitive interaction, and a visually pleasing experience, harmonizing the technical and aesthetic aspects.

The roadmap of this creative journey is illuminated by an unwavering commitment to **user-friendliness and seamless transitions.** The user's navigation through various interface elements is akin to a harmonious combination. Every interaction is orchestrated to ensure fluidity and grace. The transitions between different steps are engineered to be seamless, eliminating friction and enhancing the user's engagement, making each interaction a delightful expression of intuitive engagements.

In this ballet of functionality and aesthetics, tools like Sketch and Figma emerge as invaluable allies. They are the canvases where creative visions morph into tangible prototypes, where every stroke is informed by a profound understanding of user psychology, behavioral insights, and aesthetic principles. These tools offer a plethora of features, facilitating the creation of interactive, responsive, and visually appealing designs that are not just operational but experiential.

A pinnacle of aspiration in this phase is the realization of a **design that supports flawlessness and intuitiveness.** Every feature is engineered to echo self-evidence, every interaction is crafted to be instinctive. Users are not just navigating an interface, but are embarking on a journey where every step, every interaction, is an echo of intuitive design, strategic placement, and aesthetic allure.

Yet, the masterpiece of visualization and wireframing is not cast in stone but is an evolving entity. It is a situation of **iterative refinement**, where feedback is the artist's muse. Each piece of user insight is revered, analyzed, and seamlessly woven into the evolving design. The interface is not just built but is sculpted, with each iteration echoing the deeper insights, refined aesthetics, and enhanced functionality, born from the crucible of user feedback and market insights.

### *The Dynamic Art of Shaping a Resilient Product Backlog*

In the variegated context of product development, an indispensable artifact emerges in the form of the product backlog. It is not merely a repository but a living, breathing entity that encapsulates the aspirations, nuances, and trajectories of the product's evolutionary journey. A blend of strategic foresight, adaptive responsiveness, and detailing shapes this dynamic document. The onset of **creating a product backlog** is marked by the crafting of a comprehensive yet fluid document. This is not just a compilation but a curated ensemble of essential features, systematic enhancements, and critical technical requirements. Every entry is a reflection of strategic insights, customer expectations, and innovative aspirations, catalogued to offer a panoramic view of the product's developmental trajectory.

In the context of this backlog, **flexibility and adaptability** reign supreme. It is not rigid but organic, mirroring the ever-evolving contours of customer needs and market dynamics. The backlog is akin to a malleable sculpture, where each feature and requirement is not fixed but adaptive, ready to morph in response to the subtle and profound shifts in the external landscape and internal innovations. In the world of adaptive backlogs, Atlassian's Jira software stands as a beacon of organized flexibility. It is not just a tool but an ecosystem where features, enhancements, and requirements are not just listed but live and breathe. Each entry is embedded in a rich, context-driven environment, offering teams a dynamic platform to prioritize, discuss, and refine work. Every feature is not just an entry but a dynamic entity, evolving through discussions, refinements, and iterative enhancements.

Yet, amidst this fluidity, **strategic prioritization** is the lighthouse guiding the backlog's evolution. Each feature and enhancement is weighed, not just against its functional value but its strategic resonance. Prioritization is not an act but an art form, where customer value, business objectives, and market trends converge to shape the hierarchy of entries, ensuring that each feature is a strategic step towards the realization of the product's North Star.

The product backlog, in its essence, is a **landscape of collaborative refinement**. It is a platform where cross-functional teams converge, where diverse insights, skills, and perspectives intertwine to shape, refine, and enhance each entry. It is a collaborative sanctuary where the collective wisdom of the team is harnessed to ensure that each feature, enhancement, and requirement is not just technically sound but strategically aligned and customer centric.

The product backlog unfolds as a dynamic blueprint of organized flexibility, strategic prioritization, and collaborative refinement. It is an approach where features and requirements are not just listed but shaped and evolved to echo the silent yet potent rhythms of customer expectations, market trends, and innovative aspirations.

Throughout the entire process, it is important to involve customers. Ideation and co-creation are critical to success when designing the journeys (visit section 3.1.2.4 Customer Community – The Quintessential Target of Collaborative Progress on page 117 to appreciate the value of **customer involvement**). By following these detailed steps and aligning your strategy with proven approaches from industry leaders, you lay down a pathway that promises not just a service, but an enriching and satisfying experience for your customers. It is a blueprint for constructing journeys that are intuitive, seamless, and deeply resonant with the target audience, guaranteeing a product that stands tall in the competitive landscape.

The customer journey, as we have explored, is more than a linear progression, it is a dynamic combination of interactions, emotions, and experiences. Crafting an impeccable journey requires insight, innovation, and iteration. But the rewards of such diligence are manifold: loyal customers, amplified brand equity, and a resonating market presence. As we stand at the confluence of technology and human experience, businesses must continually reimagine these journeys, ensuring they are not just efficient but also empathetic, not just logical but also memorable. The journey, after all, is as significant, if not more, than the destination.

Find more and updated information in the **Digital Arena**. Connect with like-minded professionals to unleash the potential and make it happen.

Seamless journeys embedded into an optimized omnichannel landscape of touchpoints define the Digital Experience as it stands today, and as a company wants to develop it. To ensure that the right priorities for the future are set, a sound Digital Strategy is required.

## 3.4 Digital Strategy

«In real life, strategy is actually very straightforward.
Pick a general direction and implement like hell.»
Jack Welch[79]

The Digital Strategy serves as the guiding beacon that aligns an organization's digital initiatives with its broader Digital Vision. Whereas the Digital North Star is the 'why' and 'what' that provides directional clarity, the Digital Roadmap outlines the 'how' – a tactical plan that lays out the steps and timelines to achieve the North Star. Together, these elements form a cohesive Digital Strategy, harmonizing long-term aspirations with actionable plans to drive digital transformation effectively.

### 3.4.1 Digital North Star

Businesses face an array of challenges and opportunities, making it imperative to identify a focused direction – a Digital North Star. This guiding concept is more than a mere strategic goal, it embodies an organization's aspirations, ethos, and future perspective.

**What the C-Suite needs to know**

1. A Digital North Star provides a strategic, aspirational 3–5-year perspective, guiding companies through the digital landscape with a clear direction that aligns and motivates all departments, ensuring sustained innovation and transformation rooted in core values and objectives.

2. Establish a customer-first, data-driven approach by continuously adapting to their shifting expectations through systematic feedback collection and behavior analysis tools, while ensuring the company's digital initiatives are tightly aligned with its business strategy through clear KPIs and OKRs.

3. Secure competitive differentiation and drive innovation by conducting in-depth competitor and cross-industry analyses, embracing SWOT for strategic insights, and proactively pursuing technological advancements to enhance or reinvent the company's offerings ahead of the competition.

4. A Digital North Star provides a clear and unifying direction for digital transformation efforts, ensuring that all actions align with the company's broader vision and strategic foundations. This focal point, backed by core beliefs that embody the company's values and expertise, facilitates coherent decision-making and tactical execution across the organization.

---

[79] Jack Welch – American business executive (General Electric). * 09.11.1935 in Peabody; † 01.03.2020 in New York City

5.  Regular assessment and reinforcement of the Digital North Star and Core Beliefs are crucial. It involves reviewing internal documentation, conducting stakeholder surveys to measure awareness and alignment, and ensuring consistent communication and visualization of these principles, as exemplified by successful integration into corporate culture by companies like Amazon and Microsoft led by senior management.

But why is a Digital North Star so important?

Building on the Digital Vision (visit section 3.1.1 Digital Vision and Leadership on page 81 to validate the foundation), a company's Digital North Star emerges as its **defining compass, shining brightly amidst technological disruptions.** This is not just another box to tick on a corporate checklist, it is a deeply considered visualization of where a company wants to be in the digital spectrum, typically spanning a **3–5-year horizon**. Such a duration masterfully harmonizes the pressing needs of today with an anticipatory gaze into tomorrow, crafting a direction that is both aspirational and steeped.

The power of the Digital North Star extends beyond just giving direction – it becomes the central pillar for **alignment and motivation**. When a company can articulate a clear and compelling digital direction, it does more than set a destination. It inspires every department, from product development to marketing, ensuring that every effort, every project, and every initiative is laced with a sense of purpose. This guiding principle is not a call to hop onto every emerging tech bandwagon. Instead, it is a thoughtful strategy, a beacon that sheds light on the maze of digital evolution, ensuring a company stays true to its core values and objectives, even as it innovates. Moreover, digital reality is not just about quick pivots or capturing the flavor of the month. While rapid digital changes can indeed offer immediate gratification, the profound transformative potential of a Digital North Star unfurls gracefully over time. By anchoring their aspirations in a 3–5-year strategy, companies are effectively saying they are in it for the long haul. They are **building a digital legacy**, layer by layer, innovation by innovation. This delicate equilibrium, where firms are fueled by groundbreaking ideas yet remain firmly tethered to practical deliverables, ensures that their innovations are not ephemeral flashes but lasting changes that redefine industries.

At its heart, a Digital North Star is not just about technology. It is about people. It is about culture. It serves as a catalyst in **fostering a digital-first culture**, transforming not just processes but mindsets. When a company radiates a clear Digital North Star, it ignites a collective enthusiasm. Employees do not just see themselves as cogs in a machine but as crucial contributors to a larger digital odyssey. Their roles, their responsibilities, their very identities within the organization become intertwined with this digital transformation journey (visit section 3.7.1 Agile and Adaptive Culture on page 324 to explore the importance of a cultural shift).

Let us get some inspiration from front-running companies, which built on a conventional legacy to craft a future-oriented Digital North Star.

---

**Daimler: Driving beyond Cars to Holistic Mobility Solutions**

Daimler AG, with its rich heritage as an automobile manufacturer, did not rest on its laurels. They foresaw the future of mobility and laid out their 'CASE' strategy.

On the Connectivity front, Mercedes-Benz, a Daimler subsidiary, introduced the 'Mercedes me' connect, providing drivers with a suite of services and features accessible through mobile apps, enhancing the overall driving experience. In terms of Autonomous driving, they have been pioneers, testing autonomous trucks and partnering with tech companies for driverless passenger vehicles. Their Shared & Services vision led to the birth of car-sharing ventures like car2go, highlighting a shift from ownership to shared usage models.

Lastly, their commitment to Electric Drive was amplified by the EQ brand, focusing on holistic electric mobility solutions. Daimler's digital drive emphasizes that staying ahead requires not just innovation but a comprehensive vision that encompasses every facet of the industry[80].

---

**L'Oréal: Blending Beauty with Tech Brilliance**

L'Oréal's journey into 'Beauty Tech' is a testament to forward-thinking. Recognizing the power of AR, they acquired ModiFace, a leading AR beauty company. This allowed users to virtually try on makeup and hairstyles, bridging the tactile beauty experience to the digital space.

Their SkinConsult AI tool, launched in collaboration with dermatologists, employed AI to offer personalized skincare recommendations by analyzing user-uploaded selfies. Furthermore, their commitment to e-commerce was solidified with initiatives like shoppable videos, virtual beauty consultations, and collaborations with influencers on platforms like YouTube and Instagram. L'Oréal's digital journey highlights that understanding customer needs and seamlessly blending technology can lead to a richer, more engaging brand experience[81].

---

[80] On the Europawire website: "Daimler takes the next step towards securing its CASE (connectivity, autonomous, shared & services and electric) corporate strategy". Published 18.12.2018, visited 08.04.2024. https://news.europawire.eu/daimler-takes-the-next-step-towards-securing-its-case-connectivity-autonomous-shared-services-and-electric-corporate-strategy-8565665/eu-press-release/2018/12/12/13/02/48/69401/

[81] Šemsa Salioski on on Trending Topics website: "VivaTech 2023: Wie Kosmetik-Gigantin L'Oréal die Tech-Branche einnimmt". Published online 20.07.2023, visited 08.04.2024. https://www.trendingtopics.eu/vivatech-2023-wie-kosmetik-gigantin-loreal-die-tech-branche-einnimmt/

**Siemens: Electrifying Traditional Industry with Digital Prowess**

Siemens' vision of the 'Digital Enterprise' went beyond mere buzzwords. They visualized industries where products were developed and improved using digital twins, a digital replica of physical assets.

Their MindSphere platform, an open IoT operating system, allowed businesses to connect their systems and physical infrastructure to the digital world, unlocking insights from data in real-time. This led to better decision-making, predictive maintenance, and optimized operations.

Siemens also championed Industry 4.0 with solutions that empowered manufacturers to have more flexible, efficient, and automated processes. Collaborative robots, AI-driven solutions, and blockchain for supply chain traceability were some of the innovations Siemens spearheaded. Their journey serves as a blueprint, highlighting that the fusion of the physical and digital is not only beneficial but vital for industries to thrive in the modern era[82].

Amidst the sprawling and often overwhelming landscape of digital evolution, **the Digital North Star shines as an unwavering, constant beacon**. With eyes firmly fixed on this luminary, companies are poised to not only venture with ambition and innovation but to ensure that every digital footprint they leave is etched with deep strategy, unwavering purpose, and a touch of realism.

But what does a Digital North Star consist of?

In the evolving landscape of digital transformation, the establishment of a Digital North Star is vital, being deeply grounded in **Strategic Foundations**. These foundations are hewn from a comprehensive understanding of customer expectations and a thorough analysis of the competitive arena. Additionally, they encompass a firm grasp of the company's strategic ambition alongside a perceptive eye on the opportunities ushered in by rapid technological developments.

---

[82] On Siemens company website: "Nächster Halt: Digitale Transformation". Visited 08.04.2024.
https://www.siemens.com/ch/de.html?gclid=EAIaIQobChMInpKqtuCGggMVAIRoCR1NNA2mEAAYASA
AEgIpJfD_BwE&acz=1

*Figure 24: Digital North Star*

### 3.4.1.1 Strategic Foundations – Understanding What Defines the Strategy

A North Star is thoroughly based on strategic foundations: Clients' expectations, competitive benchmarks, and best practices, as well as technological developments set the range within the North Star should be developed. Through close alignment with the company's Digital Vision and business strategy the Digital North Star is defined and visualized. But only through broad endorsement across the organization it becomes alive.

**Awareness: Building on Strong Foundations**

Crafting a resilient Digital North Star is essential in navigating the complexities of the digital transformation, and it rests heavily on establishing sound strategic foundations. These foundations become the bedrock that ensures the Digital Strategy is customer-centric, business-savvy, competitively superior, and technologically adept.

At the heart of these foundations is a deep understanding of **customer expectations**, a critical facet that molds the direction, ensuring that the resultant strategies align well with the target audience. In addition, aligning with the **company's business ambitions** is fundamental in ensuring that the North Star not just illuminates the path to digital transformation but also significantly contributes to achieving the overarching business objectives.

Awareness and understanding of the **competitive arena** are another cornerstone, helping the organization to carve out a unique path, one that leverages its strengths to offer a differentiated value proposition. This involves a keen scrutiny of the marketplace, identifying gaps and opportunities where the organization can offer unparalleled value.

Moreover, a sharp eye on the possibilities ushered in by **technological developments** is vital. It is about harnessing the dynamic technological advancements, turning them into enablers that drive innovation and present opportunities to scale and evolve.

Defining a **Digital North Star** grounded in strong strategic foundations becomes a beacon of clarity, steering the organizational journey with a vision that is both forward-looking and grounded in the realities of the current business landscape.

**Assessment: Testing the Strength of the Foundation**

 To drill deeper on the quality of the North Star, it is worth-while to validate how the company has elaborated it. To understand, whether **customers have been involved** in defining the Digital North Star, start with a straightforward count of customer surveys sent out and the rate of responses. Beyond these basic metrics, dive into the quality of surveys. Are they designed to probe deep into customer sentiments, employing analytical techniques like conjoint analysis? For empathy maps, a foundational review should check if all customer segments are represented. A detailed assessment could involve using these maps as a foundation for qualitative interviews with customers to validate or revise the conclusions drawn. Behavior analysis should begin with basic metrics like site visits or purchase frequency, but also encompass more sophisticated metrics like segmented Customer Lifetime Value (CLV) and churn rates. In this context, it is also crucial to understand how the Digital North Star can **contribute to the achievement of the company's business objectives**, ensuring the KPIs are met, and the ORKs are achieved.

When it comes to **taking competitor assessment into consideration**, basic evaluation starts with an inventory of competitive intelligence reports. These reports should be categorized based on focus – such as pricing, product features, and customer service – and then scrutinized for their depth and coverage. Do they also include market substitutes or potential disruptors? For unique value propositions, the first assessment is to check internal documents to see if they are explicitly stated and supported by preliminary market research.

To understand, whether **Technological Opportunities** have been embraced, a foundational count of pilot projects initiated and completed sets the stage. Beyond the numbers, look at the criteria for project success. Are they well-defined, and do post-implementation audits verify if the projects met these success criteria? For innovation workshops, the foundational assessment involves simply listing their frequency and attendance. A deeper evaluation would scrutinize the quality of ideas generated and track how many have moved into the proposal or implementation stage (visit 3.6.2 Innovation and Experimentation on page 313 to explore how to test emerging ideas).

## Action: Elaborate the Strategic Foundations

 To lay the foundation for the North Star, it is essential to understand the customers' expectations, the company's (business) strategy and priorities, to differentiate in the competitive arena and to leverage the opportunities stemming from technological developments.

### *Deciphering Customer Expectations*

'**Customer First**' has never been more important than when a company defines its Digital North Star. As it defines the resources allocation over the coming years a company needs to get it right for the customers. Merely capturing the clients' mindset is not enough. It is about continuously evolving based on their ever-shifting desires and needs. This understanding is achieved through systematic methods and data-backed strategies, transforming passive feedback into active engagement.

When we broach the subject of **surveys & questionnaires**, it is not just about ticking boxes. Modern tools like SurveyMonkey or Typeform are equipped to present engaging, visual, and even interactive questions that capture nuanced feedback. The idea is to resonate with the audience on an emotional level, understanding the 'why' behind their preferences, not just the 'what'. Take Amazon for instance: their post-purchase questionnaires often dive into the depths of packaging satisfaction, delivery experience, and product quality. By doing so, they collect data that goes beyond the product itself, optimizing every facet of the customer journey. Another global player, Zalando from Europe, leverages similar strategies, often asking for detailed feedback on fit, material, and style after clothing purchases, painting a holistic picture of client expectations.

**Empathy mapping** is more than a casual brainstorm. In structured sessions, companies deploy tools like Miro or MURAL to visually plot potential customer feelings across diverse scenarios. These sessions often involve role-playing, with team members assuming client personas, navigating hypothetical situations to feel what the client might feel. This approach helps in bridging the cognitive gap between the company's offerings and client perceptions. It is no secret that China's Alibaba has been setting benchmarks in this domain. They regularly organize live interactions with real users, making them navigate potential platform updates and noting their reactions. These sessions do not just stop at noting the feelings, they drill deep into understanding the root causes, ensuring that their platform's upgrades are not just intuitive but also emotionally resonant. Through these sessions a company also better understands the users' learned behavior through other digital applications[83].

Now, the saga of **user behavior analysis** is not linear, it is a rich narrative of twists, turns, pauses, and accelerations. With tools like Hotjar and Google Analytics, every click, scroll, and hover speaks volumes. For example, Amazon diligently evaluates these metrics. If a user spends considerable time on a product page but leaves without making a purchase, the system might interpret this as interest without conversion. Consequently, the user might get a gentle nudge in the form of an email displaying related products, or even a discount code. This is not just about pushing sales, but also about assuring the user that their preferences are noted and valued. Similarly, Spotify, the Swedish music streaming giant, dives deep into the listening patterns of its users. If someone has been repetitively listening to relaxing tunes, they might get a personalized playlist titled 'Winding Down'.

Essentially, we want to understand the relative importance of the offering components a company has, to identify gaps vs. customer expectations, and to pinpoint most needed improvements in products and services from customers' perspectives.

### *Implementing the Company's Strategy*

Understanding the company's **business ambitions** is a crucial step in crafting a successful Digital Strategy. It begins with delineating the broad business goals and identifying the core objectives that underpin the organization's vision for the future. Once these overarching ambitions are clearly defined, it becomes imperative to breakdown these high-level objectives into actionable **KPIs (Key Performance Indicators)** and **OKRs (Objectives and Key Results)**. The process necessitates a detailed and collaborative discussion across various stakeholders within the organization to come to a consensus on the KPIs that would act as the performance meters, continually assessing the progress and ensuring alignment with the business ambitions. Concurrently, defining OKRs facilitates the translation of strategic objectives into actionable, quantifiable outcomes, thereby setting a clear trajectory for the teams to follow. With the KPIs and OKRs serving as guiding tools, it is time to envisage how the **Digital North Star** can dovetail into this framework. The Digital North Star should effectively serve as a lighthouse, illuminating the path that aligns digital transformation efforts directly with the business ambitions. It encapsulates the digital philosophy of the organization, defining the ultimate digital aspirations that are rooted in the practical pathway demarcated by the KPIs and OKRs. Crafting

---

[83] Ming Zeng in Harvard Business Review: "Alibaba and the Future of Business: Lessons from China's innovative digital giant". Published September 2018, visited online 08.04.2024.
https://hbr.org/2018/09/alibaba-and-the-future-of-business

the Digital North Star, thus, involves the amalgamation of the Digital Vision with the grounded, measurable outcomes defined by the KPIs and OKRs. It helps in forging a path that is not just aspirational but grounded in real, attainable objectives, fostering a digital environment that is ripe for innovation while being steadfastly directed towards achieving business success (visit section 1.1 What is Digital Success on page 13 to revisit the Digital Success criteria).

### *Navigating Competitive Dynamics*

In the sprawling maze of the digital world, understanding one's unique value proposition is crucial. Yet, it is not just about self-awareness. Navigating the tumultuous seas of **competitive dynamics** requires a blend of introspection, awareness, and strategic agility. The nuances of this navigation are enriched using analytic tools, strategic frameworks, and constant vigilance. Conducting **competitive analysis** is not a mere game of numbers. It is an effort that decodes the strategies, strengths, and shortcomings of market peers. Tools like SEMrush or Ahrefs are indispensable. They do not just chart out competitor website traffic, they illuminate patterns, spotlighting gaps in content, SEO strengths, or paid advertising strategies. Take, for instance, Samsung, a tech titan from South Korea. In their bid to continuously innovate in the smartphone sector, they regularly analyze the offerings of their competitors, such as Apple. They examine the features, price points, and even marketing campaigns, ensuring they craft a compelling narrative that differentiates. Meanwhile, L'Oréal uses similar tactics against its cosmetic competitors, dissecting ingredient lists, marketing angles, and even social media presence, striving to stay a cut above the rest. For many reasons it is worth looking beyond the walls of your company and conduct a **best practice assessment** of your competitors, but also look at successful companies in other industries. This analysis serves as an external lens, providing invaluable insights into what others in your industry are doing well, and revealing gaps that you can fill or areas where you can excel. For instance, Instagram keenly observed the success of Snapchat's 'Stories' feature. Rather than merely copying it, Instagram integrated its own version, 'Instagram Stories', enhancing the service to include additional functionalities like Boomerangs, filters, and easy linking to other Instagram content[84]. Similarly, Microsoft studied Slack's early success in team collaboration software and introduced Teams. By deeply integrating Teams with its existing Office 365 productivity tools, Microsoft did not just replicate Slack's success, it elevated it, thereby redefining collaboration for its large enterprise customer base. In both cases, the companies learned from their competitors and took those lessons to enhance

---

[84] Kaya Yurieff on CNN Business website: "Instagram Stories is twice as popular as Snapchat". Published 28.06.2018, visited 08.04.2024. https://money.cnn.com/2018/06/28/technology/instagram-stories-users/index.html

their own digital offerings. This process of identifying successful strategies in the market can serve as a crucial steppingstone in shaping your Digital North Star, ensuring it is not just ambitious but also well-aligned with market realities and opportunities for differentiation.

The process of **SWOT analysis** transcends mere bullet points. When done right, it is a deep dive into the heart of an organization's DNA, juxtaposed against the market mosaic. Platforms like MindTools and Lucidchart offer templates and workflows, ensuring that the SWOT process is comprehensive, actionable, and dynamic. Japan's automotive juggernaut, Toyota, employs SWOT religiously[85]. By recognizing their strengths in hybrid technology, they have doubled down on research and development, creating cars like the Prius. Acknowledging threats, they are investing heavily in electric vehicle technology, preparing to challenge industry disruptors like Tesla. On another front, Unilever, a consumer goods conglomerate with roots in the UK and Netherlands, taps into SWOT to navigate the competitive waters of personal care, food, and household sectors, aligning their diverse brands with emerging global trends and demands. Based on all the above inputs, **strategic differentiation** is about creating lasting value. Beyond brainstorming sessions, tools like Trello for idea organization or MURAL for collaborative sketching create an environment where innovative differentiators can be nurtured. The success of Taiwan's ASUS in the crowded PC market can be attributed to this principle. By carving out niche markets such as high-end gaming through their ROG (Republic of Gamers) line, they have differentiated themselves in a saturated market. In the luxury sector, France's Louis Vuitton harnesses differentiation by intertwining heritage with innovation. Their classic designs get modern twists, and collaborations with contemporary artists ensure they stand distinct in a sea of luxury brands.

We want to understand the competitive arena and differentiation spaces for your company through digital. In addition, a close look at our competitors and beyond our own industry also unearths best practices to build into the own offerings, or failures that we want to avoid.

### *Embracing Technological Opportunities*

In a world where the only constant is change, and where technology evolves at a breakneck pace, staying ahead means not just adapting but pioneering. Technological opportunities beckon organizations with the promise of transformative

---

[85] Edward Ferguson on Panmore Institute website: "Toyota SWOT Analysis". Updated 11.10.2023, visited 08.04.2024. https://panmore.com/toyota-swot-analysis-recommendations#:~:text=The%20SWOT%20framework%20pinpoints%20the,company%20effectively%20addresses%20such%20factors

growth. But seizing these opportunities requires foresight, innovation, and a keen understanding of the tools and trends reshaping industries.

**Technological exploration** begins with research. Platforms such as Gartner and Forrester provide insights into emerging trends and predictions. They act as the compass for companies navigating the digital terrain, highlighting innovations on the horizon. Huawei, China's telecommunications and consumer electronics giant, frequently taps into such insights to drive their R&D efforts. Their forward-looking approach has enabled them to be pioneers in 5G technology, ensuring they are not just part of the conversation but leading it. Similarly, Sweden's Spotify constantly scours technological trends, integrating features like AI-driven song recommendations, elevating the user experience to new heights (visit section 3.6.1 Anticipating future trends on page 304 to explore the power of future developments).

**Pilot projects** stand as the proving grounds for these technological endeavors. Tools such as Jira for agile project management or Slack for team communication ensure these projects run seamlessly. They provide teams with frameworks to test, iterate, and refine their initiatives. Adidas, the renowned German sportswear brand, has been at the forefront of integrating technology into their products. Their pilot projects have given birth to innovations like the 'Futurecraft.Strung' – a shoe designed with data-driven thread placement[86]. On the other side of the globe, South Korea's Hyundai tests autonomous driving technologies in controlled environments, inching closer to a future where cars drive themselves.

**Innovation workshops** are where ideas transform into tangible solutions. Here, creative solutions are born, challenges are addressed, and pathways to technological integration are carved. Brazil's airplane manufacturer, Embraer, regularly hosts innovation workshops. These sessions have led to advancements in aviation technology, pushing the boundaries of what is possible in the skies. In the context of e-commerce, India's Flipkart frequently hosts such workshops, resulting in features like 'Flipkart Ideas' where curated content enhances the shopping experience[87].

Essentially, we want to understand where technological (or other) developments open up new opportunities to enhance or re-invent our offerings. Opportunities must be assessed before other competitors do. In addition, the thorough understanding of the technical landscape also helps to identify future threats and hinderances.

---

[86] Matt Burgess on Wired website: "Adidas's ingenious new way to make shoes? Robotic string theory". Published online 08.10.2020, visited 08.04.2024. https://www.wired.co.uk/article/adidas-strung-futurecraft-shoe

[87] On the Flipkart company website: "Flipkart introduces 'Flipkart Ideas'". Published online 17.08.2019, visited 08.04.2024. https://stories.flipkart.com/flipkart-ideas/

Now, based on these sound strategic foundations, a company can craft its Digital North Star.

### 3.4.1.2 Digital North Star and Core beliefs – Describing the Digital Ambition

Derived from the strategic foundations, establishing a Digital North Star provides companies with a focused, unwavering goal that guides their digital transformation journey. This strategic focal point is further bolstered by Core Beliefs, a set of guiding principles derived from a company's values and expertise, which aid in navigating the complexities of digital initiatives and ensure that every step taken aligns with the broader vision encapsulated by the North Star. Together, the Digital North Star and Core Beliefs forge a resilient framework for sustaining a competitive edge in the digital age.

**Awareness: Importance of a Clear Direction**

A **Digital North Star** serves as the guiding light in the complex landscape of digital transformation, rooted deeply in strategic foundations that are paramount to steering digital product implementations adeptly.

Complementing the Digital North Star are the **Digital Core Beliefs**, which act as the pillars making the North Star tangible and implementable. These core beliefs break down the broader direction into principles that govern the day-to-day decision-making process in the digital transformation journey. They are rooted deeply in the company's culture and ethos, guiding the tactical executions that are aligned with the strategic North Star, and might encapsulate commitments to customer-centricity, innovation, agility, or sustainability, providing a structured yet flexible framework that empowers teams to work towards the North Star with a clear understanding of the company's values and objectives. Through these core beliefs, the abstract notion of the North Star is transformed into concrete actions and strategies that drive the company forward, ensuring a coherent and unified approach to achieving digital success.

A well-articulated Digital North Star, complemented by a set of resilient and insightful Digital Core Beliefs, offers a comprehensive blueprint for navigating the complex digital landscape.

**Assessment: Challenge the Existing Digital North Star and Core Beliefs**

In the bustling corridors of today's digital enterprises, the conversation often begins with the **clarity of direction** that a Digital North Star provides. A cogent vision is not just about a catchy phrase on a boardroom slide, it is the pulse that every stakeholder, from a top-tier executive to an intern, can feel and articulate. Picture a scenario where different teams across an organization interpret this direction in varied ways. Such divergence is not a mere miscommunication, it can hinder unified progress and warrants a re-evaluation of how the Digital North Star has been communicated and integrated.

First and foremost, the initiative to **determine the existence of a Digital North Star** begins with fundamental assessments. You will want to review corporate Digital Strategy documentation to ascertain if the term 'North Star' (or alternative wording) is explicitly mentioned. Conduct a quick document audit to find out where this strategy is archived. Is it easily accessible in a cloud storage system, a secure Intranet, or perhaps within specialized strategy software? Furthermore, distribute a quick survey to key stakeholders to determine their awareness of a designated owner or team responsible for the North Star strategy. A detailed follow-up could involve interviews with these stakeholders, asking them to elaborate on the North Star's specific components and how often it serves as a decision-making guideline.

In the next step, evaluating the **overall quality of the Digital North Star** involves layered scrutiny. Count the frequency of citations or mentions in high-impact meetings and internal communications. Is it discussed during board meetings, mentioned in quarterly reports, or referred to during departmental meetings? To gain a deeper understanding, conduct employee surveys that use a Likert scale to assess their perception of the North Star's efficacy. A more advanced evaluation could involve cross-referencing these survey results with performance metrics to understand if higher awareness correlates with better outcomes.

Finally, try to understand whether the **Digital North Star Ethos** is broadly supported at a basic level. This involves monitoring the frequency and types of communications concerning the North Star. For a deeper dive, look into the quality of these communications. Are they easily understandable and actionable? Use comprehensive pulse surveys that not only gauge awareness but also the depth of understanding and alignment. Conduct follow-up interviews or focus groups to gain nuanced insights into any gaps in alignment or understanding.

Integrating these layered assessments – ranging from basic foundational checks to intricate, detailed evaluations – provides an exhaustive, multi-faceted picture of your Digital North Star's existence, quality, and operational impact. This comprehensive approach ensures that you have all the information needed for effective fine-tuning and successful implementation.

### Action: Craft a Digital North Star and the Core Beliefs

Organizations unequivocally require a Digital North Star, a beacon to chart a course that is both resilient and adaptable to changing dynamics. This initiative is not a mere declaration but a rigorous process that leverages both technology and insights and epitomizes the core principles and objectives of an organization.

The inception of this journey commences with harnessing robust tools such as Tableau and Power BI. These platforms stand paramount in driving the **synthesis of varied insights**, facilitating the harmonization of disparate data types including qualitative nuances extracted from customer feedback, prevailing market trends, and technological shifts into a coherent tableau of actionable insights. The automotive giant, Toyota of Japan, serves as an illustrative example in this domain. Their unwavering commitment to hybrid technology gave birth to the iconic Prius, a brainchild borne from environmental sustainability principles integrated with cutting-edge data insights, thus paving a pathway for groundbreaking innovations in the automotive sector[88].

As organizations find themselves amidst a deluge of insights garnered, the urgency to discern and **prioritize insights** that resonate profoundly with the organization's core objectives escalates. Techniques such as the Eisenhower Matrix, facilitate businesses in sieving and ranking insights effectively. Such prioritization aids companies in avoiding whimsical decisions, rooting their strategies in principles that foster human well-being and nurture global tech ecosystems.

Embarking on this voyage necessitates more than crafting succinct statements. It calls for the assimilation of the company's ethos into a **Digital North Star statement**, an endeavor to encapsulate the core and vision of the company into a resonant statement. Leveraging tools such as MindMeister aids enterprises in crystallizing divergent ideas into a singular, tangible vision that mirrors the company's heart and soul.

Equally important is the establishment of **Core Beliefs**, a steadfast set of principles that form the fundamental bedrock of every organizational decision. This compass remains unwavering amidst the perpetual flux of technological and market dynamics, offering a beacon of consistency and direction. Giants like IKEA and Adidas have remarkably illustrated this principle. Their core beliefs, deeply rooted in enhancing daily life and nurturing athletic potential, reverberate in every digital venture undertaken, from augmented reality apps to invigorating online communities that echo their dedication to supporting well-being and athleticism in the digital domain[89].

---

[88] On Toyota company website: "The Story Behind the Birth of the Prius, Part 1". Published 11.12.2017, visited 08.04.2024. https://global.toyota/en/detail/20209700
[89] On adidas company website: "Profile". Visited 08.04.2024. https://www.adidas-group.com/en/group/profile/

Crafting a **Digital North Star** is akin to creating a navigational chart guiding organizations through the tumultuous seas of the digital reality. From synthesizing profound insights to crafting an overview of guiding principles that reflect the organization's heartbeat, every nuanced step holds intrinsic value in this endeavor.

Defining the Digital North is just the beginning. **Real transformation happens when the entire organization is synchronized to this guiding force.** To ensure success, every department, from R&D to marketing, needs to actively channel the spirit of the Digital North in their initiatives. Consider, for instance, how multinational conglomerate Unilever managed to do this. By centralizing their guiding principles around sustainability and innovation, their diverse portfolio supports this commitment, as seen in their 'Sustainable Living' brand campaigns[90]. Such alignment is no small feat, and businesses must actively employ strategies like change management to keep everyone on the same page. Crafting a compelling Digital North Star is a seminal first step but bringing it to life within your organization demands **endorsement and active propagation**. One of the most powerful tools for this is **visualization**. For example, Salesforce creates engaging internal videos that crystallize complex strategic concepts into digestible insights, thereby making their North Star easily understandable for every team member. At Spotify, wallpapers and screensavers across company computers and meeting rooms echo their Digital North Star, serving as a constant visual cue for what the company aims to achieve.

Yet, visualization alone is insufficient, it must be bolstered by **active communication led by Senior Management**. Jeff Bezos' annual letters to Amazon shareholders are a prime example. These letters consistently reiterate the company's customer-centric North Star, giving employees, stakeholders, and even customers a clear understanding of the company's core mission. Similarly, Satya Nadella at Microsoft incorporates the company's mission of 'empowering every person and every organization on the planet to achieve more' in almost every public address and internal communication. It is not just part of speeches but is embedded in policy briefs, performance reviews, and strategic planning sessions.

The Digital North Star demands more than mere navigation, it requires a holistic embrace of its ethos. It is a philosophy, a set of values, and an actionable strategy all rolled into one.

---

[90] On Unilever company website: "Unilever Sustainable Living Plan 2010 to 2020: Summary of 10 years' progress". Published March 2021, visited 08.04.2024.
https://www.unilever.com/files/92ui5egz/production/16cb778e4d31b81509dc5937001559f1f5c863ab.pdf

### 3.4.2   Digital Roadmap

**A Digital Roadmap breathes life into a company's Digital North Star.** It is not just a strategic document but a dynamic, working plan that guides organizations in implementing their Digital Vision. It bridges the gap between what needs to be achieved (the Digital North Star) and how to get there, offering a structured pathway that spans prioritizing initiatives, resource allocation, and timelines to eventual execution.

**What the C-Suite needs to know**

1. Holistic Planning: The Digital Roadmap should be conceived through a systematic approach that involves breaking down various components contributing to the Digital North Star. Each element should be carefully planned, including technological solutions, customer expectations, and competitive advantages.

2. Prioritization is Key: It is essential to prioritize options systematically based on customer expectations, contributions to the Digital North Star, business impact, and feasibility. This helps in making informed decisions about what to implement first, thus aligning resources and efforts efficiently.

3. Timeline and Resources: Crafting a realistic timeline, considering priorities and available resources, is crucial. Without this, even the best-laid plans can fail due to a mismatch between objectives and execution capabilities.

4. Stakeholder Validation: The Roadmap should not be a siloed document. It should be validated with both customers and internal stakeholders to ensure that it is resonating and to gather additional insights for refinement.

5. Operational Integration: The final but on-going step involves integrating the Digital Roadmap into the backlogs of Product Owners, turning strategy into actionable tasks. This includes assigning clear responsibilities, setting performance metrics, and regularly adapting the Roadmap for alignment with real-world outcomes and strategy shifts.

But why it is so important to have a clearly defined Digital Roadmap?

**Awareness: Step-by-Step to Success**

At the heart of any Digital Roadmap lies the **translation of the Digital North Star.** This stage is where a company's high-level direction gets broken down into more manageable and actionable components. For example, Philips once known primarily for its electronics, used its Digital Roadmap to pivot towards healthcare, particularly focusing on telemedicine. The Roadmap guided them through the complexities of regulatory compliance, the nuances of patient data security, and the challenges of remote healthcare delivery. The result was not just a new direction but a carefully executed transformation that saw them become leaders in remote healthcare services. Their roadmap acted as a translator, turning broad strokes of vision into details of execution, a masterpiece of strategic planning meeting tactical finesse.

Derived from the Digital North Star, the Digital Roadmap becomes a **Blueprint for Transformation**. Barnes & Noble, once a brick-and-mortar stalwart, did not just jump to e-commerce, their Roadmap helped them identify the necessary milestones. They began by digitizing their inventory, moved on to building an intuitive and user-friendly e-commerce platform, and then took the bold step of integrating augmented reality features. This layered approach ensured that each phase was a foundation for the next, optimizing both customer experience and operational efficiency. The roadmap served as the architect, laying down the structural integrity for an enterprise-wide digital transformation.

However, creating a blueprint and translating a vision would be futile if not everyone is on the same page. This brings us to **Transparency and Clarity**, which is crucial for multi-department organizations. Siemens, a global industrial powerhouse with diverse sectors like healthcare, energy, and manufacturing, utilized their Digital Roadmap to create a unified direction. They incorporated key performance indicators, assigned specific milestones to different departments, and made sure the roadmap was accessible to all, thereby reducing misunderstandings and misalignments. The roadmap became their operational lingua franca, a shared language that every stakeholder could understand and act upon.

The next layer is **Focused Organizational Effort**, which cannot be overemphasized. Early versions of digital assistants like Siri and Google Assistant were comparatively primitive, capable of only basic voice recognition. However, guided by a detailed roadmap, development teams knew which elements needed refinement and in what order. The initial focus was on improving voice recognition algorithms, which then evolved into enhancing natural language processing capabilities, and incorporating advanced AI features like contextual understanding and predictive analytics. This stair-step approach ensured that each phase built upon the last, leading to a continually improving product.

Finally, an effective Digital Roadmap is crucial for **Resource Optimization**. Consider Amazon's approach to global expansion. Their roadmap did not just say 'expand globally', it broke this down into more manageable steps, using data analytics to identify markets ripe for entry. Before entering India, for instance, the company conducted in-depth market research, identified potential local partners, and even adapted their service offerings to better suit local needs. Such detailed planning ensured that resources were not squandered on less promising ventures, optimizing ROI and ensuring long-term success.

A Digital Roadmap is a strategic asset that has guided companies like Philips, Barnes & Noble, Siemens, Siri and Google Assistant, and Amazon in their respective journeys. It offers a nuanced approach to translating broad visions into actionable tasks, transforming entire business models, enhancing transparency and focus across departments, and optimizing resource allocation for maximum impact.

**Amazon's Digital Roadmap is an Embodiment of its Customer-Centric Digital North Star, which is to be 'Earth's most customer-centric company'.**

The roadmap is broken down into a multitude of initiatives, each with a clear customer-value proposition. They have multiple services from Amazon Prime, AWS, and Amazon Fresh to Kindle, all serving different customer segments but aligning with the singular vision of customer-centricity. The company uses its proprietary 'two-pizza teams', small enough to be fed by two pizzas, to manage these diverse initiatives, thereby decentralizing command and speeding up implementation.

In terms of prioritizing initiatives, Amazon uses a robust framework that includes 'Customer Obsession' as a core metric, alongside ROI and technical feasibility. The famed 'Working Backwards' approach starts with the customer experience and works its way back to the technology, prioritizing based on customer expectations and needs.

Their timeline planning includes rigorous risk assessments and 'Plan B' scenarios, ensuring minimal disruptions in their delivery timelines. They employ 'Just Do It' and 'Six-Pager' methods for fast decision-making and deep-diving into issues, thereby streamlining the execution and adhering to schedules.

Stakeholder validation is not just an afterthought, it is built into the DNA of their planning process. Amazon involves its employees in decision-making via its 'PR/FAQ' method, where a mock Press Release and a Frequently Asked Questions document are created to consider various stakeholder perspectives even before an idea goes into development.

The Digital Roadmap is a living document at Amazon, updated continuously and communicated effectively across different departments. Town halls, internal wikis, and an array of internal communication tools keep everyone in the loop.

Finally, the roadmap effortlessly transitions into tactical tasks through a very mature agile ecosystem. The backlogs for Product Owners are not just lists of tasks but are connected to KPIs that align with the Digital North Star. They use metrics like Customer Satisfaction Scores and Net Promoter Scores to continuously validate that the tactical steps are in alignment with the strategic objectives.

Amazon's systematic approach to creating and executing its Digital Roadmap makes it a benchmark for other organizations aiming to achieve their Digital North Stars[91].

Concluding this exploration, a Digital Roadmap is a transparent plan that can illuminate the path for external stakeholders, particularly in **Building Stakeholder Confidence**. Envision an EduTech company, fervently seeking investments to fuel its digital transformation initiatives. Merely articulating a Digital North Star might not suffice in the eyes of discerning investors. Yet, presenting a crystalline Digital Roadmap not only unfurls the company's vision but offers potential investors a tangible, actionable plan. Where is your company when it comes to planning the digital priorities along a sound Digital Road Map?

---

[91] Damian Jolly on Nukon website: "What Amazon can teach us about digital transformation in manufacturing". Published online 29.09.2017, visited 08.04.2024. https://www.nukon.com/blog/what-amazon-can-teach-us-about-digital-transformation-in-manufacturing

**Assessment: Scrutinizing the Existence and Efficacy of a Digital Roadmap**

 The mere existence of a Digital Roadmap is not enough. It should be robust, precise, and actionable. The dual mandate of assessment calls for determining its existence and subsequently evaluating its effectiveness. Let us embark on this exploration.

To adequately scrutinize the existence and efficacy of a Digital Roadmap within an organization, one must embark on a multi layered examination. The first critical query is the **simple existence of a formally documented Digital Roadmap**, a binary but fundamentally crucial indicator. To confirm its existence, one can verify if the document is widely available across different departments and included in the company's strategic repositories. Access logs can offer additional insights into how often the document is being consulted.

Moving from existence to quality, it is essential to assess the **alignment of the Digital Roadmap with the Digital North Star**. This involves a detailed examination of the specificity and clarity of the objectives laid out, along with the granularity of the task breakdowns and assigned timelines. Creating an alignment index, a composite metric reflecting these variables, can help quantify this alignment, providing a tangible measure of quality.

Once the basic criteria are satisfied, the real depth of the scrutiny lies in examining how well the company has navigated through the **preparation of the Digital Roadmap.** To thoroughly scrutinize the effectiveness of a company's Digital Roadmap, the first item on the checklist should be the comprehensive structure that translates the Digital North Star into actionable initiatives. In practice, this means looking for a detailed breakdown that goes beyond generalities. For instance, if the Digital North Star is to become a leader in customer experience, the roadmap should specify initiatives such as implementing a next-gen customer service platform, incorporating AI-driven chat bots, and adopting customer journey analytics. Each initiative should be mapped to specific objectives, metrics, and timelines.

Next, focus on **how rigorously the organization has prioritized these initiatives**, using a quantifiable framework. Best-in-class organizations often employ a weighted scoring model, where initiatives are evaluated based on their anticipated customer impact, technical feasibility, and alignment with the Digital North Star. The scoring should be part of the roadmap document, ideally complete with a matrix that shows how each initiative measures up against these criteria. Priority scores can guide the allocation of resources and the sequencing of initiatives.

The third area of scrutiny is the thoroughness of planning in terms of timelines, risk assessments, and contingency plans. A well-crafted roadmap will identify potential roadblocks – be it technical constraints, budget overruns, or regulatory changes –

and outline fallback plans. These should include pre-allocated resources or a buffer time and describe trigger conditions that activate the contingency plans.

Fourth, assess the level of **engagement with both internal and external stakeholders** in validating the roadmap. Have the plans been reviewed by not just the top management but also by key operational teams who will be executing it? Additionally, have external experts, customers, or industry peers been consulted for their feedback? This could be in the form of advisory boards, beta-testing, or peer reviews, and should be documented as part of the roadmap validation process.

Fifth, scrutinize **the completeness of the documentation and how well it has been communicated across the company**. A comprehensive Digital Roadmap should be complemented by a communication strategy that ensures full organizational buy-in. This could involve regular all-hands meetings, department-specific briefings, or even an internal digital dashboard that tracks real-time progress. The goal is to ensure that every team and employee understands their role in the digital transformation journey.

Finally, evaluate **how effectively the Digital Roadmap has transitioned into the tactical execution phase**. This is best assessed by examining its integration into Product Owners' backlogs. Each initiative on the roadmap should correspond to a set of well-defined tasks, complete with assigned owners, deadlines, and requisite resources, in the backlogs of the respective Product Owners. Regular audits of these backlogs against the roadmap can indicate how effectively the strategic vision is being translated into day-to-day operations.

By applying these detailed layers of scrutiny, one can gain a nuanced understanding of the quality and efficacy of a company's Digital Roadmap, from its conceptual rigor to its operational implementation.

**Action: Prioritize a Digital Roadmap**

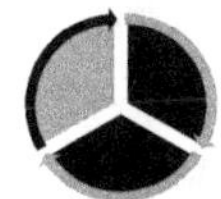

To breathe life into your Digital North Star, developing a well-structured Digital Roadmap is essential. This detailed blueprint will not only guide your digital transformation journey but also act as a communication tool for stakeholders across the organization and beyond. Here is how to go about it.

### *Crafting a Multi-faceted Digital Roadmap Approach to Achieving Your North Star*

The first critical step to creating a successful Digital Roadmap lies in dissecting your overarching Digital North Star into its **component objectives, initiatives, and products**. Whether your North Star aims for customer service excellence or technological innovation, breaking it down into achievable objectives is crucial.

During this phase, it is essential to tap into cross-functional expertise, from engineers to marketers, to brainstorm multiple avenues for each objective. These options could range from minor tweaks in existing systems to revolutionary changes in business operations.

However, change is happing every day. What is cutting-edge today might be obsolete tomorrow. That is why, while brainstorming, **consider multiple avenues** for each component objective. For instance, improving data security could include a transition to blockchain technology, implementing advanced encryption methods, or adopting a multi-cloud strategy. Each technological option has its implications for cost, speed, and effectiveness. Moreover, timing is of the essence. **Contemplating varying timeframes for each option** helps to strike a balance between quick wins and long-term gains. Some objectives might achieve substantial benefits through short-term projects, while others could necessitate longer timelines for noticeable impact. Lastly, even in these initial stages, it is beneficial to **flag potential risks associated with each option**. Identifying these risks early can assist in setting a balanced tone for the options on the table, providing a span from low to high-risk avenues, each with its set of rewards.

By the end of this exhaustive exercise, you should have a **diverse and comprehensive list of options** that serve as the foundation for the next steps in developing your Digital Roadmap. This process ensures that your roadmap will not only be robust but also flexible, setting the stage for a digital transformation journey that is both strategic and adaptable.

### *Navigating the Complex Landscape of Choices: How to Prioritize Your Options*

Once you have dissected your Digital North Star into its foundational elements and brainstormed a multitude of options, the next task is prioritization. It is essential to **align these options directly with your original North Star**, much like what leading global companies have successfully done. Take Amazon, for example. Known for its customer-centric ethos, the e-commerce giant consistently makes prioritization decisions based on **customer expectations**. Amazon leverages extensive data analytics and customer feedback to weigh every potential initiative[92]. When they launched Amazon Prime, it was not just a new service, but a strategic decision aimed at enhancing customer satisfaction. This perfectly illustrates the importance of aligning your options with customer expectations, which can be achieved through customer surveys, feedback loops, and advanced analytics tools.

---

[92] Ellen Merryweather on Product School website: "Prioritizing Roadmaps Based on Data by Amazon Senior Product Manager". Published 09.01.2023, visited 08.04.2024.
https://productschool.com/blog/product-strategy/prioritizing-roadmaps-amazon-senior-product-manager

However, customer satisfaction is just one piece of the puzzle. **How each option contributes to achieving your Digital North Star** is equally important. This involves analyzing how well each initiative helps you get closer to your ultimate vision. For instance, Airbnb's decision to diversify their offerings to include experiences, not just accommodations, serves as a strong example[93]. This new initiative was prioritized because it closely aligned with their North Star of helping people 'Belong Anywhere', showcasing how initiatives can and should contribute towards achieving your overarching goals.

**Business impact** is another crucial consideration, which Netflix exemplifies remarkably well. When the streaming giant transitioned from a DVD rental service to offering streaming and original content, it was a strategic move evaluated for its long-term business impact. They looked at potential ROI, market share gains, and brand recognition to decide that this was not just an operational shift but a core business strategy. Thus, it is vital to consider options that offer the most significant positive impact on your key business metrics.

However, any option that looks great on paper must also pass the **feasibility test**. Tesla serves as a prime example here. Even though the company's North Star has been to accelerate the world's transition to sustainable energy, Tesla had to consider technological constraints, infrastructure, and cost. They opted to first focus on high-end models before venturing into more affordable options like the Tesla Model 3. This demonstrates the importance of practicality in the prioritization process, considering technological limitations, resource allocation, and timelines.

By **integrating these four critical criteria** – customer expectations, contribution to the North Star, business impact, and feasibility – you can craft a holistic view of your priorities of your options. This multi-faceted approach to prioritizing ensures that you make informed decisions that align with both your immediate needs and long-term vision.

### *Navigating the Timeline: Bringing the Digital North Star into Reach*

Now that we have tackled the complexities of breaking down the Digital North Star into actionable options and prioritized those options, the next logical step is to craft a realistic timeline that considers both priorities and available resources. This is where strategic planning merges with operational logistics, ensuring that your digital transformation initiative is not just aspirational but attainable.

---

[93] Thibault Vernier on LinkedIn: "From an accommodation disruptor to a tourism giant: Experiences by Airbnb, story of a successful diversification strategy". Published 11.02.2020, visited 08.04.2024. https://www.linkedin.com/pulse/from-accommodation-disruptor-tourism-giant-airbnb-story-vernier

Creating a timeline requires more than just slotting in dates next to initiatives, it demands a comprehensive understanding of your resources. Salesforce serves as an illuminating example here. The company is renowned for implementing their 'V2MOM' model – Vision, Values, Methods, Obstacles, and Measures – to craft timelines. **Your timeline should account for human resources, financial budgets, technological readiness**, and any other critical factors that would impact the successful implementation of your chosen options.

As you are mapping out this timeline, it is essential to build in flexibility to accommodate unforeseen changes. The tech industry offers numerous examples, but a standout is Spotify with their Agile methodology. **The timeline you construct must be able to adapt without losing sight of the overarching Digital North Star.** Moreover, the synchronization of multiple timelines across different departments or business units becomes crucial, as digital transformation is rarely confined to a single area of the business. Microsoft's shift to cloud services like Azure can be instructive. **Cross-functional coordination is indispensable when aligning the moving parts of a complex digital transformation initiative.** Finally, review mechanisms need to be integrated into your timeline. Regular check-ins and performance metrics should be used to assess progress. Google, known for their OKRs (Objectives and Key Results), provides a useful model for setting measurable goals and revisiting them regularly[94]. **Incorporate regular check-ins and key performance indicators** to ensure that the timeline remains aligned with both the Digital North Star and the ever-evolving business landscape.

Crafting a realistic timeline is a balancing act that involves juggling various moving pieces. **It is about plotting a course that is aggressive enough to keep you competitive, yet realistic enough to be achievable.** The end goal is a timeline that is not just a series of dates but a dynamic roadmap that can adapt to both the expected and the unexpected, serving as your operational blueprint for reaching your Digital North Star.

### *Validating the Pathway: Ensuring Stakeholder and Customer Alignment*

Having crafted a planned timeline, the next crucial step is to validate your Digital Roadmap with both internal stakeholders and customers. This validation process serves multiple purposes: it ensures buy-in, tests assumptions, and offers a chance to refine the plan before it is set in motion. **Validating with internal stakeholders** first is crucial because they will be the ones implementing the plan. Companies like Procter & Gamble often set up cross-functional teams specifically for validating strategic roadmaps, reflecting the importance of internal stakeholder buy-in for successful implementation. Therefore, each department involved – be it marketing,

---

[94] John Doerr: "Measure What Matters". Published by Penguin Business, 2017

IT, or product development – should be consulted, and their feedback should be actively incorporated. Once internal validation is achieved, the focus shifts to **customer validation**, which can often provide surprising insights that can pivot the entire direction of your roadmap. Adobe, a leader in the software industry, often employs customer beta testing and feedback loops to validate new features before fully integrating them into their product suite[95]. In the same vein, use customer surveys, interviews, or even prototype testing to ensure that the initiatives on your roadmap resonate with your customer base. The key to successful validation is the flexibility to adapt the plan based on feedback while still maintaining alignment with your Digital North Star. Amazon's relentless focus on customer-centricity is a shining example. Their constant iteration based on customer feedback without deviating from their larger goals shows that a Digital Roadmap is not set in stone but is more like a living document that can and should be updated. Lastly, validation is not a one-off event but an on-going process. **Continuous refinement** based on real-world feedback ensures your roadmap stays both current and effective. Companies like Tesla, with their over-the-air software updates, show the benefits of a continually evolving roadmap that adapts based on user experience and feedback.

Validation is where the rubber meets the road. It is a critical juncture where your Digital Roadmap is exposed to real-world scrutiny, providing an invaluable opportunity for refinement and course correction.

### *Documenting the Journey: Communication as the Cornerstone*

Upon validation, the next imperative step is documenting your Digital Roadmap for communication. This stage is not merely about creating a paper trail but serves as an essential vehicle for aligning everyone on the path towards the Digital North Star. A well-documented Digital Roadmap becomes the **playbook, detailing the how, when, and who of your digital transformation journey.**

Companies like IBM have made documentation an integral part of their road-mapping, often hosting webinars, workshops, and publishing whitepapers to disseminate their strategies[96]. The same rigor should be applied to your Digital Roadmap. From a C-level executive overview to granular action items for individual team members, **different versions of the roadmap should be prepared to suit varied audiences.**

---

[95] Michael Muchmore on PC website: "Adobe Launches Photoshop Beta Program". Published online 17.08.2021, visited 08.04.2024. https://uk.pcmag.com/photo-editing/135113/adobe-launches-photoshop-beta-program

[96] On IBM company website: "IBM Unveils New Roadmap to Practical Quantum Computing Era; Plans to Deliver 4,000+ Qubit System". Published online 10.05.2022, visited 08.04.2024. https://newsroom.ibm.com/2022-05-10-IBM-Unveils-New-Roadmap-to-Practical-Quantum-Computing-Era-Plans-to-Deliver-4,000-Qubit-System

The roadmap should also be **easily accessible, not just physically but also in terms of understanding.** Google Drive, SharePoint, or any other collaborative platform should host the roadmap, making it accessible to all relevant parties. Furthermore, it should be drafted in a language that can be comprehended at all organizational levels.

But documentation extends beyond just the roadmap itself. Creating **supplemental materials**, like FAQs, explanatory videos, or even an internal podcast series, can help to elucidate complex points. Salesforce, for example, often employs multimedia documentation methods, using everything from blog posts to video explainers to get their roadmap understood across diverse internal audiences.

Communication also **involves training sessions and workshops** to educate team members on the plan's implications and their roles in its execution. Companies like Microsoft provide extensive training modules for new initiatives, allowing team members to understand not just what is changing, but why, and how they fit into that change.

Ultimately, your Digital Roadmap's effectiveness is directly proportional to how well it is communicated. An inadequately communicated roadmap can result in misalignment, confusion, and inefficient resource allocation.

### *Operationalizing the Vision: Integrating the Digital Roadmap into Product Backlogs*

Once your Digital Roadmap is documented and disseminated, the last major step is bringing it into the **backlogs of Product Owners**, transforming strategic vision into **tactical execution.** The backlog becomes the operational layer of your Digital Roadmap, where grand strategies are distilled into implementable tasks.

Companies like Spotify excel at seamlessly integrating roadmaps into agile backlogs, employing frameworks like 'squads', 'tribes', and 'guilds' to connect high-level objectives to daily tasks. Similarly, each item on your Digital Roadmap should map to a set of actionable tasks in the product backlog.

Vital to this operational layer is the use of **Minimum Viable Products (MVPs).** These MVPs serve as focused experiments that allow for quick validation of roadmap items. They can be assigned to specific mission teams to ensure rapid development and deployment, adding a layer of tactical agility to your product backlog. The MVPs also offer a framework for testing assumptions, validating initiatives, and making agile adjustments based on real-world feedback[97].

This involves more than mere task allocation, it calls for a deep understanding of dependencies between tasks, the resource load for each, and the time-sensitive

---

[97] Jonathan Smart: "Sooner, Safer, Happier". Published by IT Revolution in 2020

nature of market demands. Companies like Netflix, for instance, employ a detailed system for tagging and prioritizing backlog items based not just on technical feasibility but also business impact and customer value. Assigning responsibilities for each backlog item is crucial. Companies like Airbnb assign 'mission teams' for each strategic objective, clearly outlining who is responsible for which part of the strategic plan and corresponding backlog items. Performance metrics tied to each backlog item further add to this dynamic ecosystem. Companies like Amazon maintain robust KPI systems that link directly back to individual tasks, enabling real-time performance monitoring. Importantly, these KPIs are designed not just to measure output but to evaluate how each task advances towards the overarching Digital North Star. Continual adaptation and refinement characterize this stage as a never-ending process. As digital technologies evolve, so too will the tasks in your backlog. Google's agile methodology, featuring frequent 'sprint reviews', serves as an exemplary model for continually updating the backlog in line with real-world results and changes in strategy.

To sum up, the final stage is not just about assigning tasks but about creating a dynamic, responsive system. It transforms the 'what' and 'why' of your Digital North Star into the 'how', operationalizing your direction into daily tasks. This ensures not just alignment but effective implementation, guiding your organization ever closer to its Digital North Star.

Find more and updated information in the **Digital Arena.** Connect with like-minded professionals to unleash the potential and make it happen.

With a defined Digital Strategy, companies can aim higher – pursuing a Digital Lead.

## 3.5  Digital Lead

> «A leader takes people where they want to go. A great
> leader takes people where they do not necessarily want
> to go, but ought to be.»
> Rosalynn Carter[98]

Businesses are constantly in a race to outperform and outshine. They are not just competing against traditional rivals, they are also up against rapidly changing consumer expectations and the relentless pace of technological advancement. At the heart of this seismic shift lies the concept of a 'Digital Lead' – a holistic approach that melds the art of **Digital Wow**, where every touchpoint becomes an opportunity to dazzle, and the science of **Digital Intelligence**, the bedrock that empowers companies to anticipate, adapt, and always be a step ahead.

### 3.5.1  Digital Wow

In an era where every organization is striving for a digital presence, standing out becomes a daunting task. While many offer functionality, fewer deliver true enchantment. The modern consumer, spoiled for choice and with the world at their fingertips, craves more than just functionality – they seek the Digital Wow. It is that indescribable feeling when an app, website, or digital service does not just serve its purpose but does so in a way that delights, surprises, and resonates.

**What the C-Suite needs to know**

1. **Transcendent Experiences:** Digital Wow is not about mere interaction, it is about curating moments of profound resonance. Brands that differentiate in today's saturated digital market are those that create not just touchpoints but memorable experiences, captivating consumers at every encounter.

2. **Deep-rooted Understanding:** Success in wowing customers is deeply anchored in a brand's ability to genuinely understand its consumers. This means going beyond basic demographics to capture nuances, preferences, and behaviors, tailoring interactions to everyone's unique context.

3. **Anticipatory Engagement:** Proactive approaches, powered by insightful analytics, are transforming the reactive nature of customer service. Leading brands are now discerning and addressing user needs even before they are articulated, delighting customers by consistently exceeding their expectations.

4. **Consistency Meets Personalization:** A Digital Wow moment is sculpted at the intersection of consistent brand experiences and hyper-personalization. Every digital interaction, be it through

---

tailored content or proactive engagement, should echo a brand's ethos while resonating deeply with the individual user's needs.

5.  **Adaptive Evolution:** The digital environment is in perpetual flux. What wows consumers today might become the norm tomorrow. Thus, brands must embed adaptability into their strategies, continuously evolving and innovating to craft new moments of digital awe, ensuring sustained relevance and engagement.

But what will trigger a Digital Wow?

## Awareness: Crafting Digital Magic through Profound Customer Insights

The Digital Wow is not a mere transient moment of admiration. It is the manifestation of a carefully orchestrated digital experience where every touchpoint, every nuance, is deliberately crafted with the user's emotional and functional desires in the foreground. At the heart of this experience is a **deep-rooted understanding of the customer**, an understanding that informs and elevates every digital interaction.

Diving deeper, one realizes that the foundation of this concept is anchored in several key pillars. **Aesthetics** form the first impression, enveloping users in a sensory embrace. It is not just about the visuals but the entire sensory tapestry – colors, typography, imagery, and even the subtle tones, like the memorable chime of Skype or the familiar 'ding' of an Apple iMessage. These are not mere sounds but auditory cues that enhance and enrich the digital journey, all fine-tuned by a profound comprehension of what is liked by the user. However, even the most visually arresting platform loses its charm if navigating it becomes a herculean task. This is where **usability** shines. An intuitive, logical, and frictionless journey, curated by expert user experience (UX) designers and backed by an understanding of user behavior, ensures that users are not just visitors but engaged participants in the digital narrative (visit section 3.3.2 Customer-centric Journeys on page 203 to recap on how to define seamless flows).

At the crossroads of modern digital experiences, **personalization stands tall, emerging as the non-negotiable aspect**. In this age of information overload, users no longer desire generic content, they seek a bespoke digital experience. Personalization is about understanding user behaviors, past interactions, preferences, and even potential future needs. It is the transformation of raw data into meaningful interactions. Brands, aware of this paradigm shift, are investing heavily in AI and machine learning to mine insights and craft experiences that feel tailor-made. Spotify's 'Discover Weekly' is not just a playlist – it is a reflection of a user's musical journey, desires, and aspirations. Netflix's recommendation engine, too, goes beyond genre classifications, diving deep into viewing patterns, pausing behaviors, and even the time of day to suggest content. Grab suggests different destinations depending on weekday and timing. Personalization, when done right, does not feel algorithmic – it feels almost human. But to truly stand out, brands need an edge. **Innovation** offers that edge. Whether it is through the magic of augmented or virtual reality or the precision of AI-generated content, innovation ensures that the digital journey remains fresh, engaging, and future-forward.

And why is all this so paramount? Because in an era of digital ubiquity, **engagement is the gold standard. It is not just about numbers, but the depth, quality, and emotional resonance of interactions.** Brands like Apple have not just understood this but made it their ethos. Their products, while individually stellar, come together in a symphony, offering users a seamless, integrated digital experience that is hard to replicate. Yet, beyond engagement lies a deeper bond – **loyalty.** In a world teeming with digital options, earning loyalty is both challenging and rewarding. Consistent 'wow' moments forge this bond, turning users from mere consumers to brand evangelists, and this loyalty is invariably rooted in the feeling of being deeply understood and valued.

However, creating ripples in the vast digital ocean requires brands to be distinctive, to have a voice, a character – **differentiation.** Alibaba's transformation of the e-commerce landscape with its gala events, celebrity tie-ins, and gamified shopping experiences is a masterclass in differentiation, all possible because they understand their vast user base's nuances[99]. But amidst all this global grandeur, the importance of **local relevance** cannot be overstated. Jumia, Africa's e-commerce torchbearer, offers a shining example in this. With its localized interfaces and content, it ensures that the vastness of the digital reality still feels intimate, personal, and homegrown, all stemming from a profound understanding of its diverse customer base.

Understanding the Digital Wow is a necessity for brands aspiring to carve their niche in the digital age.

---

**Apple Inc.: Crafting Seamless Experiences in the Digital Epoch**

In 1976, a Cupertino garage became the birthplace of not just a tech giant but a beacon of experiential innovation. Founded by visionaries Steve Jobs, Steve Wozniak, and Ronald Wayne, Apple Inc. embarked on a mission far grander than creating devices – it aimed to weave magic into every digital interaction, setting the gold standard for customer touchpoints.

Central to Apple's ethos is a compelling conviction: Every interaction, no matter how minuscule, holds the potential to 'wow'. This philosophy permeates through their carefully designed devices. From the

---

[99] Raymond Zhang on New York Times website: "A Chastened Alibaba Tones Down Its Singles Day Retail Bonanza". Published 10.11.2021, visited 08.04.2024.
https://www.nytimes.com/2021/11/10/technology/china-alibaba-singles-day.html

tactile sensation of unboxing an iPhone to the gentle haptic feedback of the Apple Watch, the sensory delight is undeniable and thoughtfully curated.

The world of Apple is not confined to just tangible products, it extends to a harmonious software ecosystem. iOS, macOS, watchOS, and even the App Store are more than mere platforms — they are immersive experiences. Crafted with a blend of intuition and intelligence, Apple's software suite exemplifies how seamlessness can be both felt and celebrated.

Yet, this would not be possible without Apple's emphasis on personalization. From tailored music recommendations on Apple Music to the dynamic continuity between devices, Apple leverages deep insights to understand and cater to individual preferences, ensuring that users do not just engage but resonate with their digital journey.

Apple's retail experience further amplifies its commitment to 'wow' at every touchpoint. Apple Stores, architecturally iconic and functionally interactive, are more than retail outlets — they are hubs of discovery. Whether it is the inviting layout, hands-on product demos, or the enlightening 'Today at Apple' sessions, the retail space of Apple is the benchmark in user engagement.

The company's foray into services, be it Apple TV+ with its original content or Apple Arcade catering to gamers, underscores the brand's vision of being omnipresent in its users' digital lives. Each service, meticulously crafted, acts as a touchpoint, creating memories, evoking emotions, and reinforcing Apple's unwavering commitment to excellence.

Supporting this labyrinth of touchpoints is Apple's robust customer support framework. From the empathetic assistance at the Genius Bar to the comprehensive online support documentation, Apple ensures that post-purchase, the enchantment does not wane but intensifies.

From its inception in a humble Californian garage to its global dominion as a tech titan, Apple's journey illustrates intent, innovation, and an insatiable desire to enchant at every digital turn. It stands as a testament to what is achievable when every interaction, every detail, and every moment is seen as an opportunity to redefine excellence. In the annals of digital history, Apple will be remembered not just for its groundbreaking products but for its visionary approach to wowing users at every conceivable touchpoint.

## Amazon: Pioneering the New Age of Digital Commerce with Unmatched Precision

In 1994, the world caught its first glimpse of Amazon, emerging from Jeff Bezos's garage as a humble online bookstore. Fast forward to today, and this e-commerce titan has reshaped the very contours of online shopping, intertwining innovation with consumer desires, and redefining the digital sales landscape.

Central to Amazon's meteoric ascent is an unwavering principle: Every digital interaction is an opportunity to 'wow' the customer. This ethos is not merely tacked onto the shopping experience — it is woven into its very fabric. From the moment a user lands on the platform, they are enveloped in a bespoke experience that seems almost predictive in its precision.

Amazon's 1-Click ordering exemplifies frictionless commerce. With a single click, purchases are streamlined, bypassing the traditional cart process, and amplifying spontaneous buying. It is a subtle nod to the future — a world where transactions are instant and hassle-free.

However, the true genius lies in Amazon's ability to personalize the shopping journey. Through precise algorithms that track browsing habits, past purchases, and even items lingered upon, Amazon crafts curated recommendations, acting as both a guide and confidante. It is not merely about suggesting products, it is about understanding individual narratives and intertwining them with the vast tapestry of options available.

The introduction of Amazon Prime was a masterstroke, fusing loyalty with unparalleled convenience. Offering an array of benefits from swift shipping to exclusive entertainment access, Prime transformed passive shoppers into brand advocates. It is a testament to Amazon's foresight – recognizing that loyalty is not just born from purchasing but from cultivating holistic experiences

Innovation is at the heart of Amazon's endeavors. Whether it is the voice-assisted shopping through Alexa or visualizing products in real-time with Augmented Reality, Amazon persistently pushes the boundaries of digital commerce. Each new feature is not just an addition – it is a statement of intent, a promise of what is on the horizon.

Yet, the digital journey is not just about buying. Amazon's transparent review system and unparalleled customer service seal the trust pact with users. The assurance that their voice matters and that support is always at hand creates an environment where buying is not just a transaction but a bond.

Spanning continents with localized marketplaces, Amazon demonstrates a profound understanding of regional nuances. From offering regional specials to hosting local sellers, Amazon ensures its global footprint is felt intimately at a local level.

From its inception as a simple online store to its reigning position as a global e-commerce leader, Amazon's journey epitomizes the fusion of vision, innovation, and relentless customer focus. In the vast digital narrative, Amazon stands tall, not merely as a marketplace but as a trailblazer, continuously reimagining and redefining how the world experiences digital sales. In every endeavor, be it in tech integration or customer interaction, Amazon echoes a profound commitment to wow, engage, and inspire in the ever-evolving digital epoch[100].

Acknowledging the ambition for a Digital Wow, let us start with assessing where your company stands.

### Assessment: Measuring the Magic of the 'Wow' Factor

 Beyond generic metrics and standard KPIs, there exists a nuanced spectrum of measures that explore deeper, revealing the essence of the customer's Digital Wow. **It is about capturing those fleeting yet profound moments** that transition a customer from mere satisfaction to sheer delight.

Central to this endeavor is the art of **Emotion Tracking & Sentiment Analysis**. In today's digital age, with vast swathes of data at our fingertips, we can tap into the

---

<sup>100</sup> Avery Hartmans on Insider website: "Jeff Bezos originally wanted to name Amazon 'Cadabra', and 14 other little-known facts about the early days of the e-commerce giant". Updated 02.07.2021, visited 08.04.2024. https://www.businessinsider.com/jeff-bezos-amazon-history-facts-2017-4?r=US&IR=T

heartbeats of customer feedback. It is not merely about classifying reviews as positive or negative, it is about discerning the fervor and intensity behind them. Tools like Brandwatch or Crimson Hexagon come into play, capturing sentiments and phrases like 'beyond expectations' or 'never experienced this before' that resonate with profound experiences. Yet, sentiment alone is not the complete picture. Enter the **Moment of Wow Surveys**. Unlike broad feedback mechanisms, these micro-surveys are surgically precise. Deployed post key touchpoints, they hone in on specific experiences, asking the critical questions: 'Did our product exceed your expectations?' or 'What elements of our service left an indelible mark?' By narrowing the focus, businesses can pinpoint and replicate those exact moments of 'wow'. These surveys must be integrated into the touchpoints and the end-to-end customer journeys. An often-underappreciated treasure trove of insights is **Customer Support Interactions**. Between the lines of support chats and calls lie golden nuggets of feedback. An experience that truly 'wows' will echo in reduced complaints and will reverberate in praises like 'I was amazed by...' or 'This was beyond anything I anticipated'.

One undeniable indicator of a 'wow' experience is when a customer becomes a brand evangelist. **Referral and Word-of-Mouth Metrics** stand as testament to a job well done. Tracking organic brand mentions, unsolicited testimonials, or even spontaneous hashtags can reveal the domino effect of a single 'wow' moment, as it ripples through the vast ocean of the digital community. Yet, the journey does not end at the point of sale. **Post-Purchase Behavior Analysis** can shed light on the lasting impact of a 'wow' experience. A customer swiftly upgrading to premium services, or fervently exploring complementary products, indicates that the initial touchpoint was not just satisfactory — it was exceptional.

Assessing the Digital Wow factor is a multi-faceted journey, blending sharpened traditional metrics with innovative techniques. It is a collection of data points, harmonizing to narrate a tale of surprise, delight, and unmatched appreciation.

### Action: Cultivating the Digital Wow Through Deliberate Strategies

 To metamorphose the abstract idea of a digital 'wow' into tangible customer experiences, a carefully crafted action plan becomes indispensable. Businesses must harmonize technology, data, and creativity to design moments that linger in a customer's memory, persuading them to return, engage, and evangelize. Here is how this transformation can be actualized.

### *Personalization: The Ultimate Key to Building Memorable Digital Experiences*

In the sprawling landscape of digital interactions, where every brand competes for a sliver of consumer attention, personalization emerges as the magic wand. This is not just an engagement tactic, it is a committed strategy that effectively tells the consumer: 'We see you, we understand you, and we value you'. To reach the pinnacle of personalization, it demands a comprehensive approach that is rooted in a **deep understanding of individual needs**, the discernment to anticipate desires, and the prowess to consistently deliver tailor-made experiences.

To foster a deeper connection, platforms can empower users to **shape their experience according to their preferences**. Spotify takes this to heart, allowing listeners to articulate their mood through music choices, creating playlists that capture different moments in life, and even defining the kind of music that matches their current emotions. Harnessing this data, Spotify goes a step further, crafting 'Daily Mixes' and the much-celebrated 'Year in Review' playlists, which not only recap a user's year in music but also present new tracks based on their listening history, turning every listen into a journey of musical discovery. This approach, grounded in detailed data analysis, transforms a user's interaction with the app into a narrative that is as unique as they are.

The true cornerstone of personalization is the **strategic and ethical collection and analysis of relevant user data to generate actionable insights**. Netflix has crafted a recommendation system that has almost redefined the viewer's journey. This system, a testament to Netflix's commitment to understanding its audience, dives deep into individual viewing habits – going beyond the obvious to observe pausing patterns, re-watches, and even the pace at which shows are binged. It is this nuanced approach that facilitates a recommendation system with a predictive accuracy that often feels uncannily precise, offering viewers a tailored selection that matches their preferences with a deep understanding.

Taking a step beyond merely reacting to user behavior, **the futuristic element of personalization is about predicting the user's next step before they even realize it**. Amazon is peerless in this dimension of personalization. Its algorithms constantly learn from a user's browsing patterns, including the products they hover over, the ones they add to their cart but never buy, and even the products they review[101]. This combination of user actions crafts a personal shopping journey, offering not just products but potential experiences and solutions, ushering users towards products they desire, sometimes before they even consciously register their want.

**Personalization, at its zenith, involves a delicate ballet of understanding, meeting, and predicting user expectations**, transforming digital platforms into personalized companions that anticipate and meet user needs with a grace that feels almost magical. It is a continuous journey to forge deeper connections, building a digital

---

[101] Larry Hardesty on Amazon company website: "The history of Amazon's recommendation algorithm Collaborative filtering and beyond". Published 22.11.2019, visited 08.04.2024.
https://www.amazon.science/the-history-of-amazons-recommendation-algorithm

landscape that feels less like a marketplace and more like a haven of curated experiences, tailor-made for everyone.

***Segment of One: Crafting Individual Content***

In the complex terrain of the digital ecosystem, today's consumers, enriched with information and choice, **crave content that mirrors their precise identities, aspirations, and the individual paths they tread in their daily lives.** The need for brands is clear: to dive into the rich context of individual narratives, crafting content that not just resonates, but feels exclusively crafted for each user.

Exploring the consumers' psyche forms the first phase of this challenging process. It involves not just understanding the superficial metrics but genuinely exploring their lifestyles, preferences, digital behavior, and even the emotional triggers that influence their decisions. For instance, Spotify's 'Discover Weekly' stands as a monumental achievement in tailored content, creating a collection of music that often feels like a friend who knows your current emotional state, the highs and lows, and offers a song for each moment. It is this profound understanding that leads to the creation of playlists that connects with each individual on a deeply personal level.

A **razor-sharp segmentation of the audience** paves the way for a rich content strategy, where each segment is a canvas for crafting messages that breathe life into unique desires and behaviors. Nike's approach embodies this principle to perfection, where they distinguish between a marathon runner and a casual gym-goer, offering stories that spotlight the technology behind each shoe, thus translating the brand's deep understanding into a narrative that directly speaks to the individual needs of each segment[102].

Transitioning to the stage of content creation, brands stand before an expansive canvas where the nuances of each segmented group form the colors and textures to paint a story that echo the precise challenges and aspirations of each group. Brands like HubSpot brilliantly manifest this by breaking down their content not merely by business size, but even diving into the unique challenges faced by different roles within an organization, thereby offering solutions through blog posts, webinars, and eBooks that feel like a mentor offering tailored guidance (visit section 3.3.1.2.3 Attractive Content: The Universal Magnet for Digital Engagement on page 193 for further inspiration).

---

[102] On Two Teachers website: "How Nike uses Behavioural Segmentation to Create Personalised Marketing Campaigns". Updated 10.09.2023, visited 08.04.2024.
https://www.twoteachers.co.uk/post/how-nike-uses-behavioural-segmentation-to-create-personalised-marketing-campaigns

In this vibrant digital narrative, **user-generated content emerges as a powerful tool, bringing an unparalleled authenticity**, a kind of raw, unfiltered lens into individual lives. GoPro leverages this, creating a mosaic of experiences that range from adrenaline-packed adventures to touching everyday moments, presenting a platform where every user can see reflections of their own experiences and aspirations.

Taking a step further, **real-time content creation stands as the pinnacle of this strategy**, bringing to life a dynamically evolving landscape that molds itself to cater to the individual preferences and behaviors of the users. Airbnb stands at the forefront of this strategy, offering a curated list of accommodations, dynamically changing not just based on past interactions but also adjusting prices in real time based on a plethora of factors, creating an experience that feels like a personal travel assistant who knows your preferences inside out. Imagine reading a blog or an online magazine that **morphs its content based on your preferences**. Medium, the popular online publishing platform, does just that. Based on reading patterns, claps given, or even writers you follow, it curates a daily feed that feels custom-built. Beyond articles, even ad placements, and promotional content are tailored, ensuring users feel the platform speaks directly to them.

In a world where content is king, crafting individual narratives demands a deep constructive collaboration of art and science, an inter-dependence between creativity and technological prowess. Brands today are not just content creators but artists, crafting narratives that form deep, lasting emotional bridges, creating a world where every consumer feels seen, heard, and deeply understood.

### Consistent Experiences: Crafting the Specific Moments

Navigating the bustling corridors of digital platforms requires brands not only to maintain a steadfast consistency but also to weave personal elements that cater to each user's idiosyncrasies. This endeavor is not about mere branding uniformity, it is an invitation for brands to understand the granular nuances of every individual and ensure that each digital touchpoint, while part of a broader cohesive brand narrative, has a distinct personal resonance.

The quest for carving out a unique space starts with an understanding and acknowledgement of the potency of a well-established brand presence. **It encompasses a journey from universal to specific, with tailored gestures that foster a deeper connection**. Take Coca-Cola. Beyond the universally recognized red and white motif, they ventured into campaigns like 'Share a Coke', where bottles carried individual names. This initiative was not just about branding, it was about making every John, Priya, or Ahmed feel they had a personal stake in the global brand. Additionally, with the advent of technology, they have enabled personalized messages on bottles ordered online, allowing for a highly individualized brand interaction. This initiative blossomed into a deeply personal interaction platform, offering consumers the delight of finding their names or even personalized messages on a Coke bottle, thereby nurturing an individual's connection with the global message, a tactful blend of global and personal[103].

In this enriched narrative, universal design layouts hold significant sway, but the masterpiece is carved in the subtleties that lie in the crevices of individual preferences. Consider Spotify. Each user, upon logging in, sees a 'Made for [Name]' playlist. Behind the scenes, complex algorithms curate this playlist based on past listening behaviors, time of day, and even mood derived from track choices. So, while every Spotify interface might seem similar, the underlying content has been fine-tuned to resonate with individual rhythms. This brings forth an **offering that feels deeply personal and curated with a careful hand**.

As brands weave these personalized stories, a harmonious amalgamation of diverse user interactions creates a tapestry rich with individual stories and preferences. Amazon nurtures this landscape, knitting together browsing histories and subtle preferences to unfold a narrative that feels not just personal, but almost bespoke, offering suggestions that echo with a user's unstated desires, creating a browsing landscape that feels less like a marketplace and more like a story woven with personal desires at its core.

Apple steers its ship through these waters with a detailed eye on integration and predictive personalization, utilizing tools like Siri Shortcuts to foster a daily narrative that feels less automated and more akin to a personal assistant that learns and evolves, **predicting needs with an intuition that feels almost human**, offering suggestions that echo the user's daily rhythms and preferences, nurturing a digital assistant relationship that evolves to become almost predictive in nature.

The narrative extends to even the feedback loops, turning them into rich grounds for fostering a personal connection. When a platform like Airbnb receives feedback about a hard-to-find feature, it does not just make platform-wide changes. For users who raised that concern, their subsequent searches might have subtle UI changes, making those features more prominent. It is a silent nod to the user, an acknowledgment that their voice has been heard and acted upon.

The above details aspire to immerse in a landscape where the digital experiences are not just consistent but richly personalized, echoing the deeper nuances of individual preferences and tastes.

---

[103] Ariela Gorshtein on Medium website: "A Lesson From Coke: The Importance of Personalization". Published 29.11.2020, visited 08.04.2024. https://medium.com/marketing-in-the-age-of-digital/a-lesson-from-coke-the-importance-of-personalization-88f0d42ee4f2

***Proactive Interactions: Anticipating Desires in a Dynamic Digital Voyage***

Navigating the digital opportunities requires an acute sense of foresight. Today's consumers, empowered by technology and spoilt for choices, expect businesses to not just cater to their explicit needs but to discern and respond to their implicit desires. This calls for a **shift from mere reactive strategies to proactive engagements** – a nuanced art of predicting user needs and seamlessly embedding solutions, even before a want is articulated. It is about transitioning from simply serving to genuinely surprising and delighting the digital customer at every juncture.

There is a subtle difference between responding to a query and predicting one. The modern digital ethos demands the latter – **Engaging even before they ask.** Brands are expected to analyze user behaviors, preferences, and patterns, and then craft experiences or offers that align perfectly with those patterns. Think of Starbucks. By smartly leveraging their mobile app, they dispatch notifications about fresh beverages or tempting discounts just as users approach or pass by a store, especially during their typical visit timings. It transcends the reality of simple promotion – it is a timely, tailored invitation that synchronizes harmoniously with the user's daily rhythm.

The crux of proactive digital interactions lies in the timely **delivery of curated content or offers.** Brands are now equipped with a wealth of user data, which when processed through advanced algorithms can generate highly personalized and timely offers. Zalando, the European fashion e-commerce stalwart, does not just rely on generic promotions. It studies browsing history, previous purchase data, and even abandoned carts to send users perfectly timed, personalized offers. Imagine receiving a special discount on that pair of shoes you contemplated buying a week ago but decided against – that is Zalando's proactive magic at work.

Beyond sales and marketing, proactive strategies have transformative potential in customer support. Instead of waiting for a device to malfunction or a system to crash, leading brands now employ predictive analytics to forecast and preemptively address potential hiccups: **Predictive Support Systems.** Dell, for instance, leverages diagnostic tests and deep user pattern analysis. If their system perceives a potential glitch or a need for an update, they proactively reach out, offering solutions or updates, often surprising users who were not even aware of the looming issue[104].

The essence of proactive interaction lies in creating an anticipatory digital aura. Brands that embrace this philosophy do not merely meet expectations, they

---

[104] Kent Allison on Dell company website: "5 Ways to See Ahead and Stay Ahead with AI Support Technology". Published online 26.04.2019, visited 08.04.2024. https://www.dell.com/en-us/blog/5-ways-to-see-ahead-and-stay-ahead-with-ai-support-technology/

consistently exceed them, creating experiences that do not just satisfy but genuinely captivate – they wow the customer.

Creating a Digital Wow is essential to lead in the digital space. However, this can only be done with superior Digital Intelligence.

### 3.5.2   Digital Intelligence

To create the 'Wow' we need to put a Digital Intelligence Ecosystem in place. This ecosystem consists of clearly prioritized Intelligence Use Cases across functions, applied Intelligence Capabilities, strong Infrastructural Foundations, reliable Data & Data Management, as well as competent Data Teams and Culture.

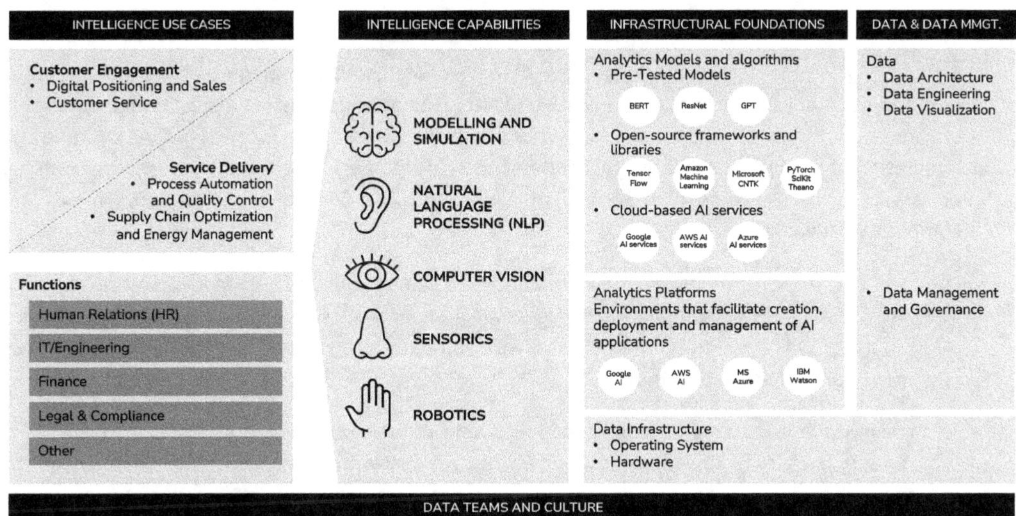


*Figure 25: Digital Intelligence Ecosystem*

This is an ecosystem that defines your future Digital Success.

**What the C-Suite needs to know**

1. Digital Intelligence consists of clearly prioritized Intelligence Use Cases, applied Intelligence Capabilities, strong Infrastructural Foundations, reliable Data & Data Management, as well as competent Data Teams and Culture.

2. Leveraging Digital Intelligence is critical for creating personalized, predictive, and prescriptive customer engagement use cases that evolve from a static approach to a tailored, data-driven interaction, enhancing customer satisfaction and optimizing business outcomes.

3. Additional mainly efficiency-oriented use cases spread throughout the organization: COOs leverage AI for supply chain and process optimization, HR benefits from AI in talent acquisition and management, and IT uses AI for code optimization and bug detection.

4. AI uses have the potential to revolutionize Finance by enhancing accuracy and strategic forecasting, to transform Legal operations with advanced analytics and efficiency, and to innovate Content Creation through automation and personalization, while underscoring the imperative of

5.  AI's evolution from a theoretical concept to a transformative force across industries is driving the future of technology, marked by milestones from the Turing Test to AGI aspirations, and powered by machine and deep learning techniques that learn and adapt, increasingly blurring the lines between human and machine intelligence.

6.  AI is designed to mimic the intricate workings of the human brain through modeling and simulation for complex decision making, and to replicate human sound recognition via Natural Language Processing for effective human-machine communication. By mimicking other human capabilities – computer vision for sight, sensorics for senses, and robotics for haptics – AI-driven technologies enable organizations to surpass human limitations, offering advanced decision-making tools that enhance precision and efficiency across various applications, from healthcare diagnostics to personalized retail experiences and collaborative industrial automation.

7.  Establishing a robust infrastructural foundation is vital for AI implementation: this includes investment in advanced hardware like GPUs/TPUs, versatile and secure data storage solutions, efficient operating systems, scalable analytics platforms with flexible, user-friendly tools, and the integration of pre-built models and algorithms from cloud-based AI services, open-source libraries, or large tech ecosystems like Google, Amazon, or Microsoft for rapid AI deployment and competitive advantage.

8.  Effective data management is crucial for deriving value from data. It involves ensuring data integrity, secure and structured storage, accessible integration, strict security practices, and regular cleanup, all of which are fundamental for leveraging data as a strategic asset in driving business intelligence and decision-making.

9.  To sustain and enhance digital intelligence, it is crucial for organizations to foster a strong data-driven culture and establish collaborative data teams, with roles from business analysts to solution architects working in concert to translate data into actionable business strategies, under leadership that actively promotes and integrates data analytics into all facets of the organization.

In the following sections, we try to outline the basics on the Digital Intelligence System, being aware that the depth and dynamic in this field is overwhelming[105].

Before we dive into the details, let us get some inspirations from selected world leaders.

---

[105] Among other the following publication takes you to the next level: Papp, Weidinger, Munro, Ortner, Cadonna, Langs, Licandro, Meir-Huber, Nikolic, Toth, Vesela, Wazir, Zauner: "The Handbook of Data Science and AI". Published by Hanser Publishers, Munich, 2022.

**Amazon:** Orchestrating Digital Intelligence to Reshape Consumer Paradigms

From those beginnings, Amazon's journey transcended the face of retail, metamorphosing into a global colossus that leverages unparalleled Digital Intelligence to redefine the consumer experience at every touchpoint.

**Intricate Algorithms for Personal Touch**: At the heart of Amazon's success is its uncanny ability to simulate a personalized shopping assistant's intuition. The recommendation engine, a blend of purchase and browsing histories interwoven with myriad of data points, suggests products with a precision that often feels telepathic. This engine does not merely react to customer actions – it anticipates, predicts, and often knows what a user might want next.

**The Echo of Artificial Intelligence**: Alexa, Amazon's voice assistant, is more than just a digital helper. She is a manifestation of the company's vision of an AI-driven future. As users interact, Alexa learns, adapts, and evolves, creating a seamless interface between man and machine. Each query and command refines this inter-play of interactions, marking Amazon's foray into spaces far beyond e-commerce.

**Empowering the World with AWS**: Amazon Web Services is not just a testament to the company's expansive reach but also to its mission of democratizing Digital Intelligence. Through tools like SageMaker and Comprehend, Amazon offers the power of AI and big data to businesses worldwide, setting the stage for countless innovations.

**Redefining Retail Dynamics with Anticipatory Moves**: One could argue that Amazon's anticipatory shipping borders on science fiction. Yet, it is real and operational. By synthesizing data like search queries, wish lists, and even cursor movements, Amazon proactively pre-ships products, narrowing the gap between desire and gratification.

**The Pinnacle of Physical Retail - Go Stores**: Stepping into an Amazon Go store is akin to experiencing the future of retail. Cashier-less, AI-powered, and sensor-laden, these stores epitomize the zenith of Digital Intelligence in physical retail, offering customers an experience untouched by traditional constraints.

**Mastery in Motion – Supply Chain Excellence**: Amazon's supply chain is not just efficient – it is predictive. Harnessing the prowess of analytics, the retail giant ensures that its vast inventory pulses in rhythm with real-time demand, a dance of numbers that ensures products are always within reach.

From its Seattle origins to global domination, Amazon stands as a beacon of how deep-rooted Digital Intelligence, when married to vision and innovation, can craft experiences that not just satisfy, but truly wow at every conceivable juncture. The essence of Amazon is not just in selling products, it is in understanding the heartbeat of every user, echoing a philosophy that Digital Intelligence is not an add-on, but the very essence of modern business.

**Alibaba Group: Pioneering the Digital Silk Road with Intelligence and Innovation**

Emerging from the bustling city of Hangzhou in 1999, Jack Ma's vision was not just to create an e-commerce platform but to build an ecosystem that would revolutionize commerce, finance, and technology. Today, Alibaba's narrative goes beyond online shopping – it is a tale of leveraging Digital Intelligence to weave a beautiful tapestry of integrated services and experiences.

**A Bazaar of Personalized Experiences**: Alibaba's Taobao and Tmall platforms demonstrate a masterclass in user personalization. Using advanced machine learning algorithms, these platforms tailor shopping experiences by analyzing user interactions, search patterns, and purchase behaviors. The result? A shopping experience as unique as the individual, turning browsing into a journey of delightful discoveries.

**Financial Acumen Meets Tech Prowess**: Ant Group, an Alibaba affiliate, reimagined financial services. With Alipay at its core, Ant Group harnesses AI and big data to offer services ranging from micro-loans to investment products, all with a few taps on a smartphone. It is not just about transactions, it is about understanding financial needs in real-time and offering solutions before they are even sought.

**New Retail - Blurring Online and Offline**: Hema Xiansheng stores, Alibaba's vision of 'New Retail', seamlessly integrate online shopping with a physical store experience. Leveraging data and smart logistics, these stores allow consumers to shop, dine, and order for home delivery, all while AI algorithms work behind the scenes to ensure inventory optimization and personalized promotions.

**Global Trade on a Digital Platter**: Alibaba's B2B platform is not just a marketplace for global trade, it is a hub of intelligence. By analyzing global trade patterns, buyer interactions, and market trends, Alibaba offers businesses insights into potential markets, emerging product trends, and partnership opportunities.

**Cloud Computing with a Twist**: Alibaba Cloud goes beyond mere storage and computing power. It offers AI-powered services, data analytics solutions, and digital transformation consultation, enabling businesses, big and small, to harness the power of their data.

**Entertainment Tailored to Taste**: Youku, Alibaba's video platform, employs AI to curate content based on viewer preferences, watch history, and even mood derived from interactions, ensuring viewers always find content that resonates.

From its inception as a digital marketplace to its evolution into a global conglomerate, Alibaba Group exemplifies the power of Digital Intelligence. Their journey showcases how understanding consumers, businesses, and even entertainment can be transformed when data-driven insights are at the helm. For Alibaba, the future is not just digital, it is intelligently digital, reshaping industries and redefining how businesses interact with their users.

Let us start with the first component of the Digital Intelligence Ecosystem, the Intelligence Use Cases.

### 3.5.2.1 Intelligence Use Cases – Benefitting from Digital Intelligence

The Digital Intelligence Ecosystem can be deployed to optimize use cases along the entire value and delivery chains. Directly supporting the interaction with customers through optimized Customer Engagement and the Service Delivery, but also taking the (internal) functions to the next level.

**Awareness: Understanding the Limitless Potential of Intelligence Use Cases**

Already today a large number of use cases can be optimized through Digital Intelligence – but every day new technical capabilities increase the potential. The space is limitless, prioritization essential.

Digital Intelligence can be used to provide the 'Wow' **optimizing the customer engagement**, by continuously increasing the understanding of the target audience, individualizing the content and the formats, by personalizing the channels and tailoring the timing. With increasing capabilities and ambition, a company can move from a static approach, through the descriptive stages to predictive recommendations (some leaders might even explore prescriptive features).

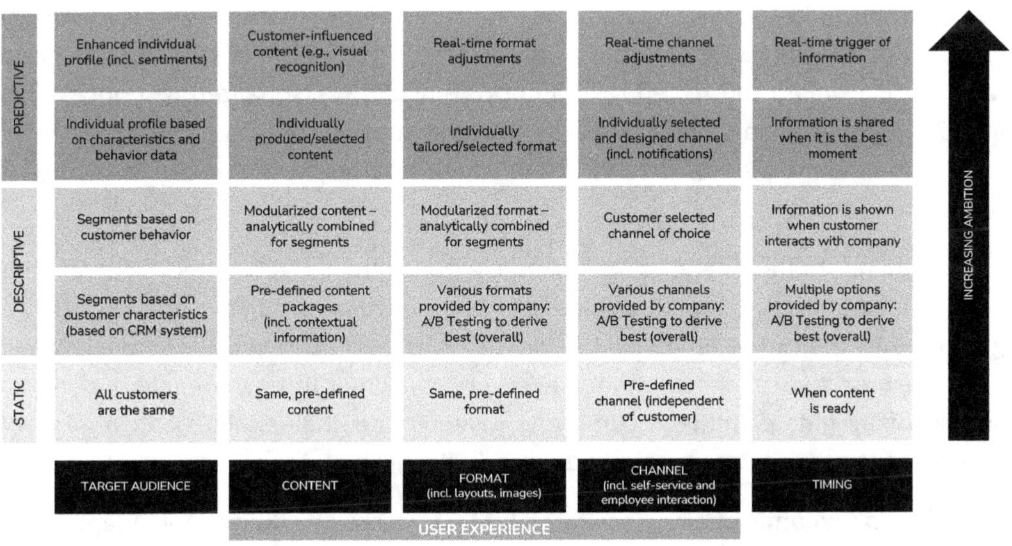


Figure 26: Modules to optimize customer engagement through Digital Intelligence

Let us have a look at some concrete customer engagement use cases spanning this matrix, reshaping the traditional approaches engrained in marketing and sales. Armed with sophisticated tools and profound insights, businesses are witnessing a fundamental shift in the dynamics of customer interaction. Every engagement, every touchpoint is enriched, laying the foundations for relationships that are not just transactional but deeply personal. The essence of this transformation is encapsulated in the nuanced combination between data analysis and modeling. With the Digital Intelligence Ecosystem, based on human and artificial intelligence, as the choreographer, consumer behavior is not just observed but understood, dissected, and interpreted. It crafts a narrative where marketing and sales are not generic but personalized, responsive, and intuitive.

In this context, the notion of **personalized marketing** is not just a strategy but an experience, curated through AI's insights into consumer data, buying patterns, and preferences. Every consumer steps into a world that is uniquely tailored, an ecosystem where products, services, and interactions echo their distinct tastes and preferences. Imagine the silent yet powerful recommendation systems on e commerce platforms, weaving through user's search and purchase histories, aligning products and suggestions with individual predilections. This extends to email marketing, where every message reflects the consumer's journey, preferences, and interactions. It is a world where communication is not broad but bespoke, echoing the individuality of each recipient, making every engagement, every message, a personal conversation.

Yet, the marvel of Digital Intelligence does not halt at personalized marketing. It strides confidently into the domain of **customer service**, where chat bots, powered by algorithms and machine learning, revolutionize engagements. Here, every query is met with immediacy, every question answered with precision, marking an end to long waiting times, and ushering in an era of instant, personalized responses. The integration of chat bots into popular messaging apps has elevated this experience, transforming these platforms into hubs of varied services, each tailored to the user's needs and preferences.

In the sphere of **sales analytics**, AI is akin to a seasoned navigator, steering strategies with a blend of insights and foresights. It is a world where predictive analytics offer a glimpse into the future, enabling businesses to transcend reactive approaches and embrace proactive, informed strategies. Every consumer interaction, every click is a source of insight, painting a comprehensive picture that enables the honing of marketing strategies to resonate deeply and effectively.

The world of **dynamic pricing**, facilitated by AI, is marked by fluidity and adaptability. Prices are not static but dynamic entities, morphing in real-time, echoing the rhythmic dance of market demands, competitor pricing, and external factors. It is a strategy that is alive, ensuring that businesses are not just participants in the market but adept navigators, optimizing profits and enhancing customer satisfaction.

**Sentiment analysis**, another jewel in AI's crown, offers businesses a real-time pulse of the consumer base. It is an era where reviews and feedback are not just read but analyzed, offering immediate insights into brand perception and product reception. Companies are not just observers but active participants, equipped to swiftly respond and adapt, nurturing positive sentiments and mitigating challenges.

These are just a few examples of Digital Intelligence use cases around Customer Engagement. However, Artificial Intelligence helps augment the outcomes and processes across all functions of a company. Let us visit some of them.

**Chief Operating Office (COO) – Enhanced Productivity and Optimized Operations**

When it comes to service delivery, the transformative wave of Artificial Intelligence (AI) has woven itself into the operational fabric of businesses, casting the role of the Chief Operating Officer (COO) in a new light. COOs are now armed with AI's precision and intelligence, a partnership that refines strategies, elevates operations, and instills a robust data-driven approach to decision-making and problem-solving. It is a combination of technology and human ingenuity, where AI is the conductor, orchestrating a performance of enhanced productivity and optimized operational avenues.

In the world of **supply chain management**, AI emerges as a revolutionary force, a navigator that predicts market changes with precision and orchestrates dynamic optimization of supply chains to meet these anticipated shifts effectively. In tandem, demand forecasting weaves through historical sales data, economic indicators, and social media trends, offering forecasts of demand that are not just predictions but precise anticipations. It is a world where inventory is balanced, where the carrying costs and stockouts are minimized, where every product is aligned with the market's pulse.

Yet, AI's contribution does not halt at supply chain optimization. It strides into the domain of **process automation** with grace, where efficiency is not just enhanced but redefined. Robotic Process Automation (RPA) emerges as the silent yet potent workforce, automating transactions, manipulating data, and delivering reports. In the nuanced context of energy management, AI is the adept custodian of efficiency and sustainability. Smart Heating, Ventilation and Air Conditioning (HVAC) Systems and Predictive Energy Analytics are the harbingers of optimization, where energy consumption patterns are not just monitored but optimized. Businesses are not just consumers of energy but custodians of efficiency, where operational costs are minimized, and sustainability is maximized.

**Quality control**, a critical operational facet, witnesses a renaissance with AI. Predictive Analytics in Quality Assurance and Visual Inspection Systems emerge as the vanguards of quality. Production lines are monitored in real-time, anomalies identified, and potential quality issues predicted and mitigated. Products on high-speed conveyor belts are not just inspected but scrutinized with a precision that transcends human capabilities, ensuring that quality is not just maintained but exemplified. Add the finesse of **Predictive Maintenance**, where AI systems are the vigilant guardians of machinery, monitoring, analyzing, and forecasting potential breakdowns. Every vibration, temperature fluctuation, and noise is a narrative, a story that AI deciphers to schedule timely maintenance, drastically reducing downtime.

As the story of AI's integration unfolds, a landscape where operations are optimized, productivity enhanced, and decision-making informed comes to the fore. AI stands as an indispensable ally to COOs. But also, other functions benefit from Digital Intelligence.

**Human Resources Management (HR) – Facilitation and Objectivity**

Human Resources Management serves as the linchpin steering a company towards success, acting as the architect that sculpts the environment of attracting and retaining top talent. Digital Intelligence has morphed this landscape, interweaving intelligent solutions that epitomize efficiency and precision in every HR task.

**Automated shortlisting** has emerged, where AI systems sift through resumes, pinpointing candidates that echo the job's requirements with precision. Each keyword, experience level, and educational background is a criterion, seamlessly analyzed reducing manual labor and the scope for errors. In addition, it reduces possible human biases (assuming objective coding of algorithms). Moreover, predictive analytics steps in as a clairvoyant, where AI tools, with an analytical rigor, forecast a candidate's trajectory of success in a role. Every pattern in career progression, each skill, and an array of multi-faceted factors are dissected, offering an overview of insights that anchor informed decision-making.

Transitioning to the **interviewing process**, AI unravels a narrative of structure and insights. Virtual interviews, facilitated by AI, scrutinize verbal and non-verbal cues, crafting a comprehensive assessment of the candidate's fit for the role. Each language nuance, technical acuity, and personality trait is evaluated, painting a holistic image of the candidate. Complementing this, intelligent scheduling emerges as the silent administrator, where the cumbersome task of aligning time slots for interviews is automated. It is a world where administrative hassles are mitigated, and efficiency is the reigning narrative.

The **onboarding process**, a candidate's inaugural journey into the company, is adorned with AI's touch. Personalized onboarding plans echo the individual's role, learning pace, and preferences. It is a welcome that is not generic but bespoke, echoing the warmth and inclusivity of the organizational culture. AI chat bots, the virtual assistants in this journey, provide real-time responses, guiding new hires through initial stages with grace and precision. It is an onboarding experience that is not just informative but engaging, ensuring every new hire is seamlessly woven into the organizational fabric.

Supporting **employee engagement and wellness**, AI is the custodian of a healthy and vibrant workforce. AI-crafted wellness programs echo personalization, offering lifestyle and fitness recommendations anchored in individual health data. It is a message of health and wellness that is not generic but personal. Sentiment analysis, another feather in AI's cap, deciphers the emotional nuances in employee communications. It is a real-time pulse check, identifying morale issues and areas of discontent, offering management the insights to proactively sculpt a positive workplace environment.

In the context of **performance analysis**, AI stands as a guardian of growth and satisfaction. Real-time feedback mechanisms foster a culture of continuous improvement, where every employee is nurtured through immediate inputs. Performance is not just observed but enhanced, sculpting a workforce that is agile and adept. Data-driven insights, extracted through AI's analytical rigor, offer a window into employee strengths and improvement areas. It is the foundation of personalized development plans and effective talent management strategies, ensuring every employee is not just a part of the organization but a contributor to its dynamic growth.

AI plays a pivotal role in revolutionizing the way **employee performance** is assessed and enhanced. Real-time analytics powered by AI enable immediate feedback, transforming traditional annual reviews into a continuous, dynamic process. AI algorithms can analyze a wide array of data points, from task completion times to the quality of work, offering instant insights into an employee's performance. Automated AI tools can facilitate immediate feedback loops, ensuring that employees receive constructive and actionable input right at the moment of task completion. For example, AI can assess the quality of a report based on predefined criteria and provide instant recommendations for improvement. This not only expedites skill enhancement but also supports a culture of real-time learning and adaptation. Moreover, AI's predictive analytics dive deeper, offering foresights not just on what has occurred but projecting future performance trends. Using machine learning models, AI can analyze historical performance data to identify patterns and predict future outcomes. This capability is instrumental in proactively addressing potential performance issues and capitalizing on opportunities for growth. **Personalized development plans** are another frontier where AI exhibits its prowess. By analyzing individual employee data, AI identifies specific strengths and areas for improvement. It then customizes learning and development resources tailored to each employee's unique needs, ensuring targeted and effective growth. For example, if an AI system identifies a gap in a sales employee's product knowledge, it can automatically recommend specific training modules or materials to bridge that gap. It is an era where learning and development are not generic but are intensely personalized and profoundly impactful. Furthermore, AI enables a holistic view of employee performance. Beyond task completion and skill sets, AI analyzes behavioral data, collaboration metrics, and even wellbeing indicators to offer a comprehensive insight into an employee's performance. It is a multidimensional approach where performance, wellbeing, and organizational fit converge to sculpt a narrative of comprehensive employee development.

In the grandeur of these transformations, AI emerges as the catalyst modernizing HR and recruiting processes, crafting a workspace where efficiency is innate, and employee needs are addressed with precision.

**Information Technology (IT) – Efficiency and Quality**

In the dynamic flux of the digital era, where software, applications, and websites are the sinews connecting the world, coding emerges as the elemental force crafting this intricate weave. As important as it has been, the advent of artificial intelligence heralds a renaissance in this domain, marking the onset of a phase where efficiency, creativity, and collaboration are not aspirations but intrinsic characteristics.

In the spectacle of **automated code generation**, the narrative of coding transforms from a laborious process to streamlined efficiency. Auto-completion of code is no longer a luxury but a norm, with AI tools weaving through the nuances of developer inputs, offering suggestions that are not just accurate but imbued with best practices. Every line of code, every syntax, is a testament to minimized errors and enhanced standards. Complementing this, code templates stand as silent repositories, a treasure trove where developers find pre-set structures echoing best practices.

**Bug detection and resolution** is adorned with AI's touch, where tools are not just responsive but predictive. Automated bug detection is akin to a vigilant sentinel, scanning codes in real-time, ensuring that cleanliness of the codebase is not just a standard but an inherent quality. Every issue is identified, every anomaly addressed, marking the dawn of coding where bugs are not just resolved but anticipated. **Predictive bug analysis** elevates this experience, where AI, with its analytical precision, deciphers historical data and code patterns, painting a forecast of potential issues.

In the area of **code optimization**, AI is the craftsman sculpting codes that are not just functional but epitomize performance and efficiency. Performance tuning emerges as a norm, where AI's scrutiny substitutes inefficient algorithms with optimized ones, ensuring codes are not just functional but exemplary. Resource allocation, another masterpiece in AI's repertoire, ensures computational resources are not just used but optimized, marking the end of wastage and the dawn of responsive application performance.

Yet, AI's contribution in the coding landscape does not halt at optimization. It strides into collaborative coding, weaving a narrative of coherence and effectiveness. **Version control**, adorned with AI's intelligence, offers automated conflict resolution and predictive analysis. Every merge, every version, is a testament to seamless collaboration, a narrative where conflicts are not just resolved but anticipated and mitigated. Real-time collaboration tools, powered by AI, craft a world where geographical locations are not barriers but mere coordinates. Developers, though miles apart, are united in a synergic environment, where multi-user coding and intelligent suggestions generate a collaborative harmony.

As this story of transformation unfolds, it is evident that AI is not just an ally but a formidable force in coding, weaving through every aspect, from generation to collaboration.

**Finance – Accuracy and Forecasting**

For Finance precision, efficiency, and strategic insights are not just desired but essential. In this context, Artificial Intelligence (AI) emerges as a transformative ally, weaving a narrative where financial outcomes and processes are optimized, and strategic foresight becomes intrinsic.

One of the essential elements where AI manifests its finesse is in **data accuracy and analysis**. Finance is a world inundated with data: every transaction, every financial movement is a data point. AI, with its intricate algorithms, sifts through this vast expanse of data, offering accuracy that is unmarred by human error. Financial data is not just collected but analyzed, interpreted, offering insights that are not just accurate but strategic. **Automated Reporting** amplifies this narrative. It is a reality where reports are not compiled but crafted with precision, offering stakeholders data that is not just current but accurate, supporting decision-making that is informed, strategic, and impactful.

**Forecasting**, a critical element in finance, is adorned with AI's predictive analytics. Budgets, financial forecasts, and predictions are not based on historical data alone but are enriched with AI's analytical prowess. It is a reality where financial trends are not just observed but predicted, where foresight is not aspirational but a standard. Financial leaders are equipped with insights, not just for informed decision-making but for crafting strategies that are proactive, agile, and responsive.

In the context of risk management, AI is the silent yet potent partner. Credit risks, investment risks, and financial vulnerabilities are assessed with AI's precision. Machine learning models are not just tools but strategic assets, offering **real-time assessments of financial risks** with an accuracy that is dynamic. Companies are not just responding to risks but are anticipating them, crafting strategies that are not just reactive but preventive.

Operational efficiency in financial processes is another frontier where AI crafts a story of excellence. Tasks that were manual, time-consuming, and error-prone are now automated. **AI-powered automation** in finance is a situation where invoices are processed, transactions are reconciled, and financial data is managed with a precision and speed that human efforts cannot parallel. It is not just about reducing operational costs but elevating operational excellence.

In the grandeur of AI's integration, the finance function transcends its traditional role. It is not just a department but a strategic ally to the corporate leadership. AI-powered data analytics and interpretations offer strategic insights that are integral in corporate decision-making. Finance leaders are not just custodians of financial data but strategic contributors, offering insights that sculpt corporate strategies, ensuring they are not just robust but resilient.

**Legal – Focus and Automation**

The legal sector, characterized by its diligent nature and the paramount importance of precision, is witnessing a renaissance where Digital Intelligence is the catalyst.

**Legal analytics**, an essential aspect of this transformation, encapsulates the use of AI to weave through extensive sets of legal data, extracting insights and patterns with finesse. In this nuanced approach, predictive analysis emerges as a formidable tool. AI's ability to analyze the historical data of court decisions crafts a narrative where legal outcomes are not just anticipated but predicted with precision. Every court decision, every legal dispute, is a data point, offering insights that are not just retrospective but prospective. Furthermore, legal research, adorned with AI's touch, transforms into an efficient and comprehensive process. Lawyers, equipped with AI tools, find relevant case laws and statutes not by sifting through voluminous legal texts but through intelligent searches. It is an approach where time is optimized, and legal landscapes are understood with depth, ensuring legal strategies that are not just informed but formidable.

As we dive into **contract analysis**, AI's role transcends traditional boundaries. Contracts, intricate and important, are scrutinized by AI tools that identify critical clauses, opportunities, and potential risks with a precision that is unmatched. In this narrative, risk assessment is not just a process but a strategic advantage. AI identifies potential contractual risks, offering legal professionals a foresight that is strategic, ensuring risks are not just addressed but anticipated and mitigated. **Automatic summarization** stands as another marvel in AI's repertoire. Lengthy contracts are distilled into summaries, where key terms and clauses are not just highlighted but emphasized. Legal professionals navigate a world where contract review is not laborious but efficient, ensuring decisions in legal negotiations and reviews are not just quick but robust. Expanding the horizon, AI's brilliance also illuminates the process of **document review** and due diligence. In a world characterized by volumes of documents, AI facilitates rapid and accurate reviews. It is not just about identifying relevant information but also about the speed and accuracy with which AI accomplishes this, ensuring legal compliance and informed decision-making.

AI-powered tools also grace the sphere of **legal document generation**. Routine documents, contracts, and legal notices are generated with AI's efficiency and precision. Every document echoes legal standards, ensuring legal communications and documentations that are not just compliant but exemplary.

In conclusion, AI's foray into the legal department is characterized by a blend of efficiency, deep insights, and strategic foresight. More applications of Digital Intelligence emerge. Let us finally look at one that has captured some attention recently – content creation.

**Content Creation – Acceleration and Personalization**

Content creation emerges as the bedrock for any entity aspiring to carve a distinguished online presence. In this vibrant arena, Artificial Intelligence (AI) emerges not merely as a tool but as a powerful engine combining creativity, efficiency, and innovation into the content creation process.

**Writing** is foundational in this creative endeavor, and with AI, it metamorphoses into a dynamic, responsive, and personalized art form. Automated journalism, powered by AI, heralds an era where news reports are generated in real-time, integrating coherent and factually accurate narratives by analyzing vast datasets. Every occurrence and event is instantly transformed into a narrative, echoing accuracy and timeliness. In this space, content enhancement emerges as a spectacle of AI's finesse. AI-based writing assistants do not just analyze text but elevate it, offering insights to enhance readability and optimize SEO, transforming the ordinary into the extraordinary.

Yet, AI's contribution is not confined to text. In **image design**, AI is the silent artist, empowering designers with automated tools and creative insights that are nothing short of revolutionary. Automated image generation unveils a world where high-resolution images are birthed from AI's imagination, influenced by mere input parameters or textual descriptions. In this world, iteration is not manual but automated, each design a harmonious blend of creativity and technology. With AI, image enhancement is not a process but an art, where images are automatically polished to echo professionalism, every color, and light corrected, every imperfection eliminated. Taking it even further, in the mesmerizing world of **video production**, AI is not just an enabler but a creator. Automated video editing is not a futuristic aspiration but a present-day reality, where AI sifts through hours of footage, selecting the best shots and weaving stories that are not just cohesive but engaging. In this dynamic sphere, deepfake and synthetic media production emerges as a testament to AI's creative prowess. It is a space where new content is birthed from existing footage, unlocking potentials in entertainment, education, and simulation, albeit echoing the need for ethical considerations. AI's emergence in content creation is not just transformative but transcendental. It is a situation where content creation is efficient, agile, and innovative, where creators are equipped with tools that are not just automated but insightful. Yet, in this mesmerizing combination of technology and creativity, the call for ethical and responsible usage of AI echoes loudly. In a world where content is king, the integrity of content is sacrosanct, necessitating a harmonious blend of AI's innovation and human ethical considerations to craft messages that are not just engaging but resonate with authenticity and integrity.

---

**Ethics in AI,** rooted in principles of fairness, transparency, and human rights, is not a lofty ideal but a concrete necessity. AI applications are being woven into the fabric of daily life, influencing decisions from healthcare treatments to job recruitments. In this scenario, the importance of AI ethics transcends theoretical discourse. It is a practical imperative ensuring that AI systems are designed and operated in ways that are inherently respectful of human rights and societal norms. AI should avoid bias, protect privacy, and be accountable.

In an era where AI's decisions have tangible impacts on individuals and communities, ethical considerations act as safeguards. Regulations like Europe's GDPR are not just legal frameworks but societal shields, ensuring individuals' privacy and offering people concrete rights and controls over their personal data. Every click, every data point, and every algorithmic decision is under scrutiny, necessitating a blend of transparency and responsibility.

To transform ethics from concepts to lived realities, certain tangible steps are indispensable. Clear guidelines for AI development and use are foundational, acting as compasses directing AI's integration into society. These guidelines become the scripts AI developers and users adhere to, outlining the boundaries of data use and ensuring decision-making transparency. For instance, the logic behind AI decisions in healthcare prioritization or job recruitment must be as clear as daylight, ensuring fairness and explicability. Regular audits of AI systems are the watchdogs of ethical adherence, ensuring that biases are not just identified but corrected. In the dynamic world of AI, these audits are the lenses that scrutinize every algorithmic decision, ensuring that hiring tools or personalized marketing algorithms are equitable and non-discriminatory. In a world pulsating with data, user control over personal information is not just a right but a cornerstone of ethical AI. Mechanisms allowing clear consent, data opt-out, or deletion are not optional but mandatory.

In the space of AI ethics, collaboration between public and private sectors crafts the script of ethical integration. It is an expression of synergy where governmental regulations and tech innovations converge to tell a story of AI that is as ethical as it is innovative. The pathway to ethical AI is paved with tangible actions, each step scripted to transform abstract ethical principles into concrete societal impacts, ensuring that AI is not just a technological marvel but a societal ally, fostering a world marked by innovation, equity, and trust.

---

Countless Digital Intelligence use cases are being developed and implemented around the world, but where does your company stand when it comes to leveraging this potential?

**Assessment: Scoping the Power of Digital Intelligence Use Cases**

When a company aspires to demystify its standing in the world of Digital Intelligence Use Cases, an honest self-assessment is paramount. This process, akin to peeling back layers, is aimed at revealing the depth and breadth of AI integration and understanding within the organization.

The first layer unfolds the **AI awareness and understanding** embedded in the company's DNA. Here, a pulse check on the level of AI literacy across all tiers and functions of the organization is essential. Tools such as internal surveys, workshops, and interactive sessions can be instrumental in gauging the depth of AI comprehension. These initiatives help in measuring not only the awareness but also the quality of understanding and the ability to envision AI's role and potential impact within the specific organizational context.

As we continue, the existence and quality of a **repository of AI use cases** come into focus. A critical assessment is needed to determine whether these use cases are clearly articulated, with well-defined outcomes and approaches. Companies can employ **peer reviews and expert consultations** to validate the robustness and relevance of these use cases. An assessment checklist that measures the clarity, comprehensiveness, and alignment of these use cases with organizational objectives can be a valuable tool.

The journey into AI maturity is marked by not just the identification but the strategic **prioritization of AI use cases**. To assess where the organization stands in this context, one might consider utilizing tools like AI prioritization matrices or scoring models. These tools evaluate use cases against criteria such as strategic alignment, feasibility, potential impact, and resource requirements. The outcome is a clear and objective lens through which the organization can view its readiness and strategic alignment in rolling out AI initiatives.

The final layer of assessment unfurls the organization's **track record in implementing AI use cases**. Here, a retrospective analysis of completed AI projects provides insights into the effectiveness, challenges, and outcomes of AI integration. **Case study analysis and performance metrics** can be employed to gauge the success and impacts of these initiatives. Moreover, the mechanism through which learnings, insights, and challenges are shared across the organization should be evaluated, offering a window into the organization's adaptive learning culture.

For a company to truly understand its foothold and trajectory in the AI landscape, a comprehensive self-assessment that embraces these four pivotal areas is indispensable.

**Action: Developing, Prioritizing and Implementing Digital Intelligence Use Cases**

 Initiating the journey with fostering **AI literacy at every tier of the organization,** envisage a landscape where educational modules tailored to each department, from marketing to R&D, are the norm. Continuous learning pathways, evolving with AI developments, are ingrained in the organizational culture. Workshops, interactive sessions with AI experts, and e-learning modules are not ancillary but integral, ensuring that AI comprehension is not siloed but ubiquitous. Here, IBM shines as best-in-class, demonstrating an ethos where AI education is pervasive, ensuring that every decision-making process is informed and enriched by AI insights and ethics. The healthcare sector is not far behind, with Siemens Healthineers embedding AI knowledge across teams, ensuring that AI's ethical and practical nuances are integral in both patient care and operational efficiency[106].

Venturing into the **development and refinement of AI use cases,** a dynamic digital repository of detailed AI applications becomes the cornerstone. Each Intelligence Use Case, accessible to every team member, outlines the problem, the AI solution, ethical considerations, datasets, and expected outcomes. It is a world where cross-departmental insights and collaborations continuously enrich AI applications. In this space, Google's culture of innovation finds its echo, with a mosaic of AI applications that are as expansive as they are collaborative. Outside the tech sphere, Under Armour stands as a testament to AI's versatility, weaving customer feedback and market trends into a picture of AI use cases that span product innovation and personalized marketing. As it evolves to the **strategic prioritization of AI use cases,** a multidimensional matrix for evaluation comes into play. AI proposals are dissected in boardrooms not just by tech experts but also by ethical advisors and business strategists, ensuring that every AI initiative is technically, ethically, and strategically aligned. Microsoft's rigorous, criteria-based evaluation, overseen by a cross-functional AI steering committee, finds its reflection here, ensuring that innovation and ethics are inseparable companions in the AI journey[107]. John Deere mirrors this ethos in the agricultural sector, where AI applications are honed to precision,

---

[106] On Siemens company website: "Siemens Healthineers". Visited 08.04.2024. https://www.siemens-healthineers.com/; and
Dirnberger, Schroll-Bakes, Schusser: "The History of Siemens Healthineers". Published by August Dreesbach Verlag 15.02.2022.
[107] On Microsoft company website: "Operationalising responsible AI". Visited 08.04.2024. https://www.microsoft.com/en-gb/ai/our-approach?activetab=pivot1%3aprimaryr5

targeting industry-specific challenges and opportunities, making AI not just a tool but a strategic ally[108].

Transitioning into **pilot projects and agile adaptations,** the innovation lab environment becomes the crucible where AI concepts are tested and refined. Real-world scenarios are not endpoints but checkpoints where feedback enriches and refines AI applications in real-time. Amazon epitomizes this ethos, where real-time feedback and immediate adaptations transform challenges into opportunities for refinement. Zipline, though a smaller entity, resonates with this agile spirit, iterating drone designs and operational protocols to meet the nuanced needs of diverse geographies and healthcare systems, epitomizing adaptability.

Based on AI literacy, expansive use cases, strategic prioritizations, and agile implementations, the harmony of **technology, ethics, and business objectives** becomes palpable.

### 3.5.2.2    Intelligence Capabilities – Mimicking and Augmenting Human Intelligence

Artificial Intelligence (AI) is a branch of computer science focused on creating systems capable of performing tasks that would usually require human intelligence. These systems are designed to mimic human cognition to execute tasks ranging from solving puzzles, understanding languages, recognizing patterns, and making predictions or decisions. AI has progressively evolved, becoming a prevalent force in our daily lives owing to the significant advancements in computing power and the vast amounts of data now accessible for training these AI systems.

**Awareness: Understanding the Scope and Potential of Intelligence Capabilities**

To fully comprehend the trajectory of Artificial Intelligence (AI), it is necessary to examine its historical timeline marked with substantial advancements and innovation.

The progression of artificial intelligence (AI) can be traced through its dynamic and multi-faceted historical context, each era marking distinct advancements and breakthroughs. In the **1950s,** AI's conceptual foundation was laid, marked prominently by Alan Turing's introduction of the Turing Test in 1950, a crucial metric for evaluating machine intelligence. The Dartmouth Conference in 1956 further epitomized this era, gathering brilliant minds focused on creating computer programs with capabilities akin to human intelligence. These efforts were complemented by the evolution of early computers and programming languages,

---

[108] Elaine Mendonça on Assembly website: "John Deere Revolutionizes Precision Agriculture with Space Technology AI and Automation". Published online 06.06.2023, visited 2023. https://www.assemblymag.com/articles/97831-john-deere-revolutionizes-agriculture-with-ai-and-automation

establishing a tangible base for AI's evolution. Transitioning into the **1960s to 1980s,** AI burgeoned with the advent of expert systems. These programs, enriched with human-like knowledge and analytical skills, carved their niche in sectors like medicine and mining. However, this era was not without its challenges. The AI winter in the late 80s marked a period of reduced funding and interest, a reflection of the hurdles in converting theoretical AI concepts into practical, scalable solutions[109].

The tides turned in the **1990s to 2000s** with the convergence of data-driven approaches and the internet boom. AI was rejuvenated by machine learning algorithms, empowered by vast datasets provided by the burgeoning internet. The influx of data and the algorithms' capacity to learn and adapt signaled AI's transformative journey. In the **2010s**, deep learning and big data became the harbingers of innovation. AI systems, empowered by deep neural networks, displayed remarkable efficacy in tasks like image and speech recognition. The automotive industry revved up with autonomous vehicles, while healthcare witnessed a change in thinking with AI technologies facilitating enhanced disease diagnosis through data and imaging analysis.

As we step into the **2020s and beyond,** the narrative is enriched by the relentless pursuit of ethical AI and the lofty visions of Artificial General Intelligence (AGI) – a form of artificial intelligence that possesses the ability to understand, learn, and perform any intellectual task that a human being can (today we are still away from that vision). AI's journey is characterized by a commitment to fairness, inclusivity, and bias mitigation, ensuring AI's evolution is not just technically advanced but ethically sound.

Recognizing the essence of artificial intelligence (AI) demands an exploration into its multidimensional existence, where diverse disciplines converge to simulate human intelligence within machines. AI emerges not as a monolith, but a rich tapestry woven from the threads of complexity and multi-faceted nature. It is an ensemble piece, choreographed not only by advancements in computer science but also contributions from psychology, linguistics, economics, and more. Each discipline, like a musician in an orchestra, plays its part in breathing life into systems capable of replicating and, at times, transcending human cognition.

Learning and adaptability stand as the keystones of AI, illuminating its intrinsic ability to evolve. Through machine learning, AI is akin to a sentient being, endowed with the capability to learn from data and refine its comprehension continuously. It is a journey of evolution, where every interaction, every piece of data, is a steppingstone leading to enhanced accuracy and responsiveness. For instance, the predictive text

---

[109] Rockwell Anyoha on Harvard University website: "The History of Artificial Intelligence". Published 28.08.2017, visited 08.04.2024. https://sitn.hms.harvard.edu/flash/2017/history-artificial-intelligence/

on your phone, becoming more adept at suggesting words, is a testament to this evolving intelligence.



At the core of many advancements in technology, particularly in the field of artificial intelligence (AI), lies Machine Learning (ML) and Deep Learning (DL). These are not just buzzwords but technologies transforming industries and enhancing our daily lives. **Machine Learning (ML)** is like teaching computers to learn from experience. Imagine a computer program that gets better and smarter at a task the more it practices – that is ML in action. For instance, ML powers recommendation systems. When you shop online, ML algorithms analyze your shopping behavior, along with the behaviors of millions of other shoppers, to recommend products that you are likely to purchase. It is like having a personal shopping assistant who knows your preferences and suggests items accordingly. **Deep Learning (DL)**, on the other hand, takes inspiration from how our brain works. It involves neural networks, which are akin to the human brain's network of neurons. In practice, this means that DL can process a vast amount of diverse data, learn complex patterns, and make decisions. A real-world application is image recognition systems. Think of social media platforms that can automatically tag you and your friends in photos – DL is the technology making this possible.

The applications of ML and DL are broad and transformative. In healthcare, ML is used to predict patient outcomes and identify potential health risks based on historical data. It helps doctors make informed decisions, enhancing patient care. In the automotive industry, DL is a key component in the development of self-driving cars, processing the multitude of data from sensors in real time to make safe driving decisions. Looking to the future, the integration of ML and DL promises a world where decision-making is more informed, processes are more efficient, and personalized experiences are the norm, not the luxury. Imagine healthcare systems where treatment plans are highly personalized, tailored to individual genetic makeup and health histories, or retail experiences that are seamlessly customized to each shopper's preferences, thanks to the weaving of ML and DL.

In a world that is becoming increasingly data-driven, ML and DL stand as pillars of a technological revolution. They promise to turn data into actionable insights, manual processes into automated efficiencies, and personalized experiences into standard practice. For businesses and individuals alike, understanding and integrating these technologies is akin to holding keys to a future where the boundary between technology and human intelligence becomes increasingly seamless.

AI's mimicry of human actions is unveiled in the conversations held with chat bots, in the identification made by facial recognition technologies, and in the execution of verbal commands by voice recognition systems in smart homes. It is a world where technology is not just a silent spectator but an active participant, engaging, responding, and personalizing experiences.

**Mimicking the Human Brain – Modelling and Simulation**

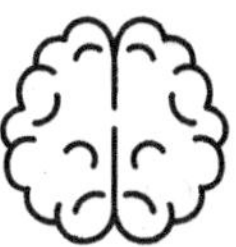

Modelling and Simulation in AI seek to imitate and reproduce the internal workings and functions of the human brain, a task that encompasses the encoding of human cognitive and decision-making processes into digital form. These models serve as intricate, digital mirrors, reflecting the multilayered neural pathways and decision-making matrices that underlie human thought processes. Imagine the human brain as a complex circuit board of neurons, each connection sparking decisions and insights. AI models attempt to replicate this complexity, mimicking the combination of electrical impulses and connections that result in human cognition. They encapsulate the intricacies of how humans think, reason, analyze, and decide, translating these into computational algorithms that can perform similar tasks but at a pace and scale far beyond human capacity.

Modelling and Simulation in AI are often used interchangeably but have distinct meanings and roles. **Models** are mathematical or computational representations that describe the behavior or activity of a system. A model serves as a static representation, a blueprint that encapsulates specific characteristics or behaviors of a system. For instance, in the space of AI, a model can represent the neural pathways of the human brain, encoding the patterns of synaptic connections and electrical activity that result in thought and decision-making. It is akin to a map, detailing the pathways, connections, and nodes of activity but is static and unchanging. Every detail, every encoded parameter, serves as a steppingstone towards a deeper understanding of the system's operation and behavior. **Simulation,** on the other hand, is the process of using a model to study the behavior and performance of a system. Together, they aim to replicate and understand the processes of the human brain, but each brings a unique aspect to this objective. A simulation brings this static blueprint to life. It is a dynamic process where the model is subjected to various inputs to study its behavior and responses. In the context of AI, simulation involves feeding data into the model and observing how it processes, analyzes, and interprets this data to make decisions or predictions. It is like watching the mapped terrain in action, observing the flow of activity, the interactions, and the outcomes to gain insights into the model's operational dynamics and efficiency. One of the principal distinctions between the two lies in their state and purpose. While a model is a well-defined and fixed representation, a simulation is dynamic and evolving. The model serves as the foundational base, the structured and static representation, while the simulation is the operational enactment of this base, active, adaptive, and responsive. The model is the theory, the simulation is the practice.

One significant area where models and simulation prove important is in their capability to process and analyze vast datasets. They can simulate the human brain's ability to sift through information, extract relevant data, discern patterns, and arrive at informed decisions. However, the speed and scale at which AI models achieve this are unparalleled. They can process and interpret complex data sets in mere fractions of the time required by a human brain, yet the decisions derived are rich in context, relevance, and applicability, courtesy of the human-like processing pathways embedded within them. For instance, in the healthcare sector, AI models that simulate diagnostic reasoning are not just algorithmic processors. They are digital replicas of the human diagnostic mind, replete with the layered reasoning, differential analysis, and context-driven decisions that characterize human medical diagnostics. They consider patient history, present symptoms, laboratory results, and more to arrive at diagnoses, much like their human counterparts, but do so with remarkable speed, ensuring timely interventions that can be critical in healthcare outcomes. In financial services, AI modelling and simulation often embody the risk-assessment and decision-making acumen of seasoned financial experts. They assess market volatility, economic indicators, and investment portfolios, making investment decisions that are not just rapid but are replete with the analytical depth, foresight, and strategic alignment characteristic of expert human financial planners. Every decision is a combination of speed, scale, and analytical depth, marking the confluence of human-like decision-making processes and AI speed and efficiency.

The creation and perfection of these models involve a continuous process of learning and adaptation. Much like the human brain, which evolves, adapts, and learns from every piece of information it encounters, AI models too are dynamic entities. They are trained on vast, diverse datasets, each piece of data serving as a learning module that refines, hones, and perfects the model's decision-making capabilities. So, every decision an AI model makes is not just a product of coded algorithms but is an outcome of a learning journey that mirrors human cognitive evolution.

**Mimicking Human Sound Recognition – Natural Language Processing (NLP)**

Natural Language Processing (NLP) acts as the foundation that fosters seamless interactions between humans and machines, grounding itself in the ability to interpret and generate human languages in a context that is both meaningful and valuable. NLP is essentially the technology behind the machine's ability to read, decipher, understand, and make sense of human languages. At its core, NLP is a branch of artificial intelligence that employs algorithms and models crafted to handle the multifarious and intricate nature of human languages. It is imbued with the capability to comprehend idioms, slangs, and colloquial phrases, ensuring machines respond not just with syntactical accuracy but with contextual relevance. This nuance in handling language enables applications like real-time translation tools and voice-activated assistants to provide users with responses that are accurate, appropriate, and contextually aligned.

In the world of business, NLP has cemented itself as a critical asset. Imagine a tool that can swiftly run through thousands of customer reviews and feedback, identifying trends and sentiments that can shape product development, marketing strategies, and customer service protocols. This is not a futuristic concept, but a current reality made possible by NLP. It translates unstructured data – text that does not follow a predefined model or pattern – into actionable insights that businesses can leverage to enhance customer experiences and drive strategic initiatives. Customer service, a critical touchpoint in the consumer journey, has been revolutionized by NLP. **Chat bots and virtual assistants,** powered by sophisticated NLP algorithms, can field customer inquiries 24/7, offering responses that are not just timely but personalized.

These AI entities can interpret the tone and sentiment behind customer queries, enabling them to respond with empathy and precision, emulating the responsiveness of a human agent. In the domain of **real-time language translation,** NLP stands as the bedrock. Visitors of Tokyo's Harry Potter musical show can enjoy real-time translations displayed into goggles while actually listening to Japanese songs. However, it is not just about converting words from one language to another but entails understanding cultural, contextual, and idiomatic nuances to provide translations that are coherent and culturally appropriate. This feature is particularly beneficial for global businesses and travelers, ensuring that language barriers are mitigated, and communication is as fluid as possible. In healthcare, the application of NLP is profound. Medical professionals are often inundated with massive volumes of data. NLP tools can quickly analyze and interpret complex medical texts, extracting critical information that aids in diagnosis, treatment planning, and research. It turns textual data, including handwritten notes and academic journals, into structured, actionable insights, ensuring that every piece of information is accessible and can contribute to patient care and medical advancements.

As we peel back the layers of NLP, it becomes evident that its capacity to transform complex, unstructured textual data into structured, actionable insights is one of its strongest suits. As advancements in NLP continue to unfold, we can anticipate a world where the interaction between humans and machines becomes as fluid, intuitive, and dynamic as human-to-human interactions.

**Mimicking Human Eyesight – Computer Vision**

Computer Vision is akin to equipping machines with a discerning eye, making them capable of understanding and interpreting the visual world. It allows computers to **extract, analyze, and understand useful information** from individual images or sequences of images. This field is rooted in multiple disciplines, including computer science, physics, and even biology, mirroring the complexity of human vision in a machine-context. One of the remarkable aspects of computer vision is its ability to **transform visual data into a tangible set of information,** a process essential in numerous real-world applications. Each image, imbued with pixels and color gradients, becomes a source from which computers, equipped with computer vision, draw data and insights. This is not just about recognizing shapes and figures, but about understanding the context, subtleties, and nuanced elements within visual data.

In a healthcare setting, imagine a machine that can quickly scan through thousands of complex medical images, pinpointing anomalies with precision. It is not just about identifying potential issues, but also about gauging their severity, predicting their progression, and offering insights that can significantly influence treatment protocols. Each image becomes a narrative, a story detailing a patient's health with precision and depth, something that human eyes might miss or take a considerable time to analyze. In retail, the adoption of computer vision elevates customer experience to unprecedented levels. As you step into a store, cameras and sensors track your movement, analyzing your behavior, and offering real-time data to in-store systems. It is a combination of technology where your preferences, gleaned from visual data, guide personalized recommendations, sales alerts, and even navigational assistance within the store. It is about turning each shopping journey into a personalized experience, with insights drawn from the subtlest of visual cues. The world of autonomous vehicles is another area where computer vision is making indelible marks. Every second, a self-driving car collects a torrent of visual data – traffic lights, pedestrians, obstacles, road signs. Computer vision is the magic that turns this data into actionable insights, ensuring that the vehicle navigates safely and efficiently. It is not just about 'seeing' but 'interpreting and responding'. Decisions, from changing lanes to stopping for a pedestrian, are rooted in the machine's ability to understand visual data in real-time. When we turn our gaze to security and surveillance, computer vision is transforming passive monitoring systems into proactive security protocols. Cameras endowed with this technology are not just recording visual data but are analyzing and responding to it. An unattended package, an intruder, or an unusual activity – the system recognizes and alerts in real-time, ensuring that security responses are timely and effective.

The power of computer vision, therefore, lies in an enhanced decision-making capability based on visual data.

**Mimicking the Human Senses – Sensorics**

Sensorics, at its core, is about integrating advanced sensing capabilities into technologies to gather real-time data, making them more responsive and intelligent. In various industries and everyday applications, sensorics has become an indispensable component. It is akin to giving machines a semblance of senses, allowing them to 'feel' and 'perceive' their environment, and respond effectively.

In healthcare, sensorics has been revolutionary. Consider **wearable technologies** like smartwatches and fitness trackers. They are embedded with sensors capable of monitoring vital signs like heart rate and body temperature with pinpoint accuracy. Each heartbeat, every spike in temperature is recorded. For instance, a sudden increase in heart rate can trigger an instant notification, alerting the wearer to potential health risks. In this sense, sensorics transforms a simple watch into a personal health assistant, constantly vigilant and ready to alert users to any irregularities. In the industrial landscape, sensorics paints a picture of **automation and precision.** Imagine a factory where machines are equipped with sensors to monitor their performance in real time. These sensors can measure factors like temperature, vibration, and humidity to assess the machine's health. If a sensor detects an abnormal increase in temperature, it can trigger an alarm, prompting immediate action to avoid potential breakdowns. This is not just about collecting data, it is about using this data to **anticipate issues and initiate preventive measures,** ensuring that operational flow remains uninterrupted. Autonomous vehicles, one of the marvels of modern engineering, are driven by sensorics. These vehicles are laced with an array of sensors, including **lidar, radar, and cameras,** each serving a unique purpose. Lidar sensors, for instance, emit light waves to measure distances and identify obstacles, playing a critical role in navigation and safety. The car, in real time, processes the data collected from these sensors to make informed decisions, like when to slow down, swerve or come to a complete halt. It is sensorics that powers this real-time decision-making ability, transforming a machine into an intelligent entity capable of navigating complex environments. For homeowners, sensorics has ushered in the era of **smart homes.** Imagine walking into your home, and the lights automatically adjust to your preferred brightness, the thermostat sets itself to your desired temperature, and the security system deactivates – all these automated and personalized responses are courtesy of sensorics. Sensors detect your presence, and the embedded AI systems take over, interpreting the data and initiating actions to cater to your preferences, turning a structure of bricks and mortar into a living, responsive environment.

Sensorics is transforming the abstract concept of data into real-world, actionable outcomes. It is about endowing machines and technologies with the capability to respond to environmental and operational cues with precision and intelligence, akin to the human senses.

**Mimicking Human Haptics – Robotics**

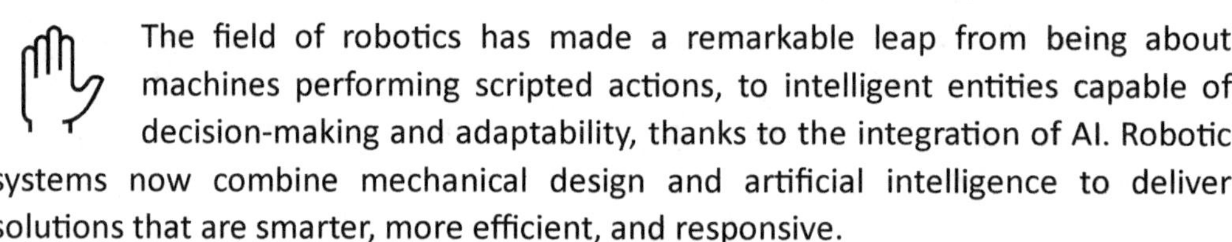

The field of robotics has made a remarkable leap from being about machines performing scripted actions, to intelligent entities capable of decision-making and adaptability, thanks to the integration of AI. Robotic systems now combine mechanical design and artificial intelligence to deliver solutions that are smarter, more efficient, and responsive.

In the context of **autonomous robots**, consider their application in a modern warehouse. These robots are not just about moving objects from point A to B. They are equipped with sensors and AI algorithms that allow them to 'see' and 'understand' their environment. If an obstacle appears unexpectedly, the robot evaluates the situation, decides the best course of action, and navigates around it seamlessly. It is a continuous process of perception, decision-making, and action, akin to how humans operate in dynamic environments. This intelligence and adaptability **reduce downtime and enhance productivity.** When we explore robotics in healthcare, particularly in robotic surgery, it unveils a blend of precision and adaptability that is transforming medical procedures. The surgeon's hand movements are translated into micro-movements of robotic instruments, offering unprecedented precision. But it is not rigid. The robotic system continuously processes visual and sensory data to adapt to the dynamic environment of surgery. Every tissue texture, every movement is analyzed in real-time, ensuring that the robotic movements are both precise and adaptive, which is crucial for patient safety and surgical outcomes. The advent of **robotic exoskeletons** merges mechanical engineering with AI to offer personalized mobility solutions. For someone with a mobility impairment, the exoskeleton is not just a mechanical support, it is a personalized mobility assistant. Sensors embedded in these exoskeletons capture data on muscle movements, body posture, and gait. AI algorithms process this data in real-time, adapting the exoskeleton's support to align with the user's natural movements and intentions. It is about transforming a piece of technology into an intuitive extension of the human body. In **our homes**, robotics manifests in devices like robotic vacuum cleaners. These are not random moving devices but intelligent systems that map your home, identify obstacles like furniture, and pets, and optimize their cleaning paths. They 'remember' the cleaned areas, detect dirt intensity, and even navigate back to their charging stations when low on battery. It is about making cleaning not just automated but intelligent, adaptive, and efficient, turning a household chore into a tech-driven, hassle-free experience. In **manufacturing**, the introduction of collaborative robots or cobots epitomizes the constructive collaboration between humans and machines. These cobots are embedded with sensors and AI algorithms that allow them to perceive their surroundings, adapt to changes, and work alongside human workers safely. If a human worker steps into the path of a cobot, it instantly recognizes the human presence and adapts its movements to avoid a collision. It is about making industrial robots not just automated but sensitive, responsive, and adaptive to the human-centric environment.

The infusion of AI into robotics is not just an enhancement but a transformation. It turns machines from tools executing scripted actions into intelligent entities capable of learning, adapting, and making decisions.

Increasingly of the human senses can be augmented with Digital Intelligence. But where does your company stand with tapping into this potential?

**Assessment: Calibrating the Intelligence Capabilities**

To gauge where a company stands in harnessing these intelligence capabilities, a keen assessment of organizational know-how is essential. The **availability of knowledge and expertise** within the company often serves as a cornerstone for innovative strategies and practical applications. Organizations should assess the presence of **centers of excellence** and dedicated teams, not only equipped with technical expertise but also enriched with a culture of continuous learning and innovation. Understanding if the staff are up to date with the **latest trends and technological advancements**, and evaluating the **depth of research and development initiatives** can offer insights into the firm's preparedness to embrace and optimize these intelligence tools. For instance, a company might possess a team of experts well-versed in natural language processing but may find a gap in the domain of computer vision. A detailed **inventory of skills and expertise** and mapping them against the dynamic needs of the market and organizational goals can pinpoint strengths and areas for development.

Transitioning to the second focal point, the integration of these intelligence capabilities into use case development and product innovation is another critical aspect. An assessment should consider how seamlessly and strategically these capabilities are woven into the fabric of the organization's operational and strategic paradigm. **Cross-functional collaboration** plays a crucial role here – the convergence of technical expertise and business acumen to transform intelligence capabilities into actionable strategies and innovative solutions. For example, does the product development team routinely collaborate with the AI center of excellence to integrate computer vision into new products? Are there established channels for the **flow of insights and innovations** from the modeling and simulation experts to the strategic planners crafting use cases? These intersections of skills and applications can be indicative of the organization's maturity in converting intelligence capabilities into tangible business value.

Assessing the depth of know-how about Intelligence Capabilities within the organization and its strategic application in crafting use cases and products can provide a comprehensive view of a company's standing in leveraging intelligence capabilities.

**Action: Building and Embedding the Intelligence Capabilities**

 When it comes to building (centralized) intelligence capabilities, establishing **Centers of Excellence (CoEs)** is paramount. Each CoE should be staffed with professionals who are subject matter experts, having a deep understanding of specific domains like Models and Simulation, Natural Language Processing, Computer Vision, Sensorics, or Robotics. These centers should be equipped with **state-of-the-art technology and resources** to facilitate cutting-edge research and development. Furthermore, the environment in each CoE should encourage innovation, creativity, and continuous learning to ensure that the organization remains at the forefront of technological advancements. Creating a **knowledge database** is an integral step that involves systematic organization and accessibility. This database should not only house theoretical insights but also practical applications, real-world case studies, and interactive learning modules to

assist in skill development. The categorization should allow for easy navigation, and a user-interface that encourages engagement from various departments within the organization, ensuring that knowledge dissemination is as efficient as possible. A systematic approach to **research and development** is necessary. Companies should consider partnerships with academic institutions and technology innovators to tap into a diverse pool of knowledge and skills. Incorporating varied perspectives can lead to breakthrough innovations and a richer knowledge base. Regular reviews and updates should be incorporated to ensure that the organization is aligned with the latest trends and developments in AI and related fields.

Embedding these capabilities into product development necessitates a well-orchestrated **collaboration and integration strategy**. Product development teams should have unfettered access to the resources housed within the CoEs (visit section 3.7.1 Agile and Adaptive Culture on page 324 to get details on empowered, cross-functional teams). These teams should be encouraged to leverage the knowledge database to incorporate intelligent features into product designs, ensuring products are innovative, user-centric, and competitive in the market. Implementing **regular training and workshops** is essential. These should be tailored, offering hands-on experiences that empower product development teams to integrate AI capabilities effectively. Learning modules should be dynamic and updated regularly, ensuring teams are equipped with the latest skills and knowledge to navigate the rapidly evolving landscape of AI. Incorporating a **feedback mechanism** is crucial. It should capture insights on the performance and integration of AI features in products, and this data should be systematically analyzed. Insights gleaned should inform iterative improvements, with the findings shared across both the CoEs and product development teams, ensuring a cohesive, organization-wide learning and improvement cycle.

To illustrate, a company like Google exemplifies this approach. Their Advanced Technology and Projects (ATAP) team is akin to a CoE, fostering deep expertise in AI[110]. The insights and innovations borne from this center are seamlessly integrated into product development, evident in AI-powered products like Google Assistant and AutoML, which have undergone iterative improvements informed by continuous feedback and learning. The symbiosis between centralized Intelligence capabilities and their integration into product development is a dynamic process.

---

[110] Harry MacCracken on Fast Company website: "Google's secretive ATAP lab is imagining the future of smart devices". Published online 13.07.2020, visited 08.04.2024.
https://www.fastcompany.com/90525392/googles-secretive-atap-lab-is-imagining-the-future-of-smart-devices

Obviously, the Intelligence Capabilities require a sound infrastructure to build on – basic data infrastructure, incl. hardware and operating system, scalable analytics platforms, and applicable analytics models and algorithms are crucial components.

**Awareness: Understanding the Infrastructural Foundations**

A comprehensive **data infrastructure** is a critical cornerstone in the context of Artificial Intelligence (AI). It is the architectural framework that facilitates the efficient gathering, storing, and processing of data, a prerequisite to developing powerful AI applications. The essence of AI lies in its ability to decipher patterns and glean insights from data. Hence, a well-structured and robust data infrastructure is indispensable. One of the primary elements of this infrastructure is the **hardware**. This encompasses **computational devices** like servers and processors, including the increasingly important **Graphics Processing Units (GPUs)** and **Tensor Processing Units (TPUs)**. These specialized hardware pieces are designed to handle the complex mathematical computations required in training and deploying AI models. They ensure that the applications run smoothly, processing large volumes of data at impressive speeds. With advancements in technology, edge devices like Internet of Things (IoT) sensors are also becoming integral, collecting real-time data that fuels AI applications. Equally critical is the **storage component**. The types of data that AI processes are diverse – from structured data in databases to unstructured data like images, videos, and audio files. The storage systems, therefore, need to be versatile, scalable, and efficient. Solutions range from on-premises servers to cloud storage options and hybrid models, each offering various levels of flexibility, accessibility, and security. The choice depends on the volume of data, the level of security needed, and the organization's operational preference. The **operating systems** and **software** that manage these hardware and storage components are tailored to maximize performance, reliability, and security. They are optimized to handle vast datasets, facilitating seamless interaction between the hardware and AI applications. Specialized software ensures that the data is accessible and usable, integrating various data sources and types into a cohesive, manageable whole, ready for analysis. **Networking** also plays a crucial role, ensuring that data can be transported quickly and securely within the system and is accessible to those who need it when they need it. High-speed internet and intranet, secure data transmission protocols, and advanced networking hardware ensure that data flows seamlessly across the various components of the infrastructure. Security is paramount. Given the sensitive nature of data processed by AI applications, robust **security protocols** are embedded within the data infrastructure. These include physical security measures for on-premises solutions and cyber-security protocols like encryption, access controls, and intrusion detection systems for online and cloud-based solutions.

**Analytics platforms** are at the heart of operationalizing and scaling AI across industries. They are engineered environments that streamline the creation, deployment, and management of AI applications, making them accessible and actionable for businesses. **Flexibility and customization** are crucial. Organizations are navigating through a diverse range of needs and challenges, requiring platforms that offer not just robust solutions but also the flexibility for tailored applications. These platforms come equipped with a range of tools and features that allow businesses to customize AI applications according to specific operational needs. They facilitate the integration of AI into existing systems and processes, ensuring that organizations can harness AI's capabilities without overhauling their established operational frameworks. **User-friendliness** is another crucial aspect. Analytics platforms are evolving to be more user-friendly, aiming to empower even those without an advanced technical background to create, manage, and deploy AI applications. They offer intuitive interfaces, easy-to-use tools, and accessible features that demystify AI, transforming it from a complex, esoteric technology to a practical, accessible solution for businesses. **Scalability and performance** are also integral. As businesses grow and evolve, the analytics platforms they use must be able to scale accordingly. They should efficiently handle increased data volumes, more complex applications, and a larger user base. Performance optimization ensures that AI applications run smoothly, offering real-time insights and actions that drive business agility and competitiveness. **Integration capabilities** amplify the efficacy of these platforms. They are designed to integrate seamlessly with various data sources, applications, and systems both on-premises and in the cloud. This ensures that businesses can access and analyze data in real-time, fostering an environment where decisions are insight-driven and timely. **Security and compliance** features embedded within these platforms safeguard sensitive business data. They are fortified with protocols that ensure data privacy, security, and compliance with regulatory standards. Features like access controls, encryption, and audit trails ensure that data is not just secure but also managed and used ethically and legally. For instance, Microsoft's Azure AI offers a suite of machine learning tools and services that allow businesses to build AI models effectively and deploy them at scale. Google AI, on the other hand, focuses extensively on making AI accessible to businesses, offering pre-trained models and tools that require minimal coding, ensuring that businesses can harness AI's powers even with limited technical expertise. AWS AI provides a wide array of machine learning services and supporting cloud infrastructure, granting businesses the computational power and tools needed to derive insights from data effectively.

Understanding artificial intelligence at a deeper level necessitates diving into the **analytics models and algorithms** – the mechanisms that imbue machines with the capability to learn, reason, and decide. They are the core that transforms raw data into actionable insights and intelligent actions. **Classification models**, for example, are paramount in applications where data categorization is essential. They are employed in healthcare for disease identification, in finance to categorize transaction types, and in e-commerce to classify customer segments. These models use tree-like graph representations to model decisions and their consequences, including chance event outcomes, resource costs, and utility. Going further **Deep Learning Models**, specifically neural networks, imitate the human brain's interconnected neuron structure to process data. They excel in managing unstructured data. Convolutional neural network (CNNs), for instance, have layers of convolutions to automatically and adaptively learn spatial hierarchies of features from images, powering applications like facial recognition and automated medical imaging diagnosis. Recurrent neural network (RNNs) are adept at handling sequential data, making them vital for analyzing time-series data, speech recognition, and language translation. **Customization and Adaptation** of these models ensure their alignment with specific business contexts. Every organization has unique data and objectives. Hence, models and algorithms are adapted and tuned. Hyperparameters, variables external to the model that configure its learning process, are adjusted. The choice of features – individual measurable properties or characteristics of the phenomenon being observed – is important, shaping the model's learning and prediction accuracy. **Explainability** is emerging as a cornerstone in AI's evolution. As AI permeates sensitive sectors like healthcare and finance, explaining model predictions and decisions is crucial for trust and regulatory compliance. Tools and methodologies to interpret model outcomes, such as LIME (Local Interpretable Model-agnostic Explanations) and SHAP (SHapley Additive exPlanations), are instrumental in decoding complex model behaviors.

There are several types of model services that can be used:

- **Cloud-Based AI Services** offer pre-trained models and algorithms accessible via the cloud, making AI implementation easier for businesses. For example, Google's Vision AI offers powerful image analysis capabilities using machine learning, while AWS's Comprehend delivers natural language processing tasks, highlighting the breadth of readily available AI services. These services enable businesses to integrate AI without building models from scratch.
- **Open-Source Libraries and Frameworks** like TensorFlow and PyTorch come with robust community support, extensive documentation, and a suite of tools for designing, training, and validating models. They support a range of neural network architectures, allowing developers to tailor their AI applications finely.
- **Pre-tested Models like BERT, ResNet, and GPT**. BERT (Bidirectional Encoder Representations from Transformers) has revolutionized the way machines understand human language, enhancing applications like chat bots and virtual assistants. ResNet (Residual Networks) has set new records in image recognition accuracy, essential in applications like automated inspection in manufacturing.

GPT (Generative Pre-trained Transformer), with its ability to generate human-like text, has significantly advanced natural language processing, powering more coherent and contextually relevant content generation, and elevating the capabilities of chat bots, content creation tools, and more.

Large players such as Google, Amazon, Microsoft, Alibaba, and others have capitalized on their expertise and resources to provide **comprehensive solutions that span across data infrastructure, analytics platforms, and analytics models**. Google, for instance, offers an all-encompassing ecosystem with its Google Cloud Platform. It provides tailored hardware and operating systems, a rich set of tools on Google AI platform for creating AI applications, and a plethora of pre-built models and algorithms that facilitate rapid development and deployment. Amazon's AWS offers a similar ecosystem, characterized by a robust data infrastructure that is optimized for performance, AWS AI platform with tools and services that cater to both novice and expert users, and AWS AI services that provide pre-built models and algorithms to accelerate AI application development. Microsoft Azure follows suit, with an emphasis on integrating their solutions seamlessly with enterprise environments, offering a robust data infrastructure, Azure AI platform for application development, and Azure AI services with pre-built models. Alibaba Cloud also extends comprehensive AI solutions, particularly optimized for e-commerce and retail industries, offering tailored infrastructure, a rich set of development tools, and extensive pre-built models that are industry specific. These tech giants have crafted ecosystems where each component – data infrastructure, analytics platforms, and analytics models – is carefully woven to offer seamless, end-to-end AI solutions. Users can leverage these ecosystems to go from ideation to deployment rapidly, with the assurance of compatibility, security, and scalability. The integration ensures that innovations and updates in one component translate to enhanced performance and capabilities across the entire AI application development lifecycle, offering businesses agility, innovation, and a competitive edge in the rapidly evolving AI landscape.

**Assessment: Testing the Stability and Performance of Infrastructural Foundations**

For a comprehensive evaluation of a company's AI infrastructural foundations, it is clear that a nuanced understanding of the data infrastructure, analytics platforms, and analytics models is paramount. These cornerstones not only define the current state of AI readiness but also shape the trajectory of future advancements.

In assessing the **data infrastructure**, companies need to consider more than just their ability to store vast amounts of data. The nuanced quality, accessibility, and security of this data are fundamental. **Data quality** ensures that AI systems are fed with accurate, timely, and consistent data, shaping the reliability of the outcomes. **Data**

**security** is equally vital. A robust infrastructure should safeguard sensitive information against breaches, ensuring compliance with regulatory standards and instilling confidence in stakeholders.

Turning our focus to **analytics platforms**, their adaptability and ease of integration become focal points. The platforms should not only host a diverse set of tools but also exhibit the flexibility to accommodate evolving business needs. **User experience** is paramount. Platforms that offer intuitive interfaces and simplified user experiences encourage broader adoption across various organizational levels, ensuring that the benefits of AI are not confined to tech-savvy individuals.

Within the space of **analytics models and algorithms**, the emphasis is on diversity and adaptability. These models should be able to handle a variety of tasks, from predictive analytics to real-time decision-making. **Transparency** in how these models arrive at their conclusions is becoming a cornerstone. As businesses and regulators alike demand explainability, models that offer insights into their decision-making processes are valued.

Taking a closer look at how companies are incorporating offerings from tech giants, the ability to weave these comprehensive AI ecosystems seamlessly into the organizational fabric is a marker of maturity. It is not just about adoption but optimizing the use of platforms like Google AI, AWS AI, and Azure AI to enhance efficiency, innovation, and competitiveness in the market.

By examining these aspects, companies can attain a granular view of their AI infrastructure maturity.

### Action: Establishing a Strong Foundation for AI

Building and utilizing AI's infrastructural foundations is a long-term process that demands a blend of strategic foresight, actionable insights, and resilient execution. For companies ready to embark on this journey, a series of concrete steps can guide the way.

Strengthening the **Data Infrastructure** foundational element requires actions like initiating comprehensive data audits to evaluate the current data landscape. **Developing a detailed data strategy** is essential. This might include identifying data sources, ensuring data quality and governance, and establishing protocols for data security and privacy. Companies should consider building dedicated teams or assigning specific roles for ongoing data management, including addressing quality, security, and governance challenges.

For the selection and optimization of these **analytics platforms**, a systematic evaluation of existing tools and technologies against the company's specific needs and objectives is a crucial first step. **Implementing training programs** to enhance workforce proficiency in using these platforms can expedite their integration into everyday workflows. A continuous feedback mechanism to understand the user experience, address challenges, and make necessary adjustments ensures that the platforms evolve to meet changing demands.

Building **Analytics Models and Algorithms** requires a deep dive into identifying the specific needs of various organizational sectors. **Developing a repository of customized models and algorithms** tailored for different applications and continuously updating them based on the latest research and trends can optimize performance. Collaboration with external AI research entities and institutions could accelerate the development and diversity of these models.

Companies can consider partnerships with comprehensive **AI ecosystems** like Google AI, AWS AI, Azure AI, or others. **Mapping out a detailed integration plan** on how these ecosystems can be tailored to fit into and enhance the existing organizational infrastructure is crucial. The strategy should include scalability to accommodate future growth and expansion.

These concrete steps underscore the ongoing nature of integrating AI into the organizational ecosystem. It is an investment in the future that promises transformative outcomes when approached with precision, commitment, and adaptability.

### 3.5.2.4 Data and Data Management – the Core Foundation for Digital Intelligence

Obviously, the key ingredient for Digital Intelligence is data – how it is sourced, processed, and cleansed, stored, and made available. Consider the types of data a company might handle. **Explicit data** represents the most straightforward interactions with consumers. Whether a user fills out a form, answers a survey, or gives direct feedback, this is the raw material from which primary insights are drawn. Netflix, for instance, takes user ratings on movies and shows and turns them into powerful engines of recommendation, delivering content that resonates. **Implicitly derived data**, on the other hand, offers a more veiled understanding of consumer behaviors. It is like the digital breadcrumbs consumers leave behind – every click, pause, and scroll tells a story. Organizations that excel in deciphering this silent narrative often stand out in the market. Google, with its search algorithms, is a trailblazer in this space. By tracking and analyzing search patterns and website visits, it offers personalized ads and content, making digital experiences feel both organic and tailored. Yet, there is a vast universe beyond a company's direct digital touchpoints. **External data** encompasses market trends, socioeconomic shifts, competitor benchmarks, and even global events. It provides context, adding layers of understanding. When Starbucks wants to launch a new outlet, they do not just rely on their sales data. Instead, they factor in demographics, nearby businesses, and even traffic patterns, illustrating the expansive potential of external data. But Data and Analytics, including Artificial Intelligence, is not without its pitfalls. **Data hygiene** emerges as a significant concern. The digital reality is rife with inconsistencies, redundancies, and plain misinformation. A minor error in data entry or an outdated customer record can cascade into misdirected marketing campaigns or inaccurate analytics. Salesforce, a leading CRM platform, emphasizes the importance of clean data, offering tools and protocols to ensure data reliability. It is a testament to the fact that **quality trumps quantity every time**.

**Awareness: Reconfirming the Importance of Data and Data Management**

Therefore, a sound planning for Data Architecture, Data Engineering, Data Visualization and Analysis as well as Data Management and Governance is essential.

**Data Architecture** stands as a foundational pillar, engineered to uphold the vast universe of data that flows through an organization. It is not merely a structural entity but a dynamic blueprint that evolves, adapting to the emerging needs and complexities of the business ecosystem. Every component, from the databases and datasets to the interfaces and integrations, is crafted to ensure that data is not just stored but is rendered accessible, usable, and insightful. In the intricate weave of data architecture, elements like **data models, database design, and data integration** emerge as crucial threads. Data models, the abstract representations of organizational data processes, are the blueprints that guide the systematic and logical organization of data. They ensure that data, in its myriad of forms and structures, is systematically organized, categorized, and indexed. The careful alignment of data models to business objectives ensures that data serves as a strategic asset, tailored to fuel business intelligence, analytics, and decision-making. The cornerstone of data architecture, database design, is where data finds its home. Databases, structured and unstructured, are engineered to not just house data but to ensure its optimal retrieval, update, and management. In the age of big data and real-time analytics, database design transcends structural rigidity, evolving into dynamic entities that support data volume, variety, velocity, and veracity. Data integration emerges as the backbone that ensures that disparate and distributed data finds a harmonious existence. It is a world where data from varied sources, formats, and structures is woven into a seamless story, ensuring interoperability and consistency. In a world driven by AI and machine learning, data integration is the bridge that ensures that data silos are obliterated, enabling a free flow of data that fuels real-time insights and analytics. Moreover, **scalability and flexibility** are embedded in the DNA of contemporary data architecture. In an era marked by exponential data growth, architectures are engineered to scale, ensuring that the influx of data is managed, stored, and processed efficiently. Flexibility ensures that architectures evolve, adapting to emerging data types, sources, and analytics needs.

**'Data Scientists dream about great things, Engineers do them'**[111]. **Data Engineering** stands as a linchpin that transforms the raw, unstructured, and complex data into a refined, accessible, and actionable asset. In a world where data volumes are burgeoning, and the diversity of data sources is escalating, the role of data engineering is instrumental in bridging the chasm between data collection and data insights. It is an effort of collecting, transforming, and preparing data, ensuring it is not just available but is in an optimal state to fuel analytics and decision-making. The **intricacies of data ingestion** cannot be understated. With data emanating from a multitude of sources, both internal and external, structured, and unstructured, the process of collecting and importing this data is a sophisticated operation. Data engineers construct and manage the data pipelines that ensure the seamless transit of data from source to destination. They are tasked with ensuring that data, in its myriad of forms, is ingested efficiently, consistently, and reliably into the organizational ecosystem. **Transformation is the alchemy** that converts raw data into a structured and usable form. Data engineers leverage a suite of tools, languages, and methodologies to clean, enrich, and transform data. They are not just coding experts but are adept at ensuring that data quality and integrity are upheld. In scenarios where data is messy, incomplete, or inconsistent, they are the magicians who ensure that it is refined, complete, and coherent. **Data storage and management** are embedded in data engineering. In a world where data is the fuel that drives organizational insights, data engineers ensure that it is stored, managed, and retrieved efficiently. The creation of **data sets and data lakes** is an art and science that falls under the purview of data engineering. Data lakes, repositories that store a vast amount of raw data in its native format, are crafted and managed by data engineers. They ensure that data lakes are optimized, scalable, and structured to support the diverse needs of data scientists, analysts, and business users alike.

In the world of big data and analytics, data lake and data mesh have emerged as significant architectural frameworks, each offering unique advantages and challenges. A **data lake** serves as a centralized repository where a massive volume of raw data can be stored, whether structured or unstructured. It is marked by its flexibility, scalability, and cost-effectiveness, traits that make it a popular choice for organizations looking to store and analyze data without the constraints of format and structure. Contrastingly, **data mesh** signifies a departure from the centralized model, championing decentralized data ownership and architecture. It is an innovative approach where data is treated as a product and cross-functional teams assume ownership of their respective data domains. This not only facilitates data accessibility but also ushers in an era of organization-wide collaboration and innovation in data use and analytics.

---

[111] James A. Michener – American writer. * 03.02.1907 in New York City; † 16.10.1997 in Austin

One of the stark distinctions lies in data ownership. A traditional data lake, with its centralized nature, is typically managed by a specialized team. Data mesh, however, thrives on decentralized ownership. Multiple teams or departments are empowered to manage and utilize their data, breaking down silos and fostering a culture of shared responsibility and innovation. The architectural divergence is also profound. The monolithic, centralized structure of data lakes is juxtaposed with the agile, distributed framework of data mesh. While both can manage vast datasets, the dynamic scalability and accessibility inherent in data mesh architectures offer enhanced agility, especially in complex organizational setups.

The choice between data lake and data mesh is nuanced, shaped by an organization's specific needs, scale, and objectives. While the former offers a robust, centralized solution for data storage and analytics, the latter promises to mitigate the complexities associated with centralization. Data mesh heralds an era where data's scalability, accessibility, and usability are intrinsic, and data-driven insights become the collective pursuit of an entire organization, not just the remit of specialized teams.

In the continuum of data to insights, **data processing** is a crucial phase where data is analyzed and processed to glean insights. Data engineers design and manage the complex processing systems that ensure that data is analyzed efficiently, insights are gleaned in real-time, and the organization is poised to respond to the emerging trends and patterns with agility and precision.

**Data Visualization and analysis** transform complex and often inscrutable raw data into coherent, intuitive, and actionable insights. This aspect is the storytelling chapter in the data journey, where numbers and statistics are morphed into visual narratives that are interpretable and decision-enabling. At the heart of this discipline is the **crafting of visual data representations**. Graphs, charts, plots, and dashboards become the canvases upon which data paints its story. The skill lies not just in choosing the right type of visualization – be it bar graphs, heat maps, scatter plots, or intricate interactive dashboards – but ensuring that they are designed to be intuitively understood, incisive in delivering insights, and tailored to the audience's informational needs and analytical acumen. Visualization also helps to better understand the data universe, to tailor the model development of the scientists. Customization and interactivity are key attributes of modern Data Visualization. Tools and technologies have evolved to offer bespoke visualization, where stakeholders can interact with data, drill down to granular details, and manipulate visual elements to explore diverse data dimensions. It allows a personalized interrogation of data, enabling stakeholders to derive insights that are specific, contextual, and aligned with their strategic objectives. Analytical rigor underpins effective Data Visualization. It is not just about presenting data aesthetically but ensuring that the visual elements are underpinned by robust analytical processes. Algorithms and analytical tools are employed to sift through data, identify patterns, trends, and anomalies and ensure that the visual narratives are not just compelling but are anchored in statistical and analytical validity. The application of advanced analytical methods, such as predictive analytics and machine learning, are integral in this context. They empower organizations to move beyond representing historical data to projecting future trends, identifying emerging patterns, and offering actionable recommendations. This prescriptive capability ensures that Data Visualization is not just a reflective mirror but a forward-looking lens that offers a vista into future opportunities and challenges. Integration with real-time data feeds is another defining characteristic of contemporary Data Visualization and analysis. In an age where data is dynamic and evolving, visualizations are designed to be equally fluid. They are connected to real-time data streams, ensuring that the visual messages are updated in tandem with the emerging data, offering insights that are not just relevant but timely.

In the world of digital business, data is often likened to oil. But like crude oil, data in its raw form is of little value. It is the refining process – **data management and governance** – that turns this raw material into a priceless commodity, powering the engines of today's digital enterprises. Effective data management not only optimizes the data's value but also ensures its security, accessibility, and relevance. Initiating this process is the crucial step of **data collection and integrity**. As businesses engage with consumers across diverse platforms, it becomes imperative to aggregate this data with utmost precision and consistency. Firms must avoid any errors at this juncture to prevent the generation of flawed insights downstream. Taking a page from Airbnb's strategy, which delineates this process clearly, it is evident that capturing a wide array of user data, including preferences and feedback, continuously tailors and refines the user experience, paving the way for a platform that is both responsive and user-friendly. Following closely is the phase of **data storage and organization**. This step necessitates the implementation of scalable and structured storage solutions to handle the ever-increasing volume of data. Services like Amazon Web Services and Google Cloud Platform have become the go-to for numerous enterprises, offering scalable and reliable solutions. Companies like Netflix further fine-tune this aspect using **sophisticated data warehousing solutions** where data is categorized, enhancing the performance and efficiency of recommendation algorithms. Integral to effective management is **Data Accessibility and Integration**. Having a treasure trove of data is of little use if it remains siloed and inaccessible to those who need it. Here, Microsoft's Power BI stands as a beacon, seamlessly integrating with various data sources and providing teams with actionable insights. This unified access ensures that whether it is the marketing team looking at campaign performance or the finance team assessing revenue streams, everyone is informed by the same, integrated data set. However, with great power comes great responsibility, particularly in the context of **Data Security and Compliance**. Protecting customer data is not just an IT responsibility, it is a trust pact between businesses and their customers. Giants like Apple emphasize this commitment. Their stringent data privacy policies and robust encryption practices ensure that user data remains confidential and secure. Moreover, with regulations like GDPR in Europe, compliance is not just ethical – it is mandatory. An important role that often goes underemphasized is that of **Data Owners**, especially for critical data or key data elements (KDE). Data owners are individuals or teams responsible for the quality, integrity, and security of a specific subset of data. Their tasks include setting data policies, ensuring data quality, and working with data stewards in operationalizing data governance. For instance, in a financial services firm, the Chief Financial Officer (CFO) may serve as the data owner for all financial data. The role is crucial as they are the torchbearer in making sure that data is not just well-maintained but also secure and compliant with regulatory requirements. Closing this discourse is the emphasis on continuous data evaluation and cleanup, a task embraced staunchly by brands like Spotify, where the practice of routinely purging redundancies and outdated information maintains a database that is both relevant and current, laying the foundation for offerings that remain fresh and resonate well with their user base.

Many companies have bits and pieces in place. But how can we assess where your company stands on Data and Data Management?

**Assessment: Stress-testing Data and Data Management**

 To gauge their professionalism and maturity in data and data management, companies should embark on a comprehensive assessment across critical facets, namely Data Architecture, Data Engineering, Data Visualization and Analysis, as well as Data Management and Governance. This evaluative journey should be marked by precise metrics and parameters, which lay down a clear pathway to ascertain both the current state and the existing gaps that need addressing.

When evaluating **Data Architecture,** companies need to consider the **adaptability of the system** to evolving business needs and data volumes. Key metrics could include the **speed of data integration** after mergers or acquisitions, the **latency in data processing and retrieval,** and the **efficiency in handling real-time data.** A review of cases where the architecture has successfully adapted, or struggled, can yield rich insights.

**Data Engineering** assessment should dig deeper into the **granularity and complexity of data handled,** examining the algorithms and processes involved. How often is data lost or misinterpreted during processing? What are the feedback mechanisms to correct errors, and how quickly are they executed? An exploration of case studies of data handling successes and failures can illuminate both strengths and weaknesses.

For **Data Visualization and Analysis,** the quality of decision-making stemming from the presented insights is crucial. How often are visualizations used in meetings and strategic decisions? A **feedback loop** involving decision-makers can elucidate the clarity and actionable nature of these visualizations. Also, an **analysis of decision**

**accuracy and efficiency** when using these tools compared to traditional methods can be telling.

The **Data Management and Governance** segment requires a microscopic view into **data quality and security protocols.** How are data breaches handled, and what preventive measures are in place? Assessing the **response time to data quality issues,** the **thoroughness of data audits,** and the **effectiveness of data owners** in safeguarding and enhancing data quality becomes essential. A **record of incidences, responses, and preventive actions taken** can be a practical tool for evaluation. Data owners, particularly, should be assessed based on their engagement levels, efficiency in handling data issues, and their proactivity in enhancing data quality and security. Their roles should be delineated and evaluated for effectiveness, with a keen eye on instances of proactive issue resolution and innovation in data handling. In evaluating compliance, beyond the quantitative metrics of adherence levels, a qualitative analysis involving stakeholder feedback, regulatory audit results, and instances of corrective actions needed can paint a detailed picture of the real-world compliance landscape.

Each aspect of data management should be dissected with both quantitative and qualitative lenses. A combination of hard metrics, real-world case analyses, and stakeholder feedback should be harmonized into a comprehensive evaluative methodology that does not just pinpoint the current standing but also illuminates the path for strategic enhancements, honing a competitive edge in the data-centric business landscape.

### Action: Solidifying Data and Data Management

In today's data-driven world, constructing a solid foundation of **Data Architecture** is paramount. Companies are tasked with initiating this process by conducting an in-depth audit to discern the strengths and weaknesses embedded in their existing layout. They are not just identifying bottlenecks but are also keenly mapping out areas where innovation and enhancement can be seamlessly integrated. This is complemented by the deployment of flexible storage and processing capabilities to adapt to the fluctuating volumes and complexities of data. A comprehensive roadmap, distinctively tailored to align with the organization's goals, paves the way for the strategic incorporation of innovative technologies, ensuring that adaptability and scalability are at the core.

Parallelly, the fortification of **Data Engineering** remains central to transforming raw data into invaluable insights. This transformation is bolstered by investing in skills development and training programs to empower engineers with advanced tools and methodologies. Standardization of data collection and processing enhances consistency, while automating repetitive tasks mitigates errors and frees up valuable human resources for more complex, analytical tasks. The integration of cloud platforms and Big Data technologies amplifies the ability to manage, process, and analyze data, turning it into a repository of actionable insights.

As the data architecture and engineering landscapes evolve, so does the necessity for advanced **Data Visualization and Analysis**. Adopting interactive and intuitive visualization tools is integral, enabling professionals to dive deeper into data, unveiling patterns and trends with unprecedented clarity. Regular workshops and training sessions keep the teams abreast of the evolving trends, ensuring that data interpretation is not just accurate but is also aligned with the business objectives. Customization of dashboards and reports, ensuring they are tailored to meet the distinctive needs of various departments, ensures that insights are both accessible and actionable.

**Data Management and Governance** fortify this transformative journey. A structured framework of policies and protocols is not just a statutory requirement but is a strategic tool that safeguards data integrity, security, and usability. Assigning data owners underscores accountability, ensuring that data is not just collected but is managed, updated, and utilized effectively. Automating compliance checks and integrating real-time monitoring tools ensure that governance is not retrospective but is a real-time, dynamic process that adapts to the evolving data landscape.

In these endeavors, details are not minute operational aspects but are strategic pillars that uphold the integrity, usability, and security of data. Each of these structured and detailed actions is quintessential, marking milestones in the journey of transforming data from a passive repository to an active strategic asset, driving insights, innovations, and growth.

### 3.5.2.5 Data Teams and Culture – Sustainable Basis for Continued Digital Intelligence

A company's capability to harness and leverage data is heavily reliant on the orchestration of Data Teams and the proliferation of a Data-Driven Culture within its organization. These two elements, though distinct, are inextricably linked, each amplifying the efficacy and reach of the other.

**Awareness: Scoping the Personal Touch to Digital Intelligence**

In the ecosystem of **Data Teams**, each member plays a crucial role, and the constructive interaction among them is essential for transforming data into actionable intelligence. **Business Analysts**, armed with a deep understanding of business dynamics and objectives, focus on deriving actionable insights from data. They interpret data, analyze trends and patterns, and translate these observations into strategic recommendations that align with business goals. Parallelly, **Data Scientists** are the technical brains behind the operation, exploring data with statistical and computational rigor. They create and deploy complex algorithms and models that can process and analyze vast volumes of data, extracting meaningful insights. They are the architects of predictive and prescriptive models that forecast trends and suggest actionable paths. **Data Engineers**, meanwhile, focus on building and maintaining the architectural groundwork. They create and manage databases and ensure the smooth and efficient processing of data. They develop the infrastructure for data generation, transformation, and conversion into analytics-ready formats. The quality, security, and accessibility of data are their primary concern. **DevOps** professionals play a key role in ensuring that the development and operations sides of a project are seamlessly integrated. They focus on the deployment of models and algorithms and ensure that the data applications are scalable, adaptable, and reliable. Their role is important in ensuring that the solutions developed are not only technically sound but are also practical and applicable in real-world scenarios. **Solution Architects** weave together the complex combination of data science, engineering, and business insights into comprehensive solutions. They ensure that the technical complexity translates into practical applications, ensuring that data initiatives align with organizational objectives and comply with regulatory norms. **The collaboration among these diverse roles is nothing short of a well-conducted orchestra.** Business Analysts provide the context, ensuring that data initiatives are aligned with business needs. They relay business problems to Data Scientists who, in turn, develop models and algorithms to extract the needed insights. Data Engineers ensure that these professionals have all the data they need in the right format and at the right time. DevOps ensure that the developed solutions are deployable and scalable, while Solution Architects ensure that all the pieces fit together, translating technical complexity into business solutions.

In cultivating a **data-driven culture**, every facet of the organization is imbued with a commitment to empirical decision-making. For instance, Airbnb systematically integrates data analytics into its service optimization and customer engagement strategies. It is not about ad-hoc or isolated initiatives but a holistic incorporation where every decision, from marketing to product development, is informed by data. The role of leadership is to be the catalyst in this transformation. Take General Electric, their leaders are not just administrators but are at the forefront of integrating data analytics into organizational strategies. They set clear objectives, allocate resources, and create policies that foster an environment where data is central. The leadership ensures that data-driven decision-making is not a theoretical concept but a practiced norm. Democratizing data is about breaking down barriers between departments and hierarchies. In the case of Spotify, it is not just the analysts who have access to data, but professionals across various functions, even those not traditionally associated with data analysis. They are equipped with tools and training to extract actionable insights, leading to a collaborative, insight-driven work environment. However, access to data is only as good as the ability to interpret it. **Training and development** programs, like those at Procter & Gamble, are comprehensive. They encompass workshops, e-learning modules, and hands-on projects to ensure employees at all levels are not just familiar with data but are adept at drawing actionable insights. There is a focus on real-world applicability to ensure that learning translates to enhanced decision-making on the job. Curiosity and experimentation are not abstract concepts but are embedded in the operational ethos. Netflix, for example, has built an infrastructure that facilitates A/B testing in real scenarios. Employees are encouraged to propose hypotheses, design experiments, and derive insights, leading to an environment where innovation is continuous and informed by real data. Celebrating victories is not just about acknowledgment but about reinforcing the role of data in these victories. In companies like Zara, success stories of data-driven decisions are documented and shared. Teams and individuals are recognized, fostering a culture where the role of data in driving success is not just understood but celebrated. To be data-driven is a tangible, actionable, and dynamic state of operation. It is characterized by specific practices, policies, and behaviors that make the role of data explicit, celebrated, and central in every aspect of organizational life. It is a scenario where the pathway to every decision, whether strategic or operational, is illuminated by data-derived insights, ensuring not just relevance but a strategic advantage in a competitive landscape.

**Assessment: Feedbacking the People Dimension around Digital Intelligence**

When assessing the maturity of data teams and the culture, a more granular approach can be beneficial. Start by looking at the **Team Composition and Skillset**. For example, examine the specific skills each member possesses. Does the data scientist have proficiency in Python, R, or machine learning algorithms? Have the data engineers been trained in handling big data technologies like Hadoop or Spark?

For **Collaboration and Interaction,** observe the tools and platforms in use. Are tools like Slack or Microsoft Teams enabling seamless communication? Look at the frequency of joint projects between data scientists and data engineers — are they collaborating on a daily or at least weekly basis, and is there documented evidence of shared outcomes and insights?

The **Project Portfolio** review should be comprehensive. Examine specific projects — for instance, did a recent project lead to a 20% increase in operational efficiency or a 15% rise in customer satisfaction? Look at the data-driven insights generated and how they directly influenced these outcomes.

**Training and Development Initiatives** should be quantifiable. How many hours of training are being provided annually to each team member? Are there certifications being earned? Is there a noticeable improvement in skill and project outcomes post-training?

When assessing **Data Accessibility,** evaluate the tools in use. Are platforms like Tableau or Power BI deployed company-wide, and what percentage of the workforce is actively using them? Is there a marked increase in data accessibility over the past year?

For **Decision-making Processes,** consider concrete examples. In the last quarter, identify major decisions and trace back – were they informed by data? Look at the analytics reports, insights, and the tangible influence they had on decisions made.

**Experimentation and Innovation** can be measured by specific projects or initiatives. Identify a data-driven project that was experimental – what were the outcomes? Did it lead to a new process or product line? Assess the risk-taking appetite – are there instances of failure, and how were they addressed?

**Data Utilization Metrics** should be tied to KPIs. Assess if there is a 30% increase in active users of data analytics platforms or a 25% increase in the frequency of data access. Look at the type of data being accessed – has there been diversification in the sources of data being analyzed?

Finally, to quantify the **Data-Driven Culture,** look at employee surveys and feedback. Is there a positive sentiment towards data? Are employees feeling empowered with data access, and are there tangible instances where data-driven insights have been celebrated company-wide? Are achievements and successful projects attributed to data insights highlighted in internal communications?

By focusing on these detailed metrics and evaluating specific instances and tangible outcomes, companies can precisely assess the maturity of their data teams and the depth of their data culture. Each observation and measurement should lead to action – addressing gaps and leveraging strengths to create a team and culture that is intrinsically aligned with data-driven insights and innovation.

### Action: Recruiting, Developing and Maintaining Best Talent

The initiation phase of building data teams hinges on a thorough **analysis of existing skills and competencies within the organization.** Businesses can employ talent analytics tools to map current capabilities against the required skills, producing a detailed gap analysis. A Business Analyst, for example, would be assessed on their ability to translate business problems into analytical queries and their skills in using Data Visualization tools.

In the hiring phase, the focus shifts to **filling identified skill gaps with precision.** For instance, the recruitment of a Data Scientist might involve creating a competency test that includes real-world data challenges to evaluate candidates' abilities to derive actionable insights from complex data sets. **Partnerships with universities and educational institutions** can also be explored, allowing companies direct access to a pool of emerging talents equipped with cutting-edge skills and fresh perspectives.

Training and development for these roles become paramount. A Data Engineer might undergo a **specific training module** on advanced database management systems and big data technologies, tailored to the organization's specific technological landscape. Cross-training initiatives could involve a structured program where a Solution Architect spends time with the Data Engineering team to understand the nuances of data infrastructure, creating a culture of mutual understanding and collaboration.

For **career progression,** each role could have a clearly mapped path. A DevOps professional might see a path from handling routine operational tasks to leading complex, organization-wide system integrations. **Mentorship programs** can be implemented where seasoned Data Scientists mentor newer recruits, driving skill enhancement and knowledge transfer.

Cultivating a data-driven culture begins with **executive endorsement,** where leaders not only advocate for data-centric decision-making but integrate data insights into strategic initiatives. **Training programs** could be amplified to include not just technical skills enhancement but also workshops on innovative thinking and creative problem-solving to maintain a culture of innovation.

**Data accessibility** can be enhanced by deploying user-friendly data platforms with intuitive interfaces, reducing the entry barrier for employees with varying skill levels. Companies might implement **monthly innovation labs,** sessions where teams present data-driven innovations, supporting a culture of creativity and recognition.

Metrics to measure the adoption of a data-driven culture could include **employee engagement scores derived from regular surveys,** tracking the uptake of data tools, and quantifying the impact of data-driven projects on business outcomes. **Knowledge sharing sessions** might be documented and archived for future reference, creating a rich database of insights and innovations.

By following this detailed pathway, organizations not only build and nurture competent data teams but also instill a vibrant, evolving data culture that adapts and grows in tandem with emerging data trends and organizational needs, positioning the company as a leader in the data-centric business landscape.

 Find more and updated information in the **Digital Arena**. Connect with like-minded professionals to unleash the potential and make it happen.

Going even beyond the Digital Lead, it is important to understand emerging technologies and opportunities. They will define the Digital Future.

## 3.6  Digital Future

«The future depends on what we do in the present.»
Mahatma Gandhi[112]

In the ever-accelerating environment of technological advancement, comprehending the Digital Future is the compass steering businesses towards enduring triumph. This chapter introduces the cornerstone principles that underpin long-lasting Digital Success: Anticipating Future Trends and living Innovation & Experimentation. By mastering these pillars, organizations cannot only weather the tempestuous waves of change but ride them to flourish in the digital terrain.

### 3.6.1  Anticipating future trends

The ability to anticipate future trends is the cornerstone of a thriving business in the long run. As the tide of technology and consumer behaviors ebbs and flows, companies that master the art of foresight position themselves not just as spectators, but as active pioneers of change.

**What the C-Suite needs to know**

1. **Awareness of Future Trends:** Successful companies like Apple, Amazon, and Tesla exemplify the importance of foresight in business strategy, with a proactive stance on market shifts and emerging technologies. They actively engage with transformative currents to anticipate and shape the future, as seen in P&G's pivot to digital relevance through continuous learning, strategic foresight, and innovation challenges.

2. **Systematic Approach to Foresight:** Evaluating a company's foresight involves assessing openness to new developments, participation in innovation, effective use of an innovation radar to identify opportunities, scenario planning accuracy, and adaptability. The key is to transform anticipation of technological trends into concrete business opportunities, illustrated by companies like Netflix and Google that continuously innovate and adapt to lead their industries.

3. **Proactive Learning and Innovation Culture:** Emphasize the importance of a culture that prioritizes continuous learning, as demonstrated by IBM's Think Academy, which fosters an environment where employees are always ahead of the curve. It is crucial to maintain a dynamic organization where exploration and anticipation of future trends are ingrained in the company's philosophy, leading to a workforce that is not only reactive but also proactive in shaping the future.

4. **Strategic Utilization of Trend Radars:** Utilize trend radars to systematically identify and analyze future technological and competitive developments, keeping ahead of the industry curve. This involves detailed competitor and technological advancements analysis, coupled with regular

---

[112] Mahatma Gandhi – Indian lawyer, anti-colonial nationalist, and political ethicist. * 02.10.1869 in Gujarat; † 30.01.1948 in New Delhi

updates to the radar, collaboration with trend researchers, and widespread organizational engagement with the findings to stay competitive and innovate effectively.

5. **Future-thinking and Scenario Planning**: Adopt a future-thinking approach to navigate through uncertainty with resilience, using strategic foresight to create a spectrum of scenarios that prepare the organization for a variety of potential futures. This readiness allows the company to adapt swiftly and robustly, ensuring strategies are in place to thrive in any future market condition, informed by a comprehensive understanding of diverse factors such as geopolitical shifts and technological progress.

But why it is so important to anticipate future trends?

## Awareness: Gazing Beyond the Horizon

The quest for long-term success hinges on the ability to anticipate future trends. Apple's astute anticipation of the smartphone revolution and Amazon's prescient grasp of e-commerce's potential illustrate the power of foresight (visit section 3.1.1 Digital Vision and Leadership on page 81 to see how anticipation translates into Digital Vision).

Embracing the future with foresight is not a matter of passive observation, it is an active engagement with the transformative currents shaping industries, markets, and societies. Just as Tesla anticipated the surge in electric vehicle demand and reshaped the automotive landscape, this awareness equips businesses with a radar that detects the faint signals of emerging technologies, shifting customer behaviors, and nascent market dynamics. Much like Netflix's early recognition of the shift to digital streaming, it is about reading the patterns of change, spotting the subtle shifts, and understanding the potential trajectories that will influence the course of business.

**Procter & Gamble** (P&G) provides a compelling example of a conventional, non-tech native company that has effectively pivoted to remain competitive in the digital age.

**Continuous Learning**: P&G's Corporate College program is an internal learning initiative aimed to constantly update the skill sets of employees. Whether it is digital marketing, data analytics, or supply chain management, P&G ensures that its workforce is updated with the latest trends and technologies. The Corporate College acts as a mini university within the company, offering workshops, courses, and seminars that equip employees to be at the forefront of change. They have 'lunch and learns' where executives share insights and updates, ensuring a culture of on-going education.

**Future-thinking**: P&G employs a strategic foresight team dedicated to long-term planning and scenario analysis. This team partners with external experts and uses data-driven tools to create a variety of future scenarios. For instance, in the beauty industry, P&G has already begun exploring the implications of augmented reality for personalized skincare. By investing in advanced simulation software, the company can explore different market conditions and consumer trends to make more informed decisions. The foresight team works across business units to ensure that each is prepared for multiple future scenarios, thereby minimizing risk, and maximizing opportunity.

**Innovation Challenges**: P&G has its own internal innovation competition known as the 'Signal Accelerator Challenge', where employees are encouraged to pitch innovative product or process ideas. The most promising ideas are then developed into prototypes. Winners often receive funding to take their ideas to the next level, and the resulting innovations have led to breakthroughs in everything from packaging sustainability to product formulations. Moreover, P&G actively engages in external partnerships through its Connect+Develop program. Here, P&G collaborates with startups, academic institutions, and even competitors to co-create innovative solutions. This open culture reflects a broader strategy to look beyond its walls for innovation, thus amplifying its creative potential and problem-solving capabilities.

By excelling in these areas, P&G has managed to not only adapt to the challenges of the digital era but also to thrive, setting a high standard for other traditional companies aiming to successfully pivot in today's fast-paced business environment[113].

To be receptive for future developments, it is essential that a company fosters an open **culture of curiosity**. Throughout the organization people do not just need to continuously increase their digital literacy, but also find encouragement to think beyond the current situation, out-of-the-box.

The heartbeat of successful businesses echoes with vigilant **market monitoring** around customers, competitors, and technologies. Netflix exemplifies this by employing advanced analytics to continuously decode viewership patterns and content preferences. Through this granular examination, they anticipate audience shifts and skillfully adapt their content strategy. By discerning the undercurrents that hint at industry shifts, they remain at the forefront of entertainment evolution. At the forefront of **data-driven anticipation**, Amazon paints a vivid picture of harnessing information for predictive insight. Their algorithms dive deep into user behavior, purchase history, and browsing patterns to craft personalized experiences. By doing so, they not only respond to customer needs but anticipate them, etching a path for competitors to follow. Drawing inspiration from Google, the technology titan renowned for innovation, offers a masterclass in **scanning technology landscapes**. Their perpetual curiosity and investments in burgeoning startups allow them to anticipate trends before they gain momentum. This proactive stance led them to champion pivotal trends like artificial intelligence, transforming the very fabric of technology as we know it.

In the energy sector, Shell embodies the essence of **scenario planning** as a powerful tool for futureproofing. With energy markets wrought with volatility, Shell diligently constructs scenarios encompassing geopolitical, economic, and environmental dimensions. These narratives of possible futures serve as guideposts, enabling the company to pivot swiftly in response to the ever-changing landscape.

---

[113] David Butler on The Streets website: "History of Procter & Gamble: Timeline and Facts". Published 21.03.2020, visited 08.04.2024. https://www.thestreet.com/personal-finance/history-of-procter-and-gamble

But does your company anticipate technological developments and identify opportunities early on?

**Assessment: Challenging the Company's Foresight**

 The journey towards anticipating future trends demands more than mere intuition, it necessitates a systematic approach to evaluation and analysis.

To understand whether a company applies a systematic approach, a first question to answer, is whether a company is genuinely open for new developments. An innovation culture is the bedrock of forward-thinking, nurturing an environment that fosters creativity and agility. An indispensable metric in this spectrum is **Employee Engagement and Participation Rates**. Companies must vigilantly track the number and diversity of employees actively involved in innovation programs, understanding that a vibrant innovation culture is reflected through high participation rates. **Retention Rate of Employees** speaks volumes about the organization's innovation climate, with higher retention rates indicating a nurturing and encouraging environment. Parallelly, conducing Innovation **Pulse Surveys** can offer deep insights into the employees' perception and help spotlight areas ripe for enhancement. Additionally, the **Number of Innovations Adopted from Employee Suggestions** stands as a testimony to a thriving innovation culture, encouraging the spirit of proactivity and engagement.

A second question circles around a company's active pursuit to identify future opportunities: Transitioning to the **Trend Radar**, it emerges as a linchpin in the strategic foresight narrative. **Number of Identified Trends and Opportunities** must be recorded to gauge the radar's effectiveness in capturing relevant market pulses. Furthermore, the **Implementation Rate of Insights** demonstrates the alignment between identified trends and organizational strategy, highlighting the tangible actions taken in response to the insights garnered. Moreover, conducting a periodic **Impact Analysis of Implemented Trends** can facilitate a grounded evaluation of the adopted trends, nurturing a proactive and informed approach to market dynamics.

A third question explores a company's willingness and ability to model anticipated developments into future business opportunities. In the landscape of **Innovation Challenges**, the focus sharpens on harnessing collective creativity to pave the path for groundbreaking solutions. The **Quality and Quantity of Generated Ideas** emerge as dual metrics, providing a balanced view of the efficacy and vibrancy of innovation challenges. Monitoring the **Success Rate of Implemented Ideas** post-implementation allows for a deep dive into their market resonance and profitability, guiding future strategies with enriched insights. Moreover, tracking **External Collaborations and**

**Partnerships** ensuing from innovation challenges can foster a culture of inclusivity, opening new avenues of growth and perspective enrichment.

A fourth and last question sheds light on whether a company is ready to think through the consequences for its franchise. Diving deeper into **Scenario Planning**, it serves as an illuminating guide in navigating the labyrinthine paths of the business world. The Scenario Accuracy stands as a sentinel, ensuring the real-world relevance and precision of the crafted scenarios, creating a culture of reflective and adaptive planning. An Adaptability Index can be crafted, encapsulating vital aspects such as response time to emerging trends and resilience to unforeseen shocks, offering a panoramic view of the organization's preparedness and agility. Significantly, the Number of Strategic Shifts Derived from Scenarios underlines the crucial role of scenario planning in shaping organizational strategy, marking a path of informed and foresighted navigation.

This assessment equips businesses with the nuanced insights required to chart a course towards informed decision-making and strategic agility.

**Action: Pioneering Tomorrow's Visions**

The pursuit of anticipating future trends is not a passive endeavor, it thrives on proactive measures and strategic actions that propel organizations into the forefront of change.

*Continuous Learning: Cultivating an Open Mindset of Exploration*

In a world where change is the only constant, supporting a culture of continuous learning is not just beneficial but essential. IBM, a vanguard in the technological arena, has instituted mechanisms like the Think Academy to epitomize this principle vividly. This establishment is more than just a learning hub, it is a powerhouse that curates a vast repository of resources, ensuring that both employees and partners do not just stay abreast of developments but are consistently ahead of the curve, foreseeing trends before they become apparent to the masses. Through a diverse range of learning modalities such as webinars, intensive courses, and collaborative forums, IBM is nurturing an ecosystem where the ethos of exploration is not just encouraged but celebrated[114].

Think of embracing continuous learning as equipping sailors with the most sophisticated navigational charts, allowing them to steer through the most turbulent and uncharted waters with confidence and foresight. It is here that **dynamic learning platforms** come into play, offering regular training sessions that dive deep into the

---

[114] On the Ragan website: "IBM's Think Academy is a model for employee education". Visited 08.04.2024. https://www.ragan.com/awards/employee-communications-awards/2016/winners/employee-education/

nuances of rapidly evolving fields such as artificial intelligence. These platforms empower teams to grasp emerging applications and visualize the ripple effect of these technologies in disrupting existing industry paradigms. But the learning landscape extends beyond artificial intelligence, venturing into the space of groundbreaking technologies like Extended Reality, Internet of Things (IoT), 3D/4D Printing or Distributed Ledger Technology/Blockchain based on underlying developments of quantum and edge computing or software 2.0 developments. By immersing employees in the rich possibilities of these evolving fields, they are nurtured to become visionaries, adept at spotting nascent trends and formulating strategies that are not reactive, but proactive, steering the organization towards paths laden with opportunities[115].

Maintaining a culture of **perpetual learning** transcends beyond just being a strategy, it manifests as a guiding philosophy that morphs organizations into dynamic entities, characterized by workforces well-versed in decoding the subtle signals of change pulsating in the industry. This culture engenders a nimbleness, transforming teams into pioneers, always ready to identify and surge ahead leveraging emergent trends, morphing them into the very vanguards of innovation. It is the commitment to continuous learning that stands as a steadfast rudder, guiding organizations with unyielding resolve. It is this dedication to learning that equips teams to anticipate shifts in the landscape, to not just adapt, but to shape the future actively, crafting trajectories that are visionary, robust, and resonate with the pulse of the ever-evolving technological forefront.

Cultivating a mindset of exploration through continuous learning is no longer a choice but a necessity, a defining pillar that will delineate the leaders from the followers in the dynamic digital landscape.

### *Trend Radar: Identifying and Communicating Future Developments*

Staying ahead of the curve is non-negotiable for companies aiming to maintain a competitive edge. It is here that the concept of a trend radar comes into play, serving as a systematic tool for identifying technological and competitive developments and discerning major tectonic shifts in the industry.

A robust trend radar ensures regular observation and analysis of both the competitive landscape and emerging technological innovations. This detailed process begins with **competitor analysis**, where strategies and developmental strides of rivals are scrutinized to identify unique opportunities and potential threats, as well as best-practices to leverage for the own success. Simultaneously, it is vital to keep abreast of **technological advancements**, including AI, blockchain, and augmented

---

[115] Don Tapscott, Alex Tapscott: "Blockchain Revolution". Published by Penguin Random House, 2016

and virtual reality. Understanding these advancements allows companies to gauge the **industry implications** and the reshaping of their value proposition and service delivery model. The insights garnered through this vigilant observation should be synthesized into a **dynamic future trend radar**, a tool updated regularly to map potential future trends, helping to navigate the evolving industry complexities and identify substantial opportunities or threats.

In addition to the trend radar, companies can benefit from **collaboration with trend researchers for validation and inspiration**, actively seeking the expertise of renowned trend research entities like the Zukunftsinstitut[116] or academia. Engaging researchers in active discussions can bring a fresh perspective, challenging and enriching existing viewpoints within the organization. It goes beyond validation, extending into a collaborative effort to foster innovation and challenging existing norms through transformative talks and seminars, encouraging employees to think beyond established boundaries and embrace innovation.

However, the synthesis of a trend radar and collaboration with researchers must be coupled with an effort to ensure engagement and awareness across all organizational levels. Translating insights into actionable strategies through regular communications, including **newsletters and management discussions**, keeps employees abreast of developments, nurturing a culture receptive to change and innovation. Creating a culture of understanding through workshops and training sessions supports readiness for upcoming developments. Moreover, establishing a feedback loop with employees promotes a sense of ownership and inclusivity, nurturing a workforce that is unified in vision.

### *Innovation Challenges: Unleashing Internal Visionaries*

In a business climate that shifts with an ever-accelerating pace, the role of innovation challenges is becoming paramount, acting as vital workshops where groundbreaking ideas germinate and flourish. Embodying the forward-thinking spirit seen in GE's Open Innovation, these challenges represent more than a strategy, they are a powerful tool and a force that galvanizes an organization's internal talent to think beyond the known horizons and uncover paths leading to undiscovered frontiers[117].

Capitalizing on the wellspring of creativity and diversified knowledge across different teams, innovation challenges are designed to foster an environment ripe for creative exploration. They create a vibrant ecosystem where employees are encouraged to

---

[116] On Zukunftsinstitute website: "Die Mega-Trends". Visited 08.04.2024. https://www.zukunftsinstitut.de/dossier/megatrends/

[117] John Donoghue on GLG website: "How Open Innovation Provides a Turbo Boost at GE". Published 19.04.2016, visited 08.04.2024. https://glginsights.com/de/news/how-open-innovation-provides-a-turbo-boost-at-ge/

traverse the landscape of the unknown, imagine the unimaginable, and translate futuristic visions into actionable strategies, leading to a garden of innovative solutions that are not just reactive but pioneering, staying one step ahead in the ever-evolving industry narrative. The bedrock of these challenges is deep collaborative exploration, where cross-functional teams engage in exercises to draft the potential impacts of transformative technological advancements on their industry's future. This immersive process instills a strong sense of ownership and enthusiasm, giving birth to a lineage of internal visionaries who are deeply engrossed in the evolving digital narrative, constantly nourishing the company's innovation pipeline with fresh, vibrant, and forward-thinking ideas. But to truly create a comprehensive spectrum of innovative solutions, it is essential to break free from the organizational silos and to create an open culture that invites diverse perspectives from external aficionados. By actively engaging industry pundits, customers, and even academicians in these challenges, organizations can benefit from a fresh influx of ideas, infusing the discussions with a rich diversity of perspectives that lead to solution generation that is both expansive and enriched. Much like the globally collaborative space of open-source software communities, this strategy garners insights from a diverse populace, creating a melting pot of groundbreaking strategies, enhanced by unforeseen creative synergies and a multitude of perspectives, transcending geographical and cultural boundaries, thus embarking on paths less traveled and envisioning solutions that are both robust and future-ready.

By pooling the collective imaginative prowess from both internal teams and external collaborators, businesses do more than stay afloat in the turbulent seas of the digital era, they forge ahead, carving pathways that lead to untapped avenues of success, sculpting a future landscape that is not only successful but is vibrant, resilient, and leads the charge in the digital revolution, creating a roadmap for success in the burgeoning digital landscape.

### *Illuminating Pathways Through Scenarios*

In a business landscape characterized by uncertainty and relentless change, leveraging a **future-thinking approach** is vital. This approach goes beyond mere prediction, it embraces complexity and uncertainty, carving out a pathway through thoughtfully crafted scenarios, a technique perfectly epitomized by the strategies employed by leading organizations.

Utilizing future-thinking stands as a lighthouse of strategic foresight, crafting a cardinal tool in their strategy arsenal. This multi-faceted approach enables companies to assemble a consortium of stakeholders from a plethora of spheres, coming together to craft a of alternative futures drawn from a rich palette of perspectives encompassing geopolitical shifts, economic variables, and innovative technological advancements.

By engaging in this proactive approach, organizations facilitate a culture of preparedness, ready to adapt and lead in periods of uncertainty, ensuring no scenario catches them unprepared. It is an exercise in foresight, allowing organizations to navigate complex landscapes with insight and agility, creating strategies robust enough to stand firm, no matter how the future unfolds. This **scenario-building process** is not about pinpointing a single predictable future but unfolding a spectrum of outcomes, each detailed narrative offering a prism through which to view potential challenges and opportunities that may arise. By tracing out these diverse trajectories, businesses prepare themselves to respond with agility and robustness to any unfolding reality, thereby not just safeguarding but strengthening its market position. Simultaneously, it holds the foresight to envisage scenarios dominated by geopolitical tensions, carving out blueprints to navigate such landscapes with nuanced strategies, ensuring a foundation robust enough to thrive in any manifested future. Future-thinking functions as a sophisticated compass in the complex world of business, illuminating viable pathways amidst a fog of uncertainties and change. Much like seasoned navigators rely on a good understanding of wind patterns and astronomic observations to chart unknown territories, future-thinking facilitates clarity in a sea of complexity. It melds imagination with strategic foresight, enabling businesses to not merely anticipate but actively shape future trends, weaving strategic roadmaps aligned with a vision grounded in deep understanding and preparedness[118].

Adopting future-thinking is akin to arming oneself with a **dynamic navigational tool**, sculpted from a blend of expertise and imagination. It invites businesses to steer with confidence through the ever-evolving digital landscape, nurturing a readiness not just to respond to changes but to shape them proactively, crafting pathways of success woven from foresight, innovation, and strategic depth. It is not just about foreseeing the changes but having the acumen to act, creating a future that is not just successful but resilient and adaptable in the face of unforeseen challenges.

The journey of anticipating future trends is not a solitary expedition but a collective endeavor fueled by strategic actions. From continuous learning that supports a culture of exploration to the profound insights gleaned from future-thinking and the unleashing of internal visionaries through innovation challenges, businesses craft a roadmap that propels them towards success in the ever-evolving digital environment.

---

[118] Rafael Ramírez, Steve Churchhouse, Alejandra Palermo, and Jonas Hoffmann on MIT Sloan Business Review website: "Using Scenario Planning to Reshape Strategy". Published 13.07.2017, visited 08.04.2024. https://sloanreview.mit.edu/article/using-scenario-planning-to-reshape-strategy/

### 3.6.2 Innovation and Experimentation

Anticipating future trends is critical to success. But just keeping the insights on paper is not sufficient. Pragmatic ways of applying these insights throughout the organization must be implemented.

**What the C-Suite needs to know**

1. **Cultivating Innovation Mindset:** Encouraging an innovation mindset throughout the organization, inspired by examples like IDEO, promotes cross-functional collaboration, regular workshops, and dedicated forums for idea sharing. This culture shift fosters a way of thinking that challenges norms, questions assumptions, and nurtures a continuous flow of creative ideas.

2. **Design Thinking as a Framework:** Design thinking, exemplified by IBM, offers a structured approach to innovation. Integrating user feedback, crafting personas, and mapping user journeys ensures that innovation is driven by empathy and user-centric insights. This approach ensures that innovative solutions align with real-world customer needs.

3. **Agile Experimentation Cycles:** Borrowing from the practices of companies like Spotify, adopting agile experimentation cycles involves rapid prototyping, testing, and iterative improvement. Cross-functional teams collaborate on short-term experiments, allowing the organization to quickly gather insights, refine ideas, and pivot strategies based on real-time feedback.

4. **Experimentation Laboratories:** Creating experimentation laboratories akin to 3M, where employees are empowered to explore without fear of failure, provides a safe space for creative exploration. These labs encourage employees to experiment with new ideas, test hypotheses, and prototype concepts, ultimately creating an environment where innovation thrives.

5. **Strategic Resource Allocation:** Strategic resource allocation for innovation, inspired by practices like Google's 20% time, ensures that time and budget are dedicated to innovative initiatives. Allocating funds specifically for experimentation and establishing innovation funds encourages employees to explore novel concepts that may lead to transformative breakthroughs.

But what is the true value of Experimentation and Innovation?

**Awareness: Cultivating Practical Applications and Tools Tuned to Future Changes**

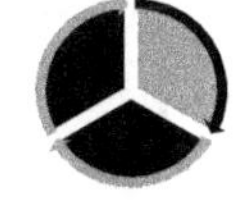

Establishing an innovation culture that comprehends and anticipates future trends is the keystone of a resilient and forward-thinking organization, a proposition powerfully brought to life through strategic insights embedded in design thinking, agile experimentation cycles, experimentation laboratories, and appropriate resource allocation for innovation.

One of the primary steps involves imparting a deep understanding and valuation of the **design thinking approach**, championed by entities like IBM. The strategy insists on a deep-seated empathy for users, striving to meet their unarticulated and existing needs through holistic solutions. This awareness induces a natural propensity to innovate, drawing from a well of understanding that involves detailed customer journey mapping, user interviews, and persona creations, painting a rich canvas that mirrors real-world scenarios. When employees immerse themselves in this rich canvas, they inherently align their innovations to address pressing issues, bringing forth solutions that are deeply empathetic and rooted in genuine challenges.

In step with this is the embrace of **agile experimentation cycles**, a strategy leveraged successfully by companies like Spotify. The focus here is to create a dynamic mindset that embraces rapid prototyping and iterative feedback loops, instilling a readiness to learn from failures and pivot swiftly. Awareness programs encouraging this mindset fuel a culture of swift action and learning, where teams can nimbly alter strategies based on real-time feedback, fostering a proactive, rather than reactive, stance towards change.

Building on this is the encouragement to forge **experimentation laboratories**, a concept nurtured by innovators like 3M and Tata Consultancy Services. These are zones of uninhibited creativity, building environments where the fear of failure is replaced by the thrill of exploration. They embody safe spaces for creative minds to experiment, iterate, and ideate, creating a culture where new concepts can be nurtured to fruition, paving paths to innovative solutions that might not adhere to conventional pathways but hold immense potential to shape the future.

Finally, to truly build a culture that anticipates future trends, it is important to align **resource allocation** towards nurturing innovation. The concept, mirrored in Google's celebrated 20%-time policy, encourages employees to dedicate part of their time to independent projects. The awareness that the organization endorses and invests in futuristic exploration sets a fertile ground for innovations to sprout, sowing seeds of trust and encouragement that nourish bold, imaginative ideas.

By holistically integrating these essential elements into the consciousness of an organization, we set the stage for an environment vibrant with potential and readiness to innovate. Each aspect, drawing from real-world successful strategies, works in synergy to build a culture poised not just to anticipate but to adeptly navigate and shape future trends. It is a rich state of awareness where curiosity meets resources and empathy meets strategy, readying organizations to not only foresee but also forge vibrant paths in the dynamically evolving digital landscape.

> **Google** has always stood at the forefront of innovation, ingraining an anticipation of future trends deep within its organizational culture. Its approach is a vivid testimony to the conscious application of the principles we have delineated.
>
> At the foundation of its innovation strategy lies a profound emphasis on design thinking. Google places a high premium on understanding user needs and preferences, often going beyond the superficial to delve into the deep intricacies of user behavior and preferences. Through systematic data analysis and a genuine desire to understand the user experience, Google crafts solutions that are not just technologically superior but also deeply empathetic to user needs.

The company further drives an agile environment through its endorsement of Agile Experimentation Cycles. It is common to see products launched in beta to glean user feedback and continuously iterate based on real-time insights. This strategy not only speeds up the product development cycle but also ensures that the final product is finely tuned to meet user expectations.

Google's innovative prowess also extends to the establishment of experimentation laboratories. The Google X laboratory, for instance, is a secretive research and development facility where audacious ideas are given the space and resources to grow. This moonshot factory, as it is often referred to, harbors projects that seek to solve huge problems through radical solutions and breakthrough technology. It nurtures an environment where the seemingly impossible is pursued vigorously, embodying the pure spirit of exploration and innovation.

Lastly, resource allocation for innovation is a significant aspect of Google's strategy. The much-acclaimed '20% time' policy allows employees to dedicate a portion of their working hours to pursue personal projects that excite them. This policy has led to the birth of several Google products such as Gmail and Google News, showcasing the profound impact of nurturing an internal environment where innovative ideas can flourish.

Through the masterful orchestration of these elements, Google stands as a paragon of innovation, seamlessly merging foresight with action, and setting a benchmark in harnessing the collective imaginative potential of its workforce to craft solutions that not only anticipate but shape future trends. It serves as a luminary guide, illustrating how a keen understanding of futuristic trends, melded with strategic insights and resources, can forge a powerhouse of innovation, ever ready to steer through the dynamic digital landscape with agility and foresight.

But where is your company in implementing pragmatic innovation approaches?

**Assessment: Navigating the Currents of Innovation Capability**

 To truly assess an organization's readiness for innovation, understanding the **innovation culture** is paramount. A true measurement of this can be seen in the way employees are not only allowed but encouraged to explore novel ideas and challenge existing norms. Here, key markers include employee engagement in innovation projects and the number and impact of cross-functional collaborations that take place within the organization.

Next, an organization's **agility and adaptability** speak volumes about its readiness to steer through the dynamic landscapes of business ecosystems. A vivid illustration can be drawn from Amazon's robust mechanism which rapidly adapts to evolving market demands. Effective assessment in this spectrum hinges on how swiftly and efficiently an organization can respond to market shifts and customer feedback. Important metrics in this domain are the speed of bringing new products or features to the market and the ability to adapt business strategies promptly and effectively to respond to market changes (visit section 3.7.1 Agile and Adaptive Culture on page 324 on how to build it).

Moreover, a crucial parameter in the innovation readiness spectrum is **resource allocation**. Successful companies like Apple have emphasized dedicated resource allocation for driving innovation. This involves earmarking a sizable portion of the budget for Research and Development, dedicating full-time employees to work on groundbreaking projects, and investing generously in the prototyping and testing of new ideas. Key metrics in this area would include the percentage of budget allocated to R&D and innovation, and the number of full-time employees engaged exclusively in innovation projects (visit section 2.6 Balancing Barriers and Priorities in a resource-limited reality on page 73 to understand the broader context of resource allocation).

Furthermore, an organization's **risk tolerance** is a significant determinant in its innovation pathway. This is evident in companies like SpaceX, which have not shied away from pushing the boundaries and embracing high-risk projects. The willingness to engage in such endeavors speaks of a company's readiness to forge new paths in innovation. Essential metrics here encompass the number of high-risk projects initiated and the level of resources allocated to such pioneering endeavors (visit section 2.4 Balancing Innovation with Risk Management on page 58 on backgrounds of balancing innovation and risk).

In tandem with internal strategies, innovation thrives in open collaborations, where organizations willingly engage with external entities such as startups and research institutions to generate fresh perspectives. Companies like Microsoft have rich histories of engaging in such collaborative ventures, yielding fruitful results. Metrics to keep an eye on here include the number of partnerships established and the innovative outcomes derived from these collaborations.

Pulling together these rich and diverse strands of metrics crafts an overview that paints a vivid picture of an organization's standing in the innovation landscape. By giving heed to these aspects, a company cannot only gauge its current position but also carve pathways to build a culture ripe for innovation, geared to adapt with agility to the evolving market dynamics.

**Action: Forging New Frontiers of Innovation**

The pursuit of innovation and experimentation is not a passive endeavor, it requires deliberate and strategic actions that propel organizations beyond their comfort zones.

***Design Thinking as a Framework for Innovation: Empathy in Action***

To institute design thinking effectively, organizations must start with a concerted effort to create **empathy and understanding** towards their user base. This means going beyond traditional market research to deeply immerse themselves in the users' environments, understanding their daily routines, pain points, and desires. Airbnb, for instance, overhauled its entire service offering by deeply understanding and addressing the needs and concerns of their hosts and guests, pivoting from merely being a service listing platform to a community-driven hospitality company. A pivotal strategy in initiating this process is **immersive research**. Teams should be encouraged to observe users in their natural habitats, effectively walking a mile in their shoes to gather rich, qualitative data that goes beyond mere statistics. This could involve home visits, contextual interviews, or even accompanying users while they use the product or service. Companies like IDEO have set the gold standard in this, often embedding themselves in the environments they are designing for to gather firsthand insights[119]. A detailed **analysis of user insights** is a fundamental next step. Insights derived from immersive research should be thoroughly analyzed to draw patterns and correlations, which could involve utilizing **affinity diagrams** to group observations and insights, helping in finding underlying themes and areas of opportunity for innovation. Procter & Gamble applied this methodology to re-imagine laundry through the eyes of the consumers, leading to a deep understanding of consumer needs and aspirations.

Subsequently, the creation of **personas** becomes essential. A persona is a detailed and semi-fictional representation of an ideal customer, crafted based on the insights gathered. It serves as a reference point in the innovation journey, helping teams to keep user needs and preferences at the forefront during the development process. Microsoft leverages personas extensively to ensure products cater to the varied needs and preferences of a global user base. **Storytelling** is an indispensable tool in design thinking. It enables teams to communicate insights and ideas effectively. Crafting narratives around personas helps in supporting empathy and keeping the user's story central to the innovation process, ensuring the development of solutions that truly resonate with users. Nike, for instance, has mastered the art of storytelling, weaving it into their innovation process to create products that meet their audience's aspirations and lifestyles[120].

**Ideation**, the process of generating a myriad of ideas without being hindered by constraints, follows next. Teams should be encouraged to brainstorm freely, fostering a **collaborative and non-judgmental environment** where every idea is welcome. Techniques like mind-mapping, sketching, and SCAMPER can be potent tools in this stage, encouraging out-of-the-box thinking. 3M, the birthplace of Post-it notes, is renowned for its collaborative and free-thinking environment, nurturing ideas that have revolutionized everyday products. To bring these ideas to life, **rapid prototyping** is essential. It entails creating low-fidelity representations of solutions to visualize concepts and test assumptions. It could range from paper sketches to digital mock-

---

[119] Jack O'Donoghue on Make: Iterate website: "IDEO Design Thinking: Process And Practice (The Complete Guide)". Visited 08.04.2024. https://makeiterate.com/ideo-design-thinking-process-and-practice-the-complete-guide/

[120] Sam Grawe on the Creative Review website: "How storytelling is at the heart of the Nike brand". Published 27.01.2021, visited 08.04.2024. https://www.creativereview.co.uk/storytelling-nike-brand/

ups. The goal is to iterate quickly, learning, and refining with each prototype based on real user feedback. Dyson epitomizes this approach with thousands of prototypes being developed before landing on the final product, ensuring refinement at every stage.

**User testing** forms the critical last mile in the design thinking journey. Solutions should be tested rigorously with users, garnering feedback to understand what works and what does not. This stage is vital in ensuring the solution meets user needs effectively before a full-fledged launch, mitigating risks, and increasing the likelihood of success. Spotify, with its frequent beta tests and user feedback loops, ensures that new features are aligned with user needs and preferences.

To embed design thinking in an organization's culture, **on-going education and reinforcement** are key. It involves regular workshops, training programs, and perhaps even establishing a **dedicated design thinking team** to foster this approach across different projects, creating a culture where empathy and user-centricity are not just buzzwords but a way of life. Companies like IBM have wholeheartedly embraced this approach, embedding design thinking principles at every level of the organization, nurturing a culture of user-centric innovation. Through a holistic adoption of design thinking, organizations pave the way for solutions that are not merely innovative but are **deeply empathetic**, user-centric, and have the potential to form deep connections with the users, offering not just products but experiences that enrich lives and build enduring relationships.

### Agile Experimentation Cycles: Rapid Iteration for Success

At the core of **Agile Experimentation Cycles** is the commitment to fast-paced, iterative progress, leveraging the strengths of cross-functional teams. Renowned companies like Spotify employ this dynamic approach to drive innovation swiftly and effectively. It is a philosophy that encourages on-going adaptation based on real-time feedback, making it a potent tool for applying innovation in dynamic markets. Central to this approach is the concept of **iterative sprints**, where teams work within a predefined time limit to accomplish specific goals. This delineated work period allows teams to maintain a sharp focus on their objectives, creating an environment of productivity and efficiency. Industries ranging from technology to healthcare have utilized this concept to streamline processes and encourage creative problem-solving. Companies adopting this strategy employ **cross-functional teams**, which are designed to bring together a variety of perspectives and skill sets. These teams, evident in the organizational structure of firms like Atlassian, work in harmony, contributing their unique expertise to short-term experiments aimed at driving innovation. Utilizing this approach, businesses can quickly pivot based on the feedback received, ensuring the most promising ideas are propelled forward while less effective concepts are promptly shelved.

A fundamental aspect that sets agile experimentation apart is its inherent acceptance of **failure as a learning opportunity**. Organizations like Fail Forward encourage this mindset, allowing teams to take risks with the understanding that not every idea will succeed[121]. This environment creates a deeper level of experimentation, where teams can pursue innovative solutions without the fear of failure, and even if a concept does not succeed, the learnings derived from the process are viewed as a valuable outcome. A substantial feature of this methodology is **responsive strategy shifts**, which entail a readiness to pivot based on the insights and feedback garnered during the experimentation process. Enterprises like Amazon have consistently demonstrated this flexibility, ensuring that they remain adaptive, swiftly modifying strategies to align with the most current insights, thereby ensuring relevance and effectiveness in their innovation journey.

Moreover, a hallmark of agile cycles is the utilization of **digital collaboration tools**. These platforms facilitate seamless communication and collaboration among team members, regardless of geographical boundaries. Tools like Slack and Microsoft Teams are central to this approach, facilitating the uninterrupted flow of information, fostering a rhythm of continuous innovation.

The agile experimentation cycles advocate for a flexible, responsive approach to innovation, where rapid iterations and a readiness to pivot based on real-time insights are not just encouraged but are intrinsic to the process. It carves out a pathway where organizations are constantly evolving, remaining in step with changing market dynamics and creating a culture of sustained innovation and adaptability.

### *Experimentation Laboratories: Safe Spaces for Creative Exploration*

Creating vibrant and successful experimentation laboratories involves weaving together a rich tapestry of elements that drive creativity, innovation, and collaboration, both from within and outside the company's ecosystem. To initiate this, **designing a conducive environment is fundamental**. Organizations need to carefully craft spaces that are both physically and psychologically nurturing for innovation. For instance, Google's famed 'Google X' laboratory is known for its futuristic and open-layout spaces, which encourage spontaneous encounters and exchanges of ideas among its employees[122]. Companies must foster a culture of openness and curiosity, where employees are encouraged to explore and experiment without fear of failure. As the lab takes form, **implementing structured yet flexible processes** to govern its operations is critical. Processes should be designed to support

---

[121] On the Fail Forward website: "Goodbye fear of failure". Visited 08.04.2024. https://failforward.org/
[122] Marziah Karch on the Lifewire website: "Google X: The Secret Google Lab". Updated 28.12.2019, visited 08.04.2024. https://www.lifewire.com/google-x-secret-lab-1616267

inclusivity and collaboration, drawing in a diverse group of individuals from various departments to nurture a rich ground for ideation. 3M, renowned for its innovation, grants its employees a percentage of their work time to focus solely on their passion projects in their labs, creating a rich ground for exploration and latest ideas. Creating a **dynamic and collaborative ecosystem** that brings together cross-functional teams, the laboratories should drive multidisciplinary collaboration. Here, Tata Consultancy Services (TCS) emerges as a role model with its Innovation Labs encouraging cross-disciplinary teamwork, allowing for a rich exchange of ideas and perspectives, nurturing ground-breaking solutions grounded in diverse expertise.

A continuous cycle of learning and development through **training programs and workshops** should be nurtured. They can include bringing in external experts for talks and sessions, as SpaceX does, encouraging an atmosphere of constant learning and growth. Undergirding the laboratory's ethos should be a supportive management style that acts more as facilitators, similar to the role of a Scrum Master in agile methodologies, removing roadblocks and fostering a nurturing environment where teams have the autonomy to explore and innovate. Leadership must encourage open dialogue, appreciating diverse perspectives, and viewing failures as opportunities for learning and growth. Crucial to the lab's triumph is the integration of its results into the broader corporate strategies. This means building bridges between the lab and other units in the company to ensure a seamless transition from ideation to implementation. Here, the role of corporate incubators such as Telefonica's Wayra, can be seen as a benchmark, as it successfully integrates startups' agility and innovative solutions into its corporate strategy[123].

Ensuring a feedback-driven and recognition-rich environment is fundamental. For instance, Adobe Kickbox, a program that provides employees with the framework to innovate, also incorporates mechanisms for feedback and success measurement, creating a culture that recognizes and celebrates innovation[124]. Lastly, maintaining **partnerships with external entities** such as academic institutions or industry pioneers can open doors to fresh perspectives and collaborative learning. Microsoft, for instance, actively engages in partnerships with startups and research organizations, tapping into the broader ecosystem for innovative solutions.

By integrating these elements conscientiously, companies can establish experimentation laboratories that are rich grounds for innovative exploration, creating a culture where creativity thrives and where ground-breaking solutions are nurtured to drive the company forward.

---

[123] On the Wayra website: "Wayra Scales Your Startup". Visited 08.04.2024. https://www.wayra.de/
[124] David Burkus on Harvard Business Review website: "Inside Adobe's Innovation Kit". Published online 23.02.2015, visited 08.04.2024. https://hbr.org/2015/02/inside-adobes-innovation-kit

*Resource Allocation for Innovation: Investment in Future Success*

Let us dive deeper into the various components that facilitate a comprehensive approach to resource allocation for innovation.

First and foremost, organizations must encourage the **allocation of dedicated time for innovation**. This approach allows employees to dive deep into their areas of interest, fostering a culture where ingenuity is not stifled by routine tasks. To enact this successfully, leadership needs to clearly communicate the expectations and objectives behind such an allowance, ensuring it is perceived not as a free time but as an opportunity to drive impactful innovations for the organization.

The next pivotal phase revolves around the **allocation of financial resources**. Beyond just creating budgets for different projects, companies should also look into forming innovation funds – designated financial reservoirs for unconventional yet promising ventures that defy traditional categorizations. A paradigm of this can be seen in corporations like Samsung, where a substantial portion of their revenues is channeled into R&D, facilitating a steady stream of innovative ideas and products. This strategy requires a comprehensive assessment process to identify projects with potential and a systematic allocation methodology to ensure that funds are utilized effectively. Implementing a **tollgate approach** provides a structured pathway where projects undergo stringent evaluations at distinct stages or 'gates'. In this method, projects move to the next phase only upon fulfilling specific criteria, thereby ensuring that only the most viable projects receive further resources and attention. The process necessitates the development of clear guidelines and checkpoints for each gate, along with a panel of experts equipped to assess projects accurately at each juncture.

---

**A Deep Dive into Resource-Infused Tollgate Approach**

In innovation management, the tollgate Approach emerges as an important instrument, marrying the art of innovation with strategic resource allocation, ensuring not just creative vigor but also pragmatic sustainability. It orchestrates a harmony where ideas, once birthed, are nurtured, assessed, and transformed into market-ready solutions, each step resonating with the echoes of strategic and financial support. Stage-gate evaluation delineates the journey of innovation into segmented phases, each marked by specific activities, outcomes, and allocated resources. At this juncture, innovation is not just a creative endeavor but a strategically guided pathway where Ideas are not just formed but forged, assessed, and honed to perfection.

In the initial ideation and exploration stage, creativity knows no bounds. It is where ideas are developed, backed by an initial infusion of funding, laying the foundational stones of innovation. Cross-functional teams, an amalgamation of diverse skills and perspectives, weave the threads of these embryonic ideas into potential innovative narratives. As the journey progresses to the first tollgate, a systematic assessment unfolds. Here, ideas are not just glanced at but gazed upon, each assessed against stringent criteria to ensure alignment with organizational imperatives and market demands. Feasibility

---

assessment becomes the crucial criteria, guiding the allocation of resources to ideas that echo potential and promise.

The ensuing development phase is where ideas metamorphose into prototypes. Backed by a robust allocation of operational budgets or project-specific funding, each prototype is crafted, tested, and refined, echoing the dance of creativity and pragmatism. Prototype validation at the second tollgate is not just a step but a leap, where innovations are not just assessed but validated, each echoing the resonance of market readiness and organizational alignment, backed by enhanced funding to ensure detailed refinement.

The execution and implementation phase emerges as the crucible, where innovations are scaled and optimized for market entry. Resource allocation is at its zenith, ensuring each innovation is not just launched but is poised to thrive and resonate in the competitive market landscape. The final tollgate is the litmus test of market readiness. Here, a final infusion of funding ensures that each innovation, now a refined entity, is not just introduced to the market but is supported to navigate the waves of competition and customer expectations.

Feedback integration and performance metrics are woven into every fabric of this journey. Each piece of feedback is a gem, and every metric is a compass, guiding the continuous refinement of innovations and ensuring strategic alignment of resources.

The Tollgate Approach stands as a testament to the harmonious combination of creativity, strategy, and execution. It is an ecosystem where every idea, backed by the pillars of strategic and financial support, has the potential to not just sparkle but shine brightly, transforming the market landscape with its radiant glow.

Through a judicious allocation of time and financial resources, coupled with structured approaches such as the tollgate method and a collaborative work environment backed by real-time analytics, organizations can create a fertile ground where innovation is nurtured and systematically applied, paving the way for a future of sustained success and growth.

Find more and updated information in the **Digital Arena**. Connect with like-minded professionals to unleash the potential and make it happen.

Being open for the Digital Future requires the right culture – A Digital Mind.

## 3.7 Digital Mind

> «Nothing is IMPOSSIBLE.
> The word itself says I'M POSSIBLE!»
> Audrey Hepburn[125]

In a world that has grown increasingly reliant on digital innovation, the most successful companies are not merely those with the most cutting-edge technologies or the sleekest interfaces. Instead, they are the companies that cultivate a 'Digital Mind' – a harmonious blend of agile culture and potent Digital Talent.

Consider the story of Tencent, the Chinese tech giant. Beyond its vast product portfolio, from messaging apps to payment platforms, what sets Tencent apart is its innate agility. In a market as vast and dynamic as China, Tencent's willingness to swiftly adapt, pivot, and redefine its strategies has ensured its dominance. This adaptive nature is not about wild gambles but stems from a deeply ingrained culture of agility[126]. Across the Pacific, we have companies like Netflix in the USA. While some remember Netflix as a DVD rental service, it is their Digital Talent pool that envisioned the future of streaming. With their fingers always on the digital pulse, they reshaped entertainment consumption worldwide. Their adaptability and vision transformed them from a mail-order DVD service to an international streaming and content-producing giant.

But what makes these organizations tick? It is their Digital Mind. The uncanny ability to foresee digital trends, adapt at a pace that leaves competitors gasping, and most importantly, nurture talent that is not just digitally proficient but can reimagine the Digital Future (visit section 3.6.1 Anticipating future trends on page 304 to dive deeper into future perspectives).

In the subsequent sections, we will explore the twin pillars that shape the Digital Mind: the cultivation of an Agile and Adaptive Culture and the rigorous nurturing of Digital Talent.

---

[125] Audrey Hepburn – British Actress. * 04.05.1829 in Ixelles; † 20.01.1993 in Tolochenaz

[126] Elie Ofek, Billy Chan, and Dawn H. Lau on Harvard Business School website: "Tencent: Combining Technology and Culture". Published December 2020, visited 08.04.2024.
https://www.hbs.edu/faculty/Pages/item.aspx?num=59411

### 3.7.1   Agile and Adaptive Culture

A company's success hinges on its ability to swiftly adapt to change, learn from every venture, and drive innovations at an unprecedented pace. At the core of this evolution lies an Agile and Adaptive Culture, a transformative force that blends the dynamism of startups with the scale of corporations.

**What the C-Suite needs to know**

1. Strategic Agility: Agile and Adaptive Culture is not just about team dynamics but a company-wide approach, aligning rapid adaptability with strategic vision. Embracing this culture ensures swift response to market shifts, fostering innovation at pace.

2. Organizational Reinvention: Traditional hierarchical structures can hinder digital-age progress. Companies like Spotify and ING have highlighted the benefits of flatter, more flexible structures that promote cross-functional collaboration and faster decision-making.

3. Continuous Learning: For sustained success, companies must prioritize continuous learning. Encouraging a learning mindset, like Microsoft's growth mindset, leads to innovation, resilience, and a workforce prepared for future challenges.

4. Flexible Work Environments: Modern productivity thrives in flexibility. Offering diverse work environments and schedules, as exemplified by GitLab and Unilever, attracts top talent and enhances overall employee well-being and efficiency.

5. Collaborative Tech Tools: The integration of tools like Slack and Zoom can bridge geographical and functional divides, ensuring seamless collaboration. Investing in such platforms supports an agile workforce, regardless of location.

But what is the power of a Digital Mind?

**Awareness: Embracing Agility and Adaptability as Cornerstones of Digital Era**

Agility and adaptability might appear as trendy buzzwords. But upon closer examination, they stand as cornerstones of modern corporate success. **Agility represents the swift response to changes**. This could be seen in areas like product development, where fast iterations and immediate action make the difference between market leadership and obsolescence. It is akin to a sprinter's reaction time at the starting gun. Historically, agile methodologies grew from the fertile grounds of software development. The approach, which prioritized fast, iterative development cycles and close customer collaboration, soon found its resonance beyond the floors of code and tech. As businesses grappled with the unpredictable speed of the digital age, the philosophy of agility began to reshape broader corporate landscapes, evolving from a software development method to a comprehensive business strategy.

**Adaptability, however, carries a deeper connotation, reflecting a company's innate capacity to evolve and transform itself.** If agility is about navigating the waves of the present, adaptability is about forecasting and preparing for the tides of the future. It concerns the company's ability to grow, to reshape its offerings, or even, at times, to embark on entirely new ventures.

An Agile and Adaptive environment offers businesses a multitude of benefits in today's dynamic landscape. Primarily, it provides a **competitive edge in the digital era.** Companies that embrace this approach are better positioned to capitalize on rapid technological advancements, ensuring they are not left behind by more responsive competitors. Such an environment also aligns with the expectations of the modern digital consumer, who craves quick solutions, constant innovation, and immediate gratification. By being agile and adaptive, businesses can swiftly tailor their offerings to cater to these demands, ensuring **greater customer satisfaction.** Furthermore, **operational efficiency is significantly enhanced** in such an environment. Companies can swiftly identify and address business challenges, streamline processes to eliminate redundancies, and rapidly adapt to fresh market scenarios. This internal proficiency manifests externally as **superior products, faster services, and a perpetually contented customer base.**

Beyond merely reacting to the present, an Agile and Adaptive environment fosters a **culture of future-oriented innovation.** This not only allows businesses to anticipate and stay ahead of emerging trends but also enables them to chart new trajectories, potentially carving out entirely new market spaces. Such an environment equips businesses with the tools and mindset to lead rather than just respond, ensuring long-term relevance and growth. To illustrate, Spotify stands as a paragon of agility. This Swedish music streaming giant is not merely reacting to the ever-shifting sands of the music industry – it is often the force causing those shifts. By leveraging agile methodologies, Spotify's organizational structure of 'squads', 'chapters', and 'guilds' ensures it maintains agility even as it scales, serving millions while continuously innovating. The rise of Paytm in India's digital payment ecosystem highlights agility's tangible impact. In the wake of India's 2016 demonetization, Paytm swiftly rolled out tailored solutions for a cash-reliant populace, turning a national challenge into a golden opportunity.

The adaptability narrative finds a compelling champion in Airbnb. When global travel nearly halted due to the COVID-19 pandemic, Airbnb swiftly pivoted. They rolled out 'Online Experiences', fostering virtual connections worldwide. From cooking classes in Italy to yoga sessions in Bali, Airbnb's platform metamorphosed, reinforcing community in an era of distancing[127]. Samsung's trajectory from a humble trading

---

[127] Denise Lee Yohn on Forbes website: "How Airbnb Survived The Pandemic – and How You Can Too". Published online 10.11.2020, visited 08.04.2024.

company to a global electronics powerhouse paints a vivid picture of adaptability. Their iterative evolution across diverse sectors displays how adaptability can shape a firm's destiny. Whether it is their shift into consumer electronics or their agile R&D approaches in the face of emerging tech trends, Samsung epitomizes the blend of agility and adaptability.

**Atlassian: Pioneering the Future of Work through Agility and Adaptability**

In the vast panorama of enterprise software giants, Atlassian emerges as a beacon of Agile and Adaptive Culture. Originating from Australia, this powerhouse, famed for tools like Jira, Confluence, and Trello, has consistently showcased how modern businesses can thrive in a turbulent environment. Central to Atlassian's success is their unwavering commitment to openness and transparency. By creating open communication and using platforms that democratize information access, they have crafted an ecosystem, where alignment and clarity reign supreme.

Yet, it is not just about keeping everyone informed. Atlassian's core strength lies in how it trusts its teams. By granting significant autonomy, they champion the philosophy that those closest to the challenges possess the optimal solutions. This decentralized approach does not merely boost processes, it supercharges morale and fosters engagement at every tier. With feedback-driven methodologies embedded in their DNA, Atlassian harnesses retrospectives and peer reviews, ensuring an organization that is perpetually in a state of learning and evolution.

Innovation is not a mere buzzword here, it is a lived experience. Their celebrated 'Innovation Days' – previously known as 'ShipIt Days' – stand testament to a culture that encourages uninhibited creativity. And tying this all together is their dynamic approach to objectives, utilizing the OKR framework to provide clarity while retaining the nimbleness to pivot when necessary.

However, beyond the structures and strategies, lies Atlassian's heart – its people. Their earnest endeavors to create a diverse and inclusive environment underpin their belief that varied perspectives catalyze true innovation. By continuously investing in learning and development, Atlassian not only equips its workforce with contemporary skills but etches a blueprint of ceaseless growth and adaptability.

In the narrative of adaptive corporate cultures, Atlassian is not just a chapter, it is a compelling prologue to the future of work[128].

Companies armed with agility and adaptability do not just survive – they thrive, shape, and sometimes even define the very markets they operate in. Is your company ready for this?

---

https://www.forbes.com/sites/deniselyohn/2020/11/10/how-airbnb-survived-the-pandemic--and-how-you-can-too/?sh=4684d6fc9384

[128] Dominic Price, Philip Braddock on Altassian company website: "24 hours of opportunity: behind the scenes of ShipIt". Published online 14.10.2019, visited 08.04.2024. https://www.atlassian.com/blog/inside-atlassian/atlassians-shipit-hackathon-for-technical-and-non-technical-teams

## Assessment: Gauging the Level of Agility and Adaptiveness

 The bedrock of transformative business lies in introspection. Deep within the labyrinth of processes, protocols, and practices, there is a pulse – a heartbeat – that signals the vitality of an organization's agility and adaptability.

Consider the nature of **feedback loops**. While most organizations have feedback mechanisms, it is the dynamism within these loops that truly sets apart agile entities. For instance, a rapidly growing startup might employ a tool like Slack to obtain instant feedback on a newly released feature, acting upon it within hours, whereas a larger, more traditional entity might take weeks to sift through similar feedback. The depth of implementation, too, is vital. In some agile companies, feedback does not just lead to process tweaks, it might spark a complete overhaul of a project or even strategic redirection. Case in point: Adobe's shift from traditional software distribution to a cloud-based subscription model was heavily influenced by user feedback.

**Project turnaround times**, while seemingly straightforward, encompass a world of sub-factors. For instance, the software development methodology employed – a Waterfall model versus Agile Scrum – can profoundly impact turnaround times. Companies like Netflix are renowned for their swift deployment cycles, pushing updates to their platform multiple times a day. This speed is not just a technical feat but a testament to their agile culture, where cross-functional teams collaborate efficiently to troubleshoot and iterate.

Speaking of **cross-functional collaboration**, it is not just about open-floor offices or team-building events. It is about having marketing experts sit down with software developers, merging user experience with technical feasibility. The success of Apple's iPhone was not just technical prowess but a harmonious blend of design, marketing, and engineering. Their collaborative culture broke down departmental barriers, ensuring that when you swipe across your iPhone screen, it is not just intuitive but technically impeccable.

On the front of **adaptability in strategy**, history is riddled with examples of giants who could not pivot in time – like Kodak, who missed the digital photography wave despite having early access to the technology. Conversely, companies that have morphed their core offerings, tapping into emerging trends, showcase exemplary adaptability. IBM's evolution from a hardware-centric company to a cloud and services entity is a beacon of adaptability. The **spectrum of diversification** is vast. While it is tempting to see adaptability in a vast product portfolio, it is the precision of this diversification that counts. Amazon began as an online bookstore but read market nuances accurately to diversify into e-commerce broadly, and later, into areas like cloud computing with AWS. This is not mere expansion, it is calculated adaptability.

The emphasis on **training and skill development** cannot be overstated in assessing adaptability. Companies that foresaw the digital wave did not just invest in new tools, they invested in their people. When Satya Nadella took the helm at Microsoft, he emphasized a 'learn-it-all' culture over a 'know-it-all' one, pushing for continuous learning. Their consistent success in new domains like cloud computing is a testament to this adaptive learning culture.

In **external assessments**, while customer feedback remains fundamental, there is an emerging trend of predictive analysis – gauging consumer reactions even before a product is launched using AI-driven tools. Moreover, the agility of a company is often reflected in its market movements. The speed at which Samsung responds to market shifts, launching new smartphone features almost instantly in reaction to competitors or user demands, is a signature of their agile stance.

Concluding, assessment in the digital era is not just a checklist but a living, breathing exercise – a blend of analytics and instincts.

### Action: Fostering and Sustaining an Agile and Adaptive Culture

In the rapidly evolving digital space, it is imperative for companies to be agile, adaptive, and prepared for constant change. Organizations that actively work to cultivate these qualities not only survive but thrive amidst disruptions.

### *Cultivating Psychological Safety: The Silent Cornerstone of Innovations*

In today's complex business arena, while 'innovation' might be a frequently echoed mantra, the bedrock of truly transformative organizations often lies in the psychological fabric they weave. Psychological safety, beyond being a mere corporate catchphrase, becomes a linchpin for fostering genuine creativity and growth.

A clear testament to this is Google's 'Project Aristotle', which emphasized the vital role of **Leadership Transparency and Vulnerability**[129]. Through their exhaustive research, Google revealed that the magic of successful teams was not about the individual talents but about team dynamics built on trust and mutual respect. When leaders and team members openly share their vulnerabilities, uncertainties, and acknowledge their mistakes, it not only humanizes them but encourages a culture of

---

[129] On New York Times website: "What Google Learned From Its Quest to Build the Perfect Team". Published 25.02.2016, visited 08.04.2024. https://www.nytimes.com/2016/02/28/magazine/what-google-learned-from-its-quest-to-build-the-perfect-team.html

open dialogue and growth. Such regular candid exchanges, be it through **town halls or open forums**, lay the foundation for a culture of continual learning.

However, it is not just about creating a transparent environment. Pixar, with its 'Braintrust' meetings, offers a vivid illustration of how companies should proactively **reward Constructive Dissent**[130]. In these meetings, Pixar encourages candid yet respectful feedback on works in progress. The underpinning philosophy is not just about critique, it is about building a culture where creators can be vulnerable and open to suggestions, knowing that the feedback aims to refine, not reprimand. By recognizing and celebrating those who challenge the status quo or offer innovative solutions, organizations emphasize the value they place on forward-thinking.

Communication remains at the heart of psychological safety. Managers and leaders, in their essential roles, must be trained in **active listening skills**. When they are genuinely present in conversations, validating and acting upon employees' sentiments and concerns, it further solidifies trust within teams. Furthermore, companies can amplify this trust by **establishing Feedback Mechanisms**. Anonymous suggestion platforms or open dialogue sessions, much like Pixar's 'Braintrust' meetings, ensure every voice, whether audibly loud or silently profound, finds its rightful space in the organizational narrative.

Organizations that prioritize and embed psychological safety into their core ethos will undoubtedly stand out.

### *Celebrating Failures: Reframing the Pathway to Success*

In the quest for innovation and digital transformation, an aversion to failure can be an organization's Achilles heel. Traditional corporate structures often vilify mistakes, resulting in a risk-averse culture. Yet, in the age of rapid technological change, it is essential to view failures not as setbacks but as invaluable learning opportunities. Taking risks and sometimes failing is an integral part of pushing boundaries and breaking new ground. It is through the trials, errors, and lessons that businesses discover uncharted territories, improve existing products, or pioneer transformative solutions.

Dyson, the British technology company known for its innovative vacuum cleaners and hand dryers, is a beacon of this philosophy. Sir James Dyson famously went through 5,127 prototypes before arriving at the design for his groundbreaking vacuum cleaner. Instead of viewing these iterations as failures, they were celebrated as

---

[130] Ed Catmull on Fast Company website: "Inside The Pixar Braintrust". Published 3.12.2014, visited 08.04.2024. https://www.fastcompany.com/3027135/inside-the-pixar-braintrust#:~:text=The%20Braintrust%20meets%20every%20few,encourage%20them%20to%20be%2 0candid

necessary steps towards the final success. This culture of persistence and iterative development is woven into Dyson's DNA, propelling their continuous innovative streak[131]. Airbnb offers a unique tale of the significance of risk-taking. In its early days, facing dwindling finances, the founders decided to sell cereal boxes themed around the 2008 presidential election. Dubbed 'Obama O's' and 'Cap'n McCain's', these quirky products generated enough revenue to keep the company afloat. More than the funds, it exemplified the founders' willingness to take risks and think unconventionally, a spirit that still drives Airbnb's global success[132]. Another paragon is 3M, the company behind the ubiquitous Post-it Notes. These sticky notepads were a byproduct of a failed attempt to develop a super-strong adhesive. Rather than shelving it as a failure, 3M saw potential in the weak adhesive, eventually leading to the creation of one of the most popular office products.

Embracing failure as a catalyst for growth and reframing it as an essential ingredient of innovation is imperative. Companies that internalize this ethos, creating an environment where setbacks are steppingstones, position themselves at the forefront of innovation, ready to navigate the multi-faceted challenges and opportunities of the digital age.

### Embracing Transparency: Building Trust in the Digital Age

In an age where digital footprints are omnipresent and every action is under the microscope, transparency emerges as more than a buzzword – it becomes the illustration of organizational success. With stakeholders wielding the power of information and demanding uncompromising accountability, businesses find themselves at a crossroads. Merely possessing information is not enough, the onus is on companies to actively share, clarify, and communicate. This push towards openness is not restricted to high-stakes boardroom decisions, it permeates every tier of an organization, binding both internal teams and external partnerships.

Buffer, a trailblazer in the space of social media management, exemplifies what radical transparency can achieve. Their pioneering 'Open Buffer' initiative was not just a marketing ploy[133]. By laying bare elements like salaries, revenue, strategies, and even their codebase, they sent a clear message: Trust is cultivated through sharing, not secrecy. The dividends of this audacity were manifold: heightened trust from

---

[131] On Wired website: "James Dyson: in praise of failure". Published 11.04.2011, visited 08.04.2024. https://www.wired.co.uk/article/james-dyson-failure

[132] On Now This News website: "Airbnb Built Its Success With Obama Political Cereal Boxes". Published online 05.09.2018, visited 08.04.2024. https://nowthisnews.com/videos/money/airbnb-built-its-success-with-obama-political-cereal-boxes

[133] On Buffer company website: "Open: Buffer's Transparency Dashboard". Visited 08.04.2024. https://buffer.com/open

users, elevated employee morale, and a magnetic pull for top-tier talent resonating with the company's ethos.

Yet transparency is not just about internal operations. Patagonia, a stalwart in outdoor clothing, seamlessly integrates transparency with ethical responsibility. Their 'Footprint Chronicles' initiative transcends traditional corporate social responsibility[134]. By detailing the supply chain journey of their products, highlighting both environmental and societal impacts, they empower consumers. This is not mere brand-building, it is about giving consumers the agency to make **informed choices based on raw, unfiltered truths**. Internally, transparency is about fostering an environment of honest reflections and continuous improvement. Spotify, with its global music streaming empire, champions this through its 'Squad Health Check model'[135]. Teams do not just work, they introspect, evaluating their performance and well-being. By sharing these insights company-wide, Spotify transcends traditional performance metrics. They spotlight both triumphs and tribulations, underlining a commitment to growth through **shared learning and candid dialogue**.

To truly embrace transparency, organizations must understand its essence. It is not about selective revelations or curated narratives. It is about unbridled vulnerability and unapologetic authenticity. In today's interconnected digital landscape, stakeholders resonate more with raw truths than polished veneers. Thus, companies that genuinely internalize and act on transparency will not merely survive, they will thrive. With more engaged teams, fiercely loyal customers, and a resilient reputation, they will stand unyielding, even when navigating the most tumultuous corporate seas.

### *Decentralized Decision-Making: Unleashing the Power of Ownership*

In today's fluid and fast-paced business landscape, the long-standing models of centralized decision-making are no longer just archaic, they can be impediments to genuine innovation and agility. Decentralized decision-making, far from being a modern buzzword, is the bedrock upon which dynamic organizations are building their future. This approach harnesses the rich tapestry of insights and expertise that lies throughout an organization, granting autonomy right at the coalface of action, rather than cloistered in boardrooms. One might ponder the tangible impacts of such an approach. More than just expediting decisions, this paradigm nurtures a profound

---

[134] On the The Drum website: "2011: Patagonia prioritizes company transparency in 'Footprint Chronicles' effort". Published 31.03.2016, visited 08.04.2024. https://www.thedrum.com/news/2016/03/31/2011-patagonia-prioritizes-company-transparency-footprint-chronicles-effort

[135] Henrik Kniberg on the Agile Academy website: "Was ist das 'Squad Health Check Model' von Spotify?". Visited 08.04.2024. https://www.agile-academy.com/de/scrum-master/was-ist-das-squad-health-check-model/

**sense of ownership and accountability** among staff. When decisions emanate from those entrenched in the work, the resultant alignment between action and outcome can be staggering. Consider the transformative journey of the Haier Group with its pioneering 'Rendanheyi' model (人单合一, where 'Ren' refers to each employee. 'Dan' refers to the needs of each individual user and 'HeYi' refers to the connection that exists between each employee and the needs of the user)[136]. By recasting traditional departments into nimble micro-enterprises, Haier did more than just streamline processes. These autonomous units, unshackled from the labyrinthine approval chains, became crucibles of innovation. The consequence? A meteoric rise that ensconced Haier as a market leader in diverse segments.

Diverging from corporate titans and tech juggernauts, Buurtzorg, a Dutch nursing organization, underscores that decentralized decision-making transcends sectors and scales. In their compassionate pursuit of community care, teams operate devoid of overarching control. Nurses, typically grouped in teams of 10-12, are not mere caregivers, they are decision-makers, stewards of patient schedules, budgets, and more. This frontline autonomy has not just streamlined operations – it has birthed higher patient satisfaction, superior care, and a cost-effective model.

Decentralized decision-making is more than a structural change – it is a cultural revolution. Organizations that recognize this, empowering their teams with autonomy and ownership, are not merely adapting to the modern business milieu, they are sculpting its very contours.

### *Reinforcing Organizational Structures: The Bedrock of Digital Age Agility*

The traditional hierarchies, defined by their rigid chains of command and compartmentalized departments, have shown cracks in their capability to handle the multi-faceted demands of the digital age and the rising inclination towards decentralized decision-making. If businesses aim to be trailblazers rather than followers, there is a pressing need for a comprehensive reimagining of organizational paradigms that are more elastic, transparent, and fundamentally aligned with cross-functional collaboration.

The call of the hour is not a blunt demolition of established structures but a calculated recalibration. Companies must first **initiate introspective audits** to pinpoint bottlenecks and redundancies in their existing structures. This process could reveal overly complex approval chains, communication blockades, or even talent underutilization. Post this diagnosis, the subsequent step is to **craft a blueprint for a rejuvenated organizational design** that emphasizes fluidity, quick decision pathways,

---

[136] L. Felipe Monteiro, Anne-Marie Carrick on INSEAD website: "Haier Europe: Bringing RenDanHeyi for All". Published 14.06.2023, visited 08.04.2024. https://publishing.insead.edu/case/haier-europe

and interdisciplinary cohesion. For many firms, this might translate to **flattening organizational layers**, thereby reducing bureaucratic drag, and expediting decision-making. But it is more profound than mere structural alterations. At the heart of this transformation is the development of a **culture that champions openness**, values diverse inputs, and treats failures as steppingstones to innovation. It is about creating an environment where every voice, irrespective of rank or role, is valued and considered. The brilliance of Spotify's 'squad' system offers a tangible blueprint. Companies can draw inspiration from how Spotify segments its vast workforce into nimble, cross-functional 'squads'. Emulating such a model, businesses should consider **establishing small, agile teams**, each armed with clear objectives but endowed with the autonomy to determine their strategies and approaches. It is pivotal to then **facilitate seamless communication mechanisms** among these units, possibly through regular sync-ups, digital collaboration tools, or inter-departmental liaisons. These mechanisms should not just serve as reporting channels but as vibrant forums for idea exchange, feedback, and co-creation.

Another actionable insight from Spotify's playbook is the concept of 'tribes', 'chapters', and 'guilds'. Companies, depending on their size and scope, can institute similar overarching bodies that ensure alignment with the larger organizational mission, while still preserving the autonomy and dynamism of individual units. This delicate balance between alignment and autonomy is the secret sauce to **nurturing a culture of innovation and ownership**[137].

---

**Spotify's Symphony of Agility: Harmonizing Autonomy with Collaboration**

Spotify, a renowned name in the music streaming industry, has not only revolutionized the way we listen to music but also how businesses can operate with agility and innovation. At the heart of this transformation is its unique 'squad' system. This forward-thinking approach involves dividing the workforce into compact, cross-functional teams, or 'squads'. Each squad, while enjoying considerable autonomy, remains aligned to Spotify's overarching mission, ensuring both swift action and consistent purpose.

To effectively weave this structure into a larger fabric, squads collaborate within conglomerates known as 'tribes', focusing on specific areas in 'chapters' and then further branching out into specialized 'guilds'. This layered yet interconnected system is emblematic of Spotify's commitment to entertaining an environment where independence coexists harmoniously with collaboration.

One of the most striking successes of this model is the balance it strikes between autonomy and direction. While squads are empowered, creating a sense of ownership and swift decision-making, their objectives are harmoniously tethered to the company's broader goals. This constructive interaction between individual empowerment and collective purpose has been a driving force behind Spotify's continued dominance in the music streaming landscape. Furthermore, the amalgamation of diverse expertise within squads has become a hotbed for cross-functional collaboration and innovation.

---

[137] Marty Cagan, Chris Jones: "Empowered – Ordinary People, extraordinary products". Published by John Wiley & Sons Inc., 2021

The benefits reaped from this agile setup are manifold. Spotify has witnessed an acceleration in its innovation pace, continually rolling out features that resonate deeply with user needs and preferences. This not only solidifies its position as an industry leader but also ensures it consistently stays ahead of the curve in the ever-evolving music streaming domain. Moreover, the culture it has cultivated – anchored in trust, shared purpose, and mutual respect – has led to higher job satisfaction levels and a palpable sense of camaraderie across teams.

Spotify's strategic embrace of the agile 'squad' system, complemented by its collaborative structural layers, stands as a compelling testament to the transformative power of agility in the modern business reality. Through this, Spotify has not only charted a course of sustained success for itself but has also illuminated the path for others in the industry.

The Dutch banking group ING offers another compelling story of organizational restructuring. Driven by the need to be as agile as tech companies and fintech startups, ING Netherlands transitioned from traditional bank hierarchies to a 'Spotify model' of squads, tribes, and chapters. This allowed the bank to react swiftly to market changes, to rapidly deploy digital solutions, and to foster a culture of continuous learning and adaptation[138]. Zappos, the online shoe and clothing retailer, has experimented with 'Holacracy', a management system that eliminates traditional job titles and managers. Instead, the power is distributed, and roles are defined around the work, not people. This shift was aimed at promoting adaptability, responsibility, and faster decision-making.

Reinforcing and realigning organizational structures is crucial in today's digital age. The goal is clear: to harness the dynamism of startups while retaining the strength and scale of established corporations.

### Encouraging Cross-Functional Collaboration: The Nexus of Innovation

The age of isolated departments, working in silos, is a bygone era. In today's interwoven business landscape, collaboration across functions is a critical ingredient for sustained success. It sparks innovation, eliminates redundancies, and often results in services or products that are far more refined and holistic. The beauty of cross-functional collaboration is that it brings together a mosaic of perspectives. Each department, with its unique insights, contributes to a more comprehensive understanding of challenges and opportunities. When these insights coalesce, the resulting solutions are robust, innovative, and finely attuned to both market demands and internal efficiencies.

Consider the success story of Amazon, a company that has rewritten the playbook on a multitude of fronts. Their 'two-pizza team' philosophy is an eloquent testament to the power of cross-functional collaboration. These teams, designed to be fed by just

---

[138] Deepak Mahadevan on McKinsey website: "ING's agile transformation". Published 10.01.2017, visited 08.04.2024. https://www.mckinsey.com/industries/financial-services/our-insights/ings-agile-transformation

two pizzas, are small but encompass varied expertise. They are self-sufficient, capable of developing, testing, and deploying projects. This design eliminates the bureaucratic lag often seen in larger teams and ensures that diverse perspectives are always at the table, leading to agile decision-making and innovative solutions. On the other side of the globe, Samsung's 'D'light' project stands as a lighthouse of integrated brilliance. Located in Seoul, this three-story showcase is not just about displaying products, it is a confluence of marketing, product design, and user experience. By ensuring that these functions operate in tandem, Samsung can present products that are not just technologically advanced but are also embedded in rich narratives, resonating deeply with consumers. It is a masterclass in harmonizing different functions to present a unified, compelling brand experience[139]. For those who believe that cross-functional collaboration is restricted to tech developments, the tale of Airbnb's rebranding is enlightening. When Airbnb decided to refresh its brand identity, it was not just a marketing endeavor. Engineers, designers, and business strategists came together, resulting in a new logo, an improved app interface, and a transformed website. This collaborative approach ensured that the rebranding was cohesive across all touchpoints, creating a seamless experience for users (visit section 3.1.2 Digital Community on page 103 to explore the power of various types of collaboration).

In the grand tapestry of modern business, each department is a thread, and cross-functional collaboration is the beautiful pattern that emerges when these threads intertwine. It is a pattern that signals an organization's commitment to holistic excellence, where every function's voice is not just heard but is instrumental in shaping the company's trajectory.

### *Institutionalizing Feedback: The Bedrock of Agile Evolution*

Feedback acts as the intersection between an organization's strategic vision and its tangible outcomes. When channeled with intention and precision, feedback can illuminate the path forward, ensuring not just growth, but sustained relevance. However, the essence of feedback is not merely in its collection. It is in its assimilation into the organization's DNA. This is where many falter, viewing feedback as an occasional check-in rather than a daily compass. To truly institutionalize feedback is to entrench it within the daily rhythms and processes of an organization.

A pivotal first step is establishing **robust and diverse channels for feedback**. This could range from digital platforms that solicit employee insights, to face-to-face focus groups that dive deep into specific issues. For instance, digital tools like Slack or

---

[139] On Samsung company website: "What is the D'light cool mode and what is its function?". Updated 25.09.2020, visited 08.04.2024. https://www.samsung.com/hk_en/support/home-appliances/what-is-the-dlight-cool-mode-and-what-is-its-function/

Microsoft Teams can have dedicated channels for feedback. Surveys, while traditional, can be revamped with tools like Typeform or SurveyMonkey to be more interactive and user-friendly. However, the sanctity of these channels rests on their promise of confidentiality, ensuring that employees feel secure and empowered to share genuine opinions. Yet, the hurdle most companies face is the **myriad of daily tasks** that seem to take precedence over feedback. The relentless hum of daily operations, deadlines, and targets often drowns out the softer whispers of feedback. To elevate Its importance, feedback needs to be woven into the very fabric of daily tasks. For instance, **implementing end-of-day reflection sessions**, where teams discuss what went well and what could be improved, can be transformative. Moreover, managers can be trained in feedback-rich leadership, ensuring they not only provide regular feedback but also create an environment where feedback is expected and valued. By **dedicating specific intervals** – be it 15 minutes at the start or end of a workday – solely for feedback, its consistent engagement is assured.

Toyota's 'Andon Cord' system epitomizes more than manufacturing prowess. It captures the ethos of a feedback-rich culture[140]. The underlying message is clear: Create a workspace where every individual, irrespective of their title, feels authorized to voice observations and concerns. This egalitarian approach to feedback is what modern organizations must aspire to. But feedback's true potency is unlocked when it is acted upon. Gathering feedback and shelving it is a futile exercise. Organizations must establish feedback response teams or committees, dedicated to parsing feedback, discerning patterns, and crafting action plans. Regularly updating the workforce about changes implemented due to their feedback not only drives trust but also cements the importance of their opinions.

> **Unpacking Netflix's Agile Feedback Loop in the Streaming World**
>
> In the competitive arena of digital streaming, Netflix stands as a testament to the power of weaving feedback directly into the fabric of business operations. Beyond its renowned content library, it is the company's agile approach to feedback that underpins its success. Embracing a 360-degree feedback system, Netflix ensures that insights flow seamlessly across every echelon, fostering a culture of mutual respect and continuous growth.
>
> What distinguishes Netflix is its unwavering belief in real-time feedback. Rather than defaulting to sporadic, annual evaluations, the streaming pioneer encourages immediate and candid conversations, positioning transparency as a catalyst for innovation. It is not merely about collecting insights, it is the dedicated focus on action. Each piece of feedback, whether praise or critique, serves as a steppingstone, sculpting the company's strategies and content decisions.
>
> Furthermore, Netflix has institutionalized platforms for open dialogues and has been strong in equipping its teams with the skills needed to both give and receive feedback constructively. Through this feedback-centric blueprint, Netflix has not only optimized its internal dynamics but has also continually fine-tuned

---

[140] On Think Insights website: "Andon Cord – How Amazon And Netflix Use Toyota Principles?". Visited 08.04.2024. https://thinkinsights.net/strategy/andon-cord/

its offerings, ensuring it remains a leader in an ever-evolving industry. This synergy between feedback and business agility is a masterclass for any organization aiming to harness the full potential of its workforce and clientele[141].

Feedback is the basics for continuous evolution. In a business world characterized by flux and change, feedback provides the steadiness and direction companies need. For those wishing to not just survive but thrive in the digital age, making feedback a cornerstone of their operations is not optional – it is vital.

### Pioneering Reward Systems: Sculpting Incentives in Agile Environments

In the vibrant landscape of agile environments, the traditional parameters for gauging success and distributing incentives often fall short. To truly harness the essence of agility and innovation, companies need to reimagine their reward systems from the ground up, weaving them seamlessly into the fabric of their operations. At the heart of an agile setup lies the principle of fluidity, which should be mirrored in the approach to target setting. Rather than setting in stone rigid annual benchmarks, the wave of the future lies in adopting a more dynamic, frequently revisited goal-setting cadence, perhaps quarterly or even monthly. This ensures alignment with the company's constantly evolving priorities and objectives. Moreover, defining success requires a broader lens. While numerical milestones such as sales figures or revenue markers retain their importance, an agile organization should equally value softer, qualitative KPIs. For instance, the innovative potential of ideas tested, proactive cross-functional collaborations, or feedback-driven improvements can be critical indicators. This perspective underscores the imperative to value the journey and evolution as much as the tangible outcomes.

Yet, the true power of an agile approach to incentives lies in its ability to balance risk with reward. In an ecosystem where setbacks are not feared but celebrated as steppingstones to innovation, the reward structure should resonate with this ethos. Employees should feel motivated to take calculated, thoughtful risks that drive groundbreaking ideas, knowing that their endeavors, irrespective of the immediate outcome, will be recognized and rewarded. A complementary layer to this paradigm is the potent tool of peer-to-peer recognition. Given the collaborative ethos inherent to agile environments, a system that allows colleagues to spotlight and reward each other's achievements can bolster teamwork, shared learning, and mutual respect. Such organic 'kudos' or 'shout-outs' go beyond monetary value, fostering a culture of shared success and appreciation.

Diving deeper into the specifics of variable pay, a comprehensive approach could entail a blend of incentives based on individual performances, team

---

[141] Reed Hastings, Erin Meyer: "No Rules Rules – Netflix and the Culture of Reinvention". Published by Penguin Press, New York, 2020

accomplishments, and broader company successes. For instance, an employee's variable pay could be influenced by their direct contribution, their team's collective achievements, and the overall company milestones. However, to stay true to an agile framework's core principles, a segment of this pay should be earmarked for insights or lessons garnered from projects that did not quite hit the mark but illuminated pathways for future exploration. To encapsulate, the secret sauce for agile companies lies in marrying their financial incentives with the overarching cultural shift towards Innovation, adaptability, and shared growth. By crafting reward systems that applaud both the peaks and the troughs of the journey, organizations can truly tap into the boundless potential of their agile framework.

Incorporating an Agile and Adaptive Culture is not a mere change, it is a revolution in how businesses operate, innovate, and thrive. The right talent brings the culture to live.

### 3.7.2   Digital Talent

Talent is the thread that weaves every innovation, strategy, and success story. As companies race to harness the power of technology, it is not just about the tools or platforms they have, it is about the people using these tools. Digital Talent is not just about possessing technical skills, it encompasses a mindset, an adaptability, and a passion to leverage digital for transformative solutions.

**What the C-Suite needs to know**

1. The Essence of Digital Talent: It is not solely about technical acumen. Digital Talent embodies a unique blend of technical skills, adaptability, and a forward-thinking mindset. From AI specialists to digital marketers, these individuals are at the forefront of digital transformation, capable of leveraging technology to craft innovative solutions.

2. Evaluating the Current Landscape: Assessment is crucial. Utilizing tools like digital skills gap analyses and continuous feedback systems will provide a clear picture of where the organization stands. Recognizing areas of strength and pinpointing gaps can guide strategic hiring, training, and development initiatives.

3. Investing in Growth and Learning: Continuous learning is the bedrock of digital prowess. From platforms like Coursera to tailored in-house training programs, fostering a culture of perpetual learning ensures that talent remains updated, versatile, and ready to tackle new digital challenges.

4. Retention is as Vital as Recruitment: In the competitive landscape of Digital Talent, retaining top performers is paramount. This requires more than just competitive compensation, it necessitates a culture of appreciation, opportunities for growth, and ensuring a feedback-rich environment attuned to cultural sensitivities.

5. Collaboration is Key: Digital transformation is not siloed. Encouraging cross-functional collaboration ensures that digital initiatives are holistic, leveraging insights from diverse departments. Whether it is marketing working with data analytics or IT syncing with HR, a collaborative ethos magnifies the impact of digital endeavors.

Let us look at the importance of the right talent for success.

## Awareness: People – The Cornerstone of Digital Talent Evolution

 It is paramount to recognize that while technology is transformative, the true catalysts behind Digital Success are the individuals adept in harnessing its potential. Digital Talent encapsulates a blend of technical acumen, adaptability, and a forward-thinking mindset. It is not just about coding prowess or digital marketing expertise, it embodies a broader spectrum, intertwining technical capabilities with the ability to visualize and drive innovation in a digital context.

The importance of Digital Talent transcends industries and geographies. For organizations, possessing the right talent is a necessity. They are the minds that grasp customer needs in a digital world, architects of innovation, and the force ensuring a company does not just stay relevant but thrives and leads. In an age where digital platforms, tools, and techniques continually evolve, it is these skilled individuals who ensure organizations are not just keeping up but are on the forefront. Consider Adobe, for instance. Traditionally recognized for its design software, the company underwent a radical transformation from selling packaged software to becoming a cloud-based service provider. This shift was not solely about restructuring their business model but required a new breed of Digital Talent. Adobe's workforce needed to understand cloud architectures, subscription models, and user experience in a SaaS environment. Their successful transition, leading to the Adobe Creative Cloud and Document Cloud services we recognize today, can be attributed as much to their technological infrastructure as to their adept digital workforce. Similarly, DBS Bank, headquartered in Singapore, embarked on a journey to become the 'Best Digital Bank' globally. Recognizing the need for top-tier Digital Talent, DBS Bank created programs to transform its workforce. The bank emphasized digital literacy, cultivating a startup culture, and creating an environment of continuous learning. Their commitment to nurturing and harnessing Digital Talent has been a key contributor to their acclaimed digital transformation journey[142].

---

[142] On Human Resources Online website: "How DBS develops future-ready digital leaders". Published 17.06.2015, visited 08.04.2024. https://www.humanresourcesonline.net/dbs-develops-future-ready-digital-leaders

**Google: Cultivating Digital Excellence from Recruitment to Retention**

In the expansive digital frontier, few names shine as powerfully as Google. Their prowess extends far beyond search algorithms and iconic products. At its heart, Google's success is powered by a distinct ethos that threads through every aspect of its talent management journey.

From the outset, Google's recruitment strategies are more about discovering potential rather than ticking boxes. They are renowned for their challenging interview puzzles and real-world problem-solving scenarios, which aim to identify innovators and disruptors. The tech giant searches for 'Googlers' – individuals who not only possess technical brilliance but align with the company's culture of continuous learning, collaboration, and a desire to make a global impact.

Once within the Google fold, employees find themselves immersed in an ecosystem designed for growth and innovation. Development is not just encouraged, it is embedded in their operational DNA. By empowering employees to dedicate a portion of their workweek to passion projects outside their primary job responsibilities, Google has not only churned out groundbreaking products like Gmail and Google News but has also nurtured a culture where lateral thinking and exploration are the norms.

Retention at Google is not merely about competitive pay scales or lavish perks, though they abound. It is about creating an environment that celebrates diversity, promotes well-being, and continuously challenges the status quo. Programs like 'Googlegeist', an annual survey that seeks candid feedback from employees, highlight Google's commitment to evolving in line with its workforce's needs and aspirations. By ensuring that every 'Googler' feels heard, valued, and integral to the company's mission, Google masterfully blends ambition with empathy.

In a world brimming with digital enterprises, Google's comprehensive approach to talent – from the initial handshake to fostering long-term growth trajectories – positions it as a beacon of how to attract and retain the digital era's brightest minds.

The global need for Digital Talent is evident, with industries from healthcare to finance undergoing digital transformations. Having the right talent pool is as important as having the right Digital Strategy. Recognizing this, understanding its nuances, and making it a priority sets the foundation for an organization's Digital Success journey.

## Assessment: Navigating the Digital Talent Landscape

 Recognizing the value of Digital Talent is just the start, truly competitive organizations go a step further to evaluate their existing talent pool's strengths, areas for growth, and alignment with strategic goals. This introspection is not a one-off checkpoint but an on-going process, ensuring that businesses remain at the forefront of digital evolution. A crucial first step in this journey is conducting a **Skill Inventory**. This holistic examination offers a bird's-eye view of current employee capabilities, drawing out areas of excellence and spotlighting gaps that might impede digital goals. It is akin to a health check-up but for organizational talent. This inventory is not merely a technical rundown but dives into essential soft skills, gauging adaptability, collaboration, and digital vision.

Yet, an internal lens can be limiting. **Benchmarking** offers a broader perspective. By comparing your organization's talent capabilities against industry standards and competitors, leaders can gauge their standing in the digital race. For instance, Netflix, known for its digital-first approach, consistently benchmarks its technical teams against the best in the business. Their ethos? To ensure that they are not just part of the digital conversation but are leading it.

But what is talent assessment without continuous feedback? **Feedback Loops** serve as the pulse of the talent pool. Implementing regular feedback mechanisms, like surveys, interviews, or focus group discussions, ensures that the aspirations, concerns, and innovative ideas of the talent align with the organization's trajectory. Companies like Google have long championed feedback processes, using platforms like Googlegeist, their annual employee survey, to gather insights and adapt strategies accordingly. The Royal Bank of Scotland (RBS) provides another illuminating case. As part of its digital transformation strategy, RBS sought to assess its Digital Talent pool depth and readiness. Through comprehensive skill assessments, competitor benchmarking, and regular feedback sessions, the bank identified key areas for talent development, shaping its subsequent training programs and recruitment strategies.

### Action: Sowing the Seeds for Digital Excellence

 Organizations are often faced with the challenge of not only identifying but also nurturing and holding onto invaluable Digital Talent. The synthesis of innovative action plans is paramount in fostering an environment that breeds digital excellence.

### *Digital Age Recruitment: Tailoring Touchpoints for Tomorrow's Talent*

Recruitment in the digital age transcends traditional vetting. It metamorphoses into a dynamic blend of branding, storytelling, and precision-targeting, ensuring that prospective talents do not just see a job offer but a beckoning digital journey tailored just for them. For companies to truly thrive in this landscape, there are concrete strategies to embrace.

First and foremost, understand your **digital brand identity**. Before embarking on a hiring spree, companies must have an unclouded vision of their place in the digital world and how they wish to be perceived. This involves introspection, crystallizing what makes the company unique, and understanding the digital aspirations they wish to create. Design **recruitment processes** that echo the company's digital ethos. Atlassian's approach serves as an apt example. They have transformed their hiring procedure into an immersive experience that is reflective of their innovative culture. By incorporating initiatives like 'ShipIt' sessions, they have turned recruitment into a collaborative venture where problem-solving, teamwork, and adaptability take center stage. Thus, companies should look beyond the CV and weave in opportunities to see candidates in action, mirroring real-world scenarios they would encounter in their roles. Further, turn job vacancies into digital narratives. This is where HubSpot shines. Using their 'inbound recruiting' strategy, they have effectively narrated the HubSpot story to potential candidates. By giving a transparent view into their world and converting vacancies into compelling tales of opportunity, they pull in individuals aligned with their digital aspirations. Companies must thus pivot from plain job descriptions to vibrant showcases of their work culture and values, making sure every post, video, or blog is a chapter in their unfolding digital story. But the nuances do not stop there. Every interaction with a potential candidate is an opportunity to solidify the brand's image. Hence, **optimize the 'candidate experience'**. Whether it is through swift responses, providing insightful feedback, or simply ensuring that the candidate's journey is seamless, these touches matter. Remember, in the digital world, perceptions spread fast, and every candidate is a potential brand ambassador. Their experience, whether they join the fold or not, can ripple through their networks, affecting the brand's reputation.

To win the recruitment game in the digital age, companies must move from passive hiring to active engagement, crafting every touchpoint to resonate with their digital spirit. It is an approach, where both the company and the candidate move in harmony towards a shared digital dream.

### *Training and Upskilling: Nurturing the Digital Growth Curve*

In the maelstrom of digital change, the static nature of traditional employee development approaches is exposed and often found wanting. For companies seeking a competitive edge, the focus is increasingly shifting from just 'having' talent to 'honing' it relentlessly. A culture of ceaseless learning and adaptability is not just an asset, it is the pre-requisite of digital prowess.

Foremost, organizations must commit to regularly assessing their training needs. The digital landscape evolves at breakneck speed. What is relevant today – think specific programming languages or digital marketing strategies – might not be tomorrow. Periodic skill gap analyses, not just at the organizational level but at the departmental and individual levels, can offer insights into areas ripe for upskilling. Furthermore, while structured training modules are essential, **blended learning environments** have proven exceptionally effective. Take the case of Amazon's 'Career Choice' program[143]. Beyond its admirable financial commitment, the genius lies in its recognition of diverse learning pathways. They understand that a warehouse employee's aspirations might differ from a software developer's. Hence, the **tailoring**

---

[143] On Path Stream website: "Maximizing the benefits of the Amazon Career Choice Program". Published 26.06.2023, visited 08.04.2024. https://pathstream.com/amazon-career-choice-program/

**of training opportunities** to individual aspirations and potential growth trajectories becomes paramount. In parallel, the rise of **digital learning platforms** has revolutionized how training is delivered. Salesforce's Trailhead, for example, is not just an online course catalog. It is a vibrant community where learners can engage in forums, earn badges, and even mentor peers. This **gamification of learning** makes it more engaging and, crucially, fosters a spirit of collaborative learning. However, not all learning happens in classrooms, virtual or otherwise. Siemens, with its '70-20-10' model, demonstrates a keen understanding of this. They champion the idea that most profound learning emerges from **real-world challenges and collaborations**. Encouraging employees to take on stretch assignments, rotate across roles, or even lead projects outside their expertise zone can supercharge their learning curve. Concurrently, supporting **structured mentorship programs** can ensure that the 20% of peer-based learning is purposeful, drawing from the rich reservoir of internal knowledge and expertise. Lastly, feedback loops are vital. After every training intervention, gather data. Were the skills acquired applied effectively? Did business metrics improve post-training? Such data-driven insights can guide future training endeavors, ensuring continual alignment with business goals.

As the digital arena's contours shift and morph, companies cannot afford a passive approach to talent development. They must be proactive, prescient, and perpetually ready to pivot. The goal is clear: Equip the workforce not just with the skills of today, but with the agility and curiosity to master the challenges of tomorrow.

### *Magnetic Retention: Cultivating an Ecosystem Where Digital Pioneers Flourish*

In the cutthroat world of digital innovation, talent retention is less about passive measures and more about active engagement. In an era where a ping from a recruiter or a new opportunity is just a click away, retention becomes a dynamic, evolving art form. It is not merely about holding on to talent, it is about creating an environment so magnetic that leaving seems unthinkable.

Take the example of Google, a titan in the digital space. By granting them the autonomy to diverge from their daily duties and chase passion projects, Google sends a clear message: they value innovation at its grassroots. And the outcomes are palpable. Breakthrough products like Gmail and Google News, originating from these very passion projects, are a testament to the harmonious constructive collaboration between employee fulfillment and organizational success.

Netflix, on the other hand, has redefined what competitive compensation looks like in the digital age. Their 'top-of-market' pay policy is not just a nod to industry benchmarks. It is a commitment to acknowledge and reward unparalleled talent. In an environment where compensation is often shrouded in mystery, Netflix stands out with its transparency, creating an atmosphere of trust and respect. Their customizable compensation structure, allowing employees to dictate the mix of cash and stock, speaks to their dedication to personalized rewards. This approach reflects a deep understanding that what motivates one might not inspire another[144]. Yet, while financial incentives are potent motivators, the ethos of true retention lies deeper. SAP, a global software behemoth, exemplifies this. Their 'Life at SAP' initiative is less about policies and more about acknowledging the multi-faceted lives of their employees. By weaving flexibility into work structures, they cater to varied life situations, from new parents to globe-trotting consultants. Health and well-being are not sidelined, they are front and center. Programs addressing physical health, mental resilience, and even opportunities for sabbaticals reflect SAP's belief in the holistic growth and rejuvenation of their workforce.

As organizations navigate the intricacies of the digital age, a clear pattern emerges. Retention is less about isolated strategies and more about a holistic tapestry of initiatives. From encouraging boundless innovation and crafting tailored reward structures to prioritizing holistic well-being, the goal is unequivocal: construct an ecosystem where digital pioneers do not just work but evolve, innovate, and flourish.

As we conclude our exploration into Digital Talent, one thing stands clear: in a world dominated by codes, algorithms, and digital interfaces, the human element remains paramount. The tools are ever evolving, but it is the talent behind them that dictates the pace and direction of this evolution. Investing in Digital Talent – by recognizing its value, nurturing its growth, and retaining its brilliance – is not just a good HR strategy, it is a cornerstone for any company's Digital Future. As we move forward, remember: In the age of machines, it is the human touch that makes the difference.

---

[144] On Slideshare: "Netflix Culture: Freedom & Responsibility". Published 01.08.2009, visited 08.04.2024. https://www.slideshare.net/reed2001/culture-1798664

 Find more and updated information in the **Digital Arena**. Connect with like-minded professionals to unleash the potential and make it happen.

As we reach the conclusion of our journey of 'Unleashing the potential' through the Digital Success Levers and Modules, we stand at the threshold of a transformative era. We have meticulously navigated through the seven Digital Success Levers. Each of these levers, with their respective modules, has been a beacon, guiding us through the complexities of digital transformation. We began with Digital Readiness, setting the stage for a culture adaptable to the digital landscape, followed by Digital Momentum, where we recognized and capitalized on our existing digital assets. Then, we shifted our focus to Digital Experience, enhancing user engagement and loyalty, and proceeded to Digital Strategy, prioritizing our digital initiatives with our overarching business goals. As we progressed, we embraced the Digital Lead, positioning ourselves as pioneers in the digital domain, and looked forward to the Digital Future, anticipating and shaping industry trends. Finally, we culminated with the Digital Mind, fostering a culture of innovation and agility.

Each step has been crucial in building a robust digital foundation, essential for navigating today's ever-evolving digital environment. We have learned to not only envision potential but also to materialize it, transforming aspirations into tangible achievements. Our journey has been about more than just understanding the 'What' and the 'How', it has been about ingraining these principles into our organizational DNA. Remember, the path to digital success is not linear. It is a continuous cycle of learning, adapting, and evolving. As you step forward from here, take with you the insights and strategies you have gained. Let them be your compass in the relentless pursuit of digital excellence – make it happen!

# 4   Make it happen

In the earlier chapters, we mapped the terrain of digital excellence through the seven Digital Success Levers and fourteen Digital Success Modules, charting a course for what to do and how to excel in the digital domain. These tools and insights are more than just a blueprint, they are the essence of a strategic playbook designed to steer any organization through the complexities of digital transformation.

The imperative for embarking on this digital journey is clear and present. Companies that ignore the signs or delay their digital evolution face the stark reality of being outpaced by more digitally mature competitors. This urgency is not just driven by fear but by the recognition of opportunities as well, framed by two pivotal questions every leader should ponder:

1.  **Is our digital trajectory set for success, or are we inadvertently courting failure?** Missteps in the digital space can have far-reaching consequences, eroding market share and customer trust. It is vital to continually assess and ensure that your digital path is leading towards growth and innovation.

2.  **Are we harnessing the full spectrum of digital possibilities for our enterprise?** It is not merely about having a digital presence, it is about leveraging digital capabilities to their utmost potential, creating new value streams, enhancing customer experiences, and achieving operational excellence.

With the stage set and the stakes understood, we turn our focus **from contemplation to action**. How can you start, sharpen, or continue our digital transformation? Let us go 'FAR'. This acronym for Focus, Application, Resilience stands as the guidance for your transition.

**Go 'FAR': What you need to do now!**

- **Focus:** Identify and prioritize the digital initiatives that will significantly impact your business. Align your resources and efforts to these strategic areas for maximum effect.

- **Application:** Convert your strategic priorities into tangible projects and programs. It is time to move from theoretical planning to practical, impactful action, leveraging proven approaches.

- **Resilience:** Fortify your initiatives against the inevitable challenges and disruptions. Maintain momentum, adapt as necessary, and stay the course towards your digital ambitions. Have the right team in place.

**Focus: Strategic Prioritization for Digital Impact**

Narrowing the attention helps to shape the digital transformation journey take shape, forming the strategic bedrock upon which all subsequent actions are built. This step is about homing in on the areas of greatest impact. **This is where you pinpoint precisely where to channel your energies and investments to kickstart or advance your digital transformation.**

Begin with an honest and detailed assessment of your organization's digital situation, informed by the comprehensive **Digital Pulse Check** – an evaluative process that examines the current state of your digital landscape. Assess whether your organization first needs to 'get the basics right', addressing gaps when it comes to Digital Readiness, Digital Momentum, or Digital Experience. Understand whether your organization is 'ready to lead through digital', exploring next steps in the areas of Digital Strategy, Digital Lead and Digital Future. Gauge the level of Digital Mind as the foundation for sustainable development. This introspection is crucial because it helps you to identify not only where you are but also where you need to bolster your efforts to stay competitive and relevant (visit section 1.3 Digital Pulse Check on page 29 to revisit the basic for an assessment). A granular look at your digital initiatives is necessary. Scrutinize your processes, evaluate your digital assets, and measure the effectiveness of ongoing digital projects. This deep dive will reveal your strengths to be leveraged, weaknesses to be addressed, and opportunities that may have been overlooked. How do your digital capabilities stack up against industry benchmarks? Are your digital skills sufficient to pivot with market demands? These questions form the basis of your strategic digital focus.

After the assessment, it is time to set specific, actionable goals. **Define what success looks like** for your organization in the digital space over the next one to three years. These targets should be rooted in tangible outcomes, such as boosting customer engagement rates, streamlining operational processes, or expanding your digital footprint across new platforms or markets. Each goal must adhere to the SMART criteria, ensuring that it is not only aspirational but also attainable within a realistic timeframe (visit section 1.1 What is Digital Success on page 13 to understand the drivers for success).

The translation of these **goals into a strategic plan** is the next critical step. This plan acts as a blueprint, guiding your organization's digital initiatives. It is not a static document but a living strategy that adapts and evolves. In this plan, each goal is broken down into actionable steps. For instance, a digital marketing goal might be disaggregated into a series of targeted campaigns, while an operational efficiency objective might translate into specific automation projects. Assign clear timelines, responsibilities, and metrics to each step, ensuring accountability and enabling progress tracking (visit section 1.1 What is Digital Success on page 13 to lay the foundations).

Focus is where the abstract concept of 'digital transformation' is distilled into a clear, practical set of priorities. It is about precision in your strategic intent, clarity in your goals, and specificity in your planning. Through this meticulous approach, you ensure that your organization's resources are concentrated on the most impactful initiatives, setting the stage for Application where these strategies are brought to life.

**Application: Concrete Implementation for Digital Progress**

With Application the strategic blueprints of the Focus phase transition into reality. This is where the **conceptual becomes operational**, where the goals and priorities become projects and outcomes. It is the domain of doing, where the Digital Success Modules, introduced previously, provide the framework and proven approaches for targeted actions. Less is certainly more in this context – it is about completing fewer projects successfully rather than spreading too thin over many. Prioritize developments that can be rapidly implemented and have a quick return on investment – including Minimum Viable Products (MVP). Quick wins are not just about immediate benefits, they also build momentum and confidence among the team and stakeholders. However, it is important to balance the desire for quick wins with the need for sustainable, long-term value creation (visit section 1.2 Digital Success Canvas on page 22 for proven approaches).

For successful Application it is crucial to be action-oriented and outcome-focused. Establish a clear process for each digital initiative, from planning to execution. Implementing the **Digital Success Modules** should follow a disciplined approach. Each module provides a pathway with steps that lead to a particular digital goal. Apply the **Triple-A approach** for each selected module. Ensure everyone has the Awareness for the relevance of the topic. Follow with a diligent Assessment of the current situation. Then initiate concrete Actions to improve (visit section 1.4 The Triple-A Approach on page 32 for a systematic methodology).

Set up **cross-functional teams** responsible for delivering on each project, with clear timelines and deliverables. These teams should operate with an understanding that their work is vital to the organization's digital transformation journey. Agility is paramount. Be prepared to adapt your plans based on real-time feedback and changing circumstances. Encourage a culture of continuous improvement, where learnings from each initiative are captured and used to inform future projects (visit section 3.7 Digital Mind on page 323 for a sustainable culture).

Application is about impact. It is a call to move beyond planning and discussion, to roll up sleeves and get to work. By focusing on concrete actions, leveraging the Digital

Success Modules, and aiming for impactful, quick wins, your organization will not only initiate but also advance its digital transformation in meaningful ways.

**Resilience: Sustain the Momentum**

Resilience in digital transformation is the sustained effort that enables organizations to navigate through uncertainty and challenges while maintaining progress towards their strategic goals.

The practice of **continuous measurement** against key performance indicators allows organizations to gauge the effectiveness of their digital strategies in real-time. This constant evaluation is vital for recognizing when adjustments are needed and for ensuring that the organization's digital efforts remain on course.

It is about fostering **a culture of adaptability and continuous improvement** that upholds the momentum, ensuring that digital initiatives are not just implemented but also continuously refined and advanced.

**Effective communication** stands at the heart of resilience. Keep stakeholders updated on progress, challenges, and successes. Transparency will build trust and support throughout the organization, which is essential when navigating the complexities of digital change. It creates an environment where objectives are clear, and every stakeholder is aligned with the organization's digital vision. This open dialogue is crucial for addressing the inevitable challenges and for collaboratively steering through the tumultuous landscape of digital change.

Building and nurturing **the right team** is essential. Resilience is not possible without people who possess the right mix of skills and the mindset to embrace change. This involves not just equipping your current workforce with new capabilities but also attracting talent that brings fresh perspectives and expertise to the digital initiatives at hand.

Finally, resilience is embedded in the organizational culture when there is a collective understanding that challenges are opportunities for growth. It is about creating **a resilient digital culture** where setbacks are learning experiences that contribute to the organization's digital maturity.

**Navigating through the ebb and flow of digital transformation requires strong leadership** – leaders who can provide clarity, make decisive adjustments when necessary, and inspire their teams to stay the course. This leadership is the compass that guides the organization through the complexities of change, ensuring that every step taken is one closer to realizing the full potential of its digital journey.

As we close this chapter – and indeed, this comprehensive guide to digital transformation – it is time to turn the page from planning to action. Managers and leaders, you are now armed with the knowledge and strategies necessary to guide your organization towards digital success. But remember, knowledge alone is not power, the true power lies in action. You stand at the helm of change, poised to steer your company through the evolving digital landscape. The journey ahead will be demanding, but the rewards are commensurate with the courage to embark on this path. It is your actions, your commitment to applying the principles of Focus, Application, and Resilience, which will transform your organization's digital potential into tangible success.

**Let this be your clarion call to action**. Embrace the responsibility with vigor and confidence. Forge ahead with a sharp vision and a steadfast resolve to implement the changes that will propel your company forward. Harness the collective strength of your teams, the sophistication of your strategies, and the resilience of your culture to overcome challenges.

**The digital era is not on the horizon, it is here, now**. The opportunities it presents are not for the distant future, they are ripe for the taking today. It is a time for doers, for visionaries who are ready to lead their organizations with conviction and agility. Digital success is not just a goal, it is an ongoing commitment to excellence, innovation, and continuous growth. As you turn knowledge into action, strategies into results, and challenges into victories, you will not only witness the transformation of your organization but also shape the future of your industry.

**Leaders, the moment to act is now.** Take these insights, strategies, and tools, and use them to carve out your path to digital success. Unleash the potential and make it happen. Let your journey be marked by bold decisions, impactful actions, and an unwavering drive to succeed. Go 'FAR' and make digital transformation your legacy.

But your journey does not end at the last page of this book. To enrich your experience  and offer a platform for continuous learning, the **Digital Arena** extends an invitation to a vibrant community. This is not just a platform, it is a growing melting pot of experts, professionals, and enthusiasts, all united by their passion for the digital opportunities. Here, the opportunity to learn is limitless. Exchange insights with peers, seek guidance from seasoned experts, share challenges, and celebrate successes. The portal transforms the book's wisdom into a living, breathing ecosystem of knowledge, expanding horizons well beyond the written word.

# Index

# About the Author

Patrick Steiner's unique blend of skills and experiences sets him apart in the world of business and leadership. His professional journey began in the rigorous and analytical world of McKinsey & Co., where he honed his strategic thinking and problem-solving skills, crafting solutions for complex business challenges with the precision and clarity that only a seasoned strategy consultant can bring.

But Patrick's talents extend far beyond traditional consulting. He possesses the imaginative spirit and innovative mindset of a serial entrepreneur. Having been involved in multiple startups, Patrick brings a creative flair to his endeavors, expertly navigating the uncertainties and challenges of entrepreneurial ventures. This experience has endowed him with an invaluable perspective on business, allowing him to see opportunities where others see obstacles.

In addition to his creative and strategic prowess, Patrick is known for his exceptional execution capabilities, a skillset he further developed during his tenure as a senior manager at UBS. Here, he demonstrated his ability to lead complex projects to successful completion, ensuring that strategic visions were transformed into tangible results. His 'get things done' attitude, combined with a meticulous attention to detail, ensures that he consistently delivers excellence.

Patrick's disciplined approach to both life and work is partly attributed to his background as a Swiss Army officer. The values of discipline, leadership, and resilience instilled during his military service as a Lieutenant Colonel have been instrumental in shaping his professional ethos.

Beyond his professional achievements, Patrick is a devoted family man, a proud father of four. His role as a parent has imbued him with patience, empathy, and a deep sense of responsibility – traits that further enrich his professional interactions and decision-making.

Patrick Steiner is a dynamic combination of rationality, creativity, discipline, and heart.

www.ingramcontent.com/pod-product-compliance
Lightning Source LLC
LaVergne TN
LVHW081302210726
843509LV00019B/198

9 783952 598818